冨 樫 義 博

The picture in vol. 3 was me. (The one who took it was my then girlfriend, now wife.)

Yoshihiro Togashi

Yoshihiro Togashi's manga career began in 1986 at the age of 20, when he won the coveted Osamu Tezuka Award for new manga artists. He debuted in the Japanese **Weekly Shonen Jump** magazine in 1989 with the romantic comedy **Tende Shôwaru Cupid**. From 1990 to 1994 he wrote and drew the hit manga **YuYu Hakusho**, which was followed by the dark comedy science-fiction series **Level E,** and finally this adventure series **Hunter x Hunter**. In 1999 he married the manga artist Naoko Takeuchi.

HUNTER X HUNTER Volume 5
SHONEN JUMP ADVANCED Manga Edition

STORY AND ART BY
YOSHIHIRO TOGASHI

English Adaptation/Gary Leach
Translation/Lillian Olsen
Touch-up Art & Lettering/Mark Griffin
Design/Amy Martin
Editor/Pancha Diaz

HUNTERxHUNTER © POT (Yoshihiro Togashi) 1999. All rights reserved. First published in Japan in 1999 by SHUEISHA Inc., Tokyo. English translation rights arranged by SHUEISHA Inc.

The stories, characters and incidents mentioned in this publication are entirely fictional.

Printed in the U.S.A.

Published by VIZ Media, LLC
P.O. Box 77010
San Francisco, CA 94107

10 9 8 7 6 5 4
First printing, October 2005
Fourth printing, May 2016

PARENTAL ADVISORY
HUNTER X HUNTER is rated T+ for Older Teen and is recommended for ages 16 and up. Contains realistic violence and mature language.
ratings.viz.com

www.viz.com

www.shonenjump.com

SHONEN JUMP ADVANCED MANGA

HUNTER × HUNTER

ハンター　ハンター

Story & Art by
Yoshihiro Togashi

Volume 5

CHARACTERS

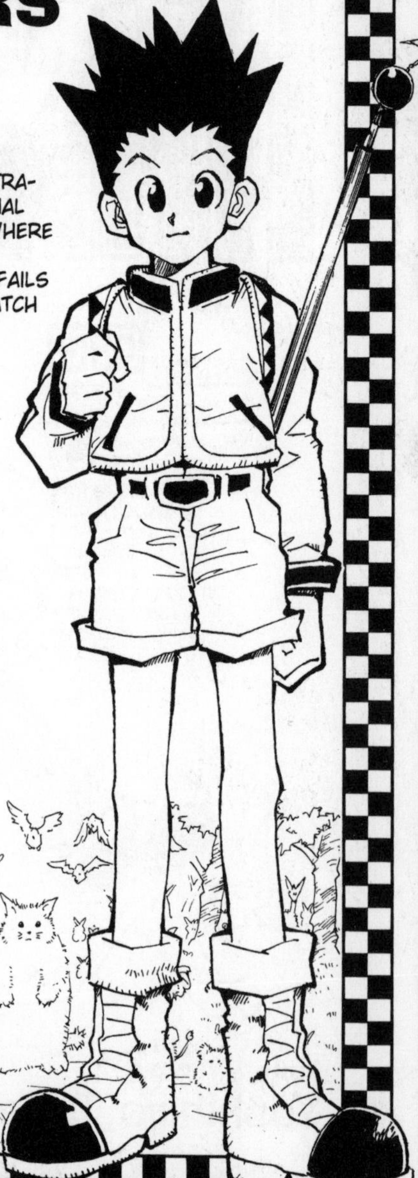

The Story Thus Far

GON DREAMS OF BEING A HUNTER LIKE HIS FATHER, AND APPLIES FOR THE ULTRA-CHALLENGING LICENSING EXAM. THE FINAL TEST IS A ONE-ON-ONE TOURNAMENT WHERE THE WINNERS FALL OUT AND THE LAST APPLICANT STANDING IS THE ONE WHO FAILS THE EXAM. THE ONLY WAY TO WIN A MATCH IS TO MAKE YOUR OPPONENT DECLARE DEFEAT—IF YOU KILL YOU ARE IMMEDIATELY DISQUALIFIED. GON, UP AGAINST THE MUCH STRONGER AND HIGHLY TRAINED HANZO, REFUSES TO BACK DOWN...AND HANZO GIVES HIM THE MATCH! KURAPIKA AND HISOKA ALSO PASS. THEN KILLUA FINDS OUT THAT HIS BROTHER HAS BEEN TAKING THE EXAM AS WELL, IN THE GUISE OF GITTARACKUR...!!

Gon

OUR EAGER HERO, WHO WANTS TO BE A HUNTER IN ORDER TO REUNITE WITH HIS FATHER!

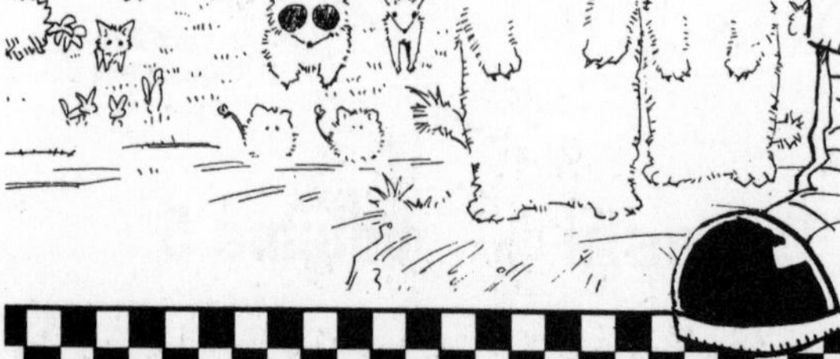

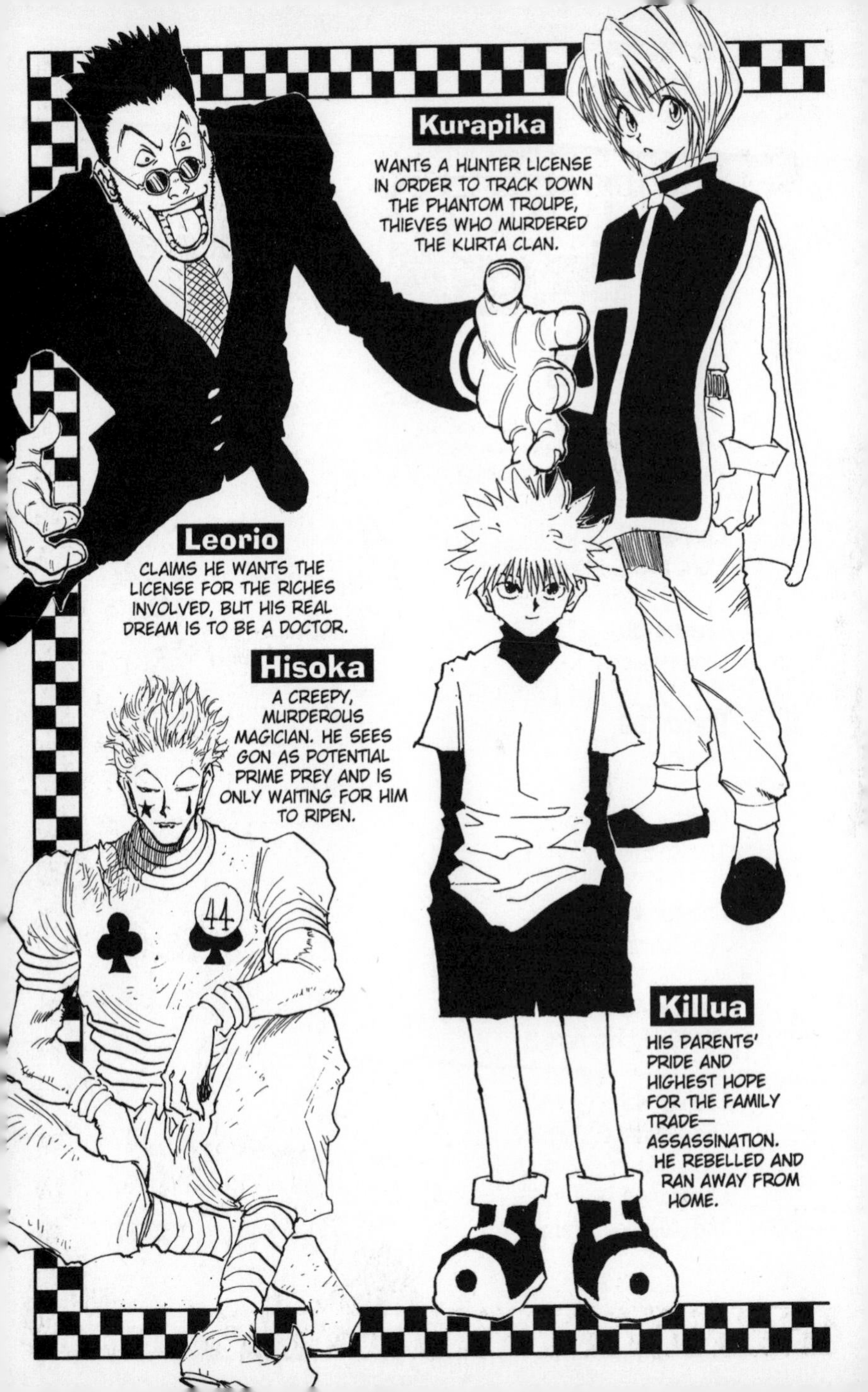
Kurapika
WANTS A HUNTER LICENSE IN ORDER TO TRACK DOWN THE PHANTOM TROUPE, THIEVES WHO MURDERED THE KURTA CLAN.
Leorio
CLAIMS HE WANTS THE LICENSE FOR THE RICHES INVOLVED, BUT HIS REAL DREAM IS TO BE A DOCTOR.
Hisoka
A CREEPY, MURDEROUS MAGICIAN. HE SEES GON AS POTENTIAL PRIME PREY AND IS ONLY WAITING FOR HIM TO RIPEN.
44
Killua
HIS PARENTS' PRIDE AND HIGHEST HOPE FOR THE FAMILY TRADE— ASSASSINATION. HE REBELLED AND RAN AWAY FROM HOME.

Volume 5

CONTENTS

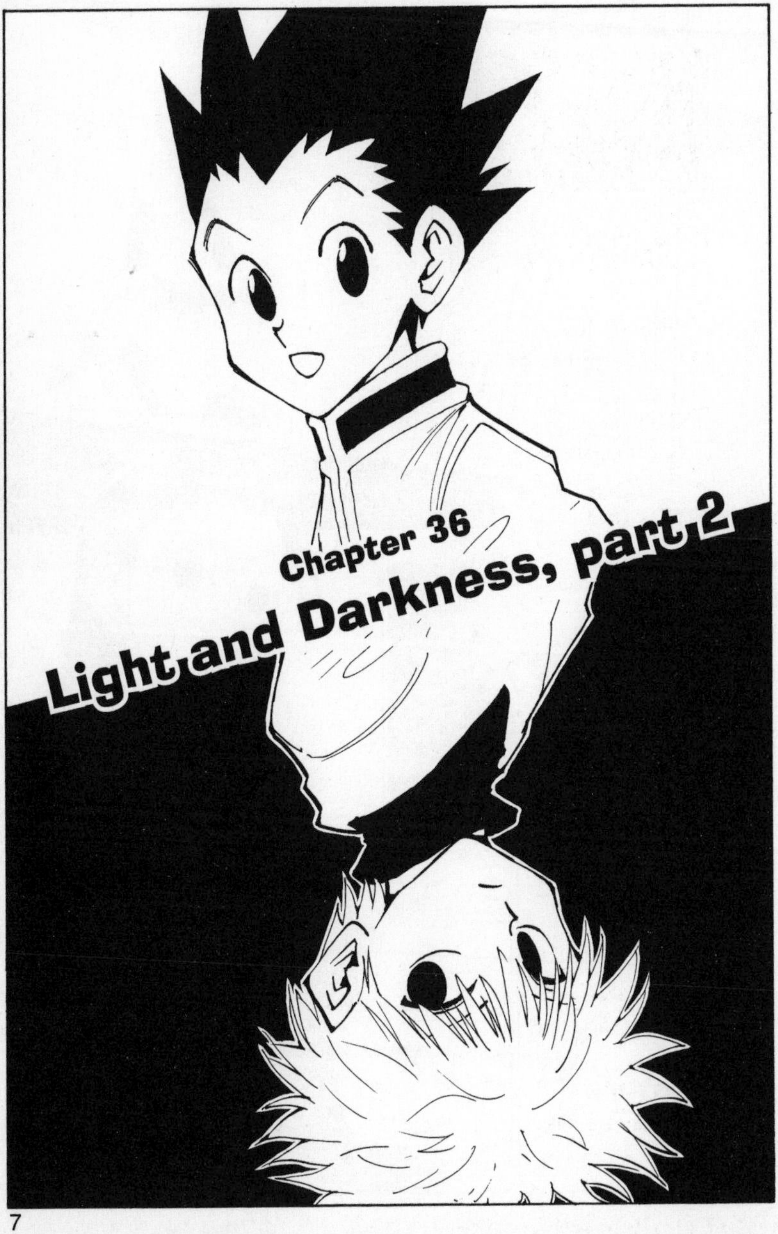
Chapter 36
Light and Darkness, part 2

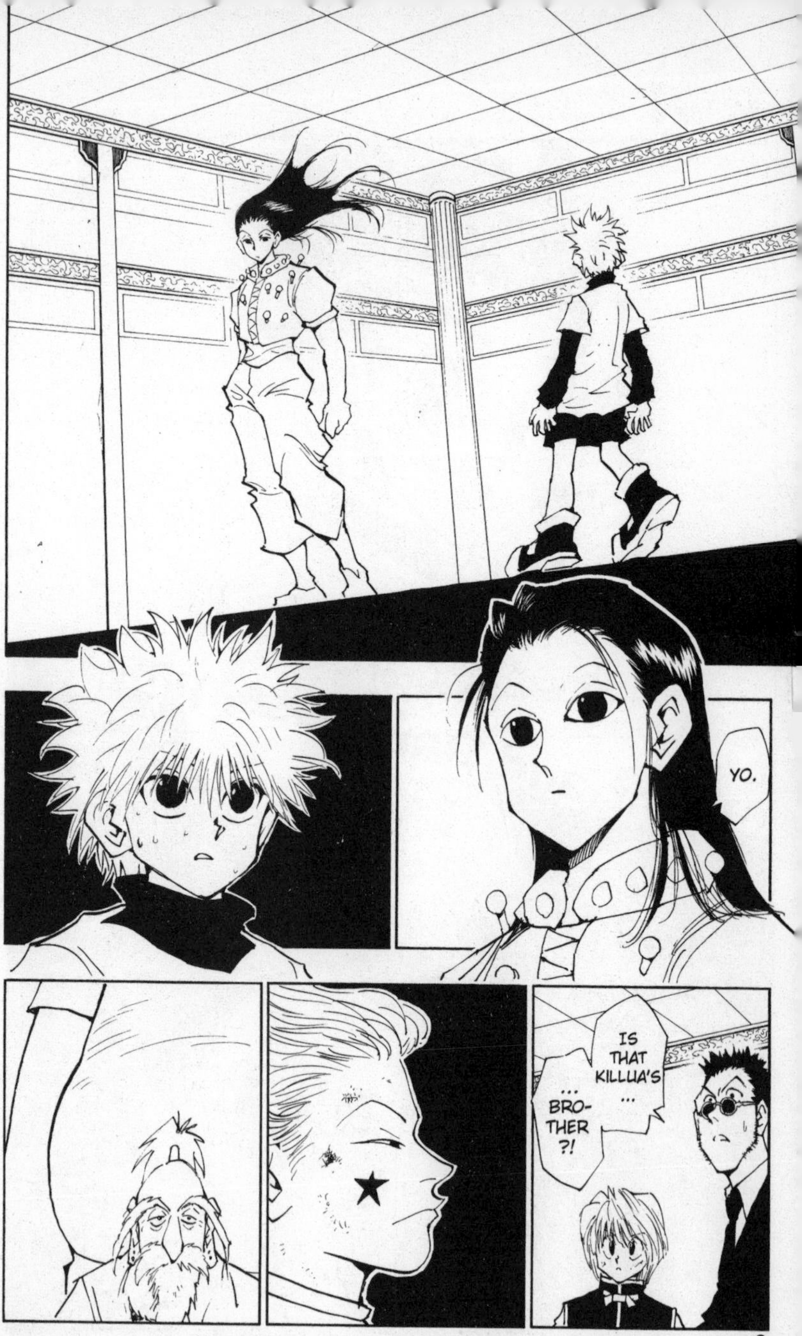
YO.
IS THAT KILLUA'S ...
... BROTHER?!

READ THIS WAY

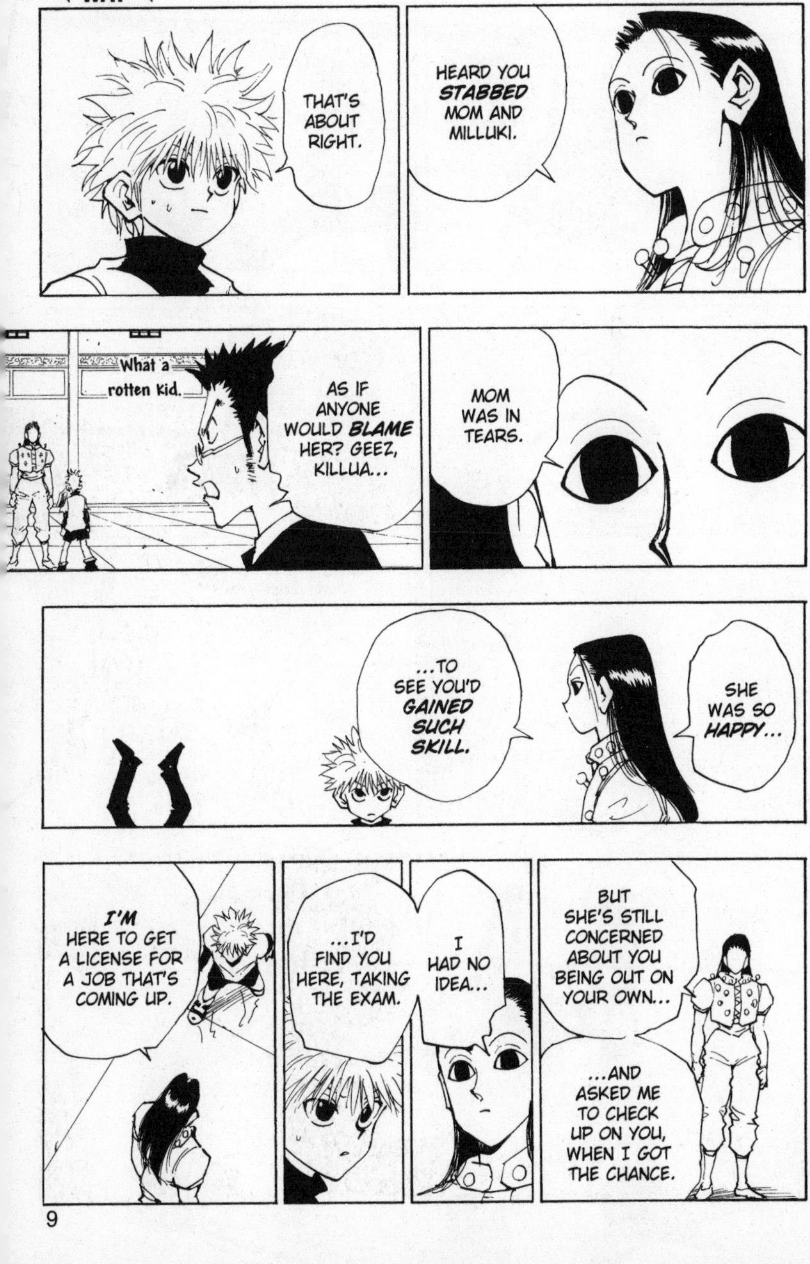
HEARD YOU STABBED MOM AND MILLUKI.
THAT'S ABOUT RIGHT.
MOM WAS IN TEARS.
AS IF ANYONE WOULD BLAME HER? GEEZ, KILLUA...
What a rotten kid.
SHE WAS SO HAPPY...
...TO SEE YOU'D GAINED SUCH SKILL.
BUT SHE'S STILL CONCERNED ABOUT YOU BEING OUT ON YOUR OWN...
...AND ASKED ME TO CHECK UP ON YOU, WHEN I GOT THE CHANCE.
I HAD NO IDEA...
...I'D FIND YOU HERE, TAKING THE EXAM.
I'M HERE TO GET A LICENSE FOR A JOB THAT'S COMING UP.

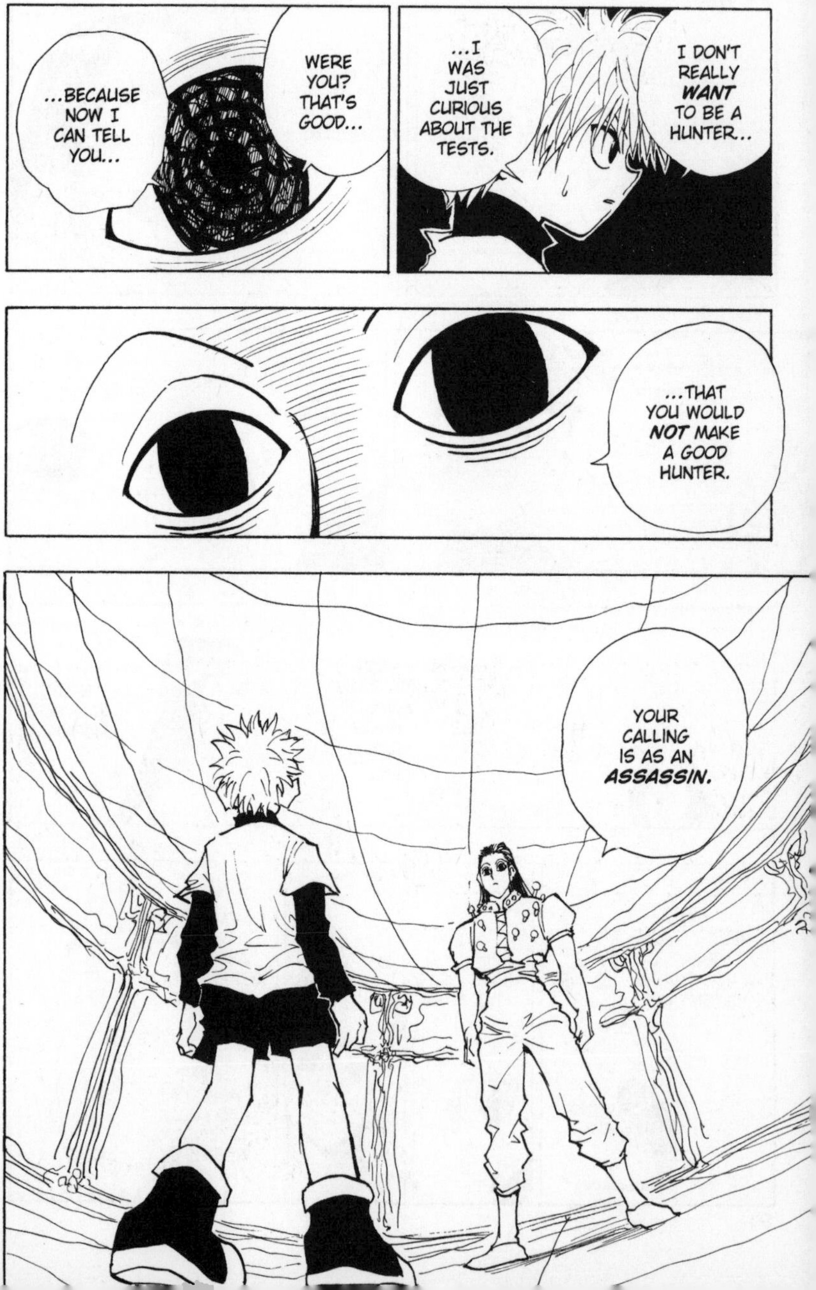
I DON'T REALLY WANT TO BE A HUNTER...
...I WAS JUST CURIOUS ABOUT THE TESTS.
WERE YOU? THAT'S GOOD...
...BECAUSE NOW I CAN TELL YOU...
...THAT YOU WOULD NOT MAKE A GOOD HUNTER.
YOUR CALLING IS AS AN ASSASSIN.

READ THIS WAY

HE ACTUALLY SAID THAT?
WHEW! WHAT A *FAMILY* KILLUA'S GOT!
AH...
...THAT WASN'T ALL.
THERE'S NO *FIRE* IN YOU, JUST DARKNESS.
IT SUSTAINS YOU, DRAINS YOU OF ANY DESIRE.
YOUR ONLY JOY IS IN CAUSING DEATH, AND EVEN THAT IS FLEETING.

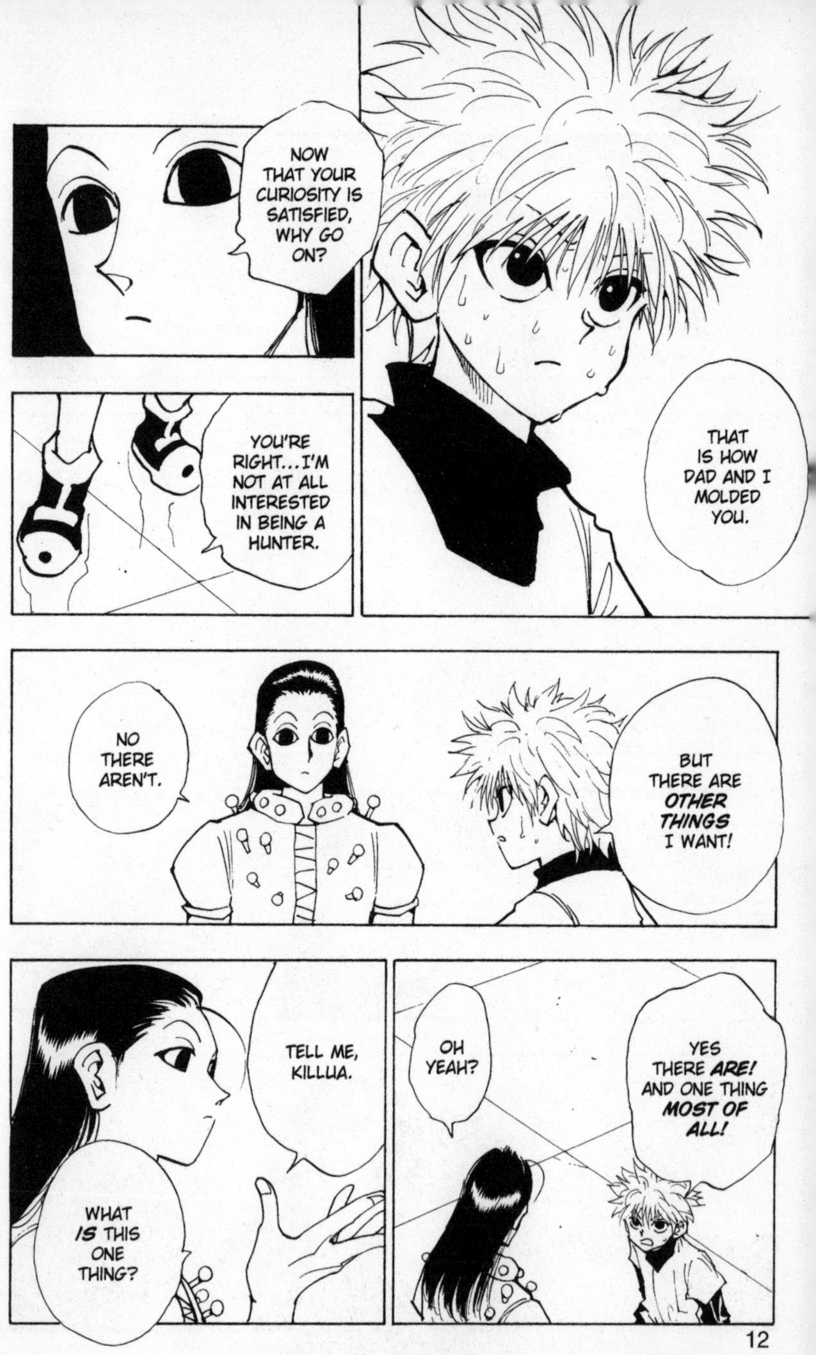
THAT IS HOW DAD AND I MOLDED YOU.
NOW THAT YOUR CURIOSITY IS SATISFIED, WHY GO ON?
YOU'RE RIGHT...I'M NOT AT ALL INTERESTED IN BEING A HUNTER.
BUT THERE ARE *OTHER THINGS* I WANT!
NO THERE AREN'T.
YES THERE *ARE!* AND ONE THING *MOST OF ALL!*
OH YEAH?
TELL ME, KILLUA.
WHAT *IS* THIS ONE THING?

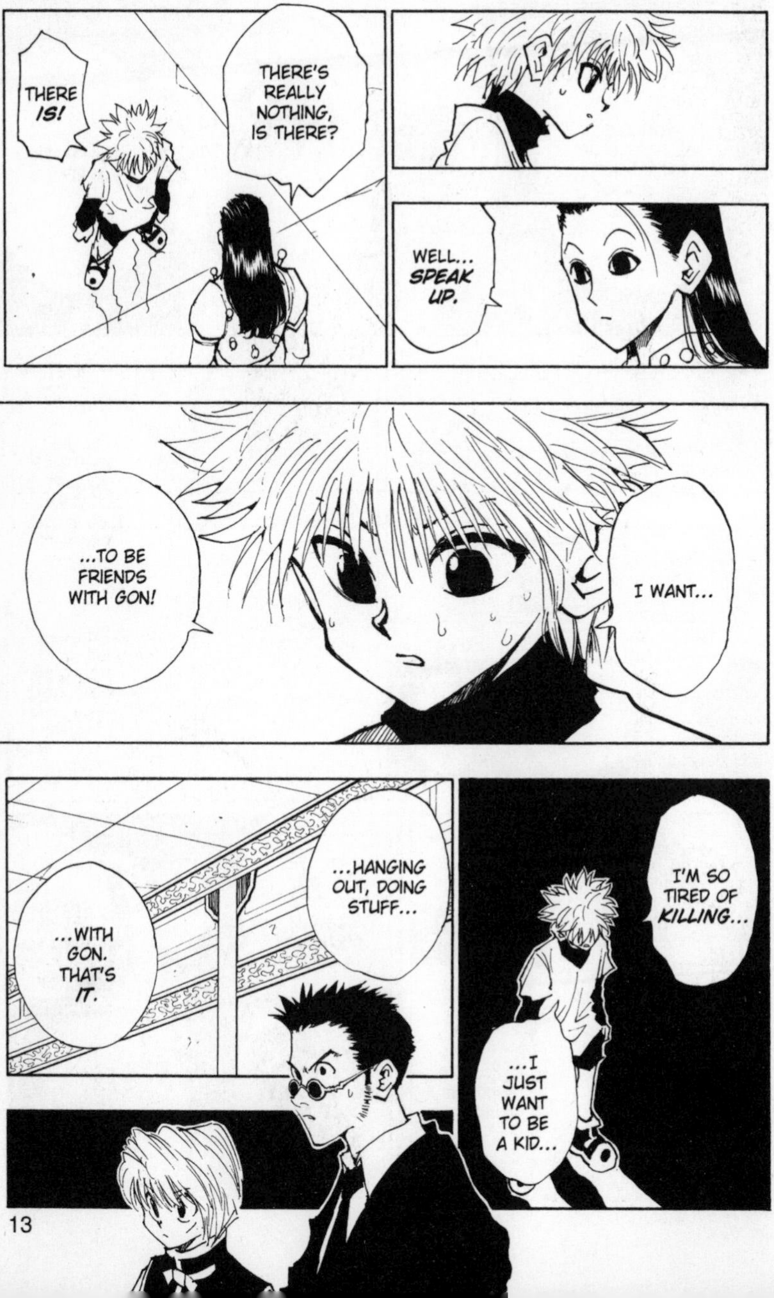
WELL... SPEAK UP.
THERE'S REALLY NOTHING, IS THERE?
THERE IS!
I WANT...
...TO BE FRIENDS WITH GON!
I'M SO TIRED OF KILLING...
...I JUST WANT TO BE A KID...
...HANGING OUT, DOING STUFF...
...WITH GON. THAT'S IT.

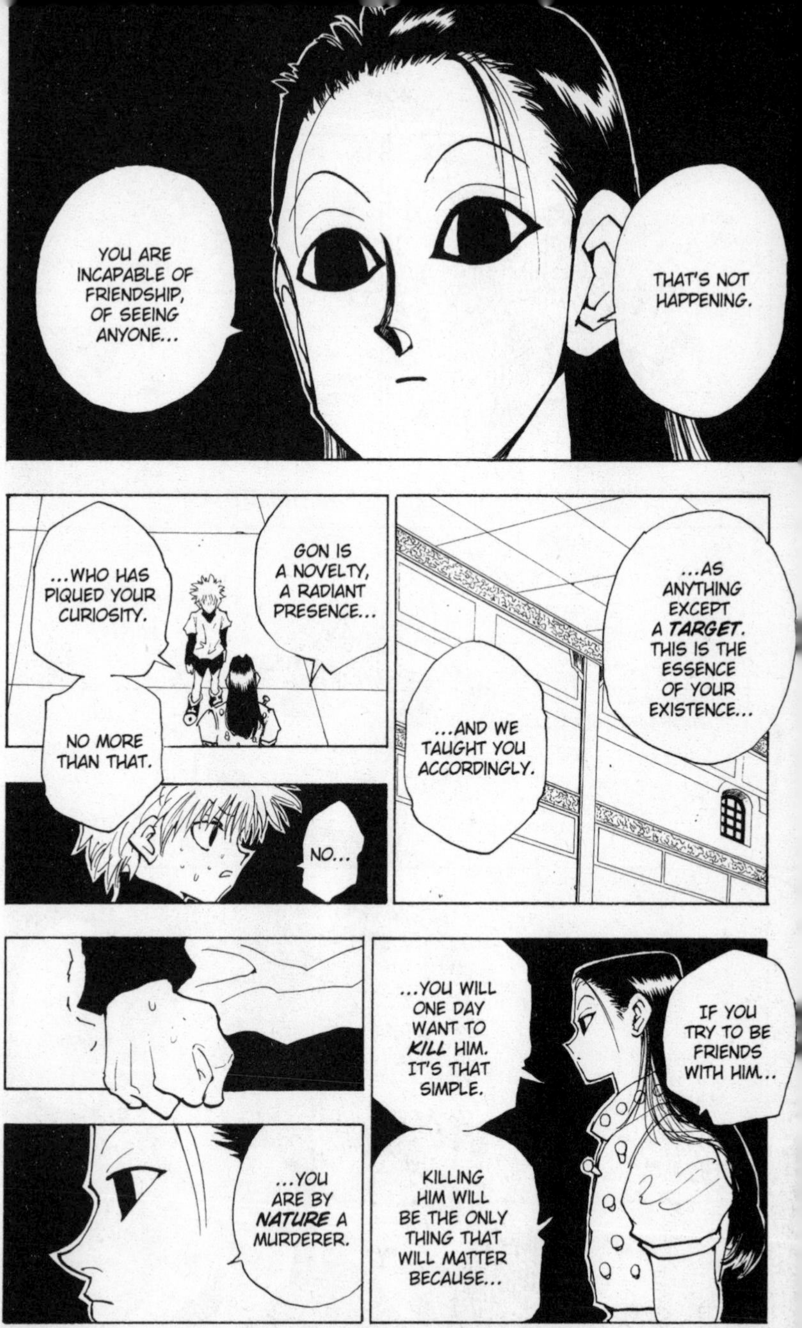
THAT'S NOT HAPPENING.
YOU ARE INCAPABLE OF FRIENDSHIP, OF SEEING ANYONE...
...AS ANYTHING EXCEPT A **TARGET**. THIS IS THE ESSENCE OF YOUR EXISTENCE...
...AND WE TAUGHT YOU ACCORDINGLY.
GON IS A NOVELTY, A RADIANT PRESENCE...
...WHO HAS PIQUED YOUR CURIOSITY.
NO MORE THAN THAT.
NO...
IF YOU TRY TO BE FRIENDS WITH HIM...
...YOU WILL ONE DAY WANT TO **KILL** HIM. IT'S THAT SIMPLE.
KILLING HIM WILL BE THE ONLY THING THAT WILL MATTER BECAUSE...
...YOU ARE BY **NATURE** A MURDERER.

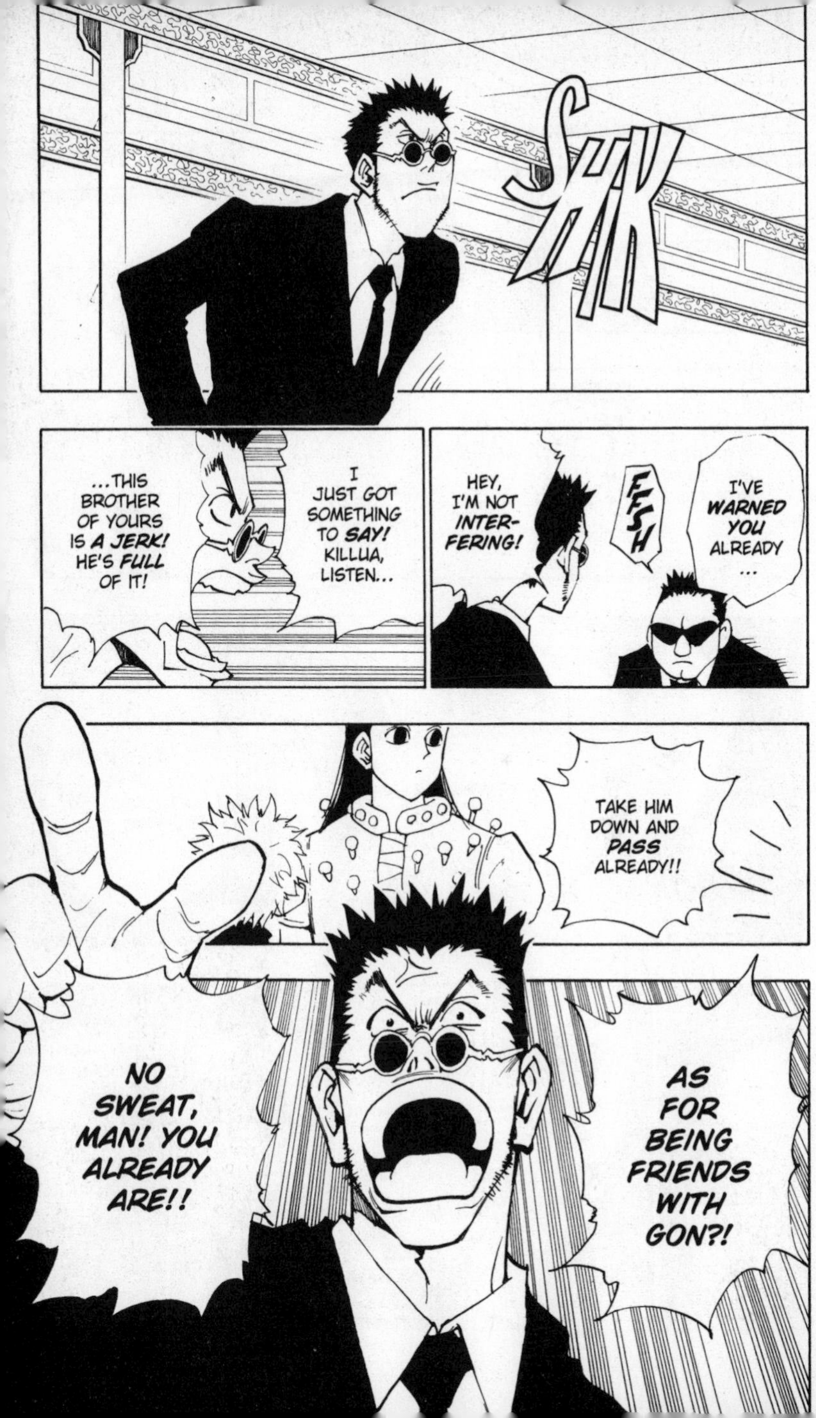
SHK
I'VE WARNED YOU ALREADY ...
FFSH
HEY, I'M NOT INTER-FERING!
I JUST GOT SOMETHING TO SAY! KILLUA, LISTEN...
...THIS BROTHER OF YOURS IS A JERK! HE'S FULL OF IT!
TAKE HIM DOWN AND PASS ALREADY!!
AS FOR BEING FRIENDS WITH GON?!
NO SWEAT, MAN! YOU ALREADY ARE!!

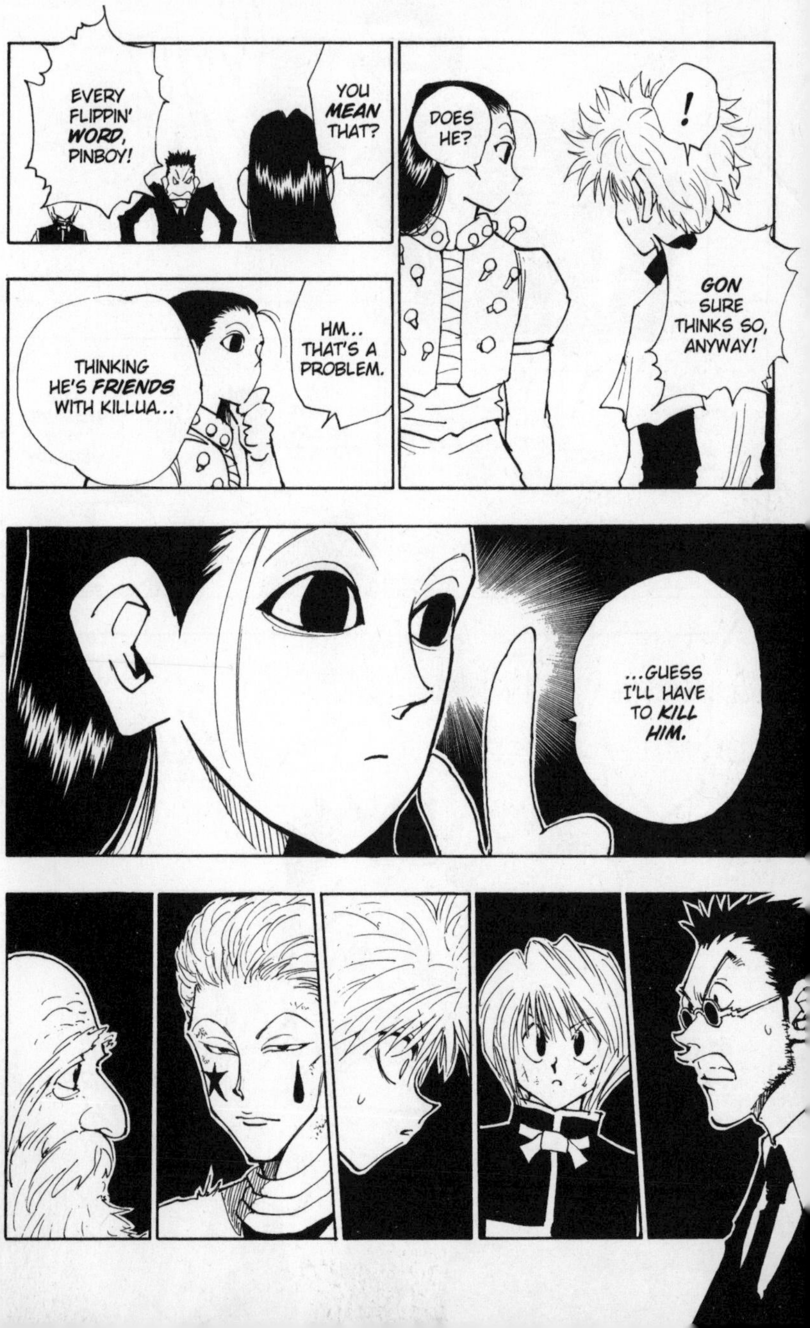
!
DOES HE?
GON SURE THINKS SO, ANYWAY!
YOU MEAN THAT?
EVERY FLIPPIN' WORD, PINBOY!
HM.. THAT'S A PROBLEM.
THINKING HE'S FRIENDS WITH KILLUA...
...GUESS I'LL HAVE TO KILL HIM.

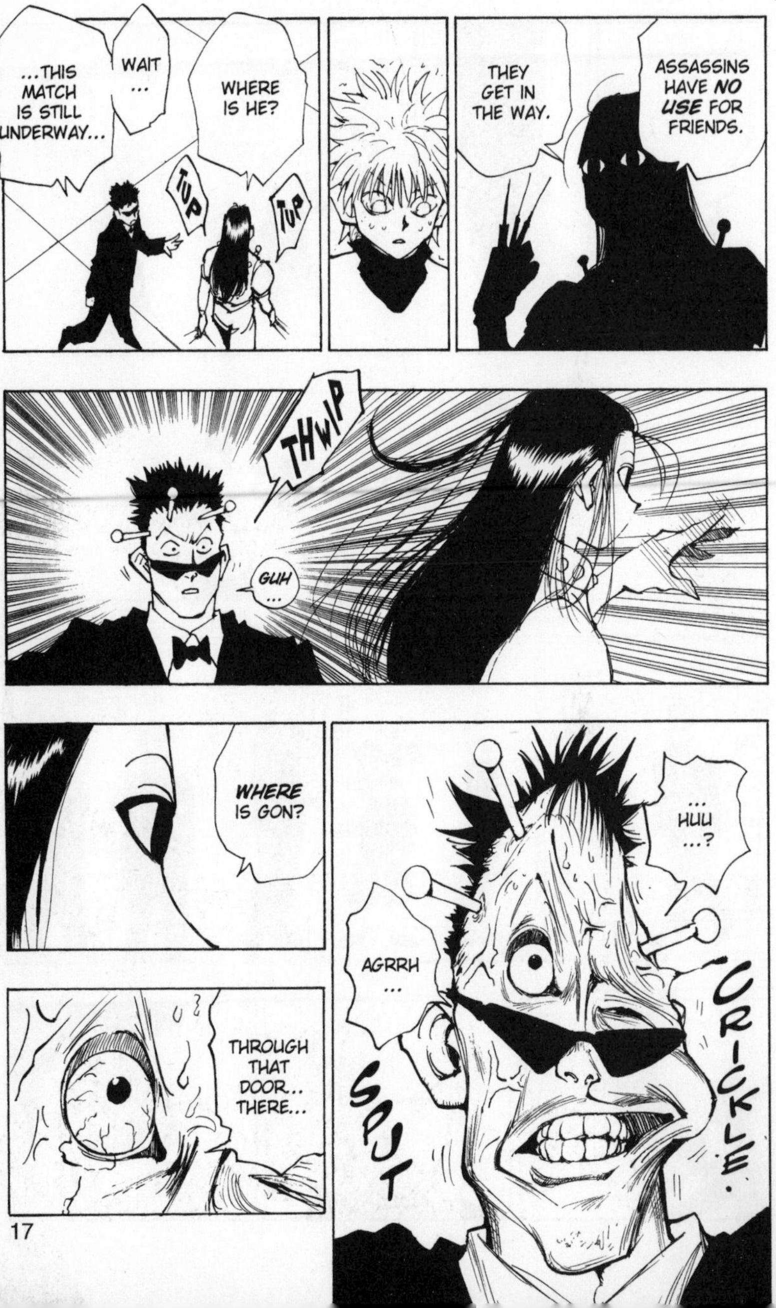
ASSASSINS HAVE ***NO USE*** FOR FRIENDS.
THEY GET IN THE WAY.
WHERE IS HE?
WAIT ...
...THIS MATCH IS STILL UNDERWAY...
TUP
TUP
THWIP
GUH ...
... HUU ...?
AGRRH ...
CRICKLE.
SPUT
WHERE IS GON?
THROUGH THAT DOOR... THERE...

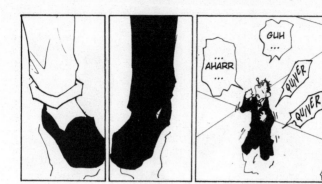

GUH
...

...
AHARR
...

QUIVER

QUIVER

THANKS.

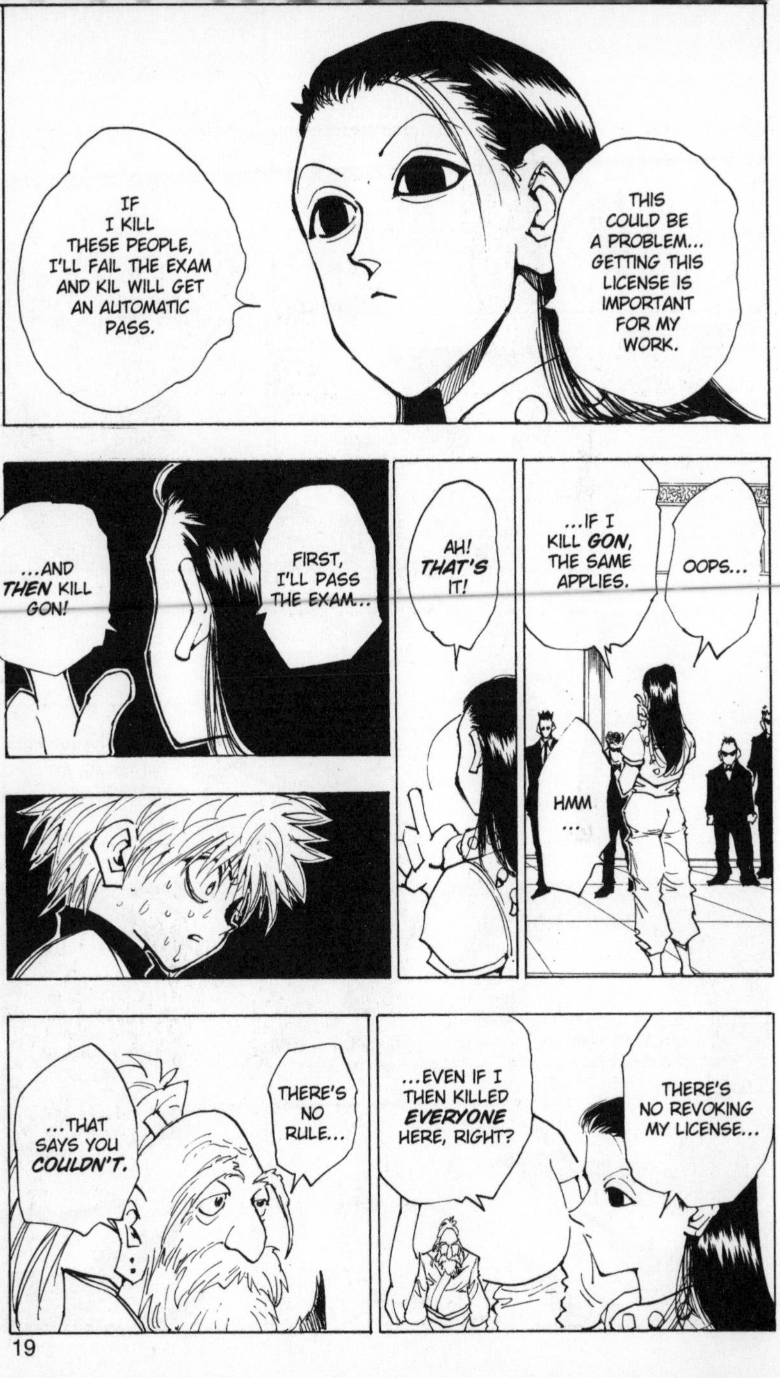
THIS COULD BE A PROBLEM... GETTING THIS LICENSE IS IMPORTANT FOR MY WORK.
IF I KILL THESE PEOPLE, I'LL FAIL THE EXAM AND KIL WILL GET AN AUTOMATIC PASS.
OOPS...
...IF I KILL **GON**, THE SAME APPLIES.
HMM ...
AH! **THAT'S** IT!
FIRST, I'LL PASS THE EXAM...
...AND **THEN** KILL GON!
THERE'S NO REVOKING MY LICENSE...
...EVEN IF I THEN KILLED **EVERYONE** HERE, RIGHT?
THERE'S NO RULE...
...THAT SAYS YOU **COULDN'T.**

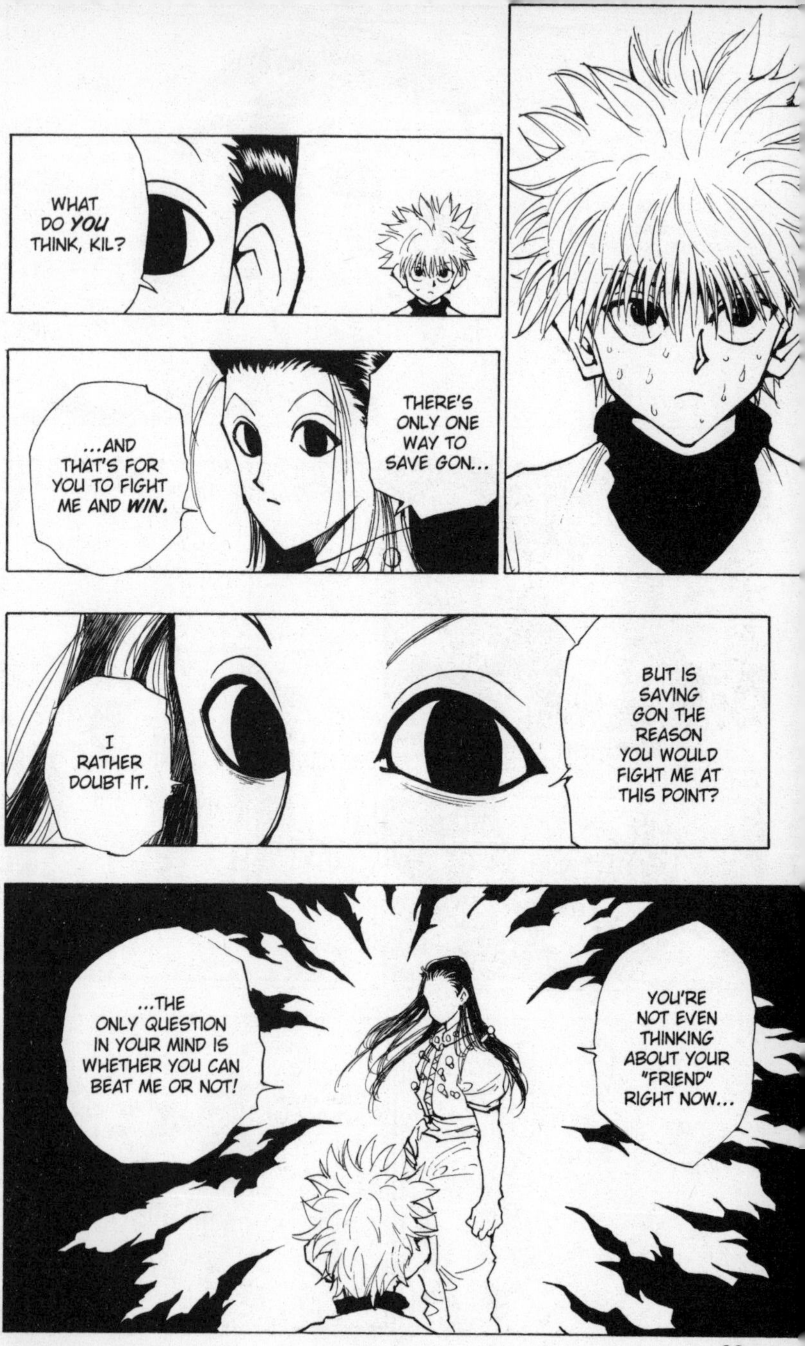
WHAT DO *YOU* THINK, KIL?
THERE'S ONLY ONE WAY TO SAVE GON...
...AND THAT'S FOR YOU TO FIGHT ME AND *WIN.*
BUT IS SAVING GON THE REASON YOU WOULD FIGHT ME AT THIS POINT?
I RATHER DOUBT IT.
YOU'RE NOT EVEN THINKING ABOUT YOUR "FRIEND" RIGHT NOW...
...THE ONLY QUESTION IN YOUR MIND IS WHETHER YOU CAN BEAT ME OR NOT!

READ THIS WAY

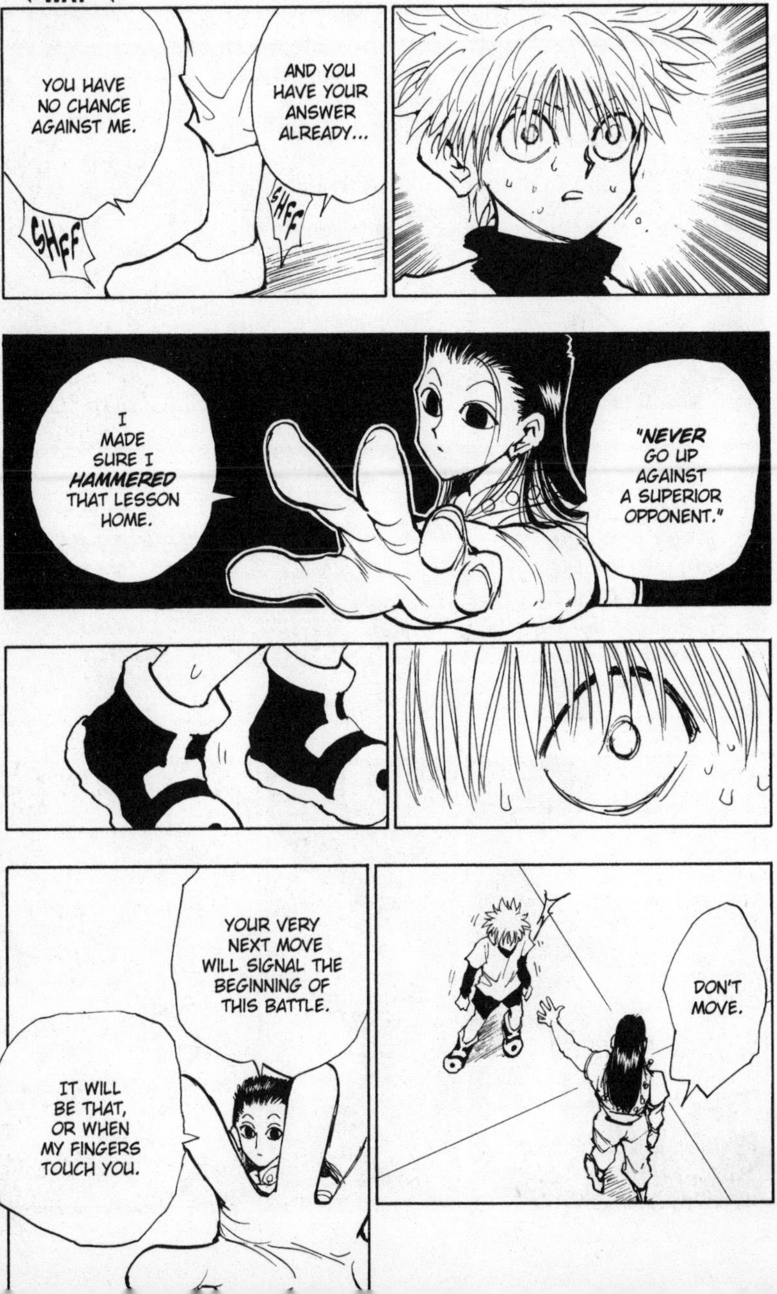
AND YOU HAVE YOUR ANSWER ALREADY...
SHFF
YOU HAVE NO CHANCE AGAINST ME.
SHFF
"NEVER GO UP AGAINST A SUPERIOR OPPONENT."
I MADE SURE I HAMMERED THAT LESSON HOME.
DON'T MOVE.
YOUR VERY NEXT MOVE WILL SIGNAL THE BEGINNING OF THIS BATTLE.
IT WILL BE THAT, OR WHEN MY FINGERS TOUCH YOU.

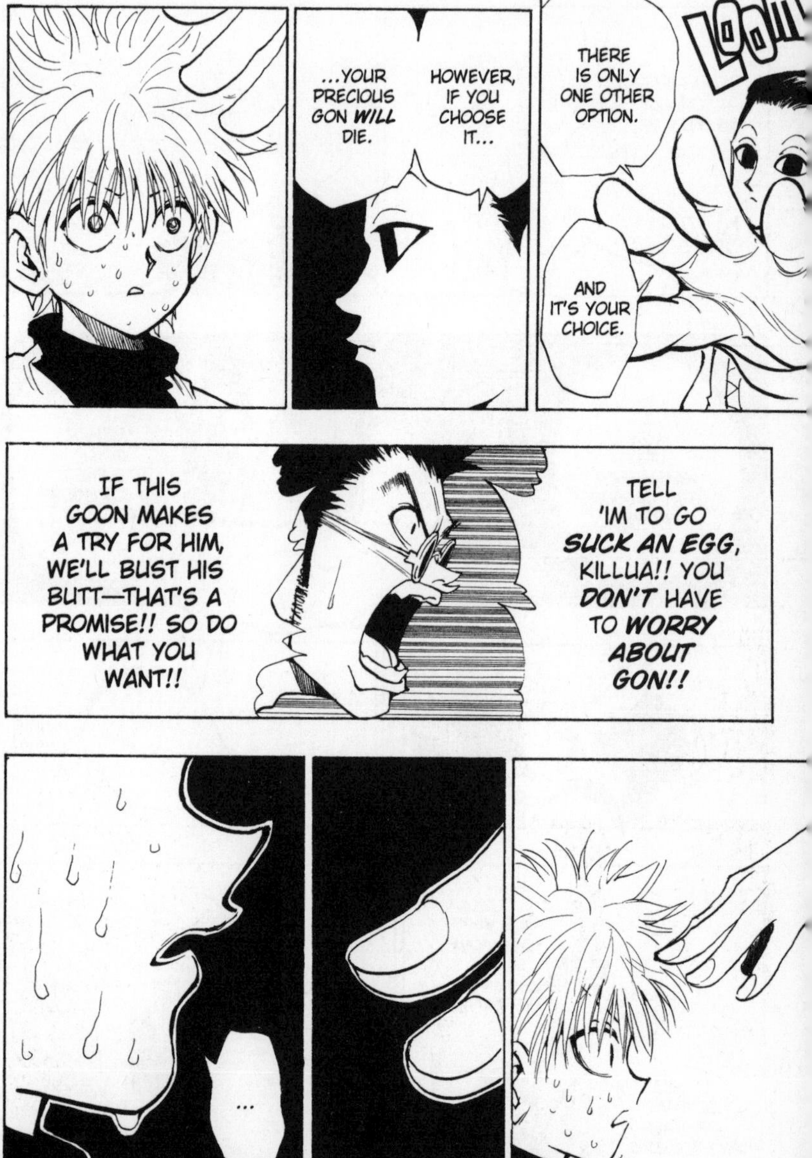
LOON
THERE IS ONLY ONE OTHER OPTION.
AND IT'S YOUR CHOICE.
HOWEVER, IF YOU CHOOSE IT...
...YOUR PRECIOUS GON **WILL** DIE.
TELL 'IM TO GO **SUCK AN EGG**, KILLUA!! YOU **DON'T** HAVE TO **WORRY ABOUT GON!!**
IF THIS GOON MAKES A TRY FOR HIM, WE'LL BUST HIS BUTT—THAT'S A PROMISE!! SO DO WHAT YOU WANT!!
...

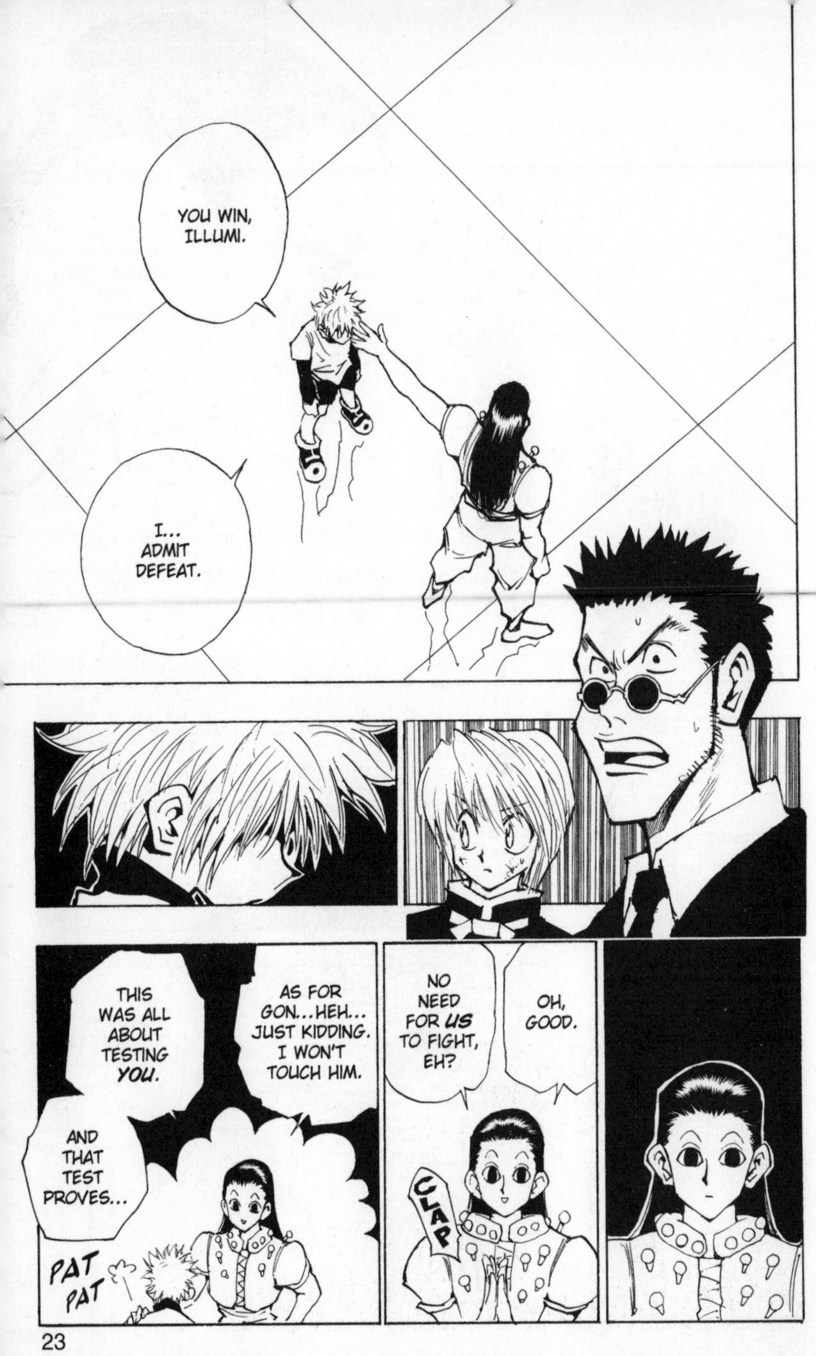
YOU WIN, ILLUMI.
I... ADMIT DEFEAT.
OH, GOOD.
NO NEED FOR US TO FIGHT, EH?
CLAP
AS FOR GON...HEH... JUST KIDDING. I WON'T TOUCH HIM.
THIS WAS ALL ABOUT TESTING YOU.
AND THAT TEST PROVES...
PAT PAT

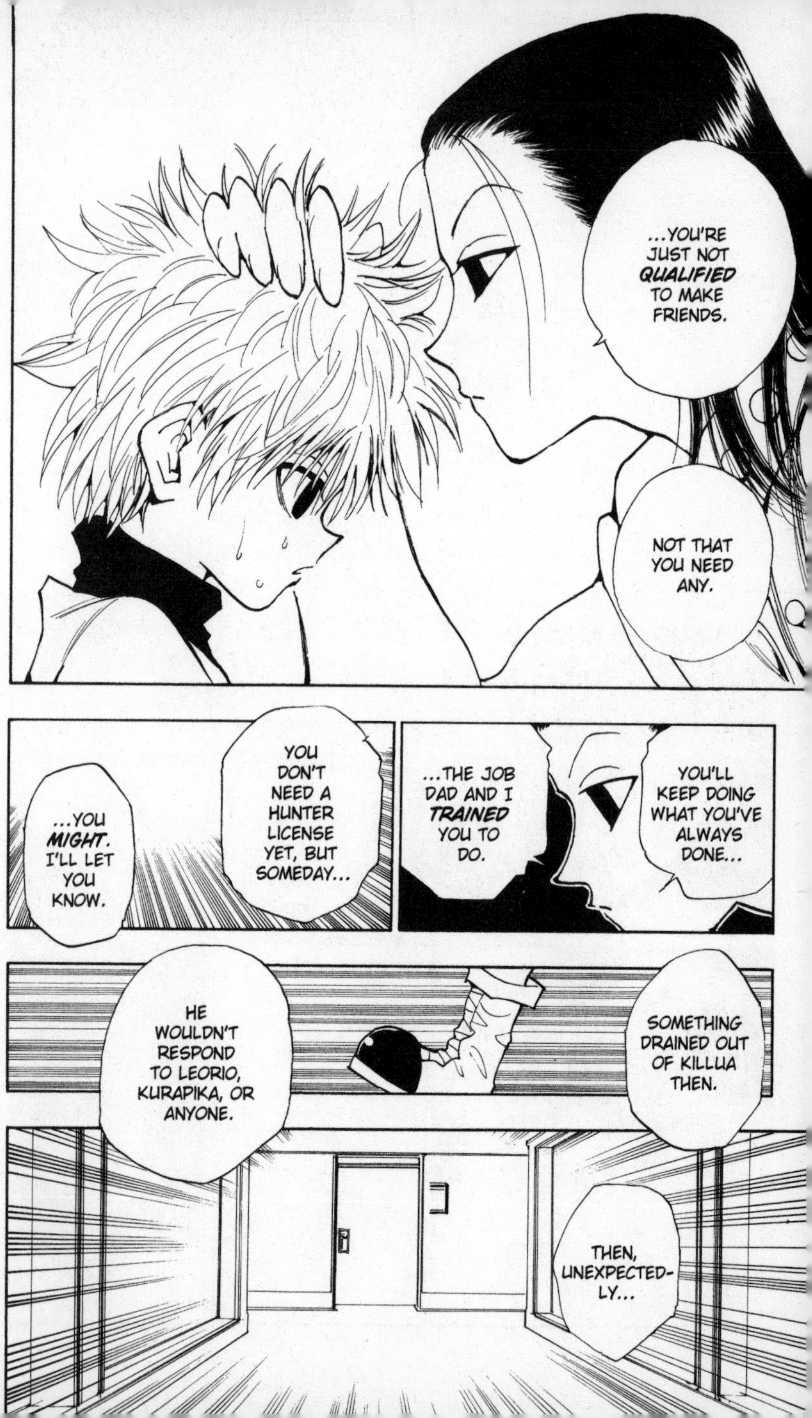
...YOU'RE JUST NOT *QUALIFIED* TO MAKE FRIENDS.
NOT THAT YOU NEED ANY.
YOU'LL KEEP DOING WHAT YOU'VE ALWAYS DONE...
...THE JOB DAD AND I *TRAINED* YOU TO DO.
YOU DON'T NEED A HUNTER LICENSE YET, BUT SOMEDAY...
...YOU *MIGHT*. I'LL LET YOU KNOW.
SOMETHING DRAINED OUT OF KILLUA THEN.
HE WOULDN'T RESPOND TO LEORIO, KURAPIKA, OR ANYONE.
THEN, UNEXPECTEDLY...

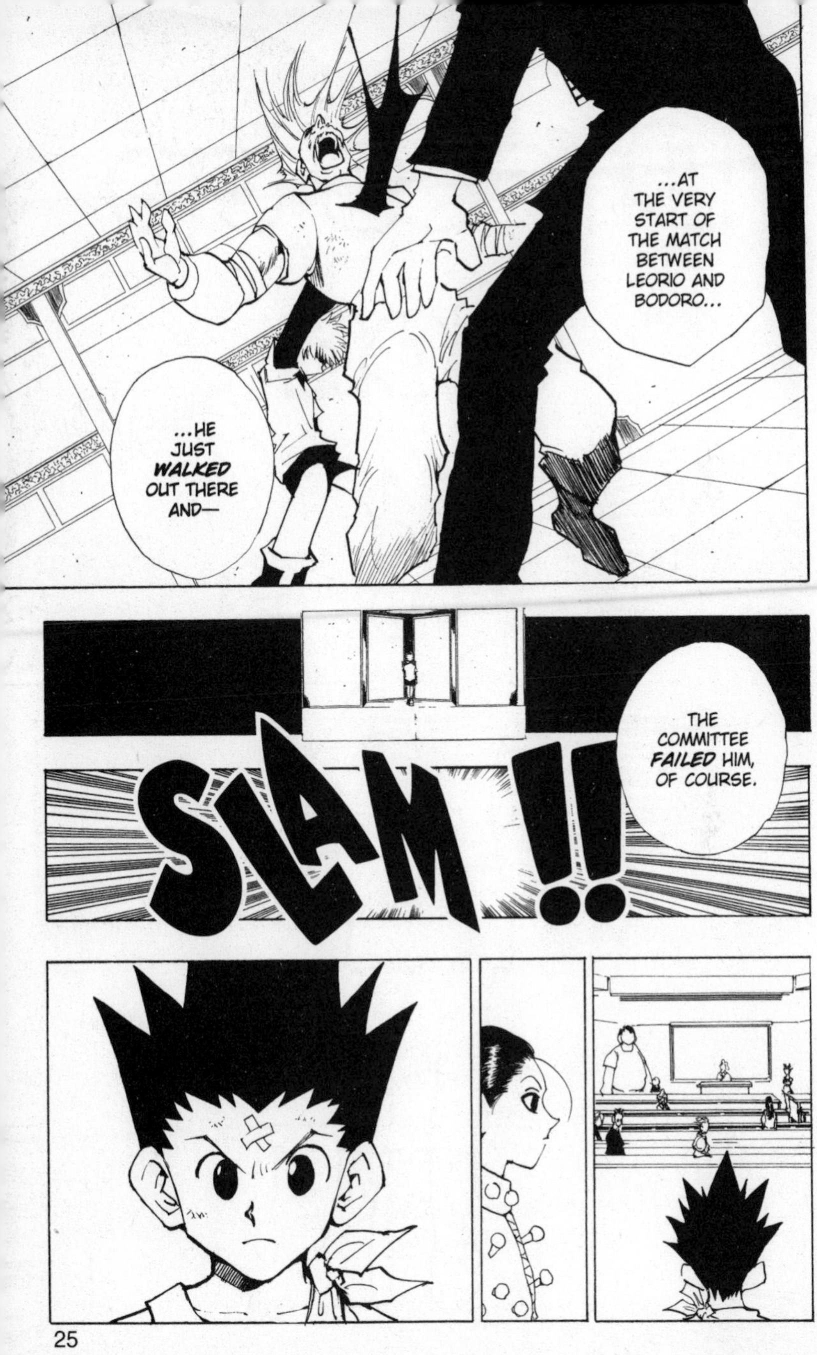
...AT THE VERY START OF THE MATCH BETWEEN LEORIO AND BODORO...
...HE JUST **WALKED** OUT THERE AND—
THE COMMITTEE **FAILED** HIM, OF COURSE.
SLAM!!

Dress-up Gon ✂

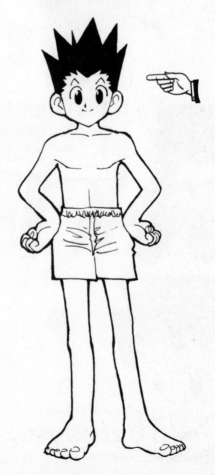

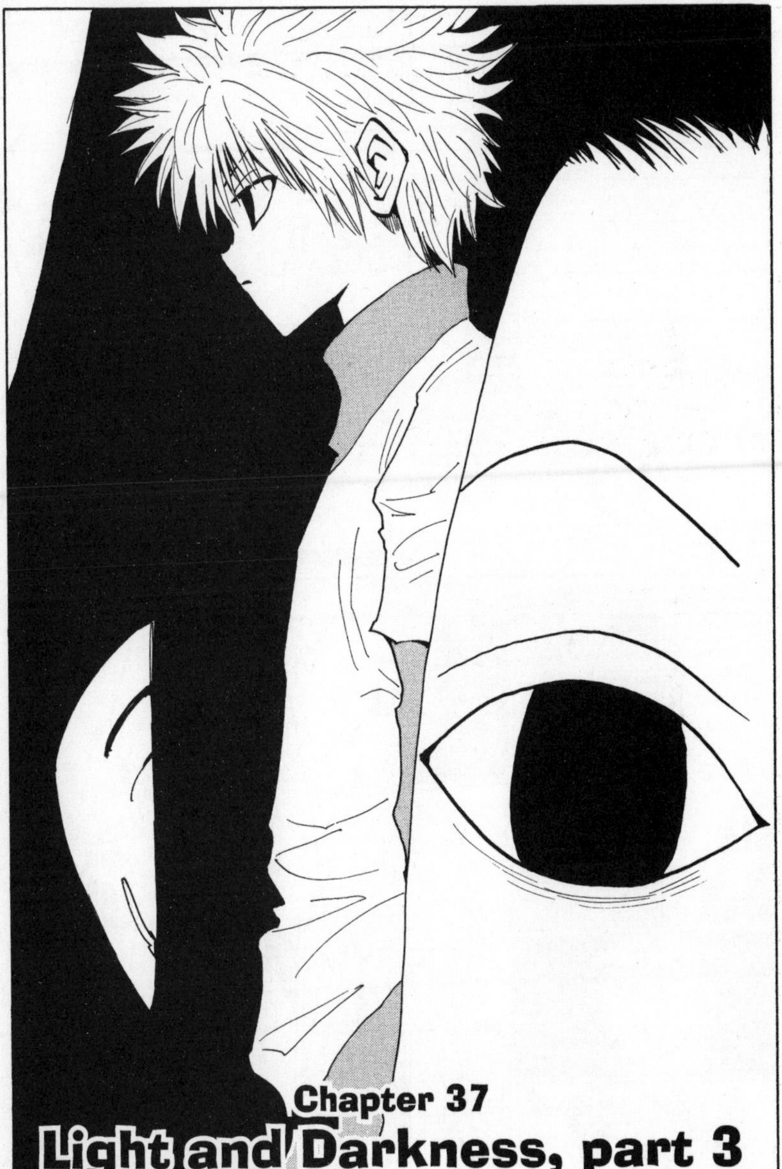
Chapter 37
Light and Darkness, part 3

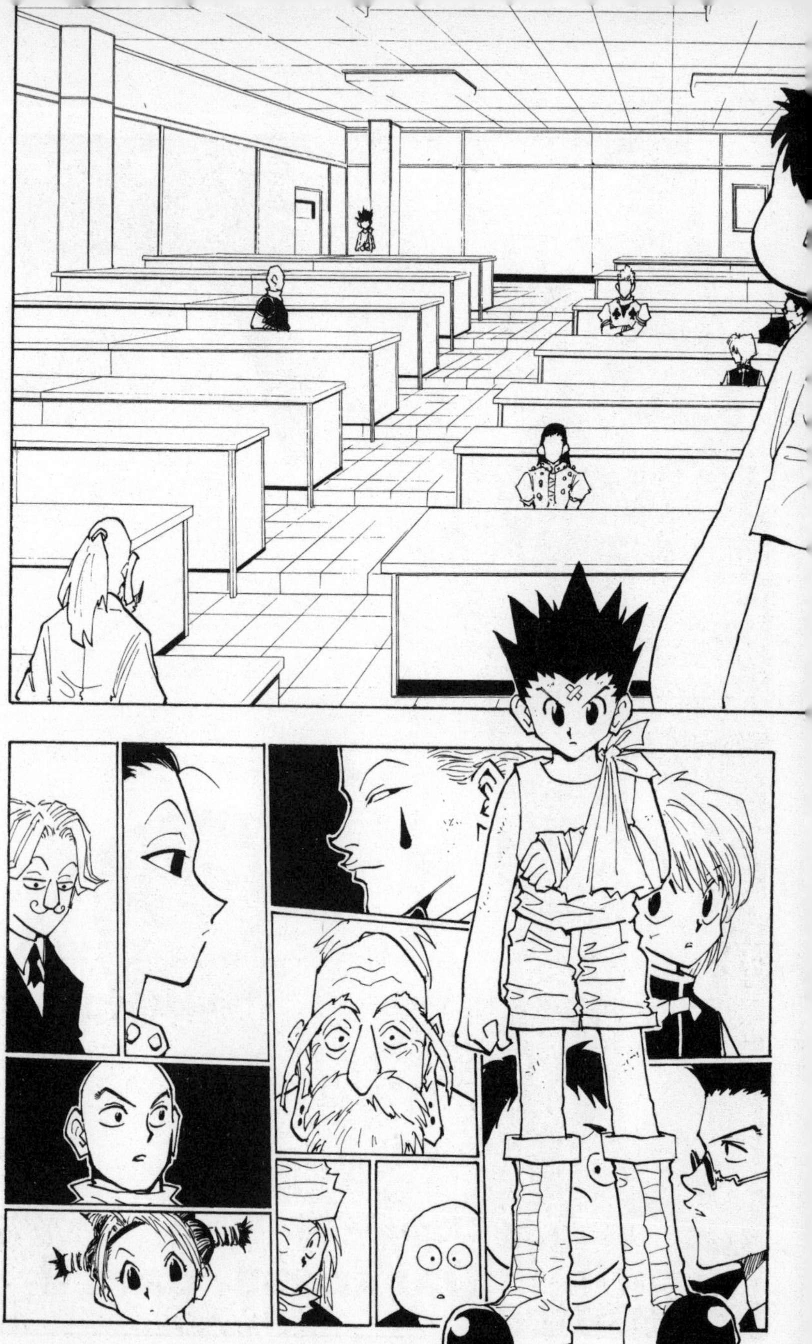

READ THIS WAY

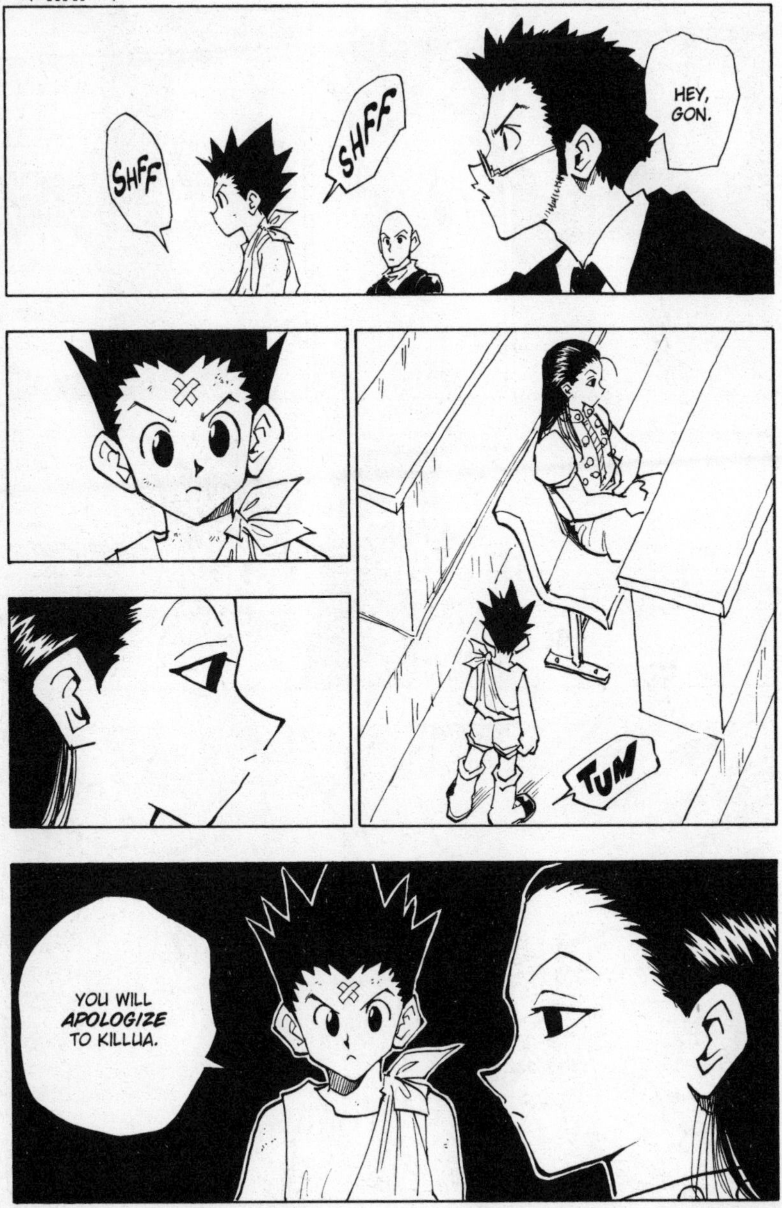
HEY, GON.
SHFF
SHFF
TUM
YOU WILL *APOLOGIZE* TO KILLUA.

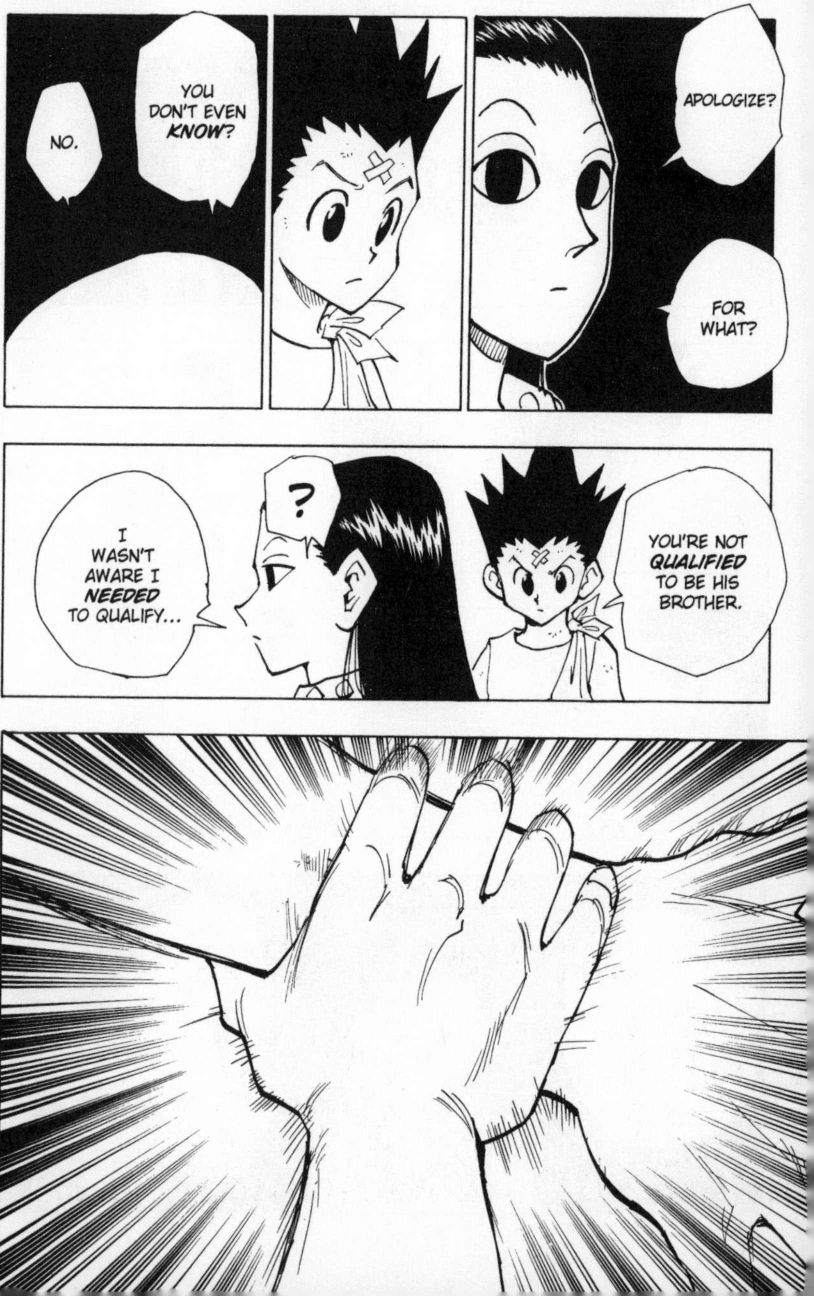
APOLOGIZE?
FOR WHAT?
YOU DON'T EVEN *KNOW*?
NO.
YOU'RE NOT *QUALIFIED* TO BE HIS BROTHER.
?
I WASN'T AWARE I *NEEDED* TO QUALIFY...

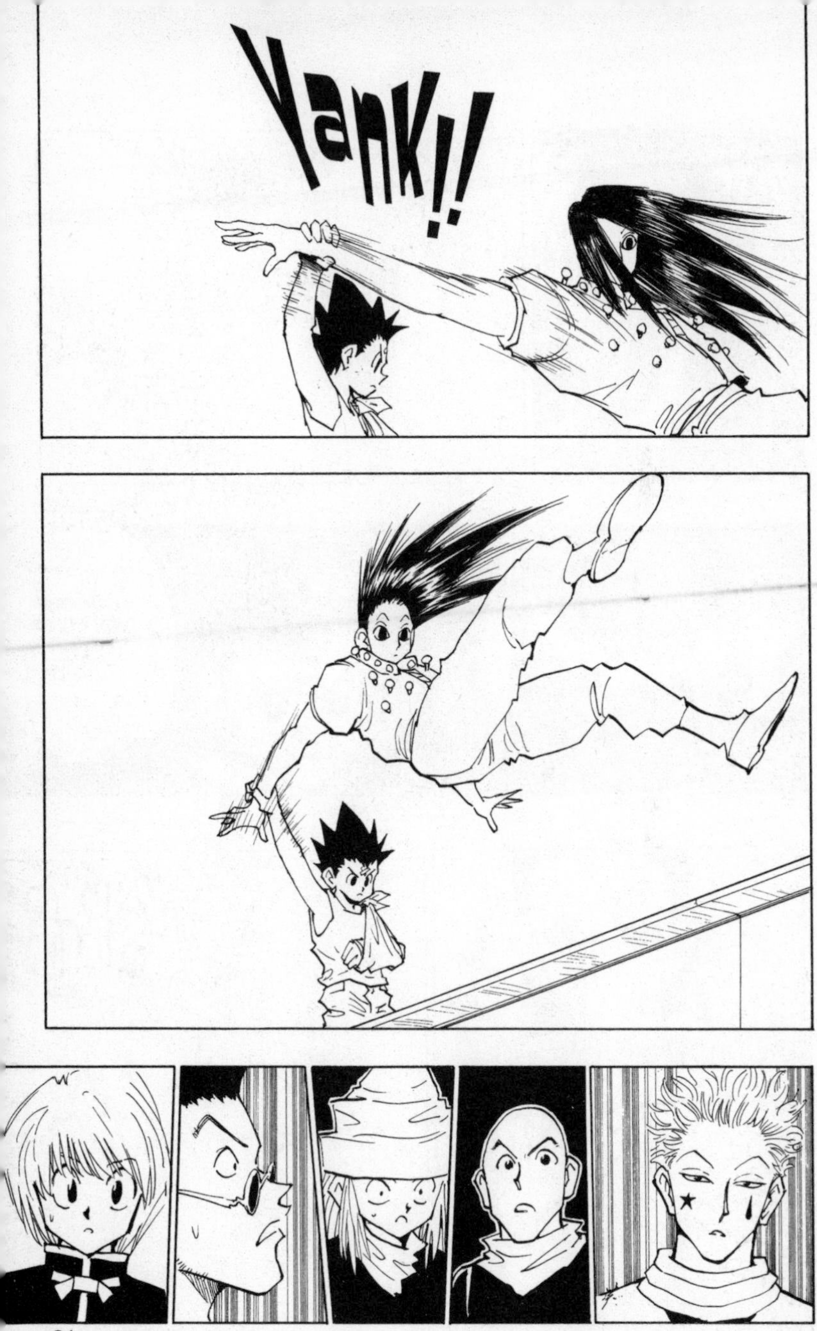
YANK!!

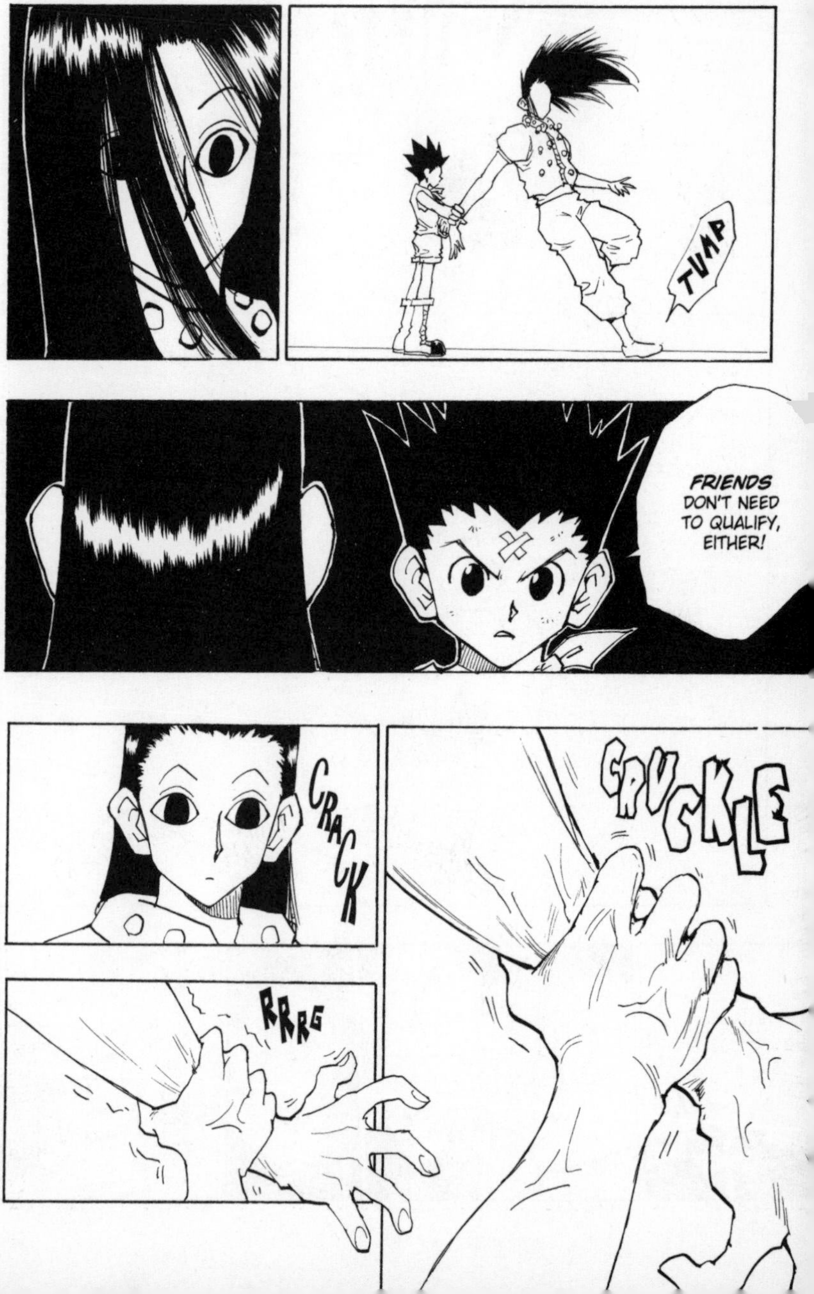
TUMP
FRIENDS DON'T NEED TO QUALIFY, EITHER!
CRUCKLE
CRACK
RRRG

READ THIS WAY

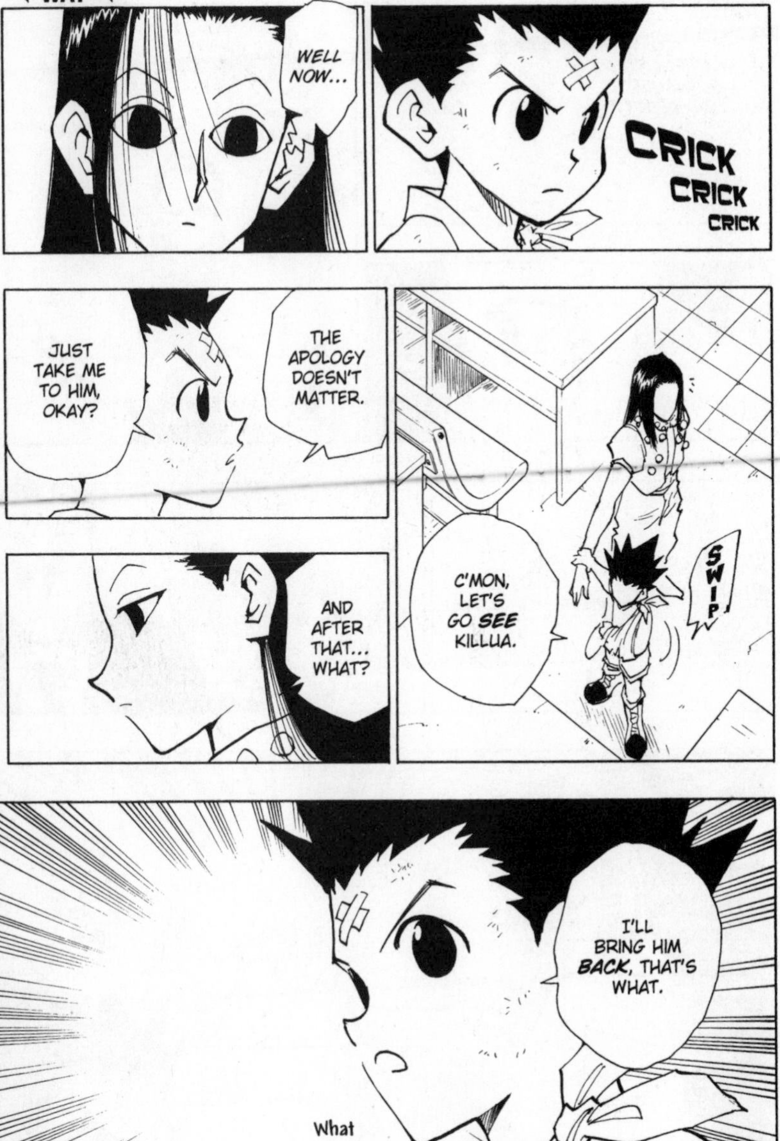
CRICK
CRICK
CRICK
WELL NOW...
C'MON, LET'S GO SEE KILLUA.
SWIP
THE APOLOGY DOESN'T MATTER.
JUST TAKE ME TO HIM, OKAY?
AND AFTER THAT... WHAT?
I'LL BRING HIM BACK, THAT'S WHAT.
What else?

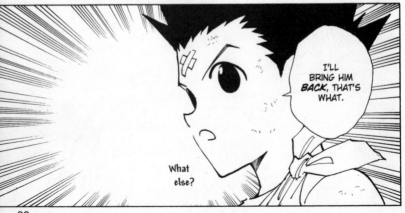

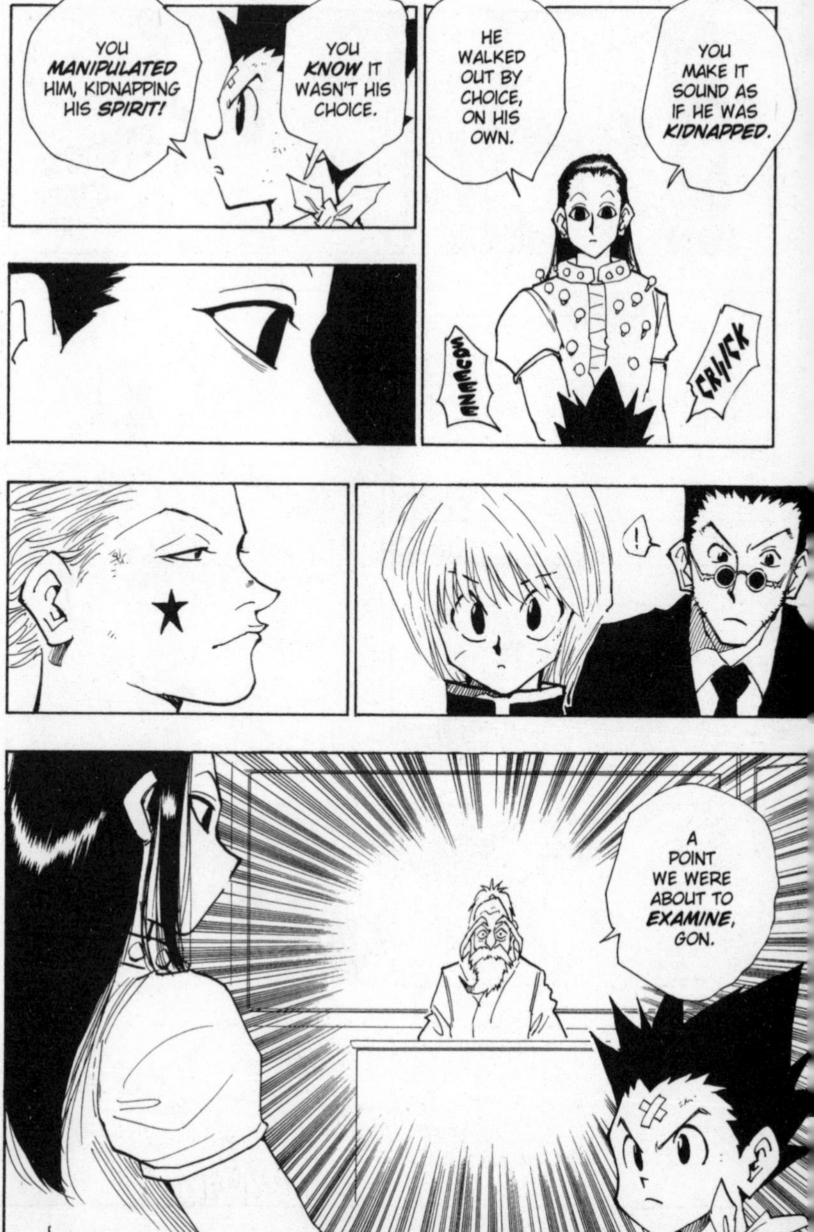
YOU MAKE IT SOUND AS IF HE WAS KIDNAPPED.
HE WALKED OUT BY CHOICE, ON HIS OWN.
CRICK
YOU KNOW IT WASN'T HIS CHOICE.
YOU MANIPULATED HIM, KIDNAPPING HIS SPIRIT!
!
A POINT WE WERE ABOUT TO EXAMINE, GON.

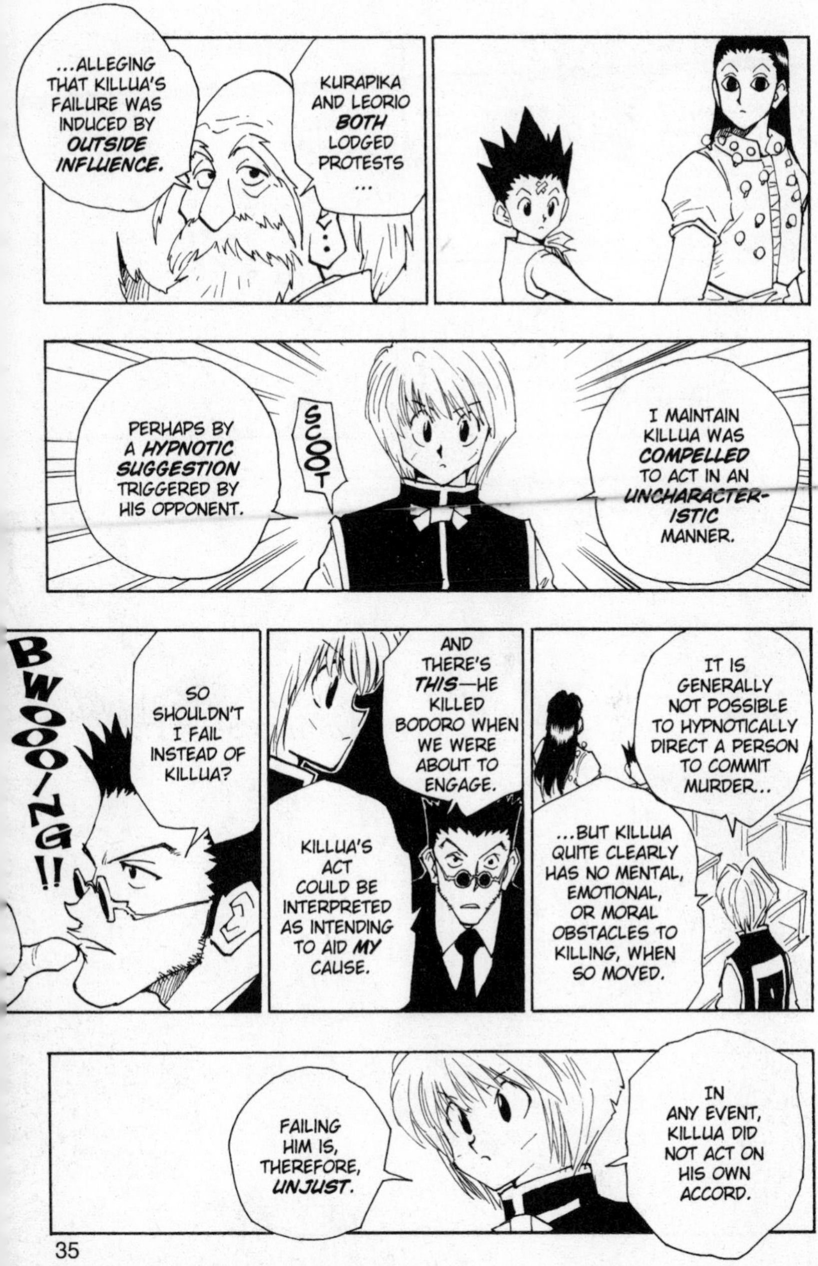
KURAPIKA AND LEORIO BOTH LODGED PROTESTS ...
...ALLEGING THAT KILLUA'S FAILURE WAS INDUCED BY OUTSIDE INFLUENCE.
I MAINTAIN KILLUA WAS COMPELLED TO ACT IN AN UNCHARACTER-ISTIC MANNER.
SCOOT
PERHAPS BY A HYPNOTIC SUGGESTION TRIGGERED BY HIS OPPONENT.
IT IS GENERALLY NOT POSSIBLE TO HYPNOTICALLY DIRECT A PERSON TO COMMIT MURDER...
...BUT KILLUA QUITE CLEARLY HAS NO MENTAL, EMOTIONAL, OR MORAL OBSTACLES TO KILLING, WHEN SO MOVED.
AND THERE'S THIS—HE KILLED BODORO WHEN WE WERE ABOUT TO ENGAGE.
KILLUA'S ACT COULD BE INTERPRETED AS INTENDING TO AID MY CAUSE.
SO SHOULDN'T I FAIL INSTEAD OF KILLUA?
BWOOOING!!
IN ANY EVENT, KILLUA DID NOT ACT ON HIS OWN ACCORD.
FAILING HIM IS, THEREFORE, UNJUST.

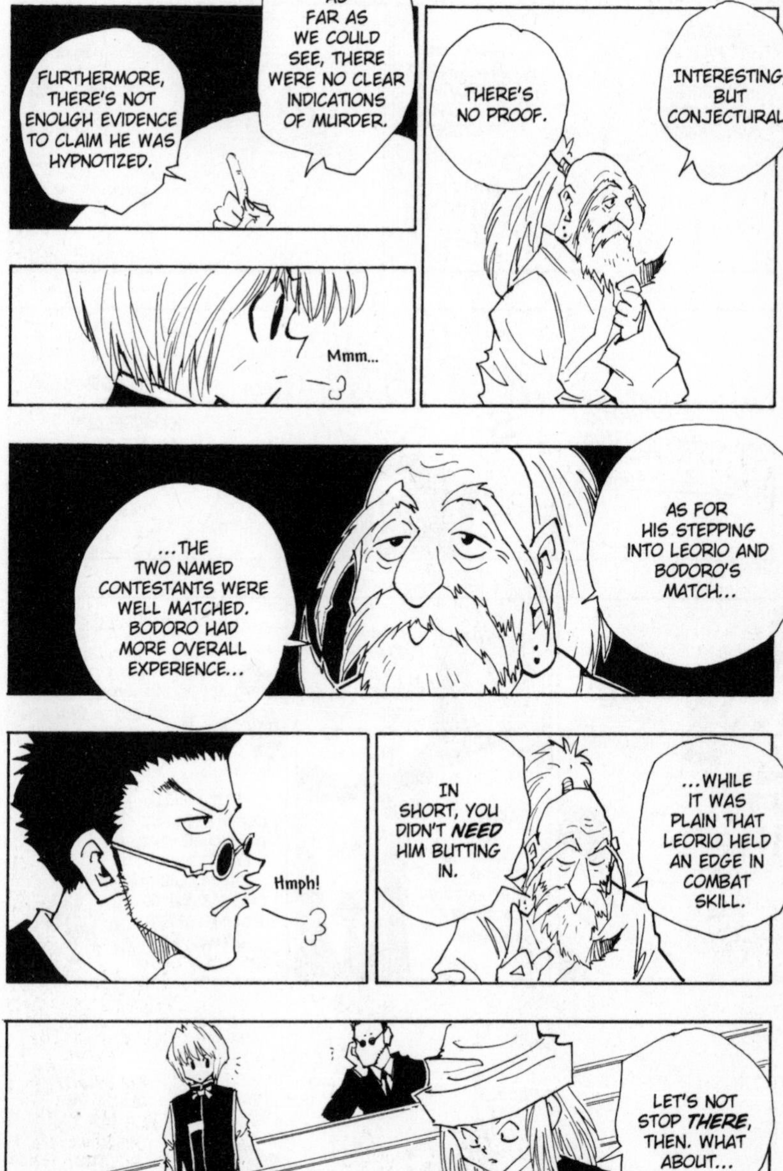
INTERESTING, BUT CONJECTURAL.
THERE'S NO PROOF.
AS FAR AS WE COULD SEE, THERE WERE NO CLEAR INDICATIONS OF MURDER.
FURTHERMORE, THERE'S NOT ENOUGH EVIDENCE TO CLAIM HE WAS HYPNOTIZED.
Mmm...
AS FOR HIS STEPPING INTO LEORIO AND BODORO'S MATCH...
...THE TWO NAMED CONTESTANTS WERE WELL MATCHED. BODORO HAD MORE OVERALL EXPERIENCE...
...WHILE IT WAS PLAIN THAT LEORIO HELD AN EDGE IN COMBAT SKILL.
IN SHORT, YOU DIDN'T ***NEED*** HIM BUTTING IN.
Hmph!
LET'S NOT STOP ***THERE***, THEN. WHAT ABOUT...

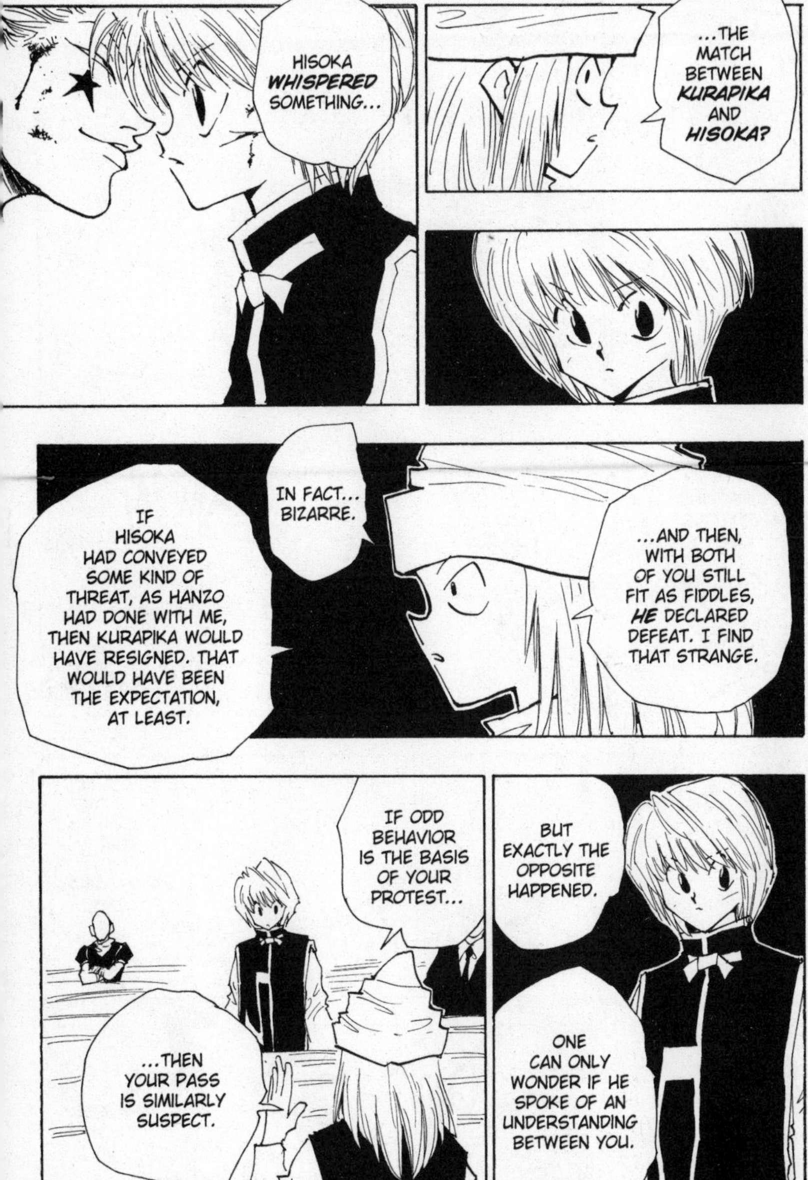
...THE MATCH BETWEEN KURAPIKA AND HISOKA?
HISOKA WHISPERED SOMETHING...
...AND THEN, WITH BOTH OF YOU STILL FIT AS FIDDLES, HE DECLARED DEFEAT. I FIND THAT STRANGE.
IN FACT... BIZARRE.
IF HISOKA HAD CONVEYED SOME KIND OF THREAT, AS HANZO HAD DONE WITH ME, THEN KURAPIKA WOULD HAVE RESIGNED. THAT WOULD HAVE BEEN THE EXPECTATION, AT LEAST.
BUT EXACTLY THE OPPOSITE HAPPENED.
ONE CAN ONLY WONDER IF HE SPOKE OF AN UNDERSTANDING BETWEEN YOU.
IF ODD BEHAVIOR IS THE BASIS OF YOUR PROTEST...
...THEN YOUR PASS IS SIMILARLY SUSPECT.

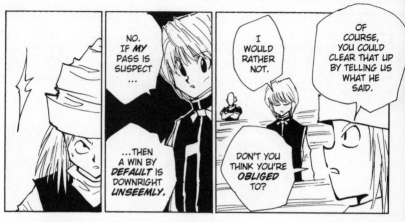

OF COURSE, YOU COULD CLEAR THAT UP BY TELLING US WHAT HE SAID.
I WOULD RATHER NOT.
DON'T YOU THINK YOU'RE OBLIGED TO?
NO. IF MY PASS IS SUSPECT ...
...THEN A WIN BY DEFAULT IS DOWNRIGHT UNSEEMLY.
SHLUNK!
SAY WHAT?!
COOL IT, SHRIMP!
LET'S JUST GET THIS OVER WITH! I'D LIKE TO GO HOME!
THIS IS ALL POINTLESS.
EVERYONE HERE HAS PASSED. EACH OF US...
...IS EITHER SATISFIED THAT HE HAS MEASURED UP, OR HE CAN DO WHATEVER IT TAKES TO BE SATISFIED.

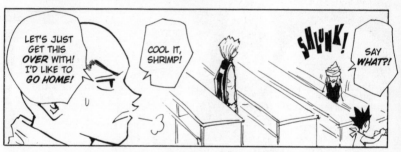

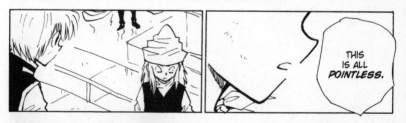

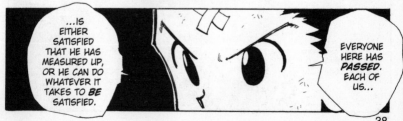

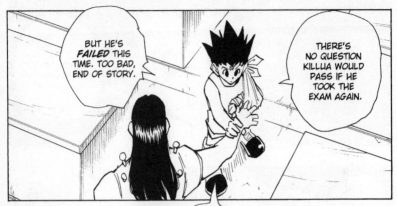

THERE'S NO QUESTION KILLUA WOULD PASS IF HE TOOK THE EXAM AGAIN.
BUT HE'S *FAILED* THIS TIME. TOO BAD, END OF STORY.
CRICKLE
CRICKLE
CRICKLE
BUT...
...IF KILLUA'S A KILLER BECAUSE...
...YOU'VE *MADE* HIM ONE, GITTARAKUR, THEN...

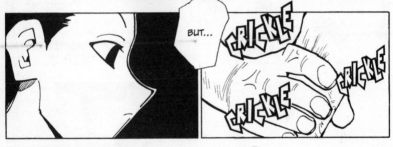

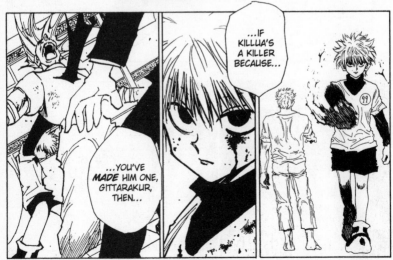

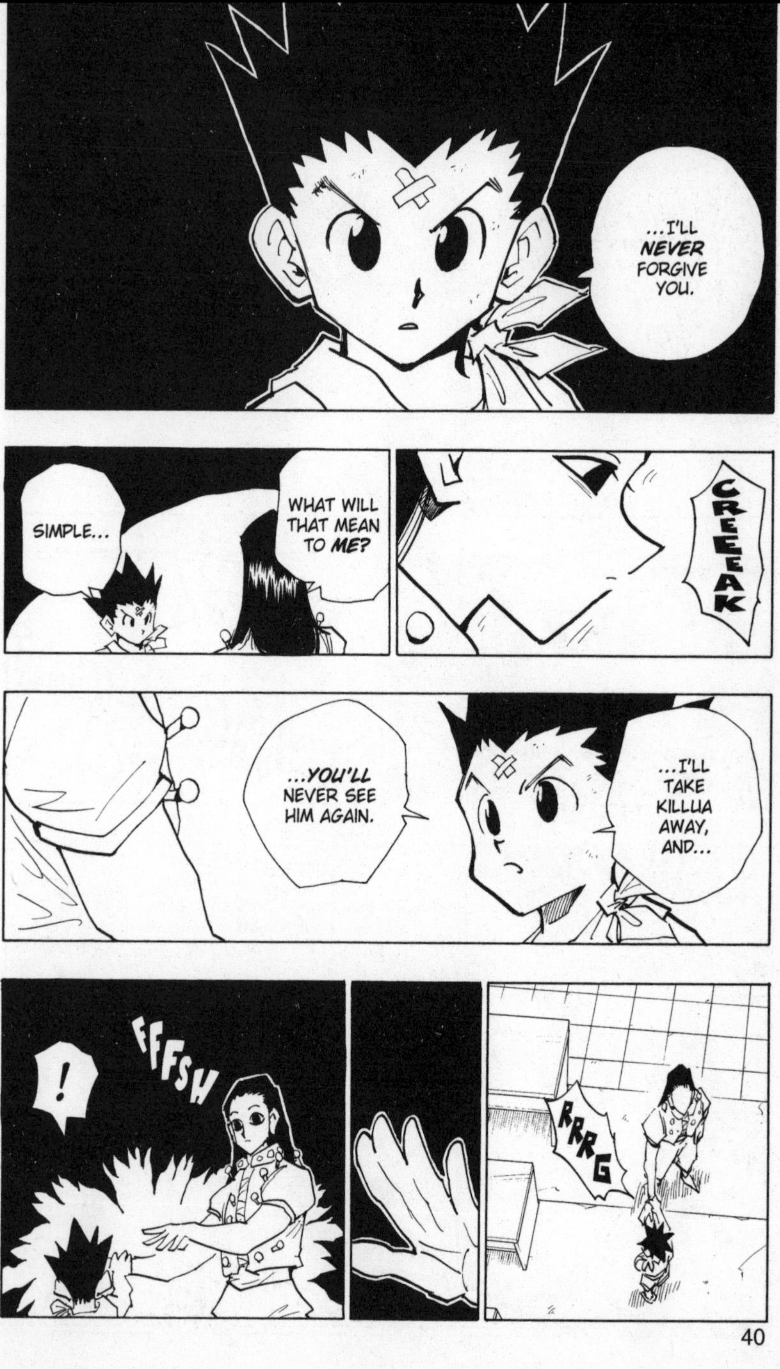
...I'LL *NEVER* FORGIVE YOU.
CREEEAK
WHAT WILL THAT MEAN TO *ME?*
SIMPLE...
...I'LL TAKE KILLUA AWAY, AND...
...*YOU'LL* NEVER SEE HIM AGAIN.
RRRG
FFFSH
!

READ THIS WAY

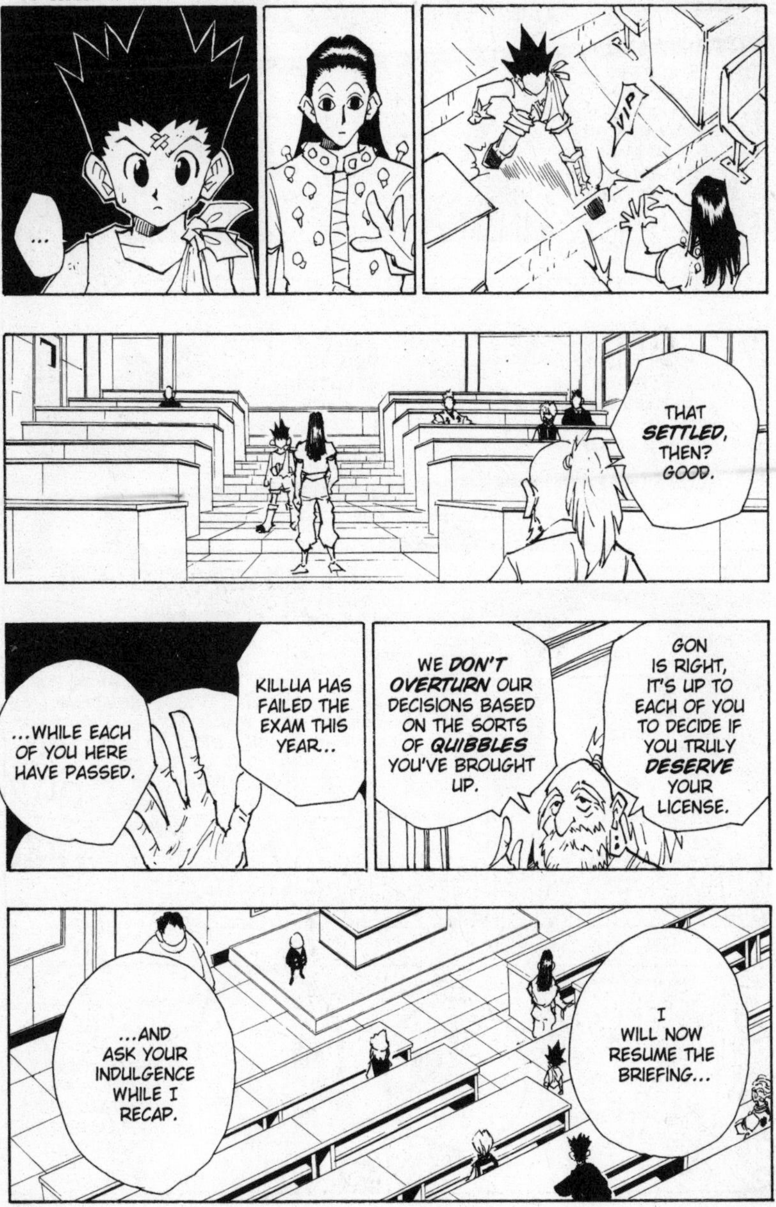
VIP
...
THAT SETTLED, THEN? GOOD.
GON IS RIGHT, IT'S UP TO EACH OF YOU TO DECIDE IF YOU TRULY DESERVE YOUR LICENSE.
WE DON'T OVERTURN OUR DECISIONS BASED ON THE SORTS OF QUIBBLES YOU'VE BROUGHT UP.
KILLUA HAS FAILED THE EXAM THIS YEAR..
...WHILE EACH OF YOU HERE HAVE PASSED.
I WILL NOW RESUME THE BRIEFING...
...AND ASK YOUR INDULGENCE WHILE I RECAP.

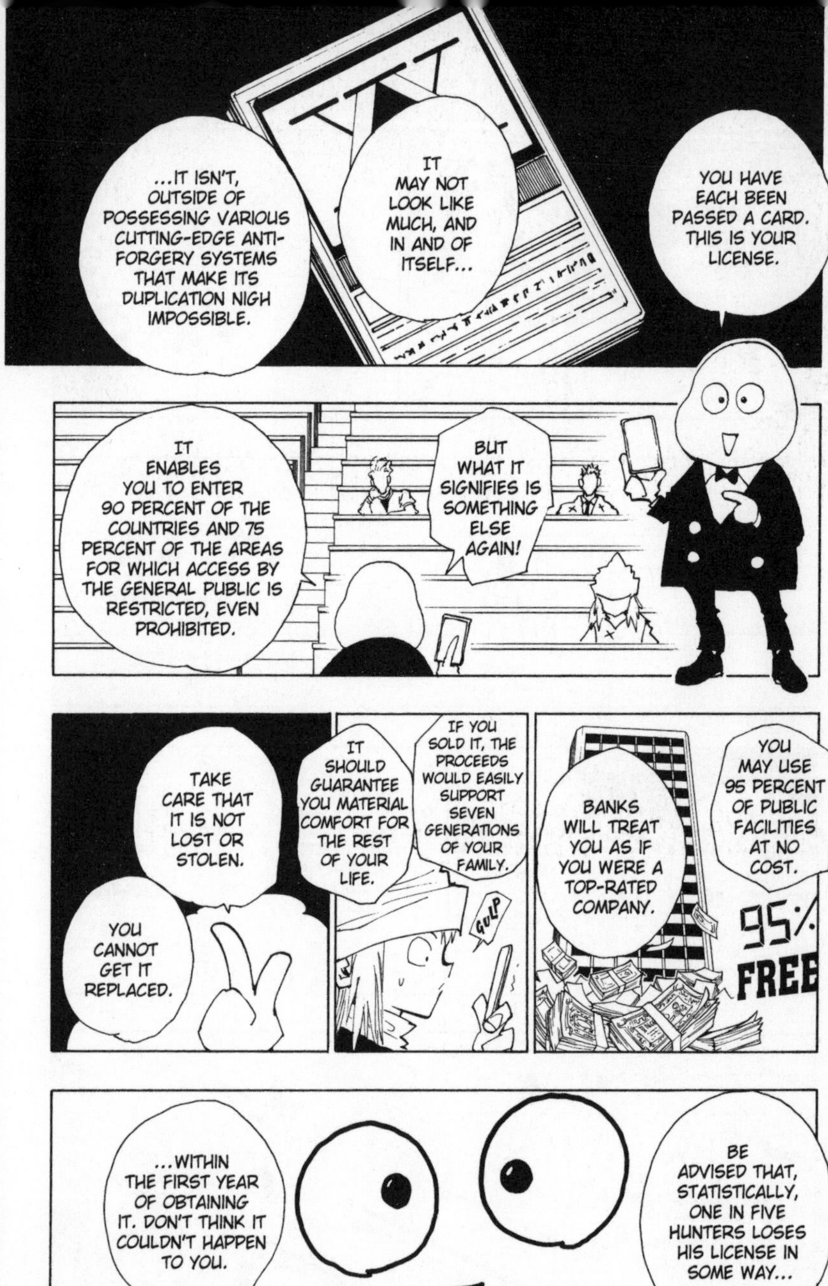

YOU HAVE EACH BEEN PASSED A CARD. THIS IS YOUR LICENSE.
IT MAY NOT LOOK LIKE MUCH, AND IN AND OF ITSELF...
...IT ISN'T, OUTSIDE OF POSSESSING VARIOUS CUTTING-EDGE ANTI-FORGERY SYSTEMS THAT MAKE ITS DUPLICATION NIGH IMPOSSIBLE.
BUT WHAT IT SIGNIFIES IS SOMETHING ELSE AGAIN!
IT ENABLES YOU TO ENTER 90 PERCENT OF THE COUNTRIES AND 75 PERCENT OF THE AREAS FOR WHICH ACCESS BY THE GENERAL PUBLIC IS RESTRICTED, EVEN PROHIBITED.
YOU MAY USE 95 PERCENT OF PUBLIC FACILITIES AT NO COST.
95% FREE
BANKS WILL TREAT YOU AS IF YOU WERE A TOP-RATED COMPANY.
IF YOU SOLD IT, THE PROCEEDS WOULD EASILY SUPPORT SEVEN GENERATIONS OF YOUR FAMILY.
IT SHOULD GUARANTEE YOU MATERIAL COMFORT FOR THE REST OF YOUR LIFE.
GULP
TAKE CARE THAT IT IS NOT LOST OR STOLEN.
YOU CANNOT GET IT REPLACED.
BE ADVISED THAT, STATISTICALLY, ONE IN FIVE HUNTERS LOSES HIS LICENSE IN SOME WAY...
...WITHIN THE FIRST YEAR OF OBTAINING IT. DON'T THINK IT COULDN'T HAPPEN TO YOU.

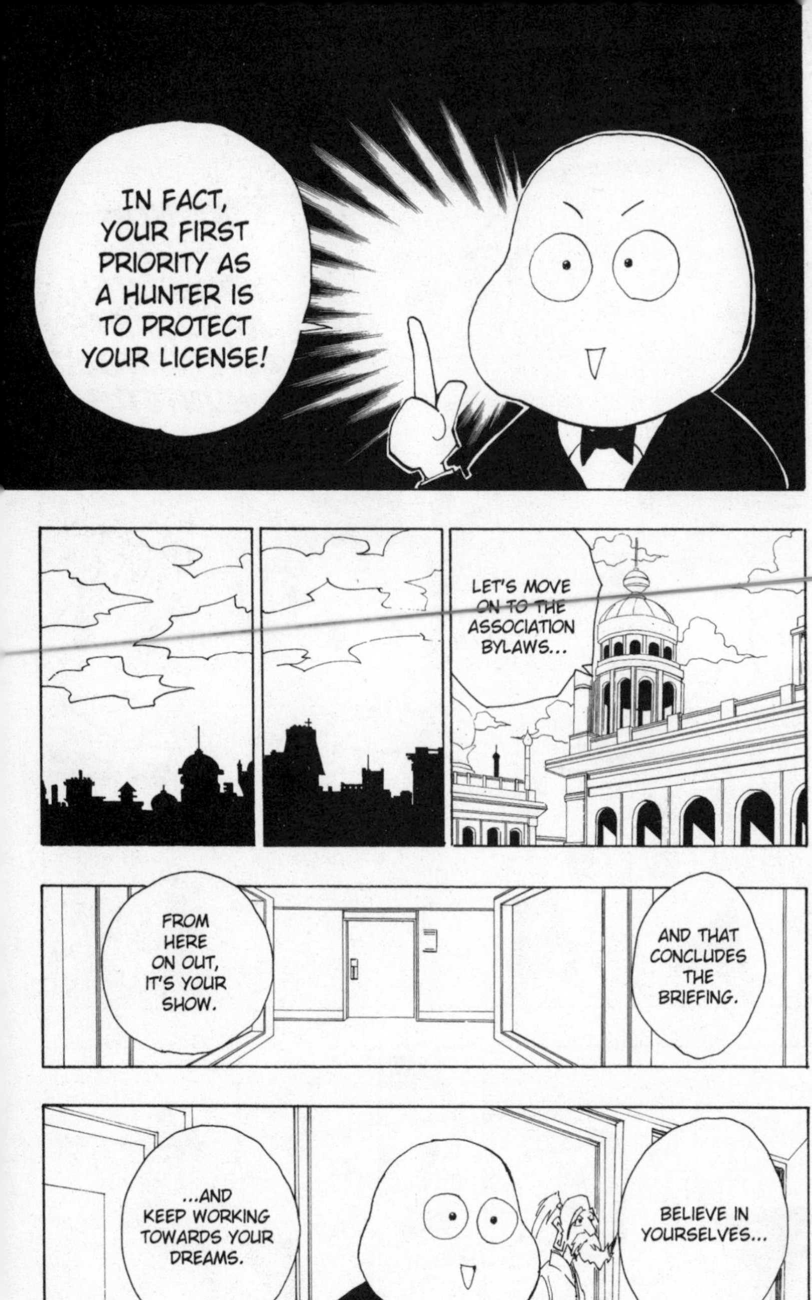
IN FACT, YOUR FIRST PRIORITY AS A HUNTER IS TO PROTECT YOUR LICENSE!
LET'S MOVE ON TO THE ASSOCIATION BYLAWS...
AND THAT CONCLUDES THE BRIEFING.
FROM HERE ON OUT, IT'S YOUR SHOW.
BELIEVE IN YOURSELVES...
...AND KEEP WORKING TOWARDS YOUR DREAMS.

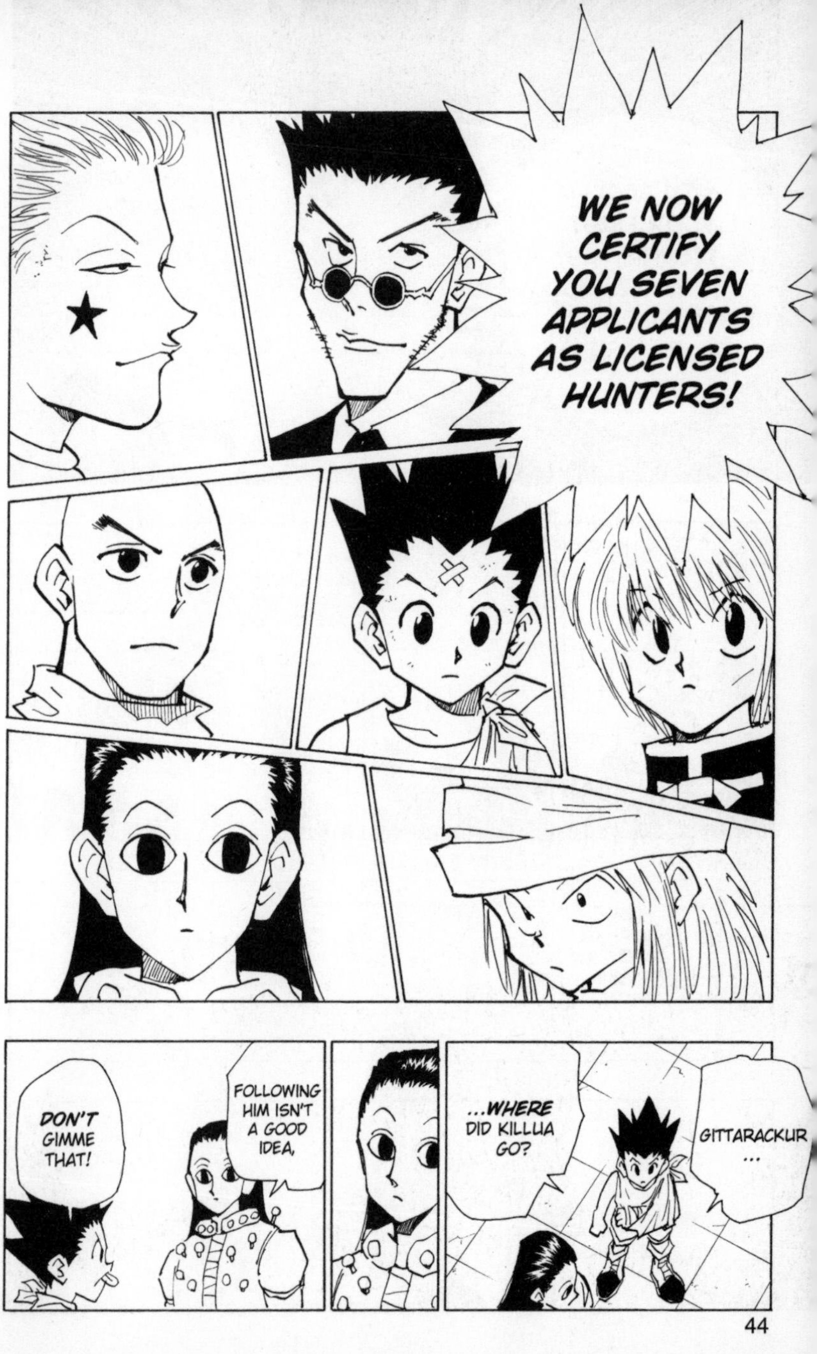
WE NOW CERTIFY YOU SEVEN APPLICANTS AS LICENSED HUNTERS!
GITTARACKUR ...
...WHERE DID KILLUA GO?
FOLLOWING HIM ISN'T A GOOD IDEA,
DON'T GIMME THAT!

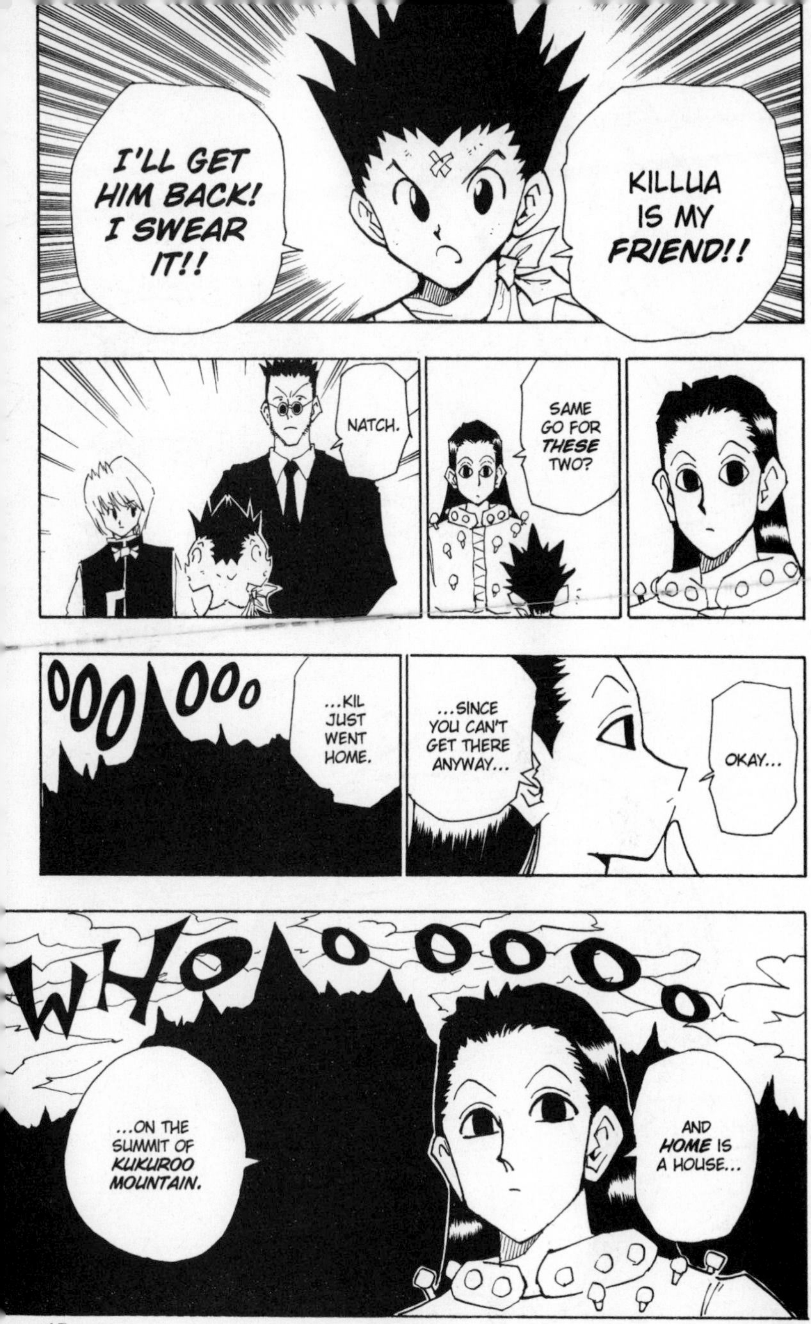
KILLUA IS MY FRIEND!!
I'LL GET HIM BACK! I SWEAR IT!!
SAME GO FOR THESE TWO?
NATCH.
OKAY...
...SINCE YOU CAN'T GET THERE ANYWAY...
...KIL JUST WENT HOME.
OOOOOO
WHOOOOOOO
AND HOME IS A HOUSE...
...ON THE SUMMIT OF KUKUROO MOUNTAIN.

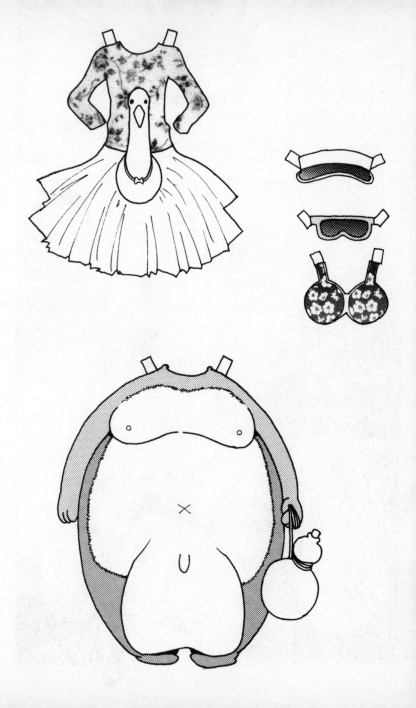

Chapter 38

Ging Freecss

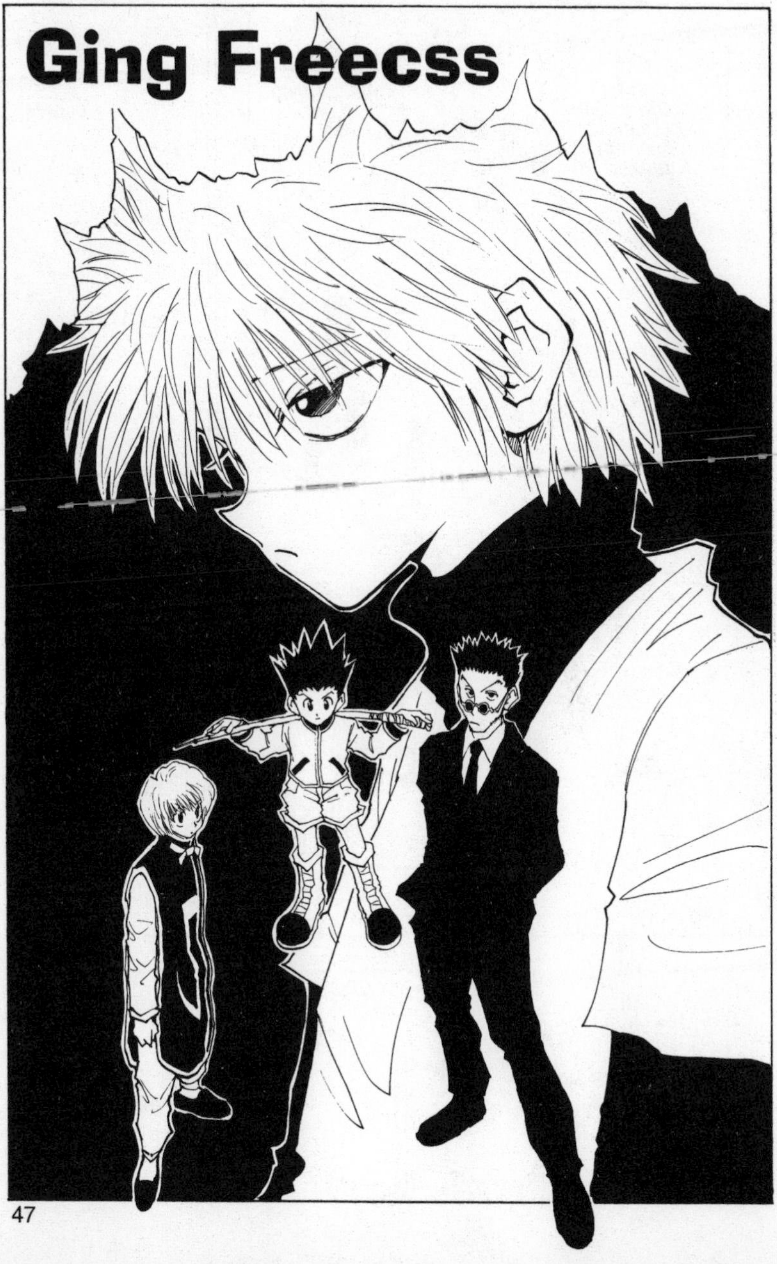

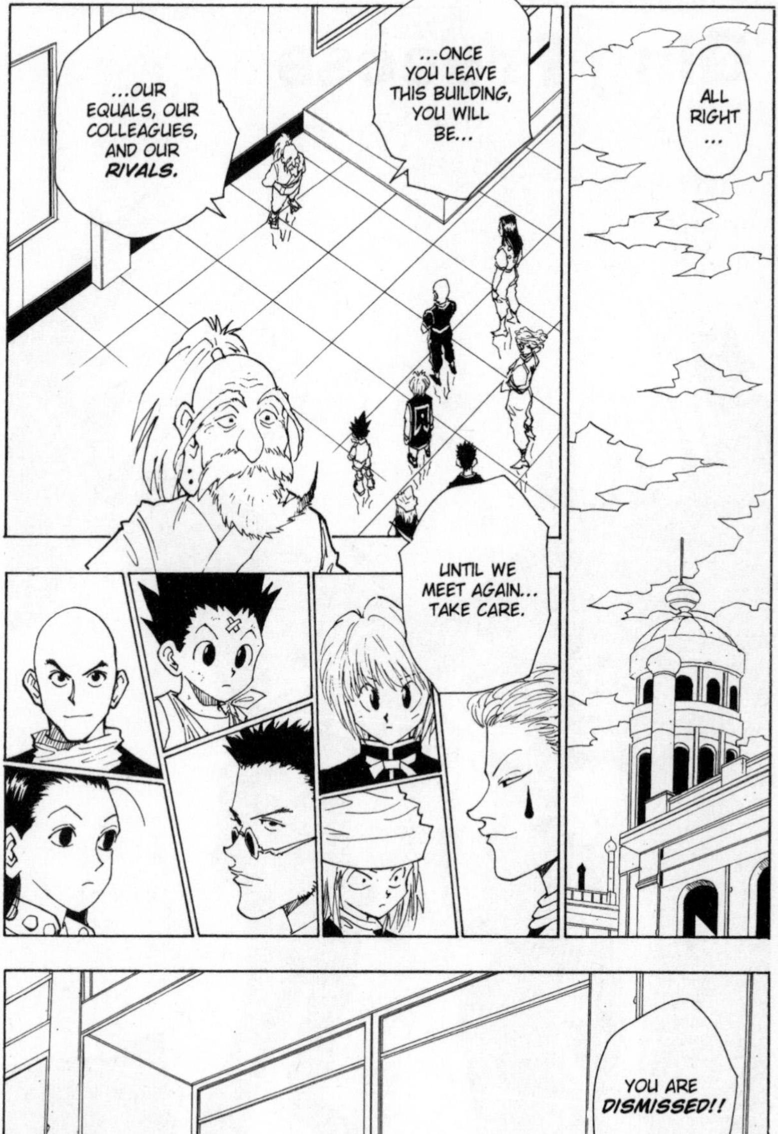
ALL RIGHT ...
...ONCE YOU LEAVE THIS BUILDING, YOU WILL BE...
...OUR EQUALS, OUR COLLEAGUES, AND OUR RIVALS.
UNTIL WE MEET AGAIN... TAKE CARE.
YOU ARE DISMISSED!!

READ THIS WAY

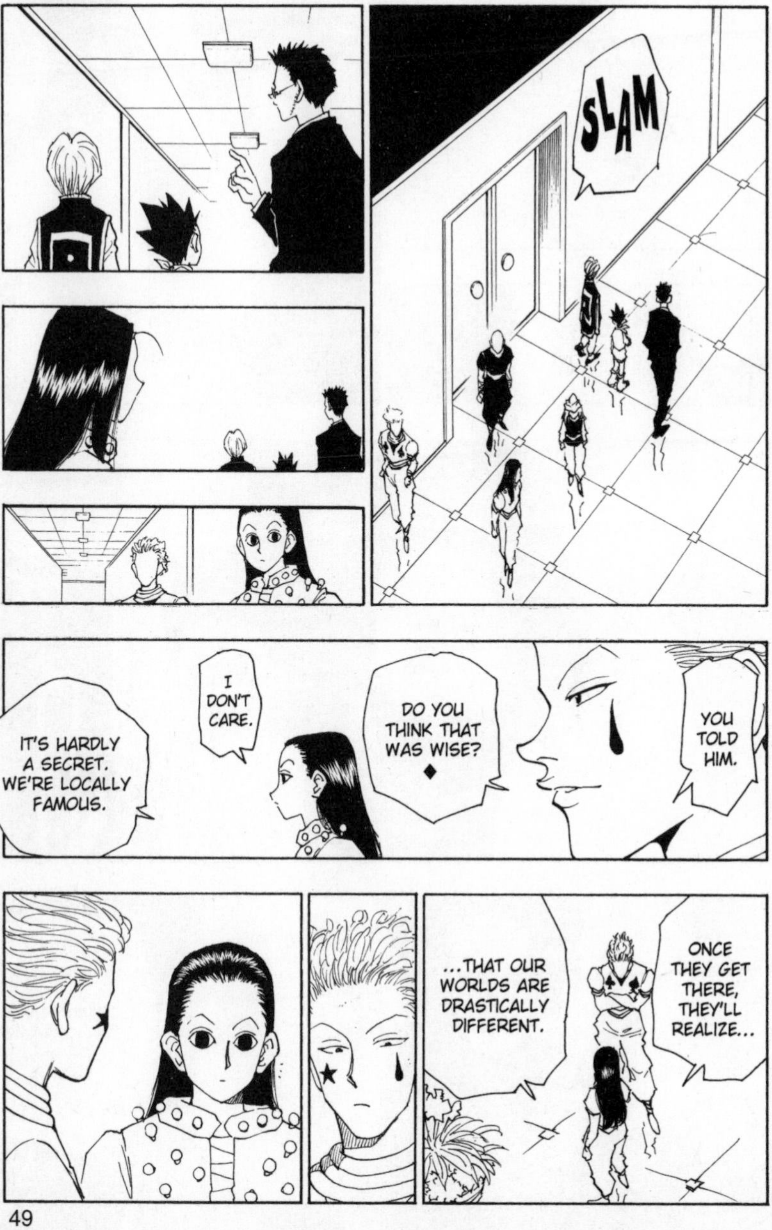
SLAM
YOU TOLD HIM.
DO YOU THINK THAT WAS WISE? ◆
I DON'T CARE.
IT'S HARDLY A SECRET. WE'RE LOCALLY FAMOUS.
ONCE THEY GET THERE, THEY'LL REALIZE...
...THAT OUR WORLDS ARE DRASTICALLY DIFFERENT.

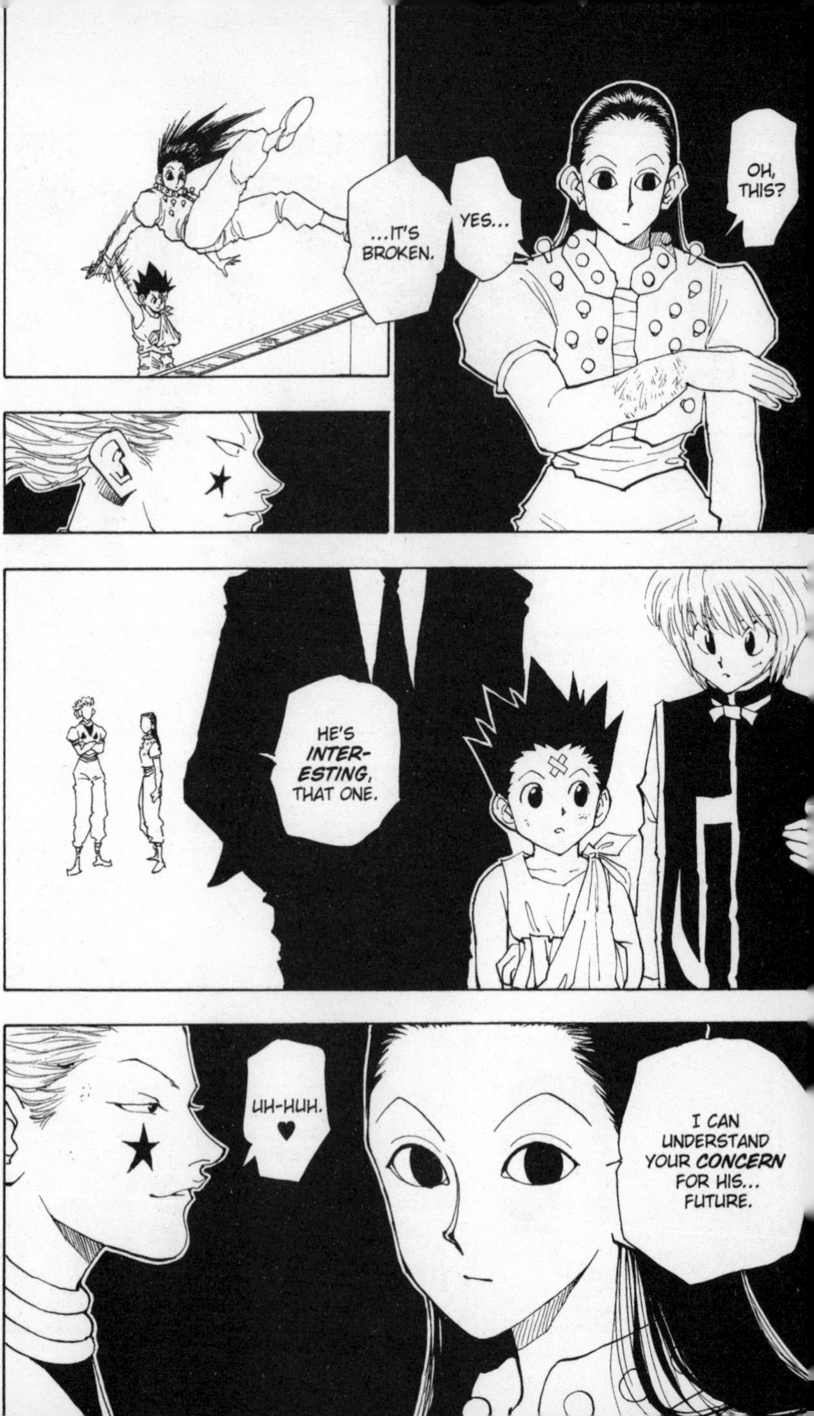
OH, THIS?
YES...
...IT'S BROKEN.
HE'S *INTERESTING*, THAT ONE.
I CAN UNDERSTAND YOUR **CONCERN** FOR HIS... FUTURE.
UH-HUH. ♥

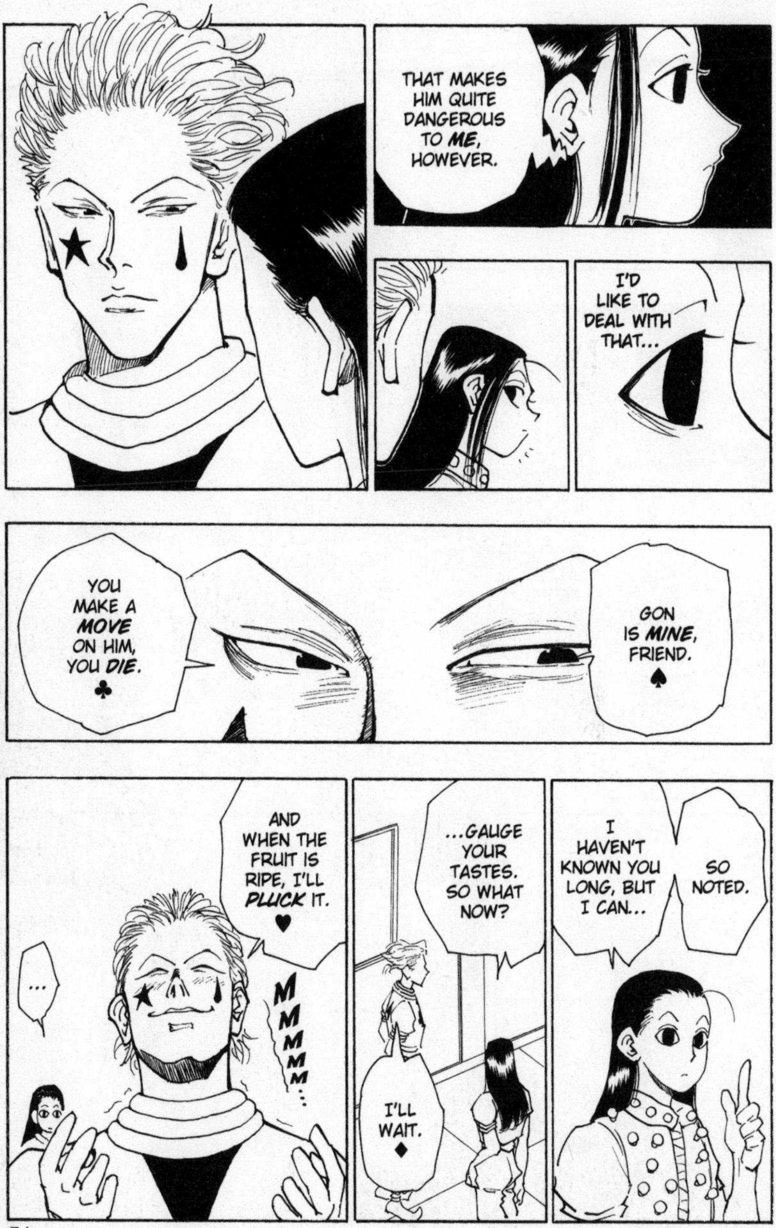

THAT MAKES HIM QUITE DANGEROUS TO *ME*, HOWEVER.
I'D LIKE TO DEAL WITH THAT...
GON IS *MINE*, FRIEND. ♠
YOU MAKE A *MOVE* ON HIM, YOU *DIE*. ♣
SO NOTED.
I HAVEN'T KNOWN YOU LONG, BUT I CAN...
...GAUGE YOUR TASTES. SO WHAT NOW?
I'LL WAIT. ♦
AND WHEN THE FRUIT IS RIPE, I'LL *PLUCK* IT. ♥
MMMMM...
...

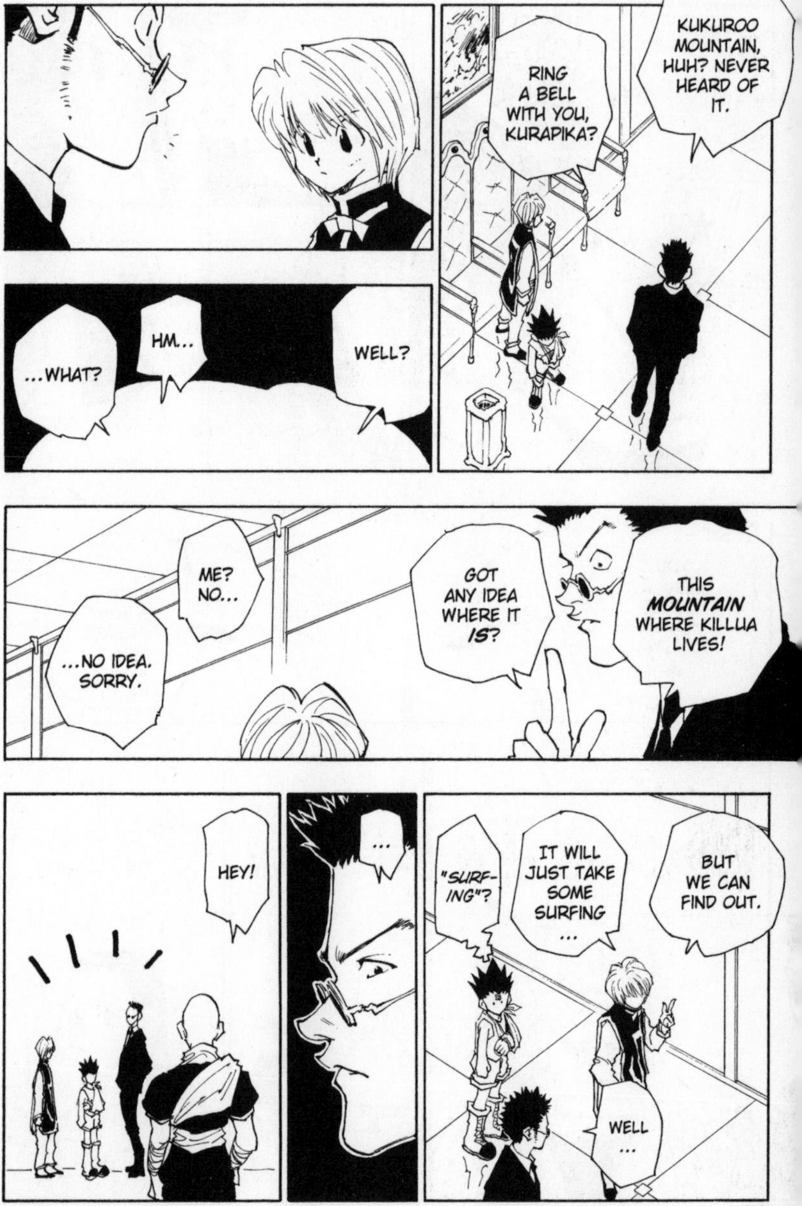
KUKUROO MOUNTAIN, HUH? NEVER HEARD OF IT.
RING A BELL WITH YOU, KURAPIKA?
WELL?
HM...
...WHAT?
THIS *MOUNTAIN* WHERE KILLUA LIVES!
GOT ANY IDEA WHERE IT *IS*?
ME? NO...
...NO IDEA. SORRY.
BUT WE CAN FIND OUT.
IT WILL JUST TAKE SOME SURFING...
"*SURF-ING*"?
WELL...
...
HEY!

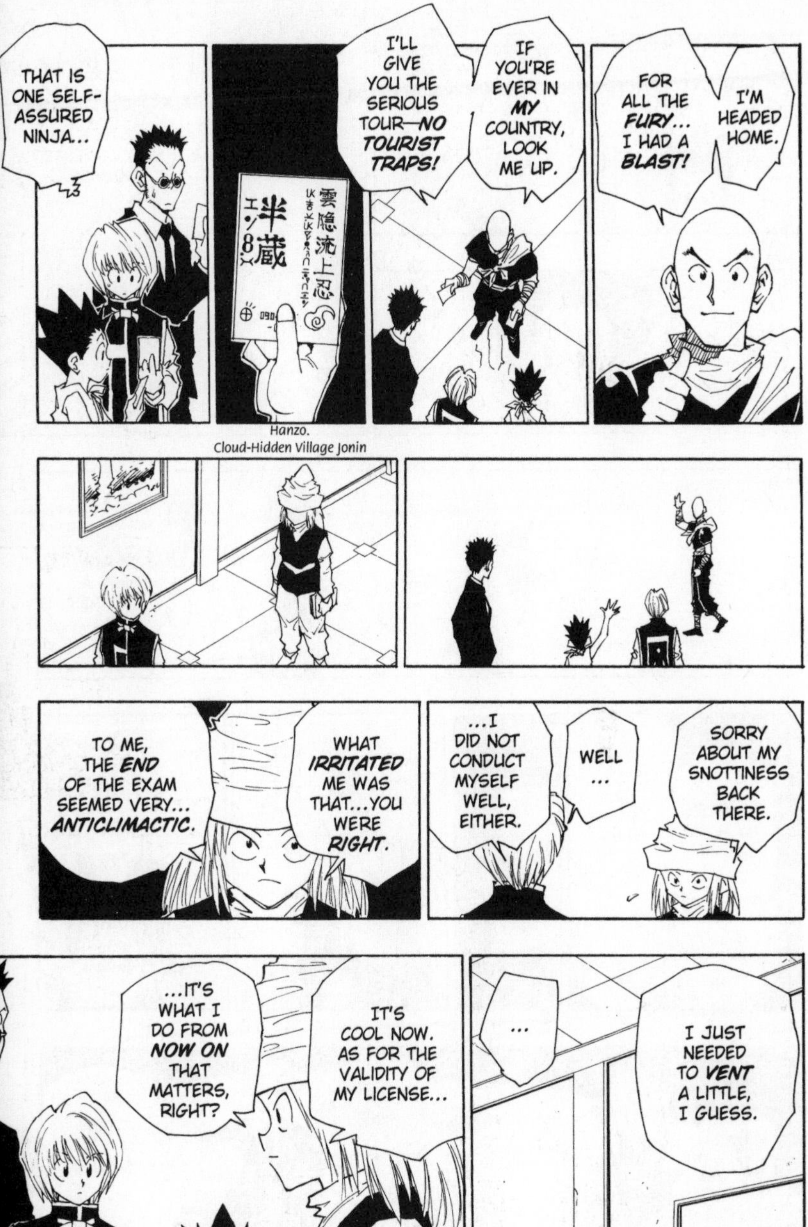
I'M HEADED HOME.
FOR ALL THE FURY... I HAD A BLAST!
IF YOU'RE EVER IN MY COUNTRY, LOOK ME UP.
I'LL GIVE YOU THE SERIOUS TOUR—NO TOURIST TRAPS!
雲隠流上忍
半蔵
THAT IS ONE SELF-ASSURED NINJA...
SORRY ABOUT MY SNOTTINESS BACK THERE.
WELL ...
...I DID NOT CONDUCT MYSELF WELL, EITHER.
WHAT IRRITATED ME WAS THAT...YOU WERE RIGHT.
TO ME, THE END OF THE EXAM SEEMED VERY... ANTICLIMACTIC.
I JUST NEEDED TO VENT A LITTLE, I GUESS.
...
IT'S COOL NOW. AS FOR THE VALIDITY OF MY LICENSE...
...IT'S WHAT I DO FROM NOW ON THAT MATTERS, RIGHT?
Hanzo.
Cloud-Hidden Village Jonin

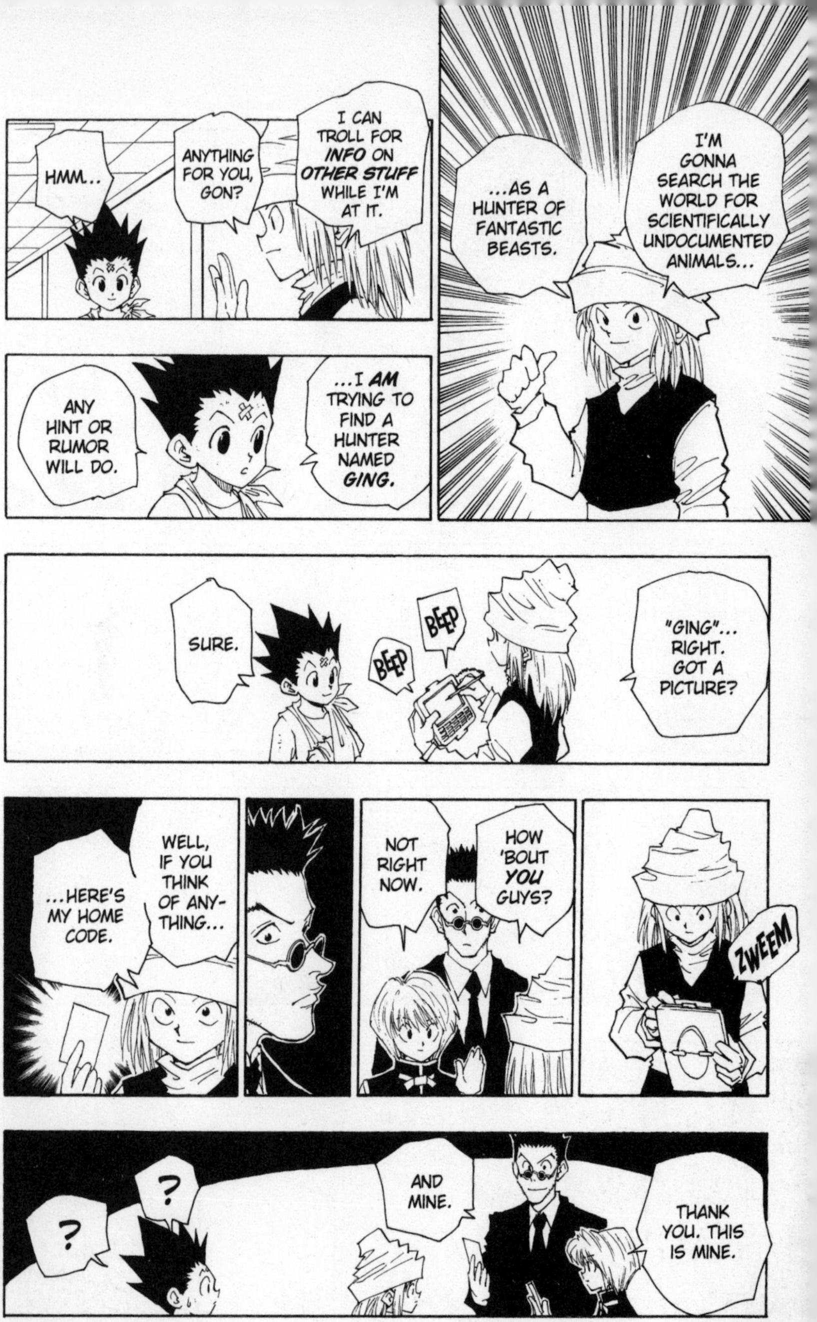
I'M GONNA SEARCH THE WORLD FOR SCIENTIFICALLY UNDOCUMENTED ANIMALS...
...AS A HUNTER OF FANTASTIC BEASTS.
I CAN TROLL FOR INFO ON OTHER STUFF WHILE I'M AT IT.
ANYTHING FOR YOU, GON?
HMM...
...I AM TRYING TO FIND A HUNTER NAMED GING.
ANY HINT OR RUMOR WILL DO.
"GING"... RIGHT. GOT A PICTURE?
BEEP
BEEP
SURE.
ZWEEM
HOW 'BOUT YOU GUYS?
NOT RIGHT NOW.
WELL, IF YOU THINK OF ANY-THING...
...HERE'S MY HOME CODE.
THANK YOU. THIS IS MINE.
AND MINE.
?
?

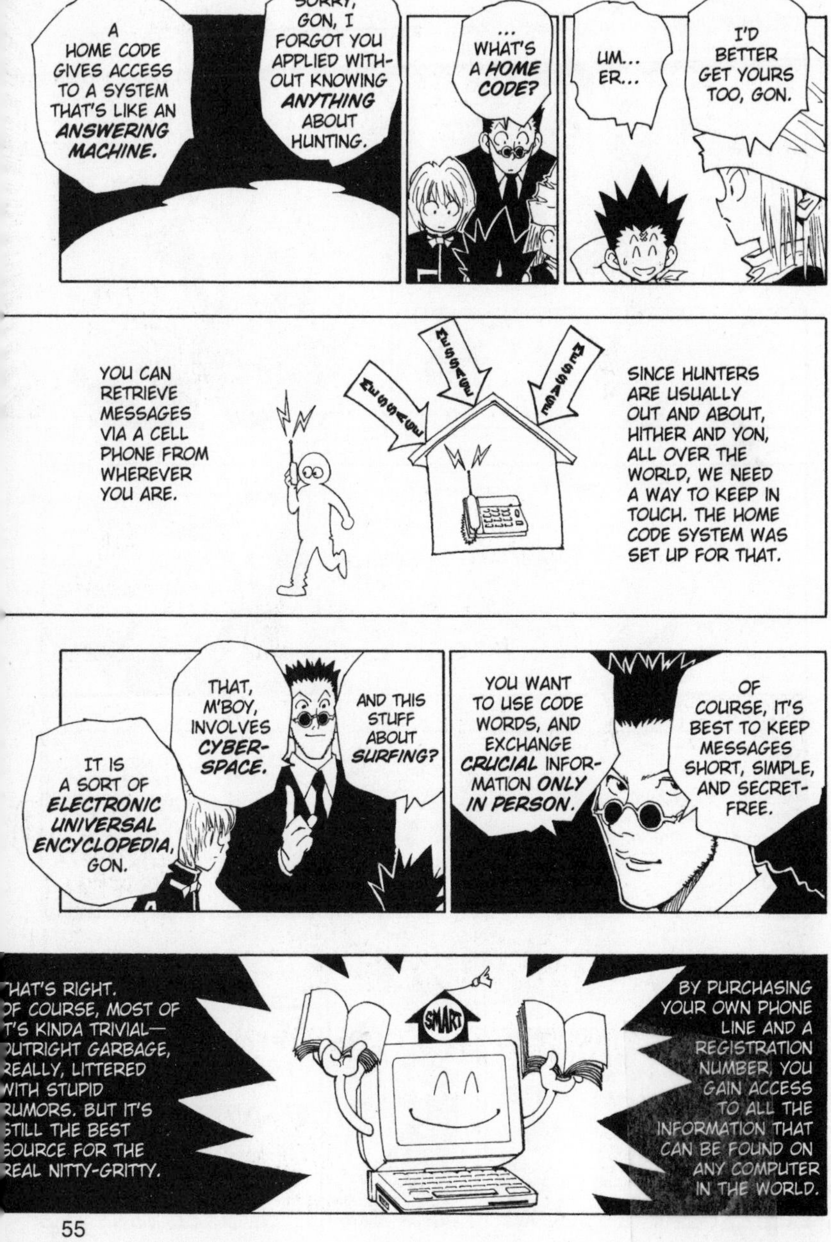
I'D BETTER GET YOURS TOO, GON.
UM... ER...
... WHAT'S A **HOME CODE?**
SORRY, GON, I FORGOT YOU APPLIED WITHOUT KNOWING **ANYTHING** ABOUT HUNTING.
A HOME CODE GIVES ACCESS TO A SYSTEM THAT'S LIKE AN **ANSWERING MACHINE.**
SINCE HUNTERS ARE USUALLY OUT AND ABOUT, HITHER AND YON, ALL OVER THE WORLD, WE NEED A WAY TO KEEP IN TOUCH. THE HOME CODE SYSTEM WAS SET UP FOR THAT.
MESSAGE
MESSAGE
MESSAGE
YOU CAN RETRIEVE MESSAGES VIA A CELL PHONE FROM WHEREVER YOU ARE.
OF COURSE, IT'S BEST TO KEEP MESSAGES SHORT, SIMPLE, AND SECRET-FREE.
YOU WANT TO USE CODE WORDS, AND EXCHANGE **CRUCIAL** INFORMATION **ONLY IN PERSON.**
AND THIS STUFF ABOUT **SURFING?**
THAT, M'BOY, INVOLVES **CYBERSPACE.**
IT IS A SORT OF **ELECTRONIC UNIVERSAL ENCYCLOPEDIA,** GON.
BY PURCHASING YOUR OWN PHONE LINE AND A REGISTRATION NUMBER, YOU GAIN ACCESS TO ALL THE INFORMATION THAT CAN BE FOUND ON ANY COMPUTER IN THE WORLD.
SMART
THAT'S RIGHT. OF COURSE, MOST OF IT'S KINDA TRIVIAL— OUTRIGHT GARBAGE, REALLY, LITTERED WITH STUPID RUMORS. BUT IT'S STILL THE BEST SOURCE FOR THE REAL NITTY-GRITTY.

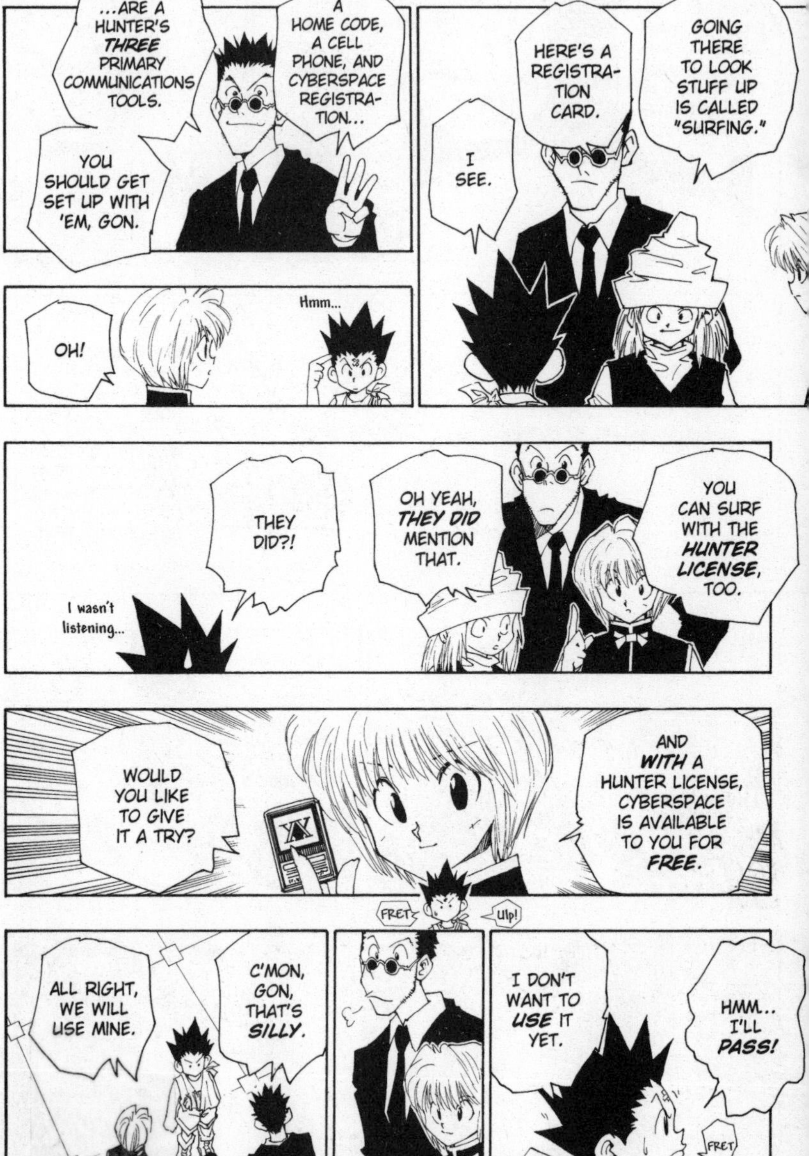
GOING THERE TO LOOK STUFF UP IS CALLED "SURFING."
HERE'S A REGISTRATION CARD.
I SEE.
A HOME CODE, A CELL PHONE, AND CYBERSPACE REGISTRATION...
...ARE A HUNTER'S THREE PRIMARY COMMUNICATIONS TOOLS.
YOU SHOULD GET SET UP WITH 'EM, GON.
Hmm...
OH!
YOU CAN SURF WITH THE HUNTER LICENSE, TOO.
OH YEAH, THEY DID MENTION THAT.
THEY DID?!
I wasn't listening...
AND WITH A HUNTER LICENSE, CYBERSPACE IS AVAILABLE TO YOU FOR FREE.
WOULD YOU LIKE TO GIVE IT A TRY?
Ulp!
FRET
HMM.. I'LL PASS!
FRET
FRET
I DON'T WANT TO USE IT YET.
C'MON, GON, THAT'S SILLY.
ALL RIGHT, WE WILL USE MINE.

READ THIS WAY

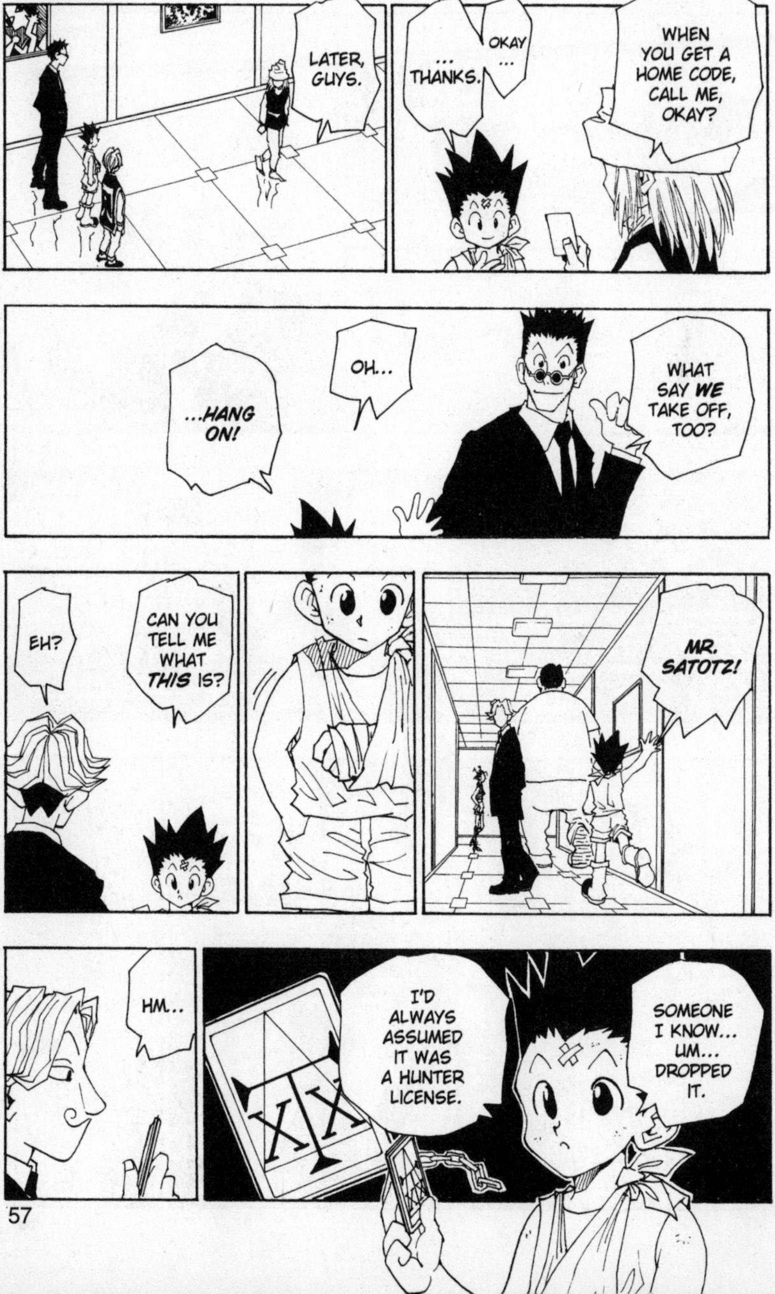

WHEN YOU GET A HOME CODE, CALL ME, OKAY?
OKAY...
...THANKS.
LATER, GUYS.
WHAT SAY WE TAKE OFF, TOO?
OH...
...HANG ON!
MR. SATOTZ!
CAN YOU TELL ME WHAT THIS IS?
EH?
SOMEONE I KNOW... UM... DROPPED IT.
I'D ALWAYS ASSUMED IT WAS A HUNTER LICENSE.
HM...

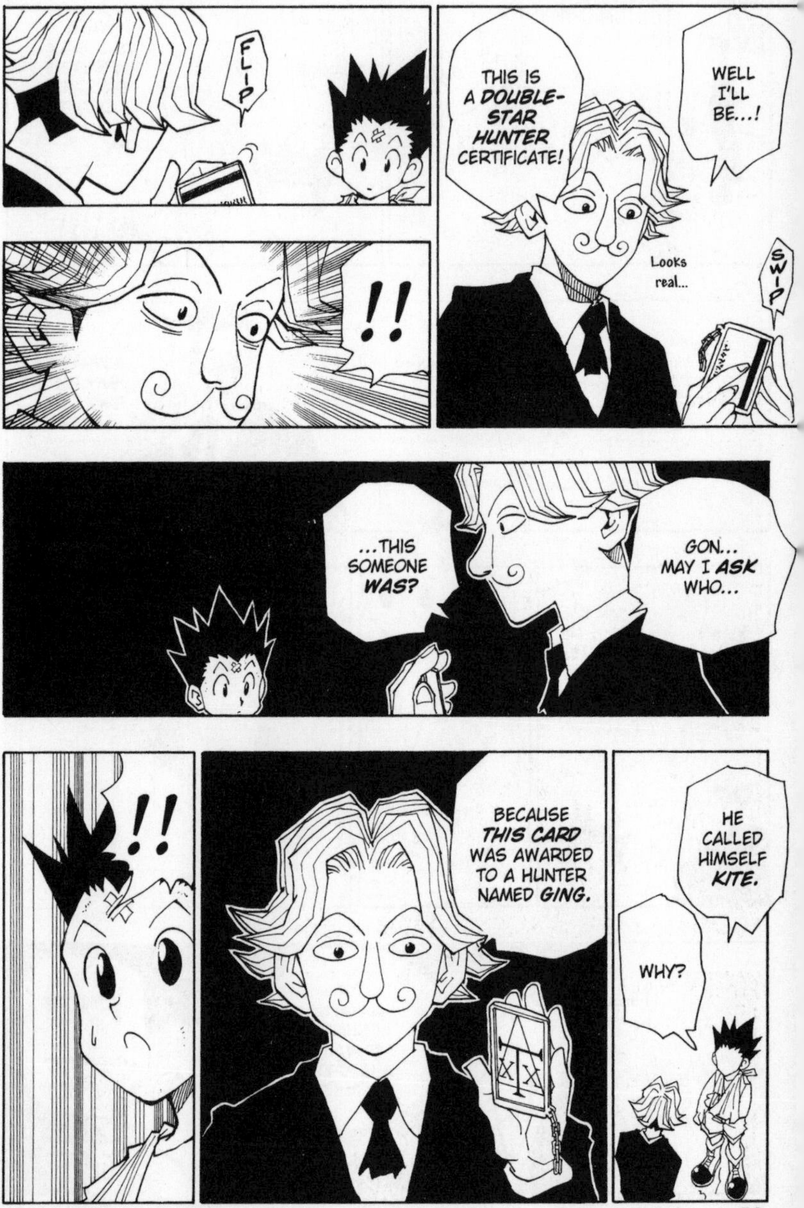
WELL I'LL BE...!
THIS IS A DOUBLE-STAR HUNTER CERTIFICATE!
Looks real...
SWIP
FLIP
!!
GON... MAY I ASK WHO...
...THIS SOMEONE WAS?
HE CALLED HIMSELF KITE.
WHY?
BECAUSE THIS CARD WAS AWARDED TO A HUNTER NAMED GING.
!!

READ THIS WAY

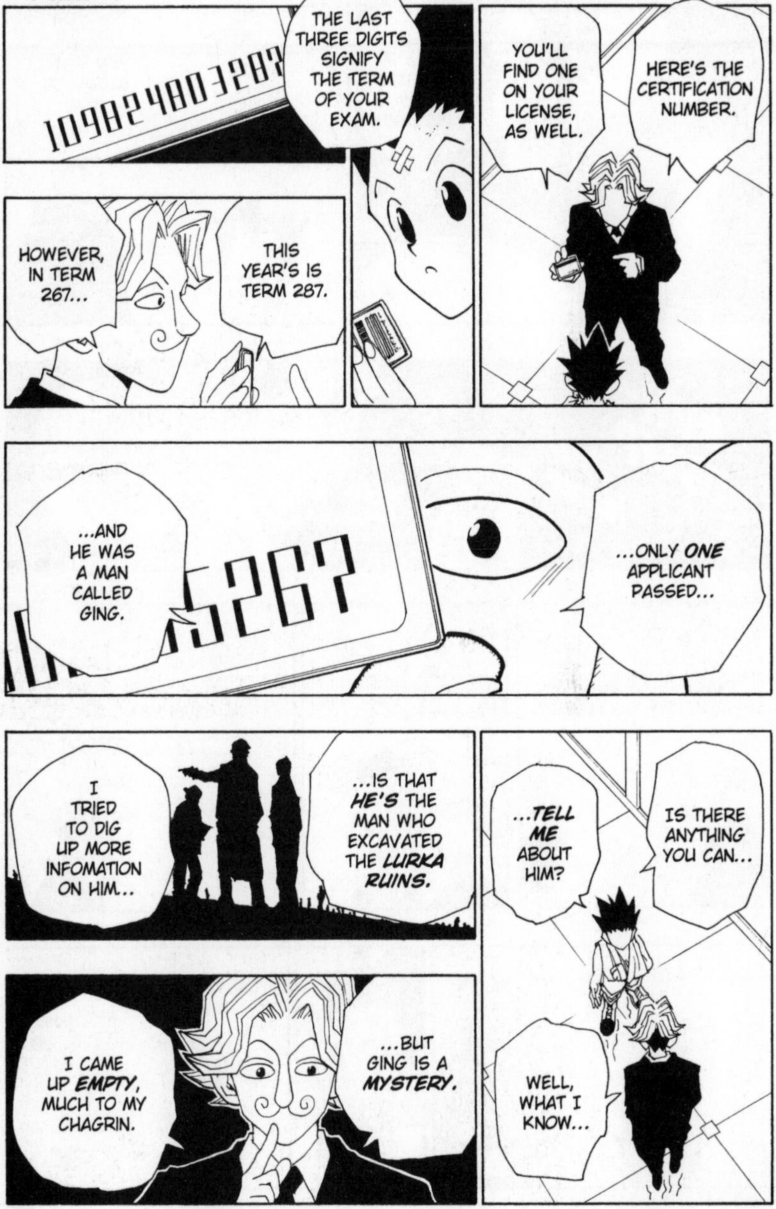
HERE'S THE CERTIFICATION NUMBER.
YOU'LL FIND ONE ON YOUR LICENSE, AS WELL.
THE LAST THREE DIGITS SIGNIFY THE TERM OF YOUR EXAM.
109824803287
THIS YEAR'S IS TERM 287.
HOWEVER, IN TERM 267...
...ONLY *ONE* APPLICANT PASSED...
...AND HE WAS A MAN CALLED GING.
IS THERE ANYTHING YOU CAN...
...*TELL ME* ABOUT HIM?
WELL, WHAT I KNOW...
...IS THAT *HE'S* THE MAN WHO EXCAVATED THE *LURKA RUINS.*
I TRIED TO DIG UP MORE INFOMATION ON HIM...
...BUT GING IS A *MYSTERY.*
I CAME UP *EMPTY,* MUCH TO MY CHAGRIN.

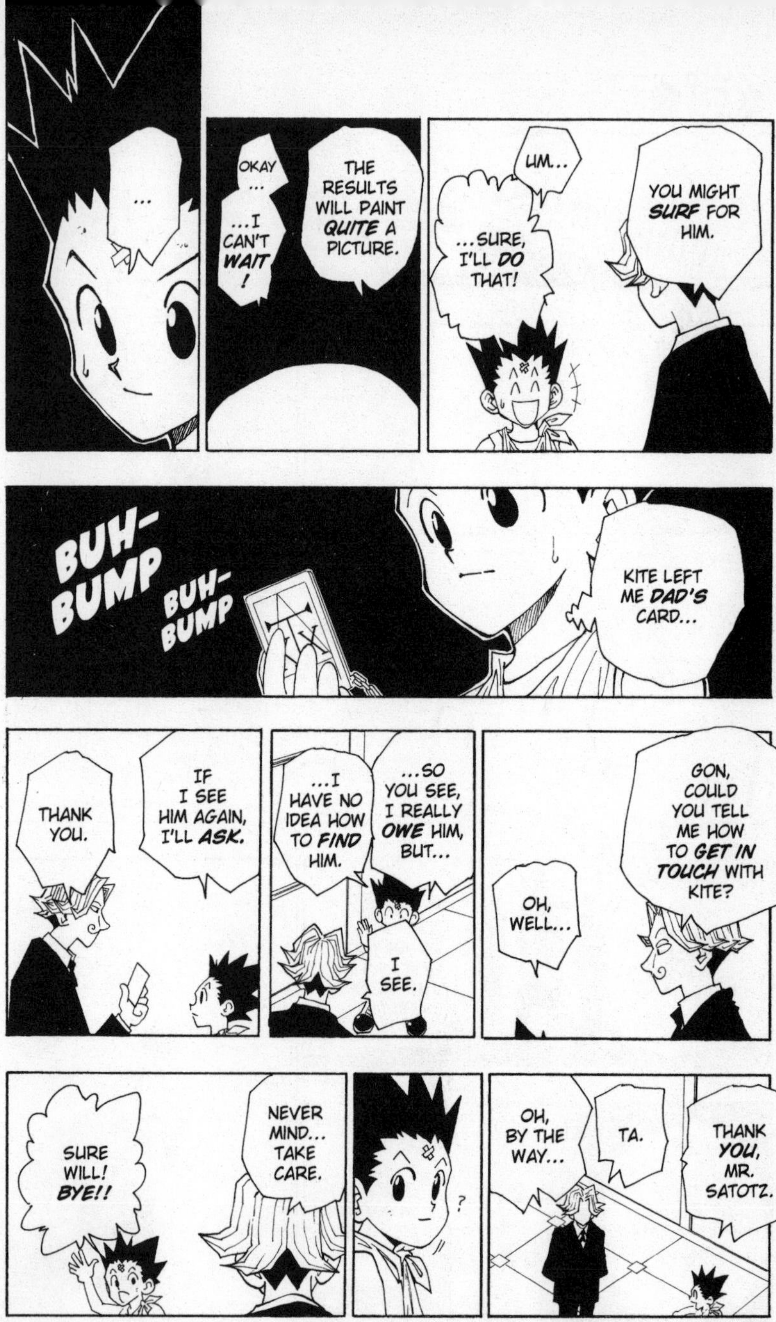
YOU MIGHT SURF FOR HIM.
UM...
...SURE, I'LL DO THAT!
THE RESULTS WILL PAINT QUITE A PICTURE.
OKAY ... ...I CAN'T WAIT!
...
KITE LEFT ME DAD'S CARD...
BUH-BUMP
BUH-BUMP
GON, COULD YOU TELL ME HOW TO GET IN TOUCH WITH KITE?
OH, WELL...
...SO YOU SEE, I REALLY OWE HIM, BUT...
...I HAVE NO IDEA HOW TO FIND HIM.
I SEE.
IF I SEE HIM AGAIN, I'LL ASK.
THANK YOU.
THANK YOU, MR. SATOTZ.
TA.
OH, BY THE WAY...
?
NEVER MIND... TAKE CARE.
SURE WILL! BYE!!

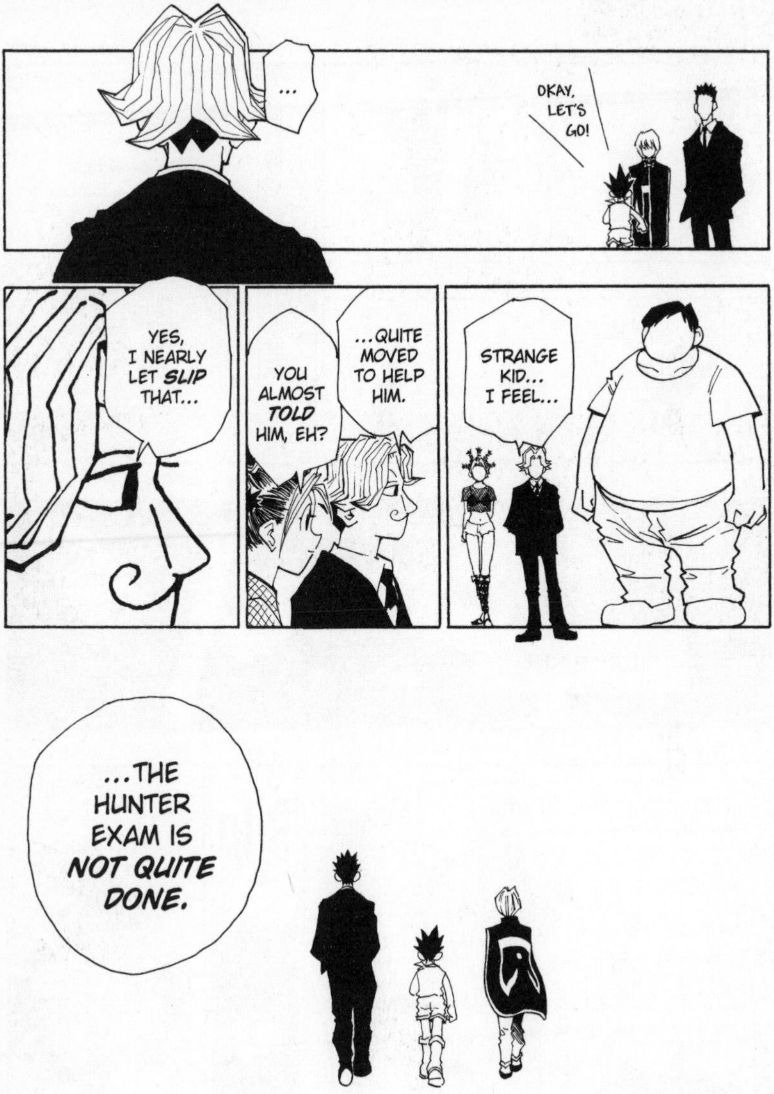
OKAY, LET'S GO!
...
STRANGE KID... I FEEL...
...QUITE MOVED TO HELP HIM.
YOU ALMOST TOLD HIM, EH?
YES, I NEARLY LET SLIP THAT...
...THE HUNTER EXAM IS NOT QUITE DONE.

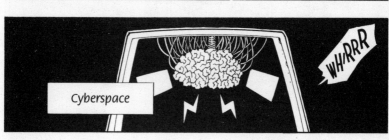

Cyberspace

WHRRR

CLICK

Kukuroo Mountain

Republic of Padokea, Dentora region. Elevation: 12,211 ft

BLIP

KUKUROO MOUNTAIN... HMM...

TAP TAP

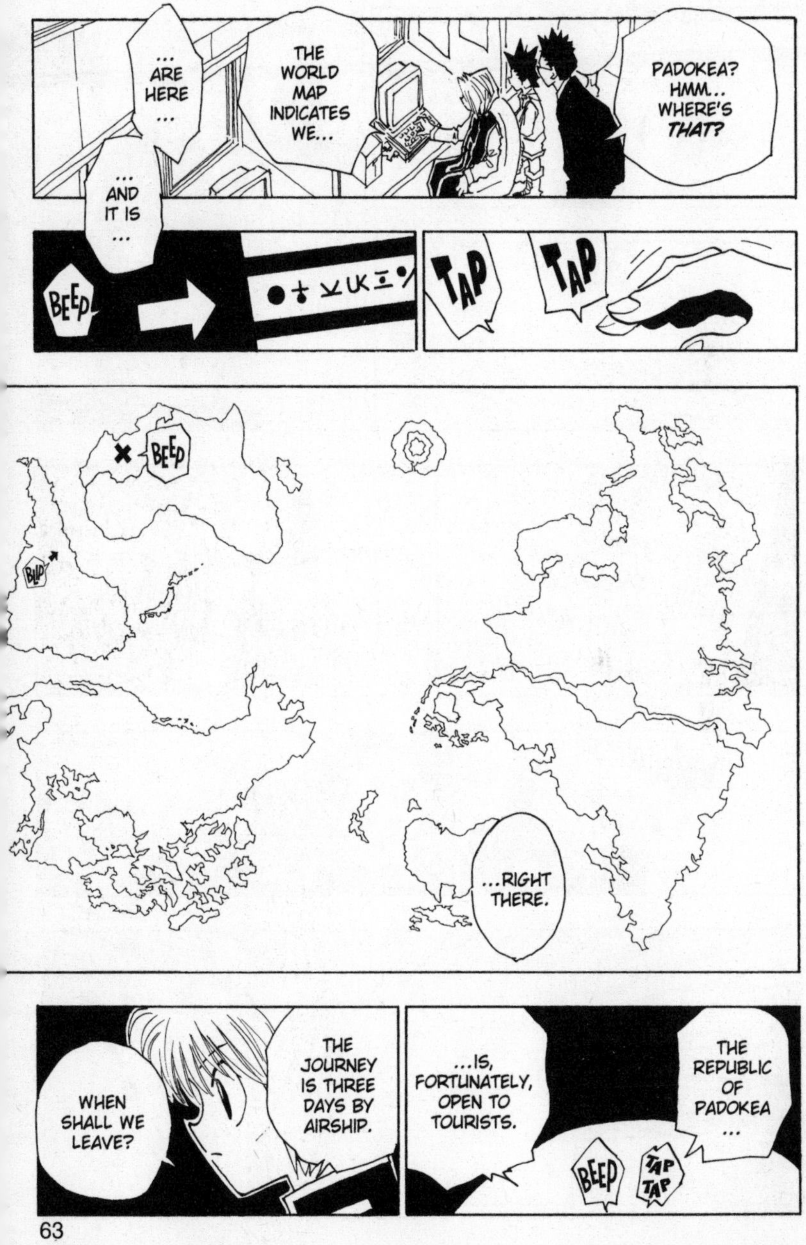
PADOKEA? HMM.. WHERE'S *THAT?*
THE WORLD MAP INDICATES WE...
... ARE HERE ...
... AND IT IS ...
TAP
TAP
BEEP
BEEP
BLIP
...RIGHT THERE.
THE REPUBLIC OF PADOKEA ...
TAP TAP
BEEP
...IS, FORTUNATELY, OPEN TO TOURISTS.
THE JOURNEY IS THREE DAYS BY AIRSHIP.
WHEN SHALL WE LEAVE?

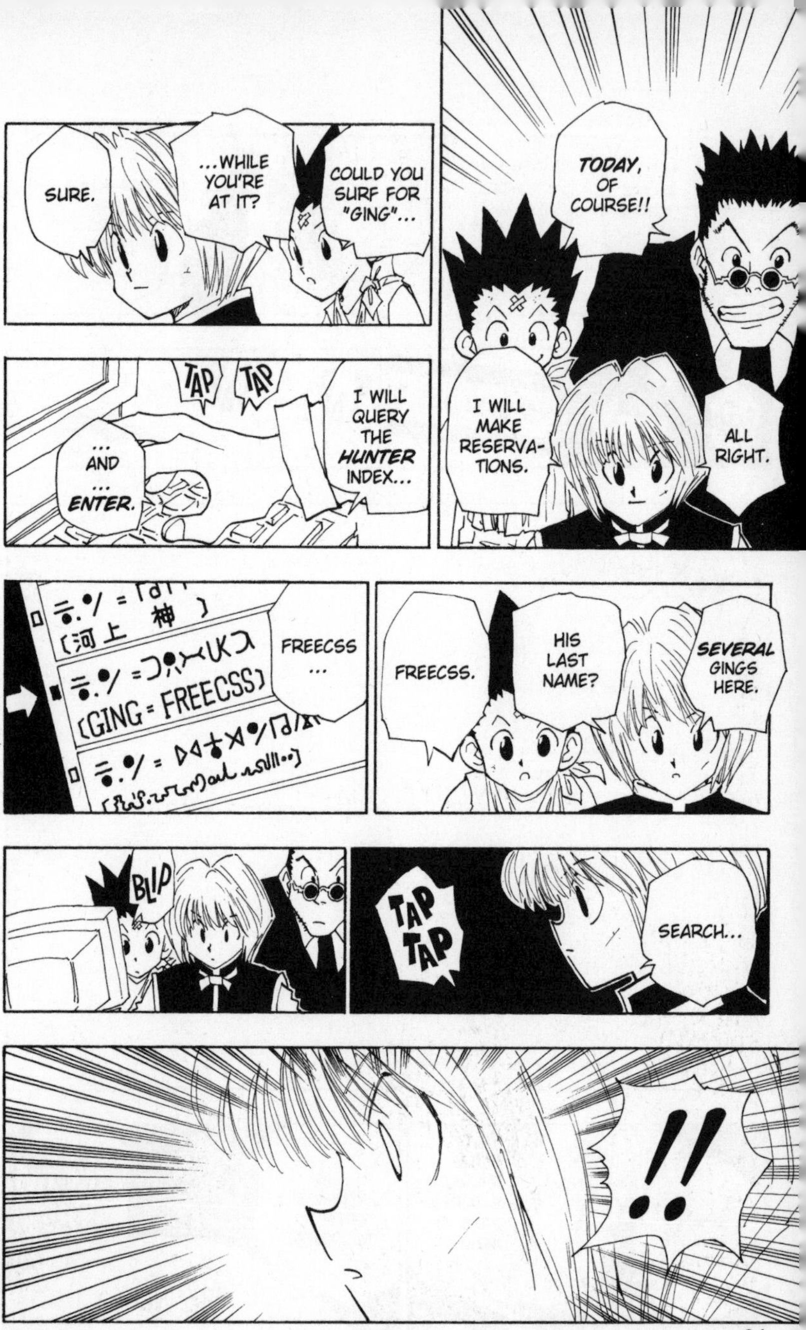
TODAY, OF COURSE!!
ALL RIGHT.
I WILL MAKE RESERVA-TIONS.
COULD YOU SURF FOR "GING"...
...WHILE YOU'RE AT IT?
SURE.
I WILL QUERY THE HUNTER INDEX...
TAP
TAP
... AND ... ENTER.
SEVERAL GINGS HERE.
HIS LAST NAME?
FREECSS.
FREECSS ...
〔河上 神〕
〔GING = FREECSS〕
SEARCH...
TAP TAP
BLIP
!!

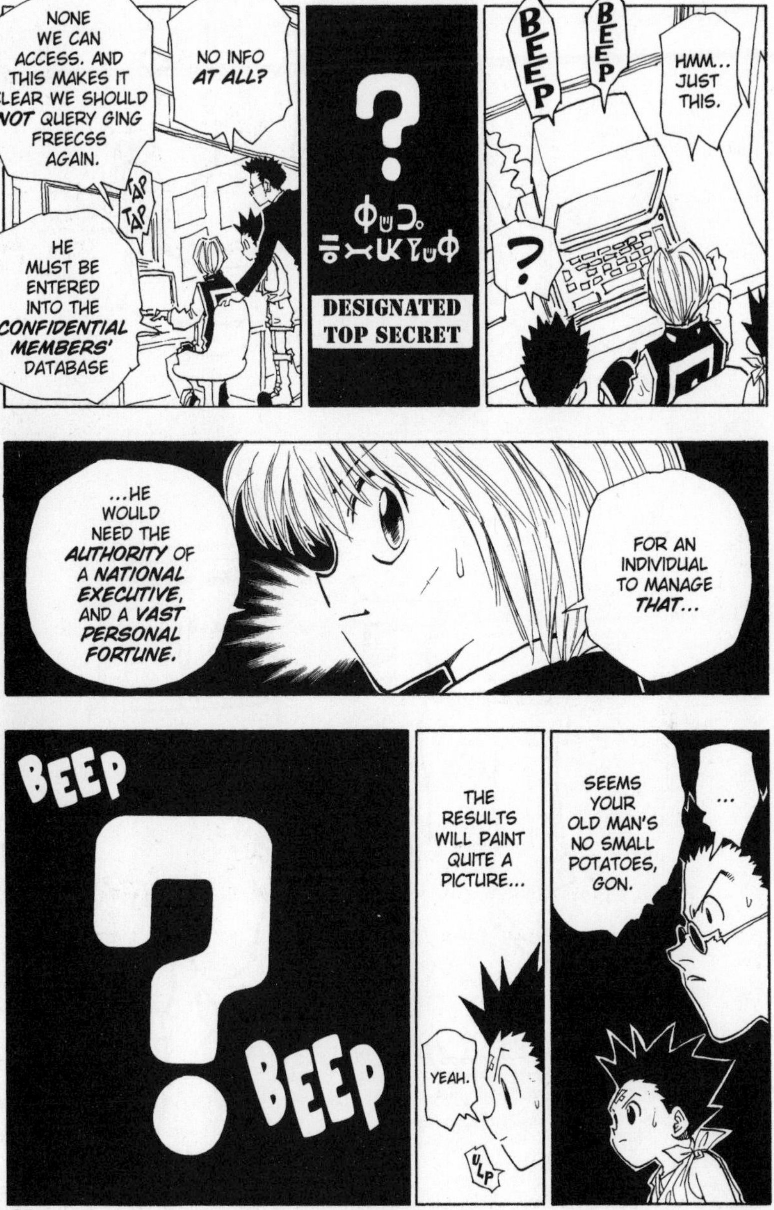
BEEP
BEEP
HMM... JUST THIS.
?
?
DESIGNATED TOP SECRET
NO INFO AT ALL?
NONE WE CAN ACCESS. AND THIS MAKES IT CLEAR WE SHOULD NOT QUERY GING FREECSS AGAIN.
TAP TAP
HE MUST BE ENTERED INTO THE CONFIDENTIAL MEMBERS' DATABASE
FOR AN INDIVIDUAL TO MANAGE THAT...
...HE WOULD NEED THE AUTHORITY OF A NATIONAL EXECUTIVE, AND A VAST PERSONAL FORTUNE.
...
SEEMS YOUR OLD MAN'S NO SMALL POTATOES, GON.
THE RESULTS WILL PAINT QUITE A PICTURE...
YEAH.
ULP
BEEP
?
BEEP

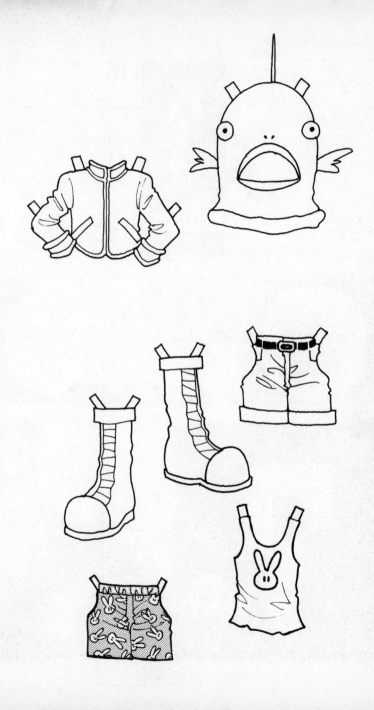

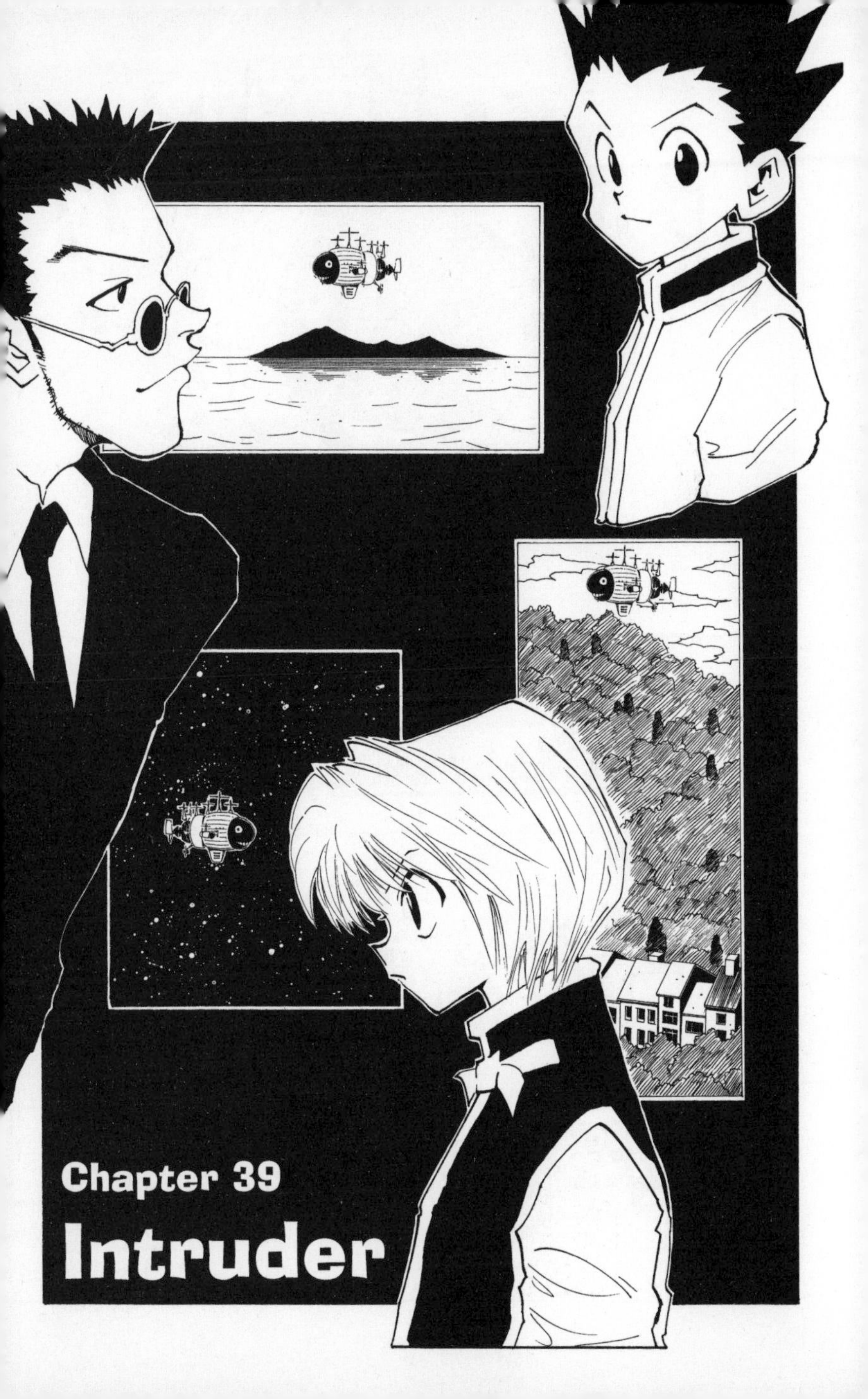
Chapter 39
Intruder

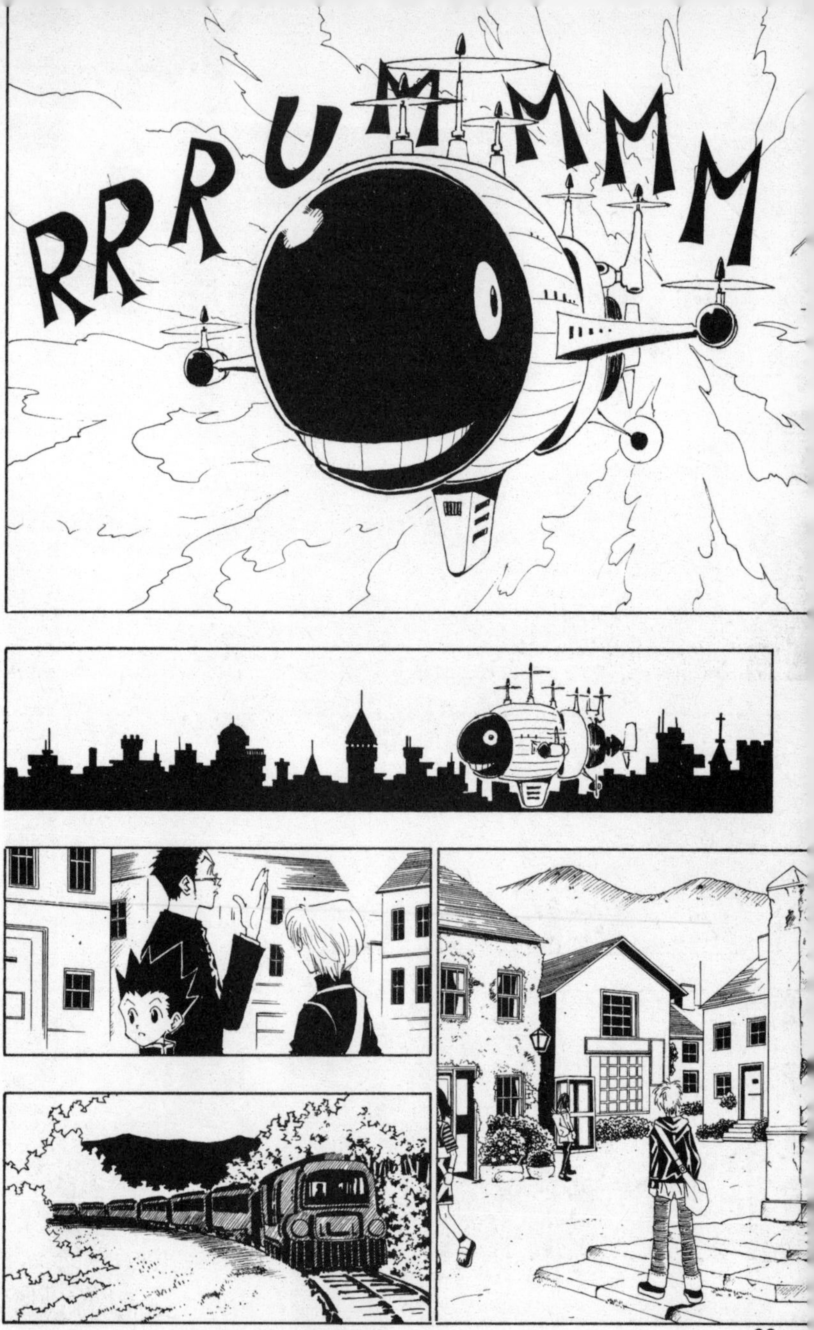
RRRUMMMM

READ THIS WAY

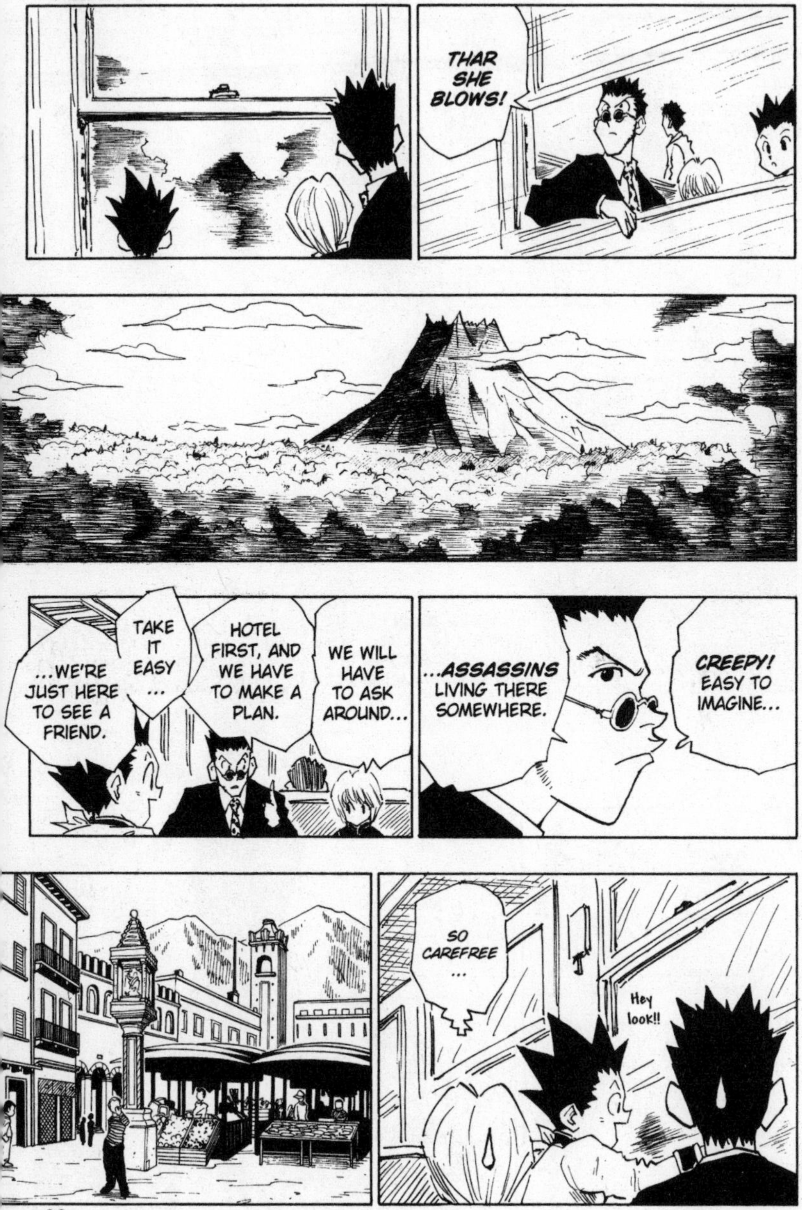

THAR SHE BLOWS!
CREEPY! EASY TO IMAGINE...
...ASSASSINS LIVING THERE SOMEWHERE.
WE WILL HAVE TO ASK AROUND...
HOTEL FIRST, AND WE HAVE TO MAKE A PLAN.
TAKE IT EASY ...
...WE'RE JUST HERE TO SEE A FRIEND.
SO CAREFREE ...
Hey look!!

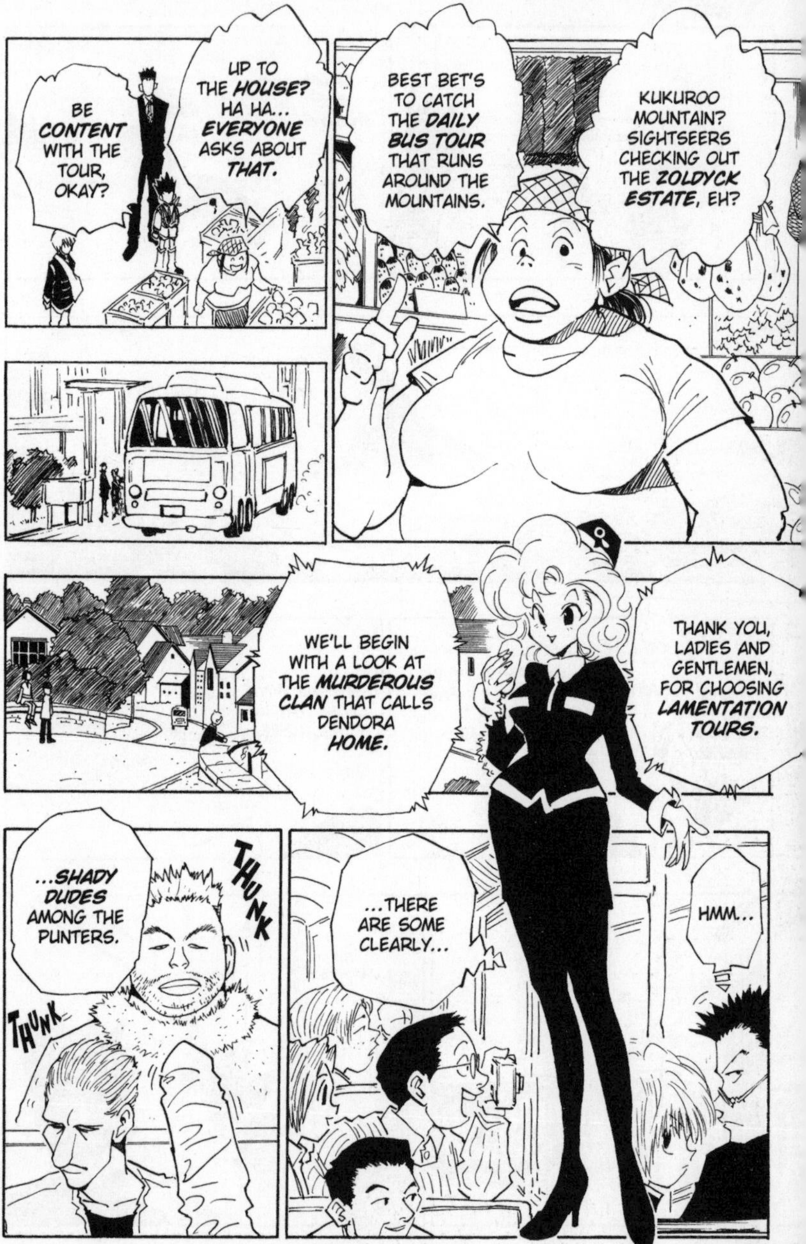

KUKUROO MOUNTAIN? SIGHTSEERS CHECKING OUT THE ZOLDYCK ESTATE, EH?
BEST BET'S TO CATCH THE DAILY BUS TOUR THAT RUNS AROUND THE MOUNTAINS.
UP TO THE HOUSE? HA HA... EVERYONE ASKS ABOUT THAT.
BE CONTENT WITH THE TOUR, OKAY?
THANK YOU, LADIES AND GENTLEMEN, FOR CHOOSING LAMENTATION TOURS.
WE'LL BEGIN WITH A LOOK AT THE MURDEROUS CLAN THAT CALLS DENDORA HOME.
HMM...
...THERE ARE SOME CLEARLY...
THUNK
...SHADY DUDES AMONG THE PUNTERS.
THUNK

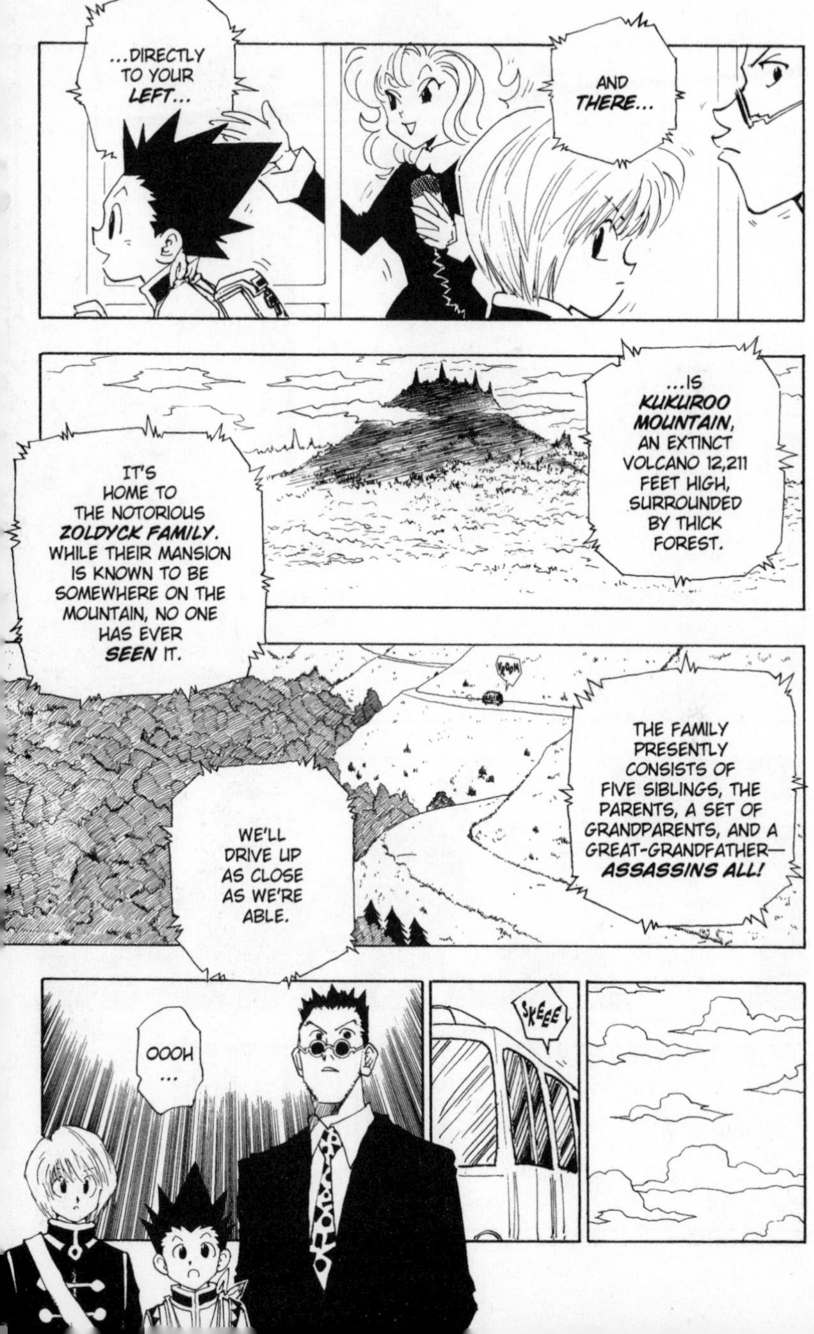
AND THERE...
...DIRECTLY TO YOUR LEFT...
...IS KUKUROO MOUNTAIN, AN EXTINCT VOLCANO 12,211 FEET HIGH, SURROUNDED BY THICK FOREST.
IT'S HOME TO THE NOTORIOUS ZOLDYCK FAMILY. WHILE THEIR MANSION IS KNOWN TO BE SOMEWHERE ON THE MOUNTAIN, NO ONE HAS EVER SEEN IT.
VROOM
THE FAMILY PRESENTLY CONSISTS OF FIVE SIBLINGS, THE PARENTS, A SET OF GRANDPARENTS, AND A GREAT-GRANDFATHER—ASSASSINS ALL!
WE'LL DRIVE UP AS CLOSE AS WE'RE ABLE.
SKEEE
OOOH...

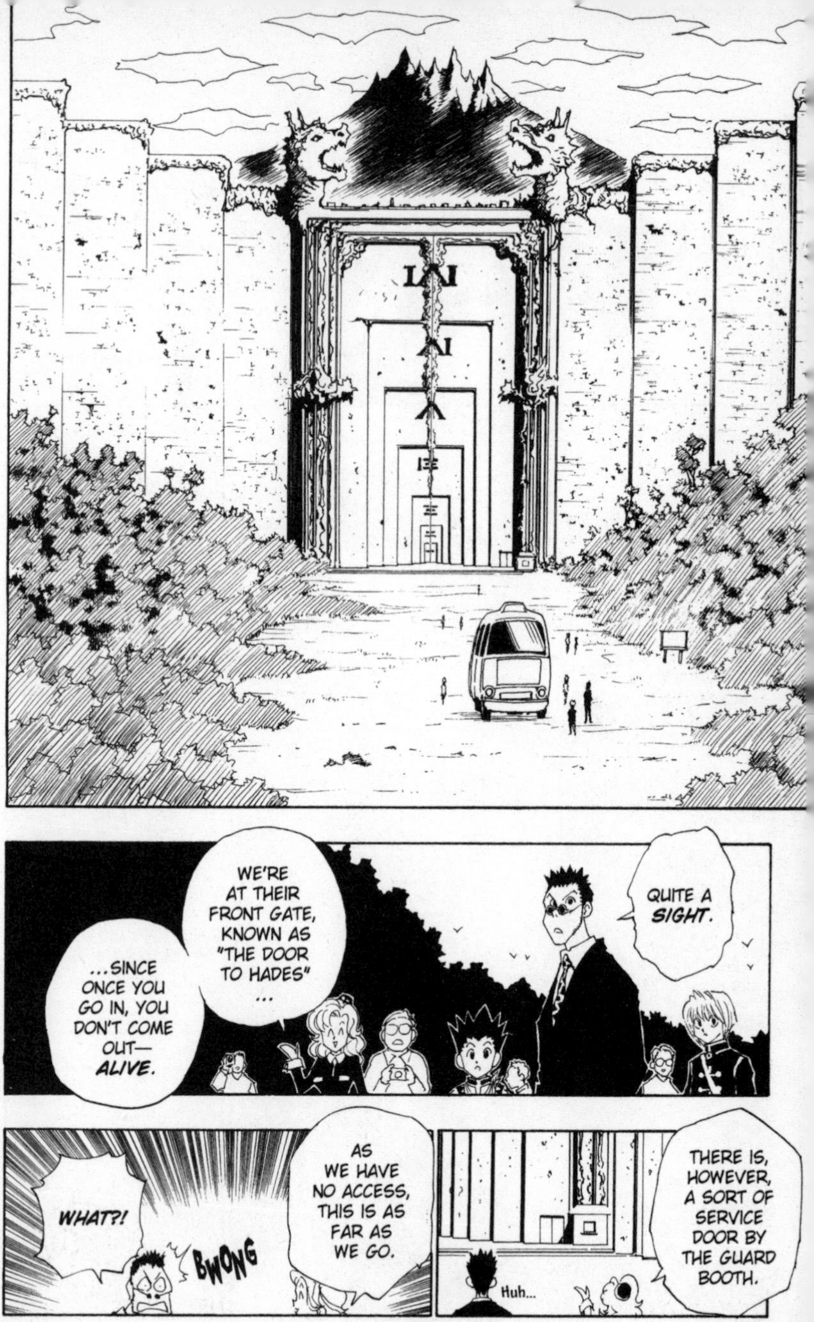
QUITE A *SIGHT*.
WE'RE AT THEIR FRONT GATE, KNOWN AS "THE DOOR TO HADES" ...
...SINCE ONCE YOU GO IN, YOU DON'T COME OUT— *ALIVE*.
AS WE HAVE NO ACCESS, THIS IS AS FAR AS WE GO.
WHAT?!
BWONG
THERE IS, HOWEVER, A SORT OF SERVICE DOOR BY THE GUARD BOOTH.
Huh...

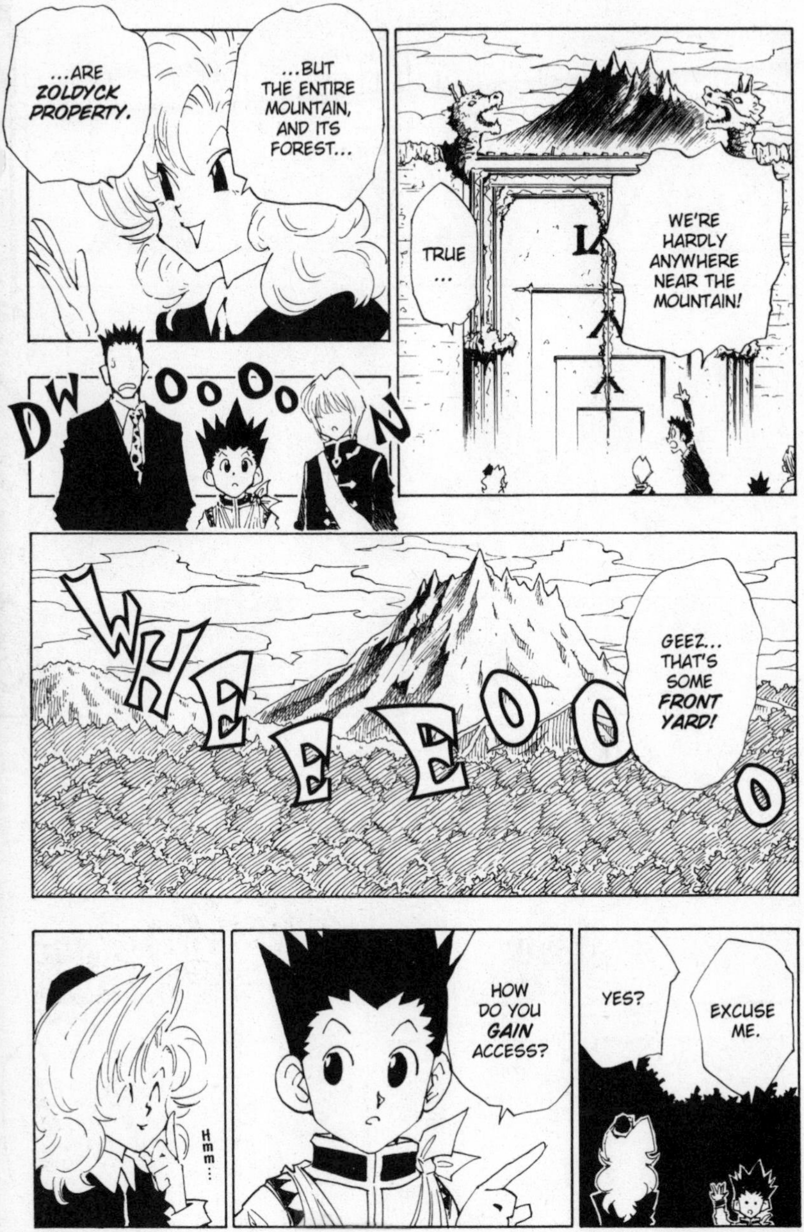
WE'RE HARDLY ANYWHERE NEAR THE MOUNTAIN!
TRUE ...
...BUT THE ENTIRE MOUNTAIN, AND ITS FOREST...
...ARE ZOLDYCK PROPERTY.
DWOOOOON
GEEZ... THAT'S SOME FRONT YARD!
WHEEEOOOO
EXCUSE ME.
YES?
HOW DO YOU GAIN ACCESS?
Hmm...

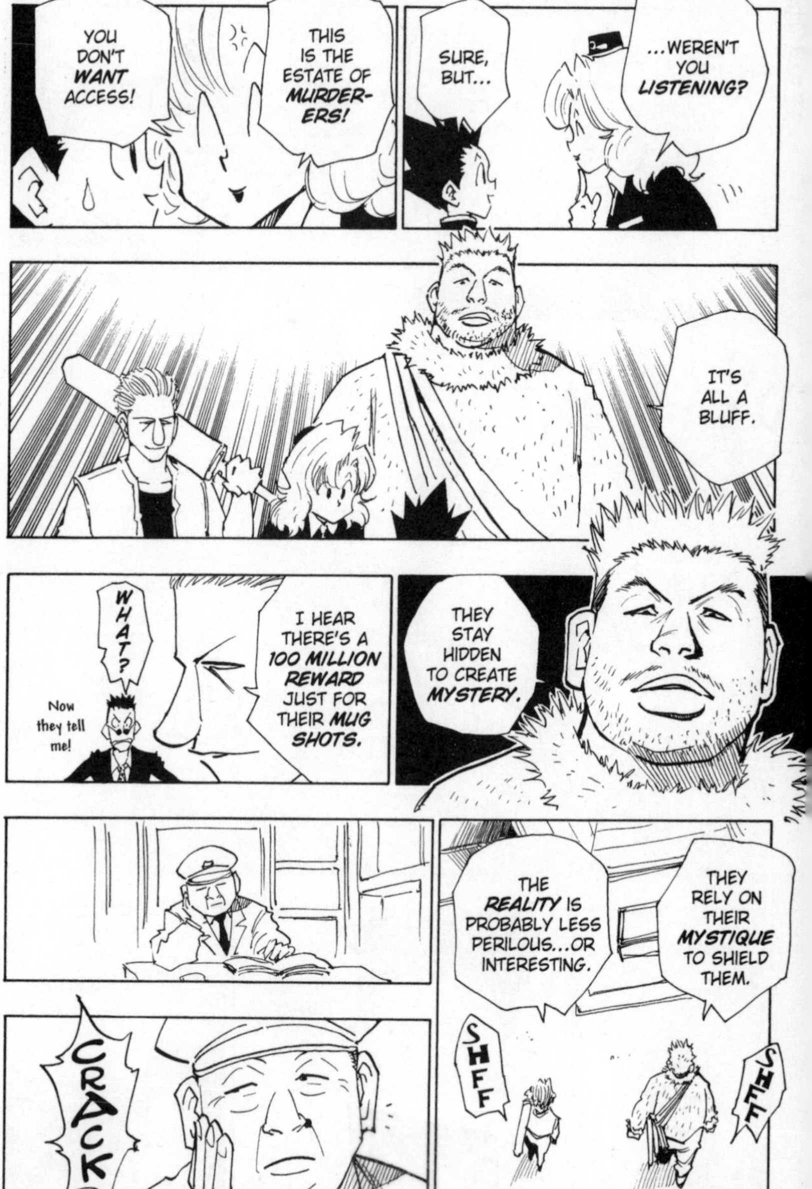

...WEREN'T YOU LISTENING?
SURE, BUT...
THIS IS THE ESTATE OF MURDERERS!
YOU DON'T WANT ACCESS!
IT'S ALL A BLUFF.
THEY STAY HIDDEN TO CREATE MYSTERY.
I HEAR THERE'S A 100 MILLION REWARD JUST FOR THEIR MUG SHOTS.
WHAT?
Now they tell me!
THEY RELY ON THEIR MYSTIQUE TO SHIELD THEM.
THE REALITY IS PROBABLY LESS PERILOUS...OR INTERESTING.
SHFF
SHFF
CRACK

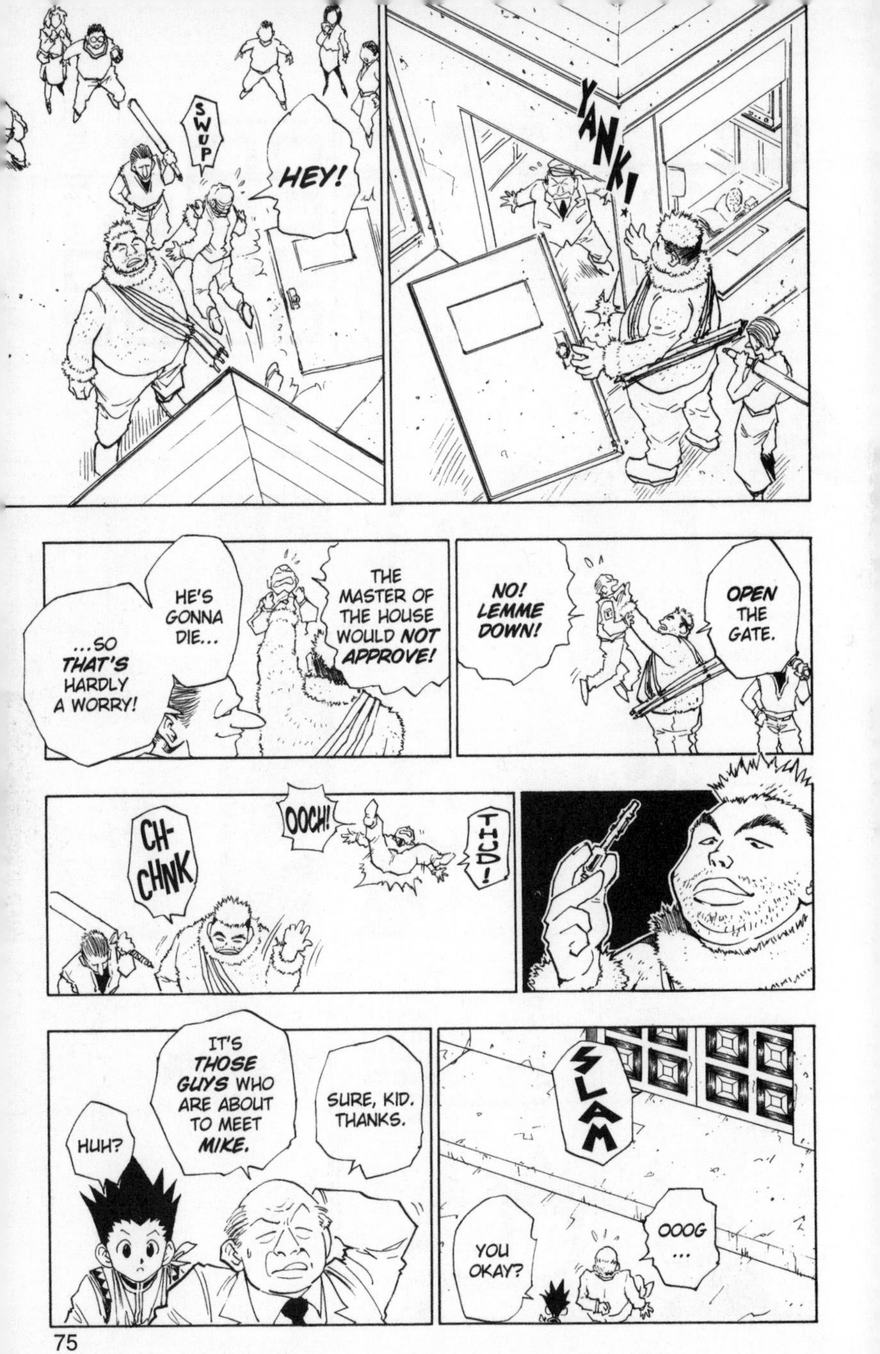
YANK!
HEY!
SWUP
OPEN THE GATE.
NO! LEMME DOWN!
THE MASTER OF THE HOUSE WOULD NOT APPROVE!
HE'S GONNA DIE...
...SO THAT'S HARDLY A WORRY!
THUD!
OOCH!
CH-CHNK
SLAM
OOOG ...
YOU OKAY?
SURE, KID. THANKS.
IT'S THOSE GUYS WHO ARE ABOUT TO MEET MIKE.
HUH?

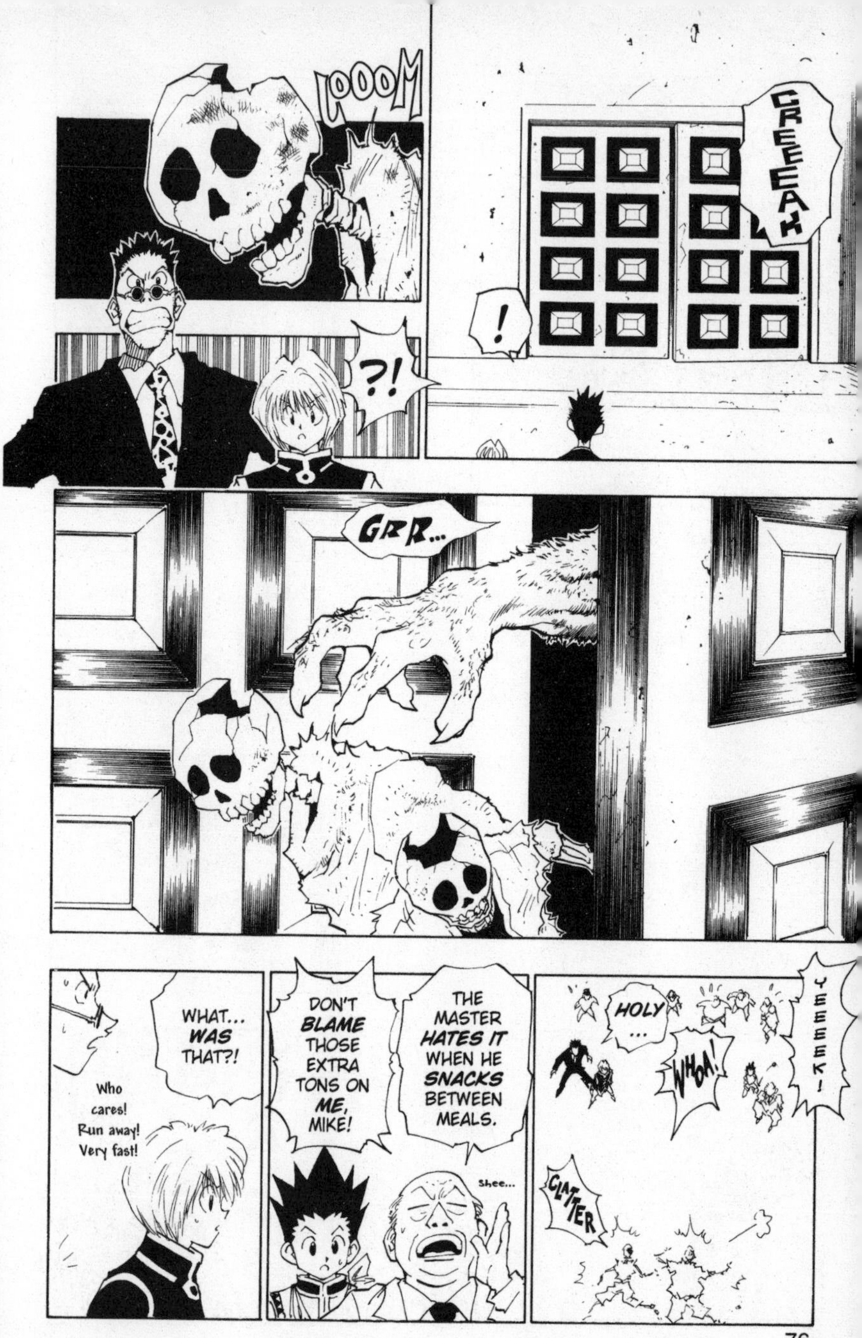
CREEEAK
!
?!
GRR...
YEEEEK!
HOLY...
WHOA!
CLATTER
THE MASTER HATES IT WHEN HE SNACKS BETWEEN MEALS.
DON'T BLAME THOSE EXTRA TONS ON ME, MIKE!
Shee...
WHAT... WAS THAT?!
Who cares! Run away! Very fast!

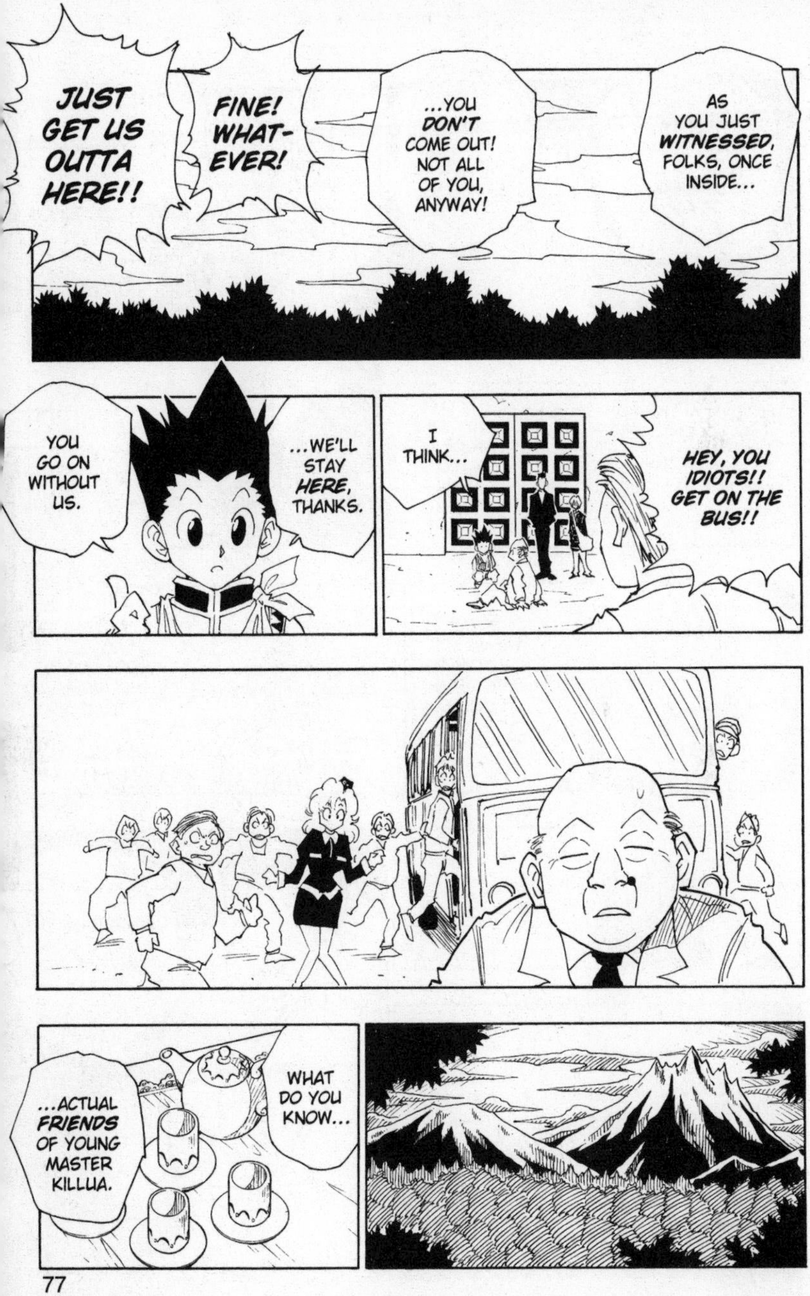
AS YOU JUST WITNESSED, FOLKS, ONCE INSIDE...
...YOU DON'T COME OUT! NOT ALL OF YOU, ANYWAY!
FINE! WHAT-EVER!
JUST GET US OUTTA HERE!!
HEY, YOU IDIOTS!! GET ON THE BUS!!
I THINK...
...WE'LL STAY HERE, THANKS.
YOU GO ON WITHOUT US.
WHAT DO YOU KNOW...
...ACTUAL FRIENDS OF YOUNG MASTER KILLUA.

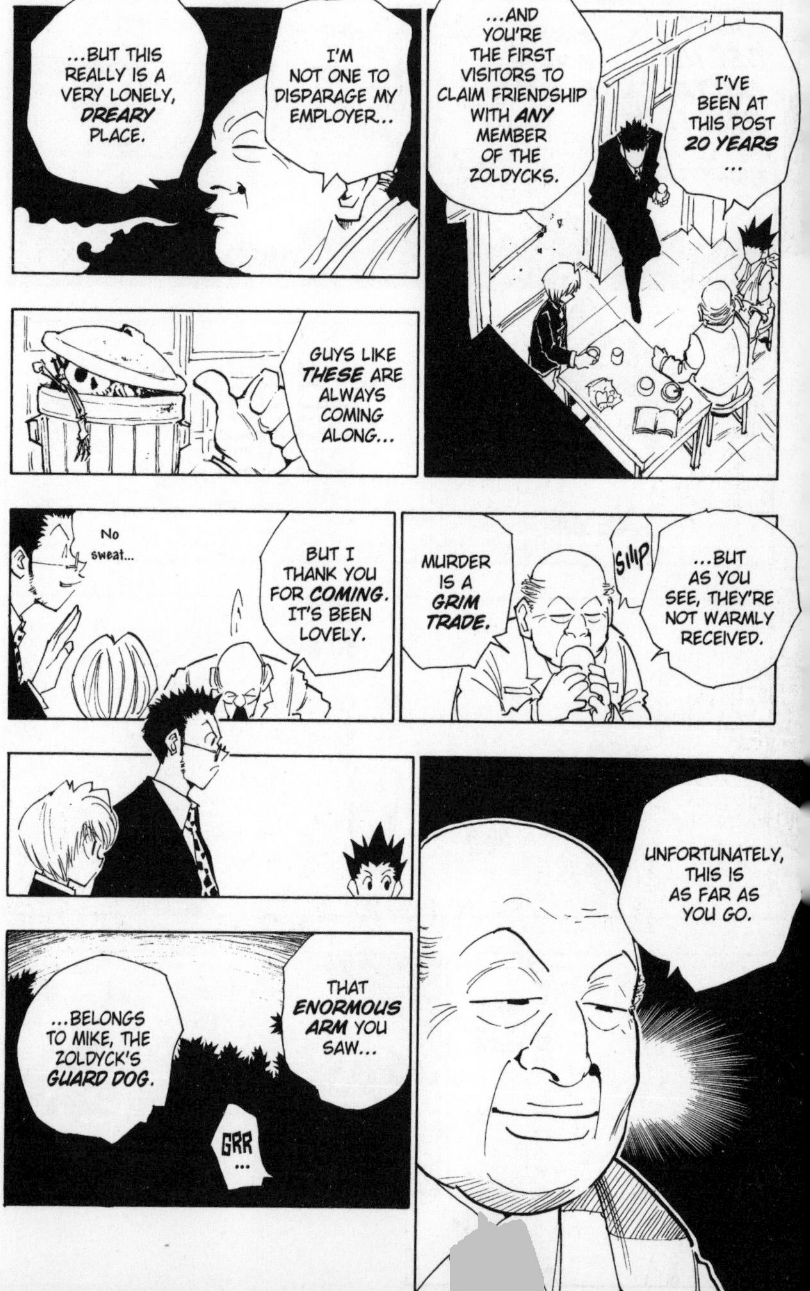
I'VE BEEN AT THIS POST 20 YEARS ...
...AND YOU'RE THE FIRST VISITORS TO CLAIM FRIENDSHIP WITH ANY MEMBER OF THE ZOLDYCKS.
I'M NOT ONE TO DISPARAGE MY EMPLOYER...
...BUT THIS REALLY IS A VERY LONELY, DREARY PLACE.
GUYS LIKE THESE ARE ALWAYS COMING ALONG...
...BUT AS YOU SEE, THEY'RE NOT WARMLY RECEIVED.
SLIP
MURDER IS A GRIM TRADE.
BUT I THANK YOU FOR COMING. IT'S BEEN LOVELY.
No sweat...
UNFORTUNATELY, THIS IS AS FAR AS YOU GO.
THAT ENORMOUS ARM YOU SAW...
...BELONGS TO MIKE, THE ZOLDYCK'S GUARD DOG.
GRR ...

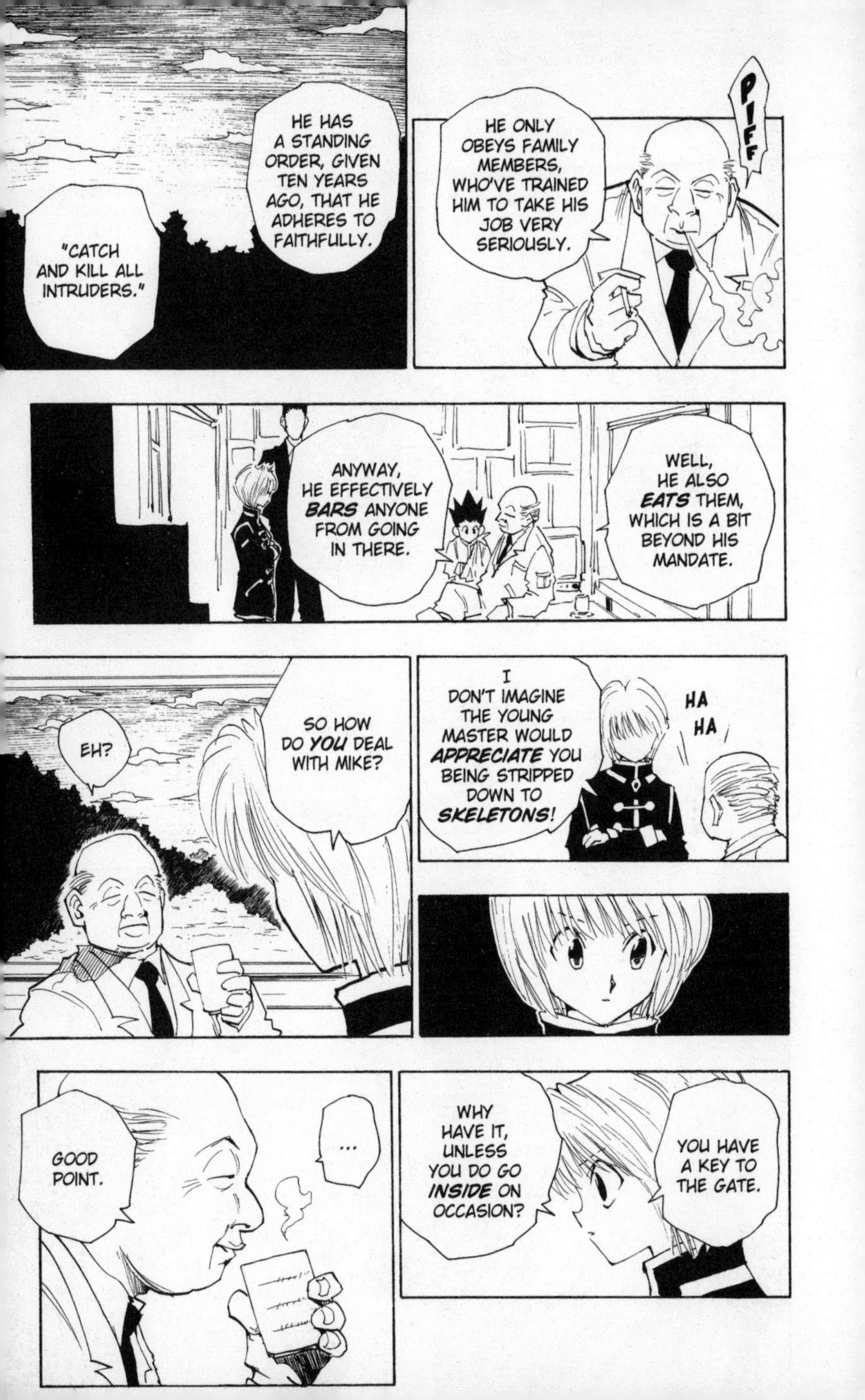
PIFF
HE ONLY OBEYS FAMILY MEMBERS, WHO'VE TRAINED HIM TO TAKE HIS JOB VERY SERIOUSLY.
HE HAS A STANDING ORDER, GIVEN TEN YEARS AGO, THAT HE ADHERES TO FAITHFULLY.
"CATCH AND KILL ALL INTRUDERS."
WELL, HE ALSO EATS THEM, WHICH IS A BIT BEYOND HIS MANDATE.
ANYWAY, HE EFFECTIVELY BARS ANYONE FROM GOING IN THERE.
HA HA
I DON'T IMAGINE THE YOUNG MASTER WOULD APPRECIATE YOU BEING STRIPPED DOWN TO SKELETONS!
SO HOW DO YOU DEAL WITH MIKE?
EH?
YOU HAVE A KEY TO THE GATE.
WHY HAVE IT, UNLESS YOU DO GO INSIDE ON OCCASION?
...
GOOD POINT.

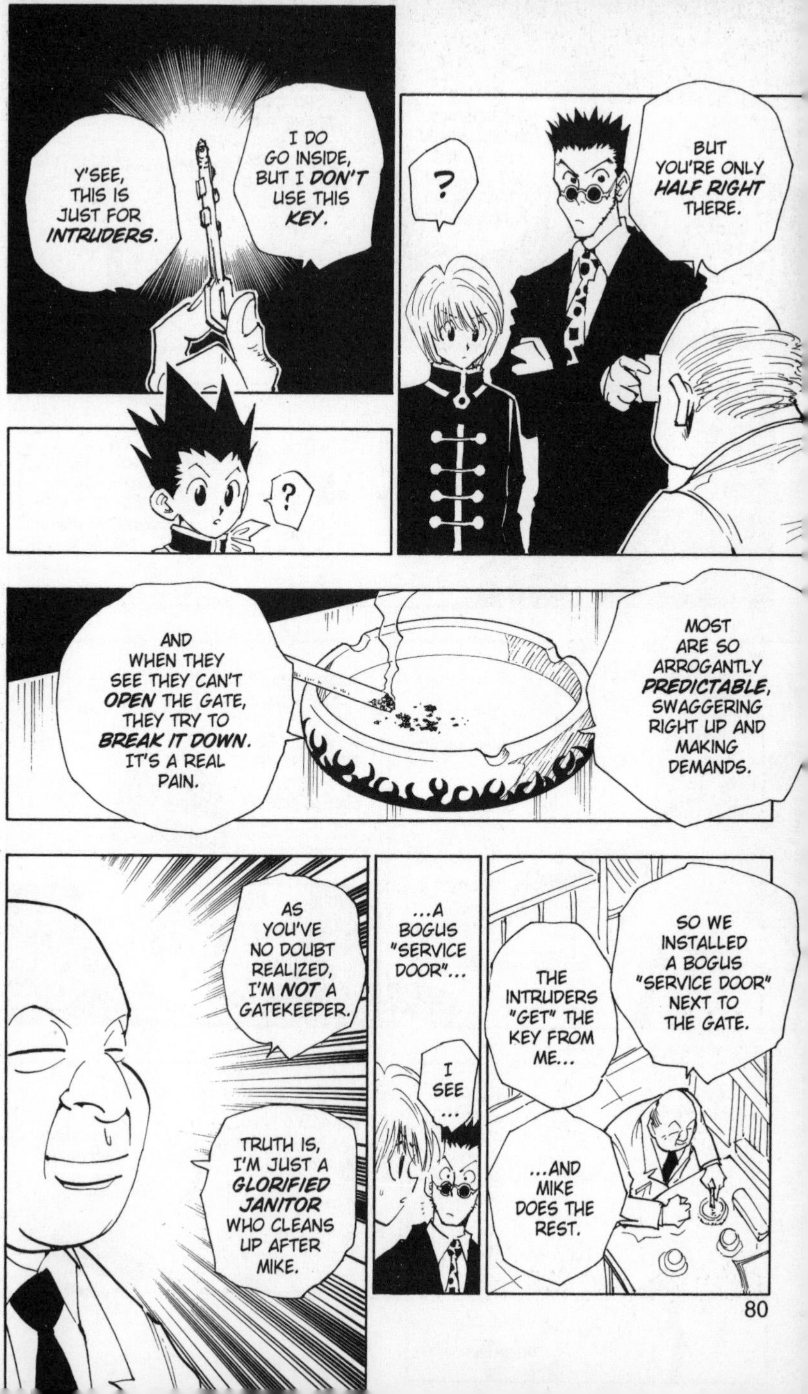
BUT YOU'RE ONLY HALF RIGHT THERE.
?
I DO GO INSIDE, BUT I DON'T USE THIS KEY.
Y'SEE, THIS IS JUST FOR INTRUDERS.
?
MOST ARE SO ARROGANTLY PREDICTABLE, SWAGGERING RIGHT UP AND MAKING DEMANDS.
AND WHEN THEY SEE THEY CAN'T OPEN THE GATE, THEY TRY TO BREAK IT DOWN. IT'S A REAL PAIN.
SO WE INSTALLED A BOGUS "SERVICE DOOR" NEXT TO THE GATE.
THE INTRUDERS "GET" THE KEY FROM ME...
...AND MIKE DOES THE REST.
...A BOGUS "SERVICE DOOR"...
I SEE...
AS YOU'VE NO DOUBT REALIZED, I'M NOT A GATEKEEPER.
TRUTH IS, I'M JUST A GLORIFIED JANITOR WHO CLEANS UP AFTER MIKE.

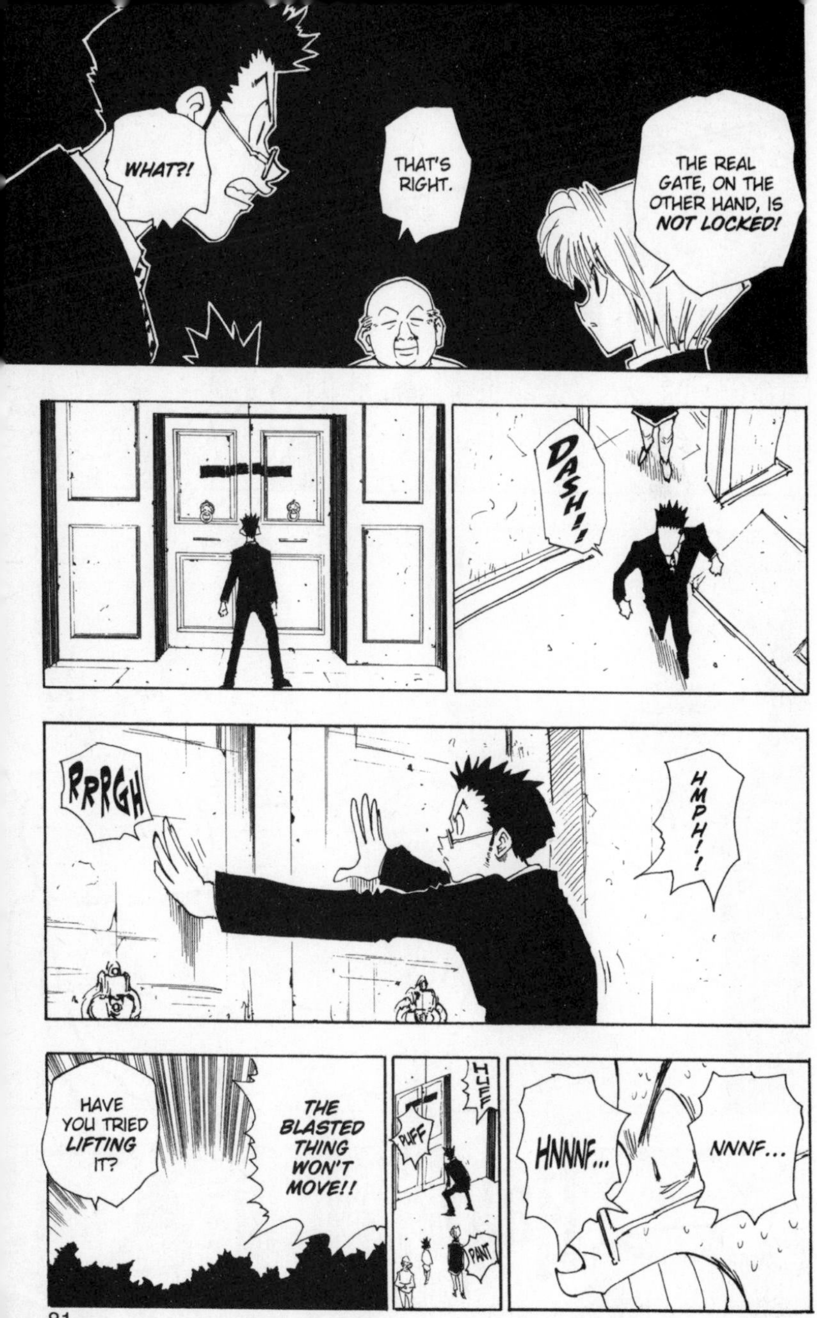
THE REAL GATE, ON THE OTHER HAND, IS NOT LOCKED!
THAT'S RIGHT.
WHAT?!
DASH!!
HMPH!!
RRRGH
NNNF...
HNNNF...
HUFF
PUFF
PANT
THE BLASTED THING WON'T MOVE!!
HAVE YOU TRIED LIFTING IT?

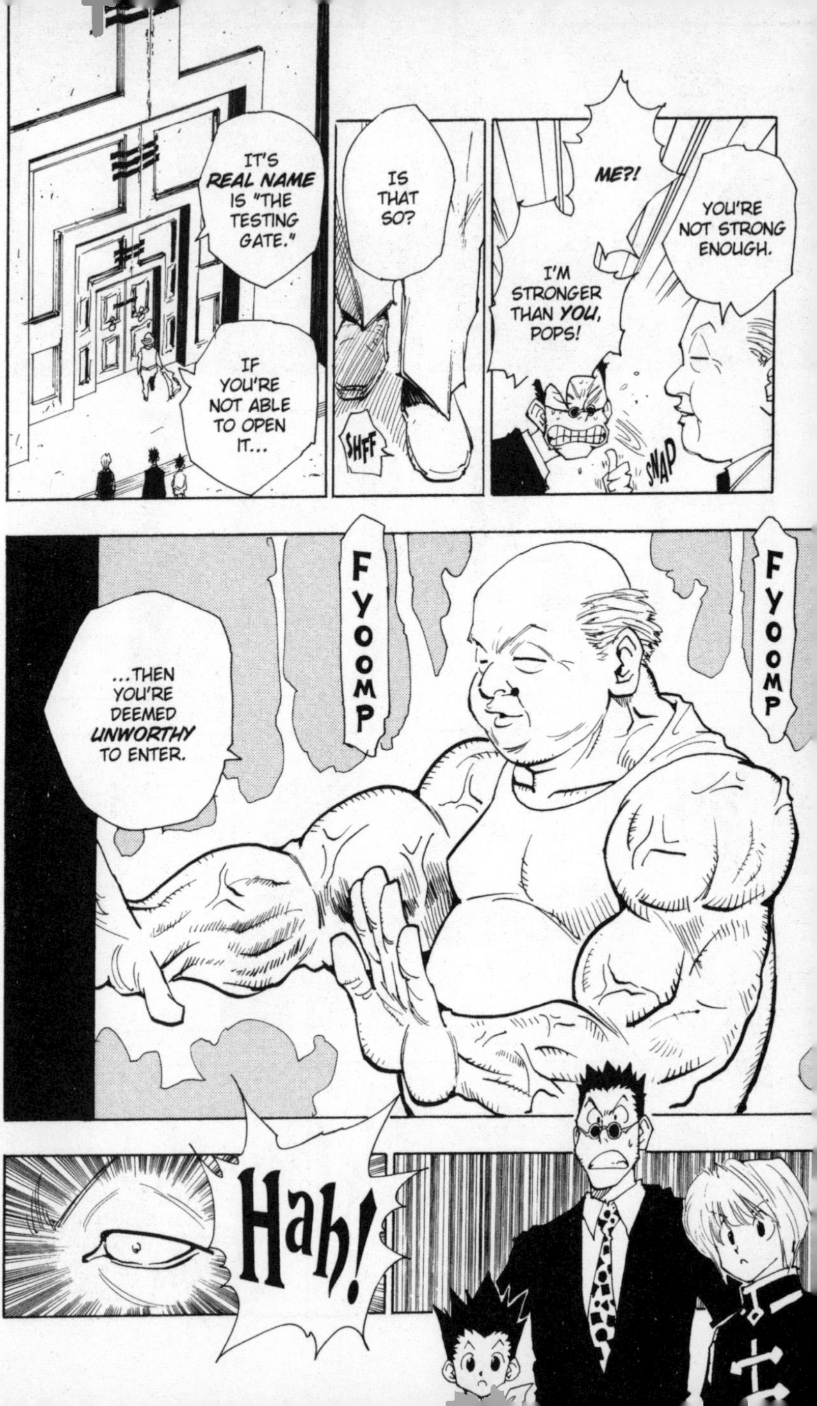
YOU'RE NOT STRONG ENOUGH.
ME?!
I'M STRONGER THAN YOU, POPS!
SNAP
IS THAT SO?
SHFF
IT'S REAL NAME IS "THE TESTING GATE."
IF YOU'RE NOT ABLE TO OPEN IT...
FYOOMP
FYOOMP
...THEN YOU'RE DEEMED UNWORTHY TO ENTER.
Hah!

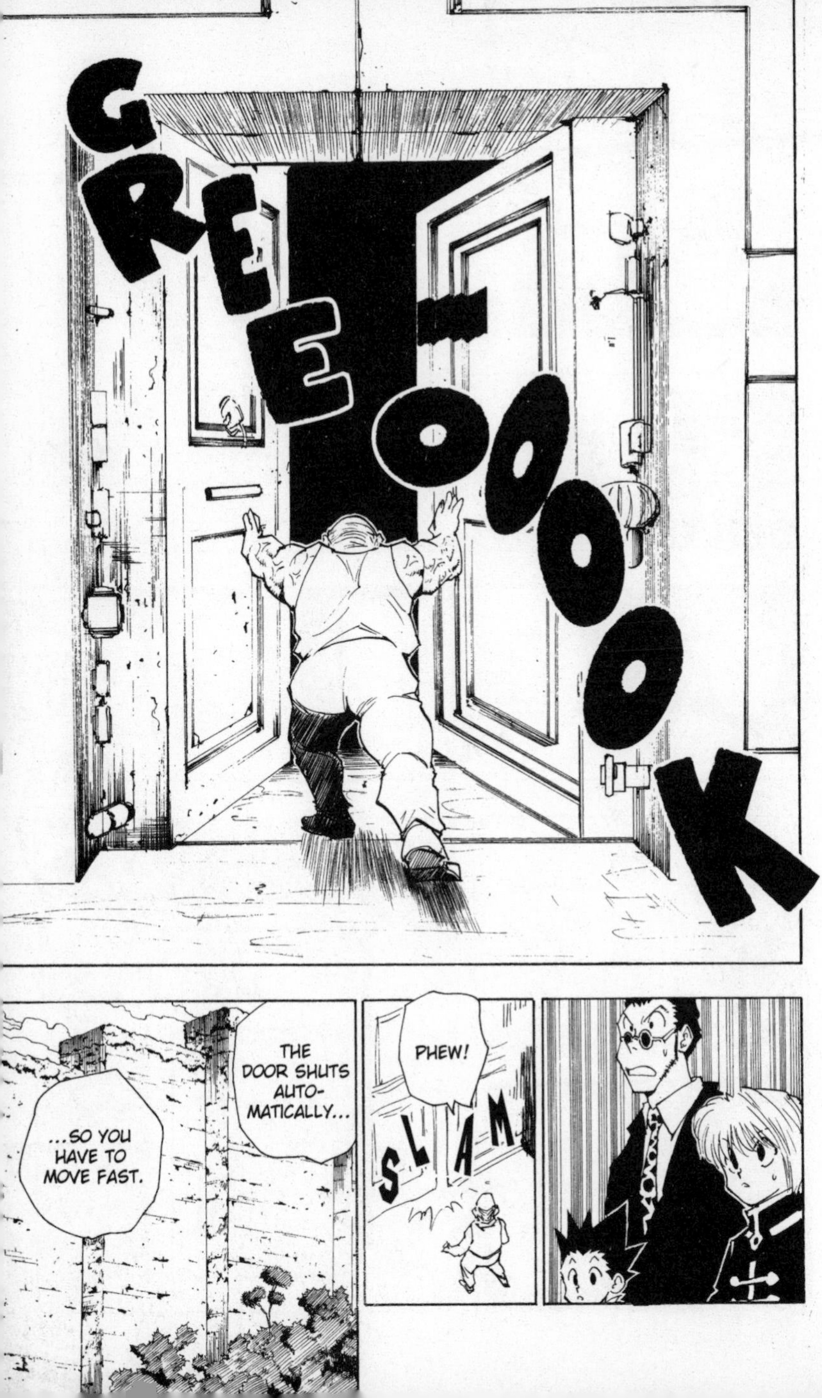
GREE-OOOOK
PHEW!
SLAM
THE DOOR SHUTS AUTO-MATICALLY...
...SO YOU HAVE TO MOVE FAST.

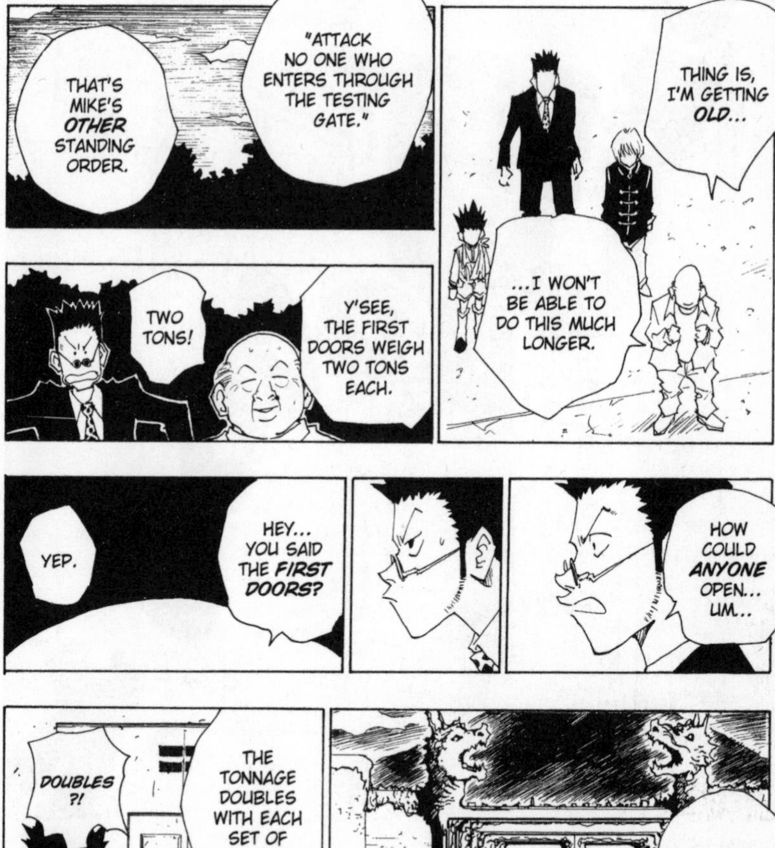
THING IS, I'M GETTING *OLD*...
...I WON'T BE ABLE TO DO THIS MUCH LONGER.
"ATTACK NO ONE WHO ENTERS THROUGH THE TESTING GATE."
THAT'S MIKE'S *OTHER* STANDING ORDER.
Y'SEE, THE FIRST DOORS WEIGH TWO TONS EACH.
TWO TONS!
HOW COULD *ANYONE* OPEN... UM...
HEY... YOU SAID THE *FIRST DOORS?*
YEP.
SEE THERE? *SEVEN* IN ALL.
OH...
THE TONNAGE DOUBLES WITH EACH SET OF DOORS.
DOUBLES ?!
THE MORE *FORCE* YOU PUT IN, THE MORE *DOORS* YOU OPEN.

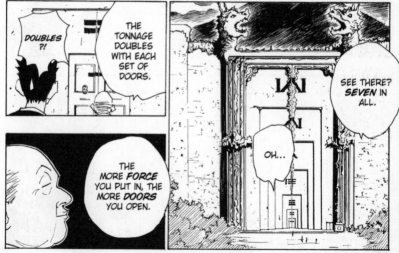

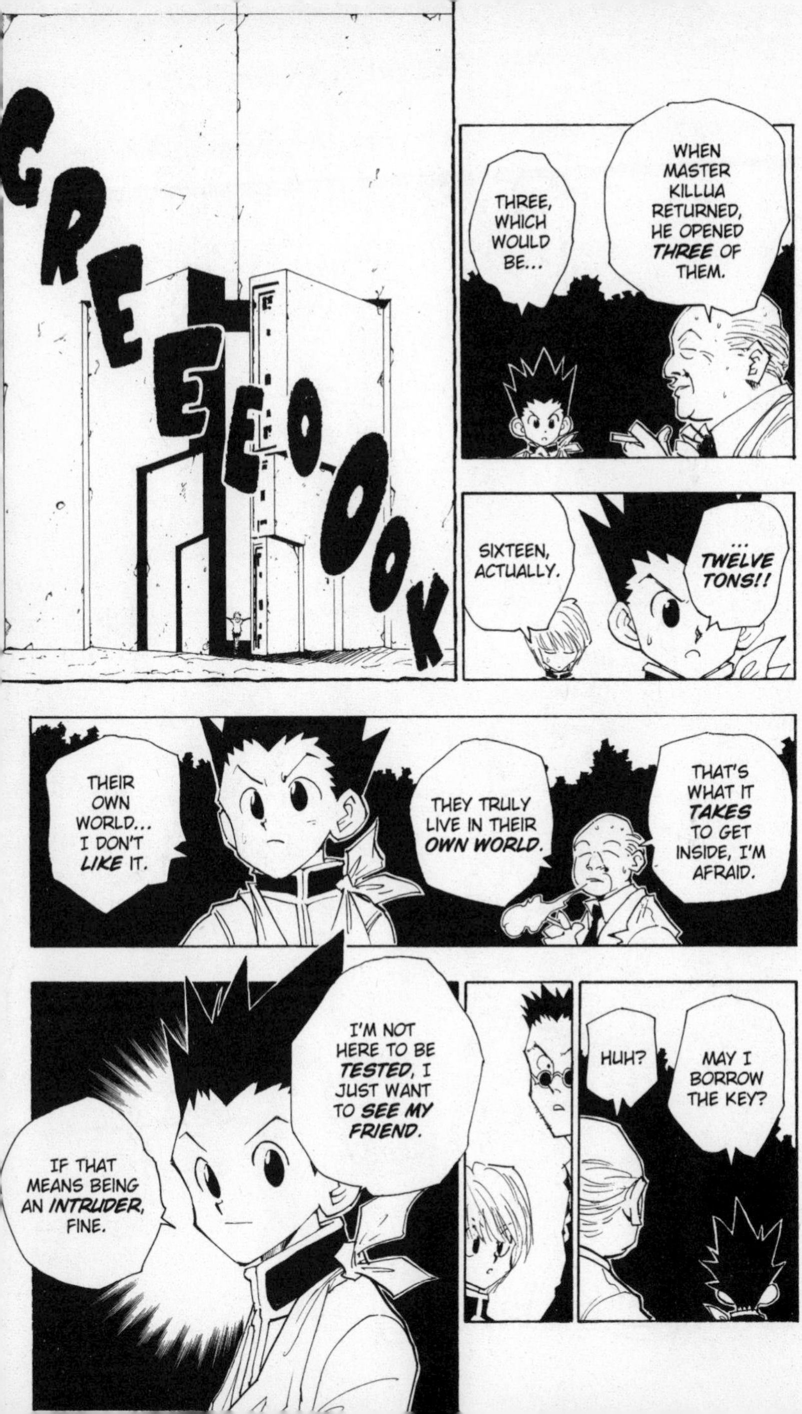
WHEN MASTER KILLUA RETURNED, HE OPENED *THREE* OF THEM.
THREE, WHICH WOULD BE...
... *TWELVE TONS!!*
SIXTEEN, ACTUALLY.
GREEEO-OOOK
THAT'S WHAT IT *TAKES* TO GET INSIDE, I'M AFRAID.
THEY TRULY LIVE IN THEIR *OWN WORLD*.
THEIR OWN WORLD... I DON'T *LIKE* IT.
MAY I BORROW THE KEY?
HUH?
I'M NOT HERE TO BE *TESTED*, I JUST WANT TO *SEE MY FRIEND*.
IF THAT MEANS BEING AN *INTRUDER*, FINE.

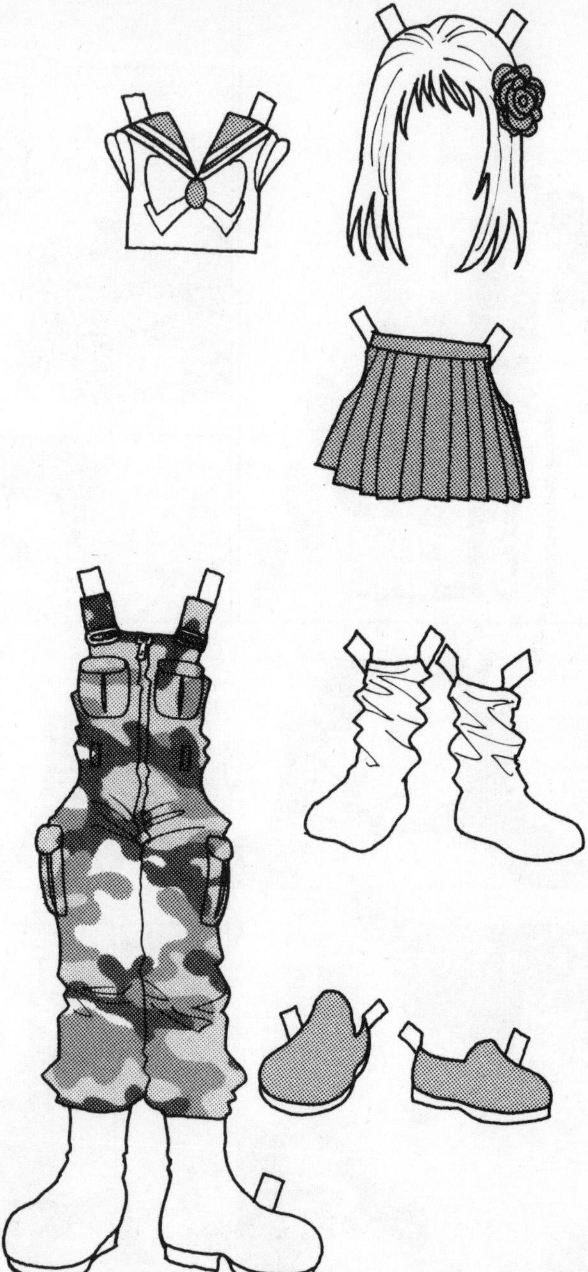

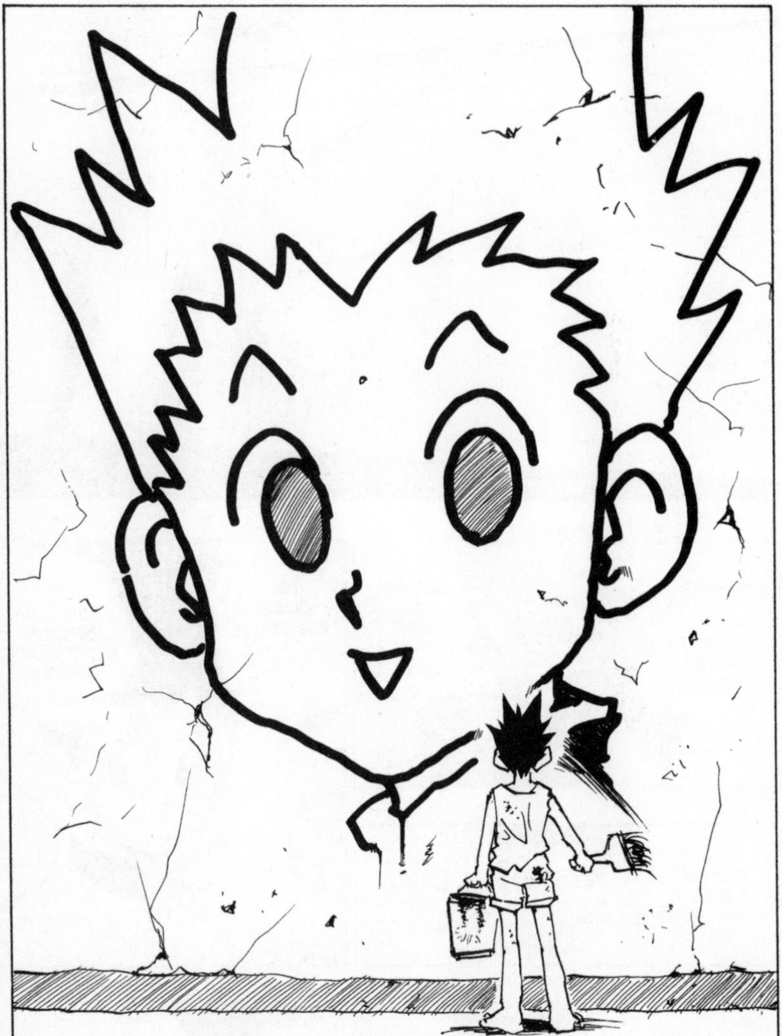

Chapter 40

The Zoldycks, part 1

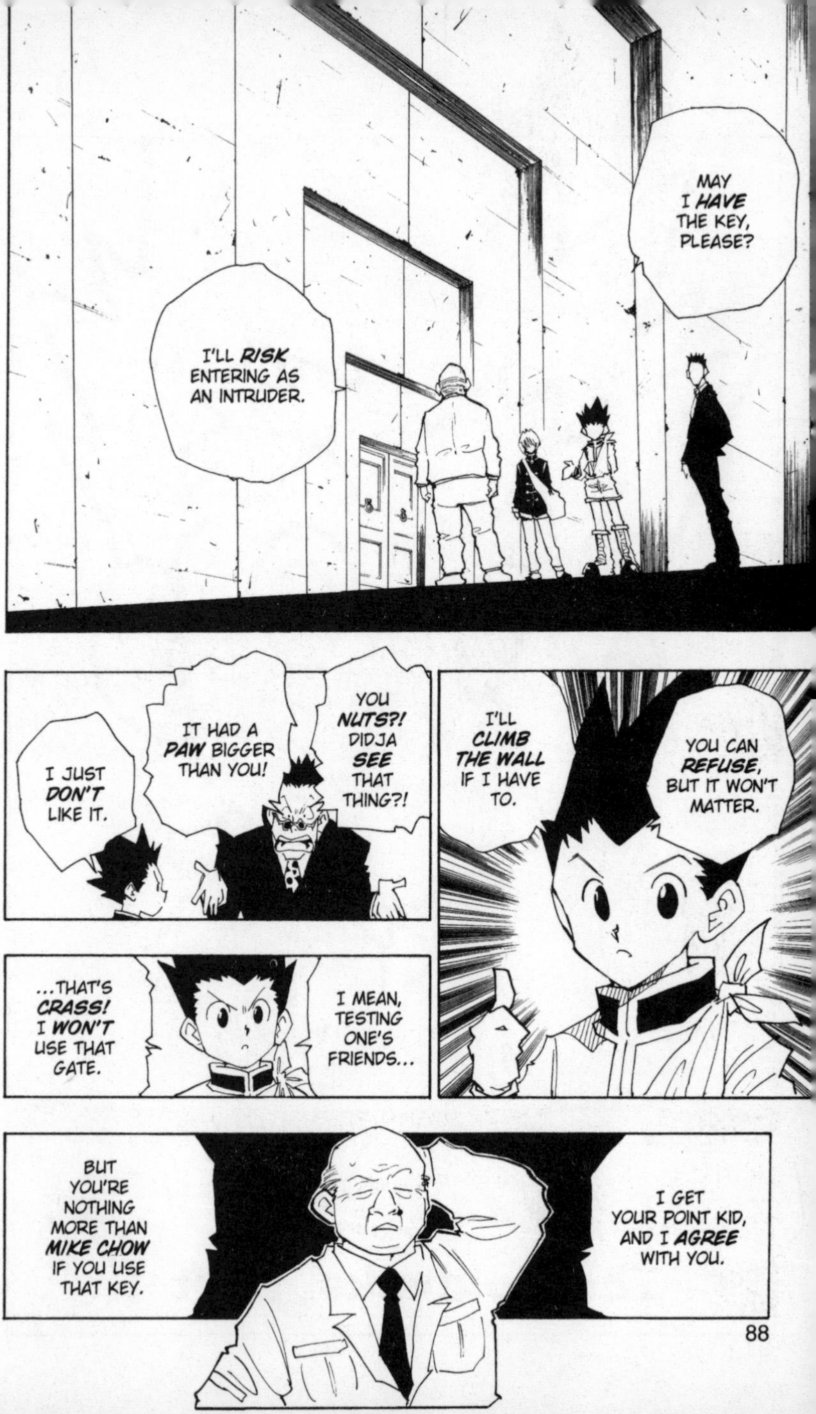
MAY I HAVE THE KEY, PLEASE?
I'LL RISK ENTERING AS AN INTRUDER.
YOU CAN REFUSE, BUT IT WON'T MATTER.
I'LL CLIMB THE WALL IF I HAVE TO.
YOU NUTS?! DIDJA SEE THAT THING?!
IT HAD A PAW BIGGER THAN YOU!
I JUST DON'T LIKE IT.
I MEAN, TESTING ONE'S FRIENDS...
...THAT'S CRASS! I WON'T USE THAT GATE.
I GET YOUR POINT KID, AND I AGREE WITH YOU.
BUT YOU'RE NOTHING MORE THAN MIKE CHOW IF YOU USE THAT KEY.

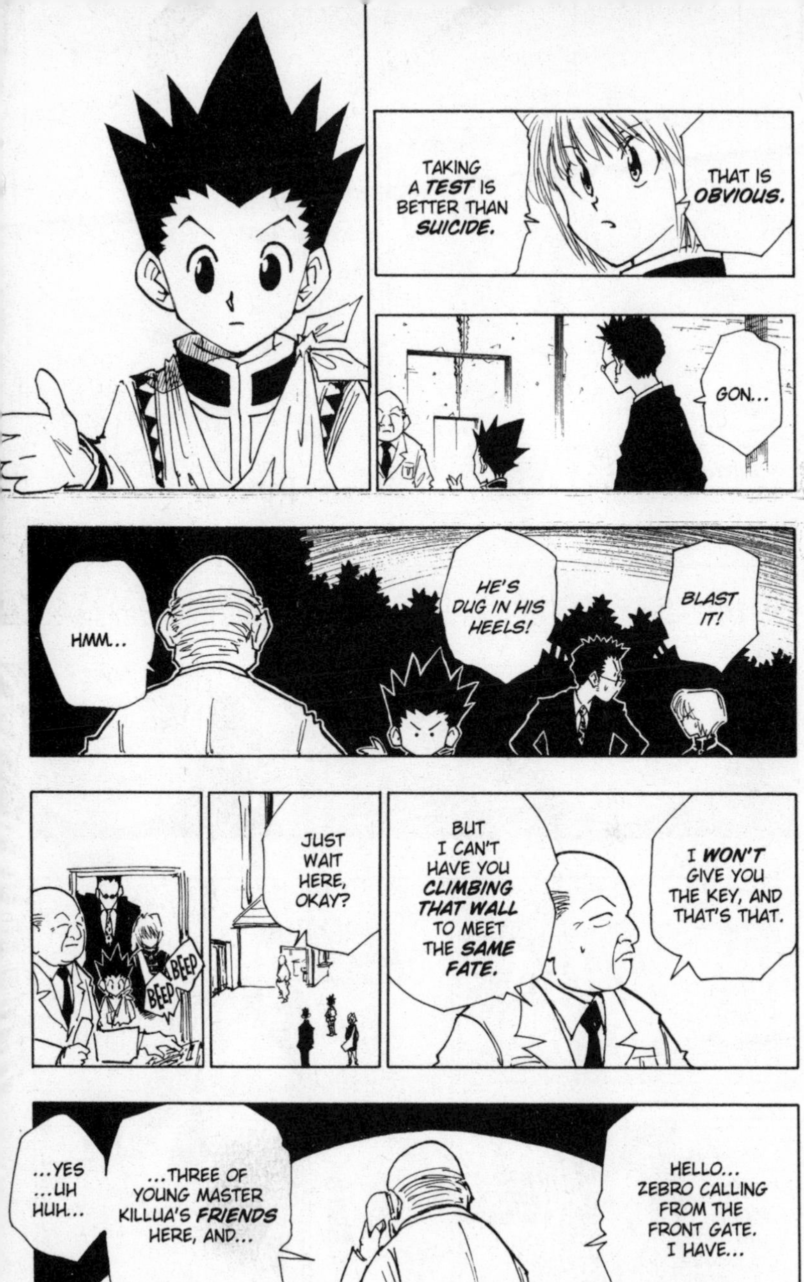

THAT IS *OBVIOUS.*
TAKING A *TEST* IS BETTER THAN *SUICIDE.*
GON...
BLAST IT!
HE'S DUG IN HIS HEELS!
HMM...
I ***WON'T*** GIVE YOU THE KEY, AND THAT'S THAT.
BUT I CAN'T HAVE YOU ***CLIMBING THAT WALL*** TO MEET THE ***SAME FATE.***
JUST WAIT HERE, OKAY?
BEEP
BEEP
HELLO... ZEBRO CALLING FROM THE FRONT GATE. I HAVE...
...THREE OF YOUNG MASTER KILLUA'S ***FRIENDS*** HERE, AND...
...YES ...UH HUH...

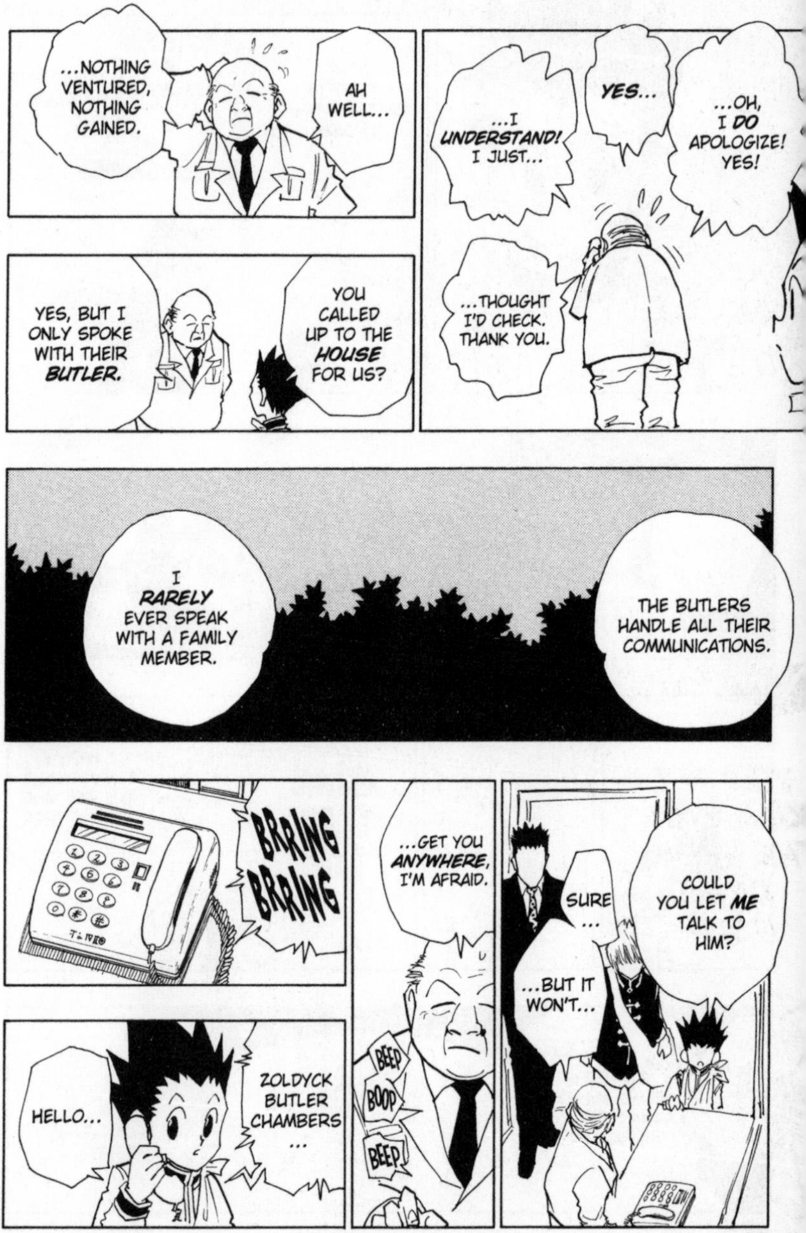
...OH, I DO APOLOGIZE! YES!
YES...
...I UNDERSTAND! I JUST...
...THOUGHT I'D CHECK. THANK YOU.
AH WELL...
...NOTHING VENTURED, NOTHING GAINED.
YOU CALLED UP TO THE HOUSE FOR US?
YES, BUT I ONLY SPOKE WITH THEIR BUTLER.
THE BUTLERS HANDLE ALL THEIR COMMUNICATIONS.
I RARELY EVER SPEAK WITH A FAMILY MEMBER.
COULD YOU LET ME TALK TO HIM?
SURE...
...BUT IT WON'T...
...GET YOU ANYWHERE, I'M AFRAID.
BEEP
BOOP
BEEP
BRRING BRRING
ZOLDYCK BUTLER CHAMBERS ...
HELLO...

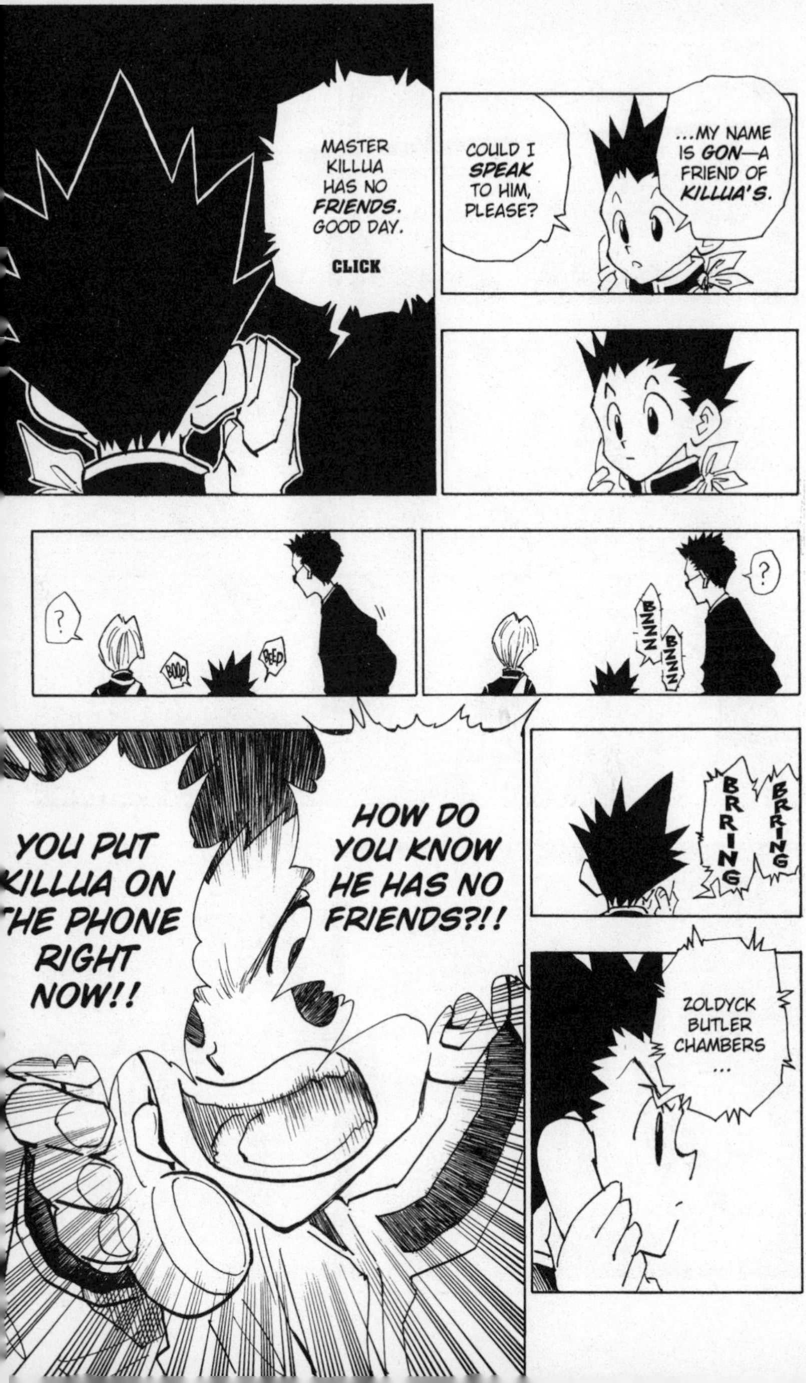
...MY NAME IS GON—A FRIEND OF KILLUA'S.
COULD I SPEAK TO HIM, PLEASE?
MASTER KILLUA HAS NO FRIENDS. GOOD DAY.
CLICK
?
BZZZ
BZZZ
?
BOOP
BEEP
BRRING
BRRING
ZOLDYCK BUTLER CHAMBERS ...
HOW DO YOU KNOW HE HAS NO FRIENDS?!!
YOU PUT KILLUA ON THE PHONE RIGHT NOW!!

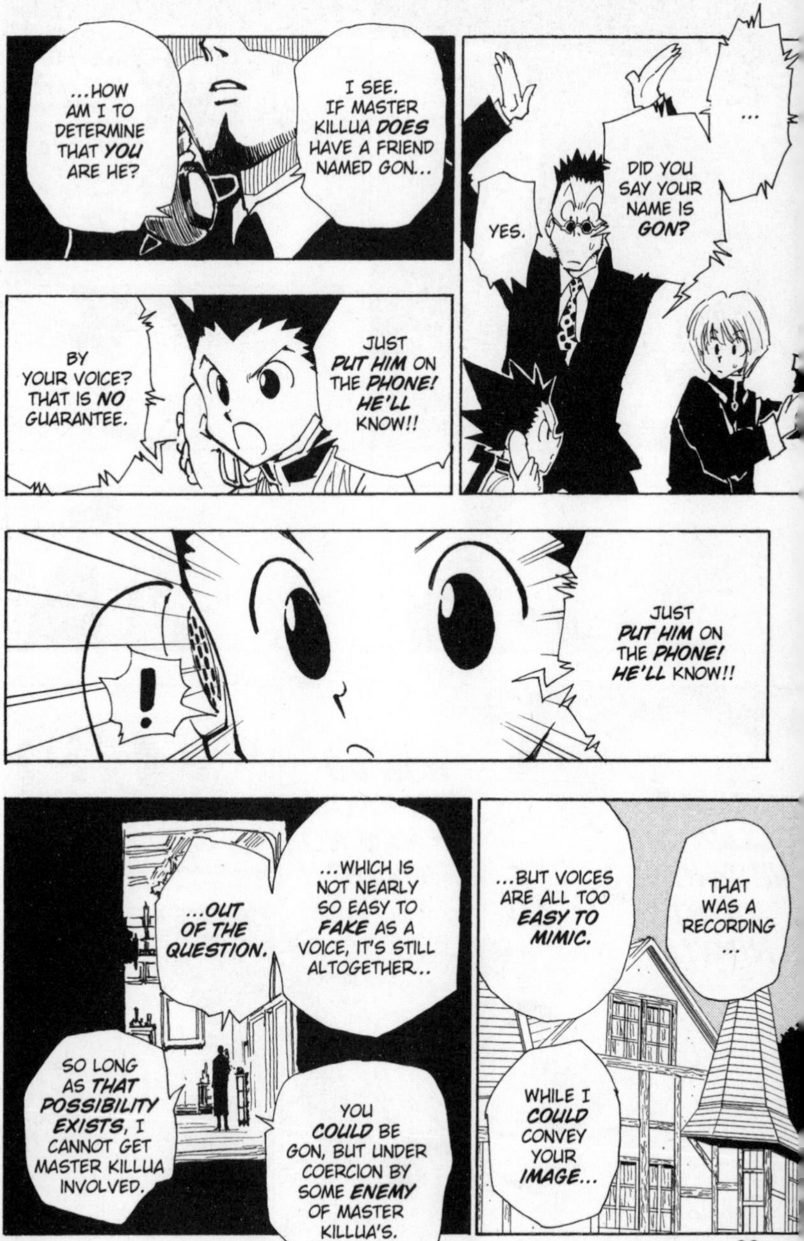
...
DID YOU SAY YOUR NAME IS GON?
YES.
I SEE. IF MASTER KILLUA DOES HAVE A FRIEND NAMED GON...
...HOW AM I TO DETERMINE THAT YOU ARE HE?
JUST PUT HIM ON THE PHONE! HE'LL KNOW!!
BY YOUR VOICE? THAT IS NO GUARANTEE.
JUST PUT HIM ON THE PHONE! HE'LL KNOW!!
!
THAT WAS A RECORDING...
...BUT VOICES ARE ALL TOO EASY TO MIMIC.
WHILE I COULD CONVEY YOUR IMAGE...
...WHICH IS NOT NEARLY SO EASY TO FAKE AS A VOICE, IT'S STILL ALTOGETHER...
...OUT OF THE QUESTION.
YOU COULD BE GON, BUT UNDER COERCION BY SOME ENEMY OF MASTER KILLUA'S.
SO LONG AS THAT POSSIBILITY EXISTS, I CANNOT GET MASTER KILLUA INVOLVED.

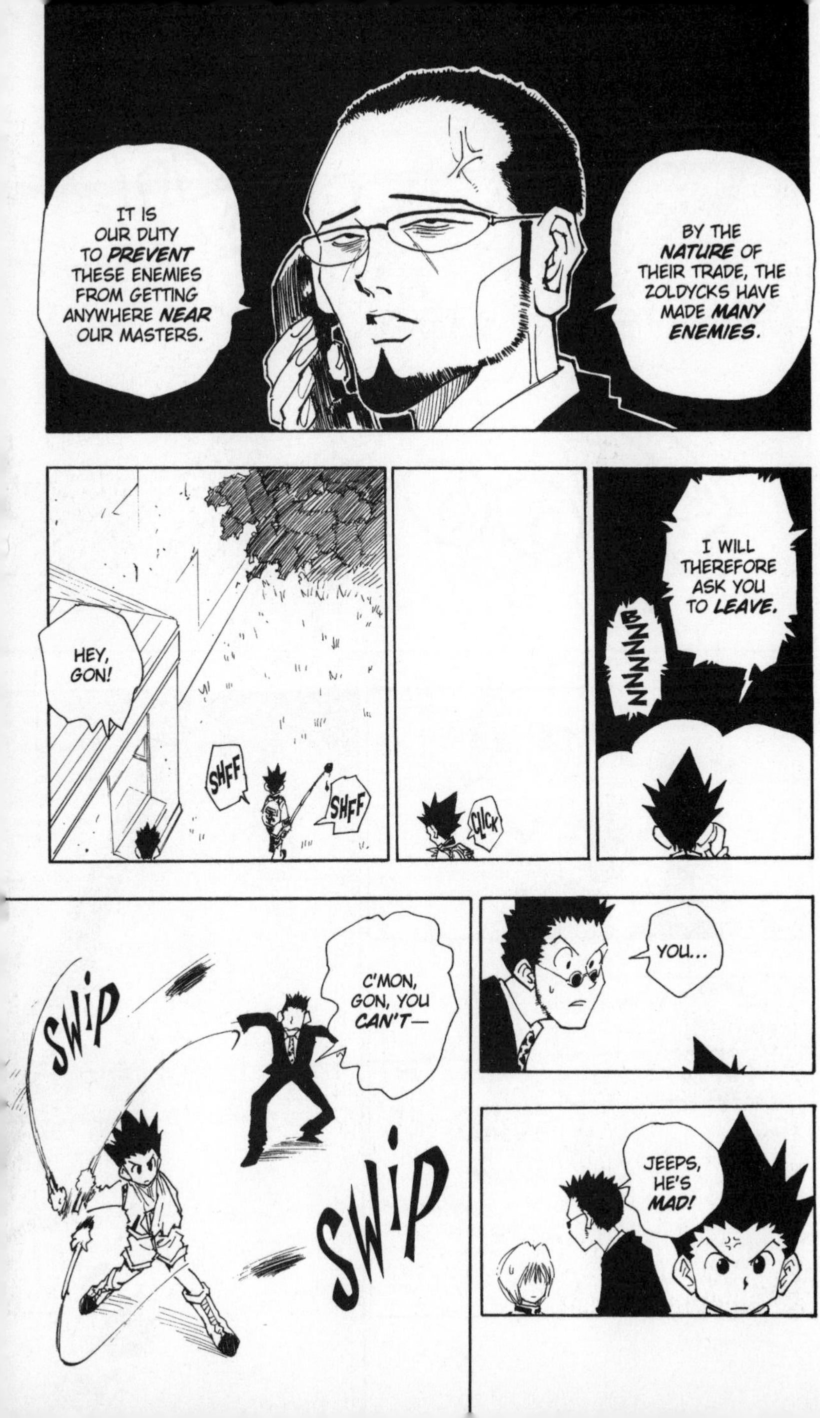
BY THE NATURE OF THEIR TRADE, THE ZOLDYCKS HAVE MADE MANY ENEMIES.
IT IS OUR DUTY TO PREVENT THESE ENEMIES FROM GETTING ANYWHERE NEAR OUR MASTERS.
I WILL THEREFORE ASK YOU TO LEAVE.
BZNNNNN
CLICK
HEY, GON!
SHFF
SHFF
YOU...
JEEPS, HE'S MAD!
C'MON, GON, YOU CAN'T—
SWIP
SWIP

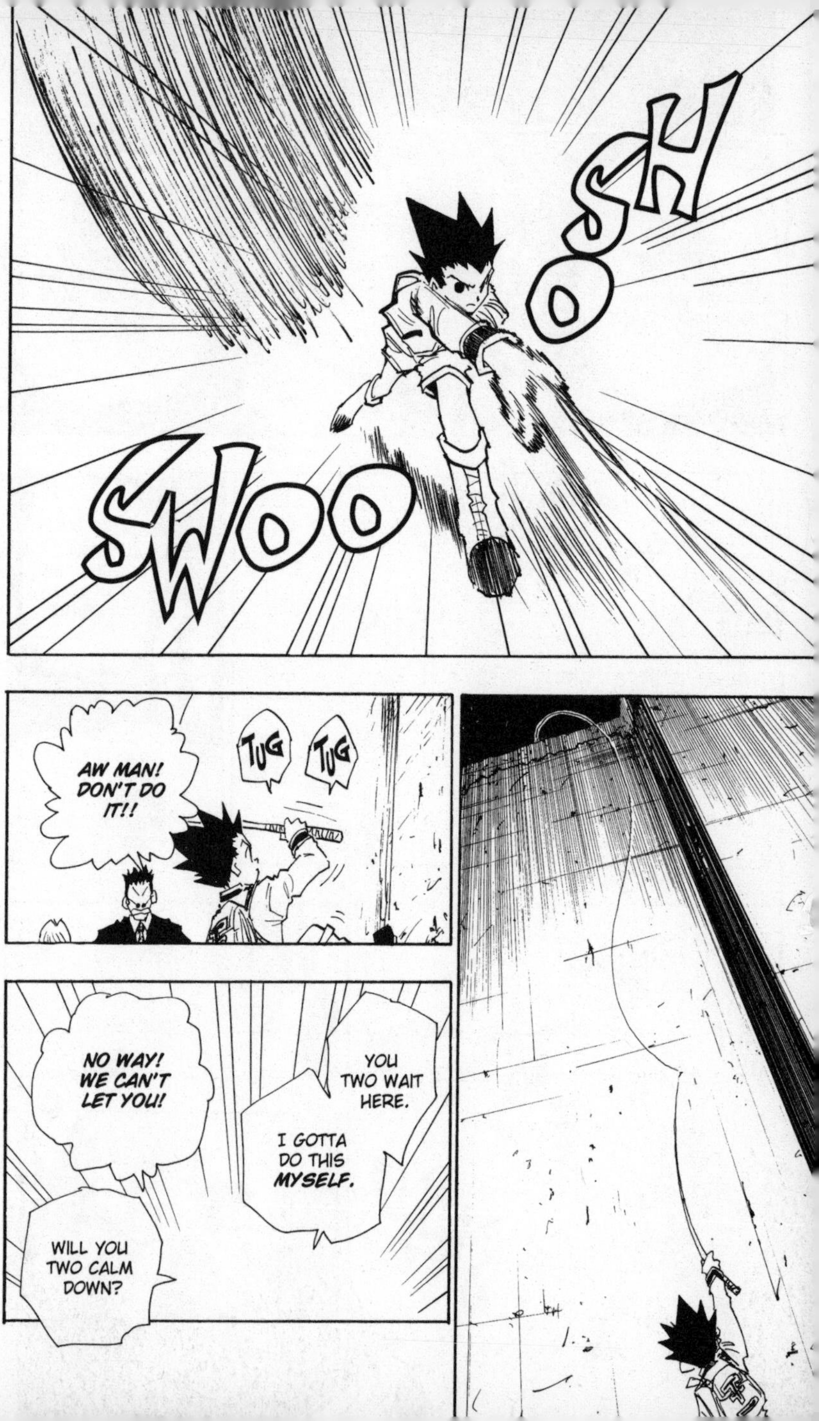
SWOOOSH
TUG
TUG
AW MAN! DON'T DO IT!!
YOU TWO WAIT HERE.
I GOTTA DO THIS MYSELF.
NO WAY! WE CAN'T LET YOU!
WILL YOU TWO CALM DOWN?

READ THIS WAY

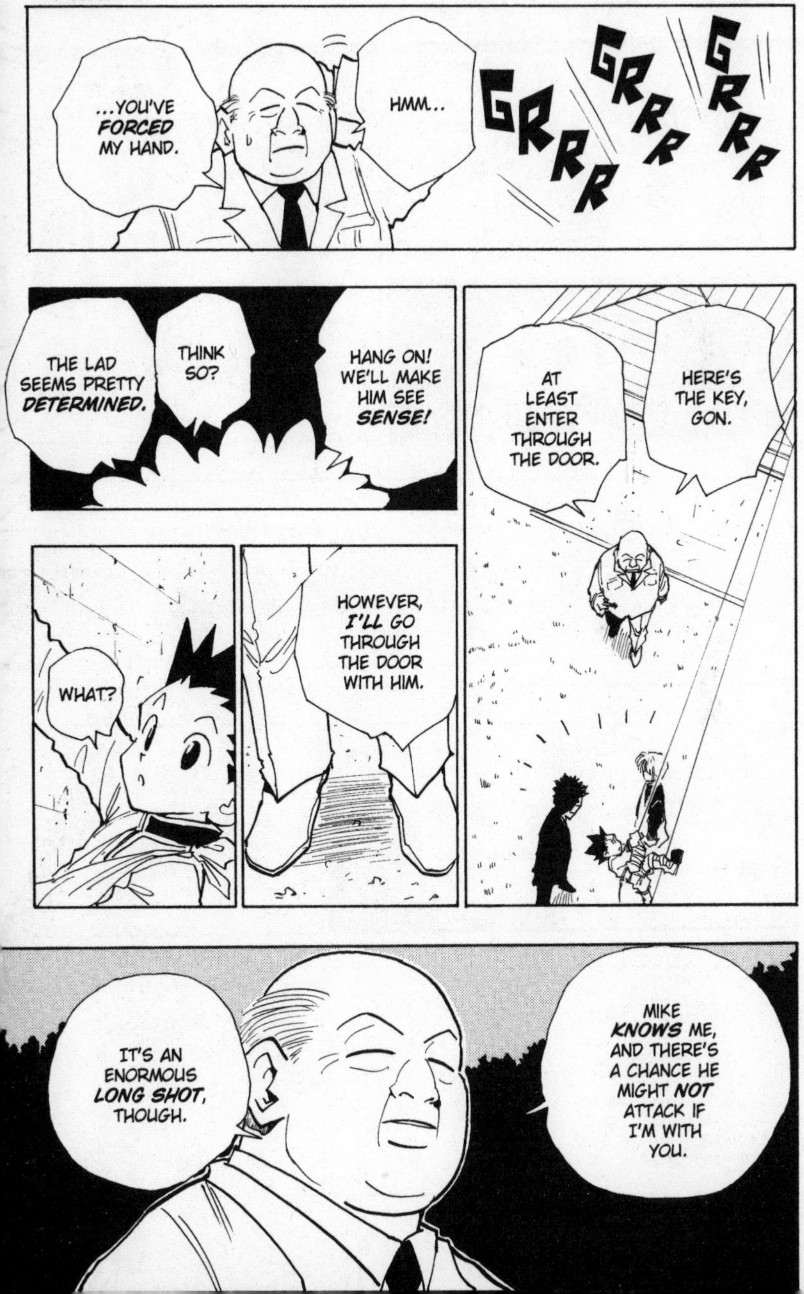
GRRR GRRR GRRR
HMM...
...YOU'VE FORCED MY HAND.
HERE'S THE KEY, GON.
AT LEAST ENTER THROUGH THE DOOR.
HANG ON! WE'LL MAKE HIM SEE SENSE!
THINK SO?
THE LAD SEEMS PRETTY DETERMINED.
HOWEVER, I'LL GO THROUGH THE DOOR WITH HIM.
WHAT?
MIKE KNOWS ME, AND THERE'S A CHANCE HE MIGHT NOT ATTACK IF I'M WITH YOU.
IT'S AN ENORMOUS LONG SHOT, THOUGH.

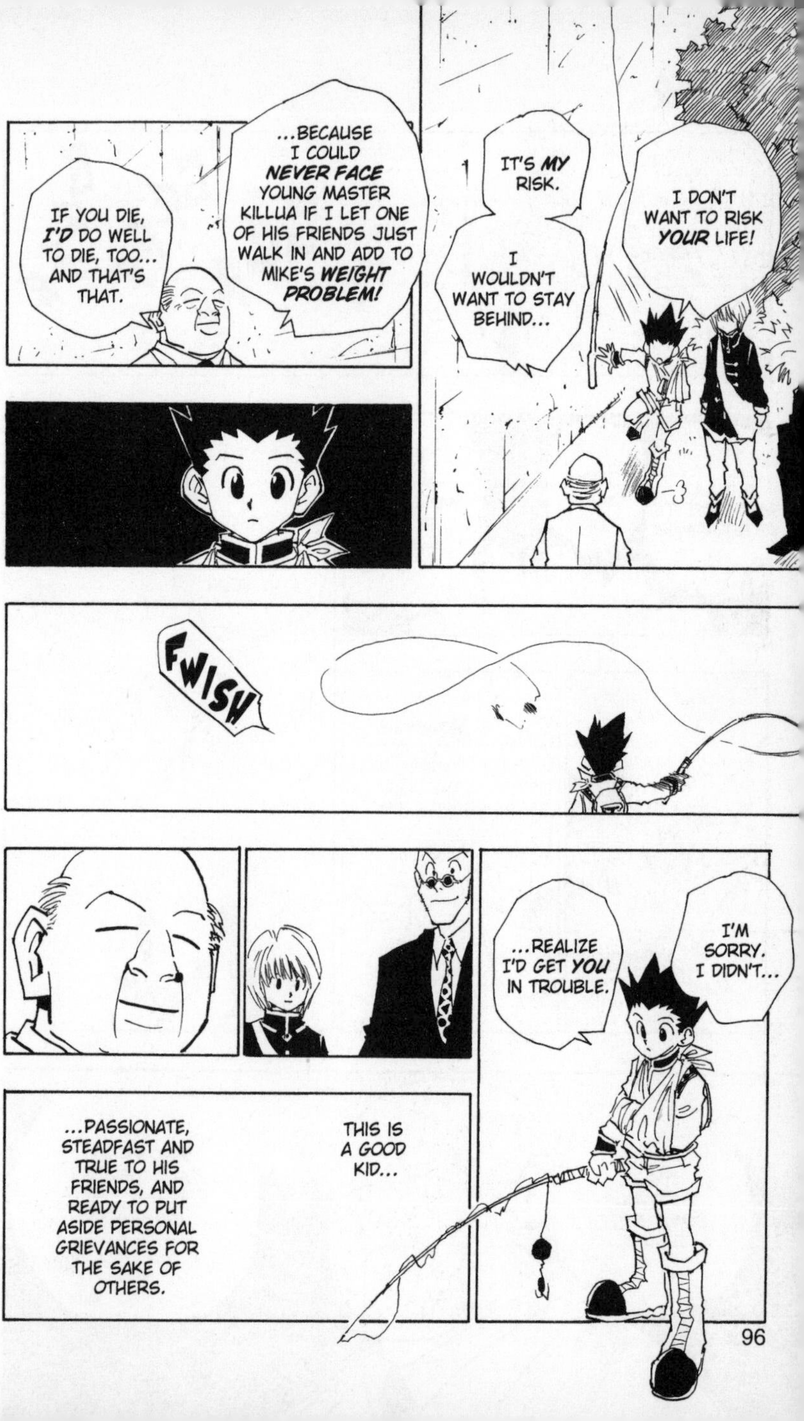
I DON'T WANT TO RISK YOUR LIFE!
IT'S MY RISK.
I WOULDN'T WANT TO STAY BEHIND...
...BECAUSE I COULD NEVER FACE YOUNG MASTER KILLUA IF I LET ONE OF HIS FRIENDS JUST WALK IN AND ADD TO MIKE'S WEIGHT PROBLEM!
IF YOU DIE, I'D DO WELL TO DIE, TOO... AND THAT'S THAT.
FWISH
I'M SORRY. I DIDN'T...
...REALIZE I'D GET YOU IN TROUBLE.
THIS IS A GOOD KID...
...PASSIONATE, STEADFAST AND TRUE TO HIS FRIENDS, AND READY TO PUT ASIDE PERSONAL GRIEVANCES FOR THE SAKE OF OTHERS.

READ THIS WAY

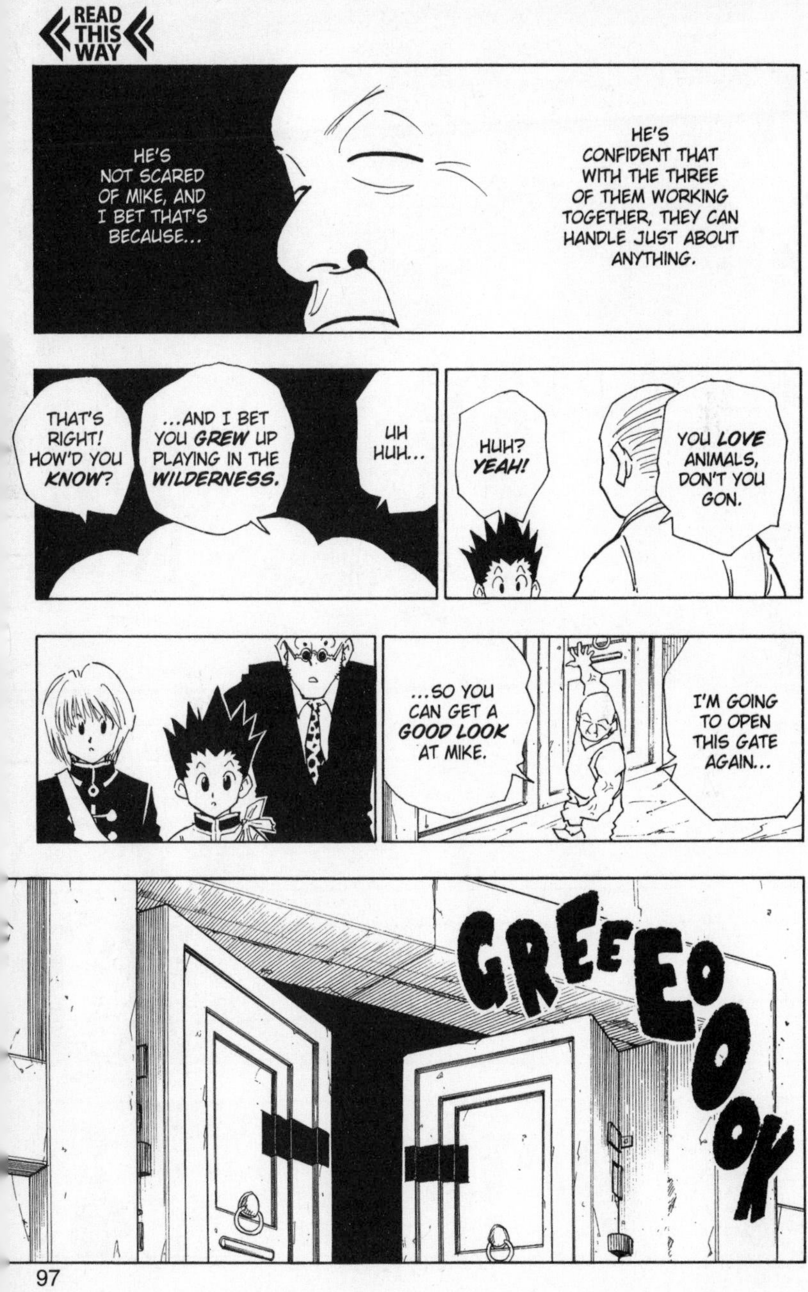

HE'S CONFIDENT THAT WITH THE THREE OF THEM WORKING TOGETHER, THEY CAN HANDLE JUST ABOUT ANYTHING.
HE'S NOT SCARED OF MIKE, AND I BET THAT'S BECAUSE...
YOU LOVE ANIMALS, DON'T YOU GON.
HUH? YEAH!
UH HUH...
...AND I BET YOU GREW UP PLAYING IN THE WILDERNESS.
THAT'S RIGHT! HOW'D YOU KNOW?
I'M GOING TO OPEN THIS GATE AGAIN...
...SO YOU CAN GET A GOOD LOOK AT MIKE.
GREEEOOOOK

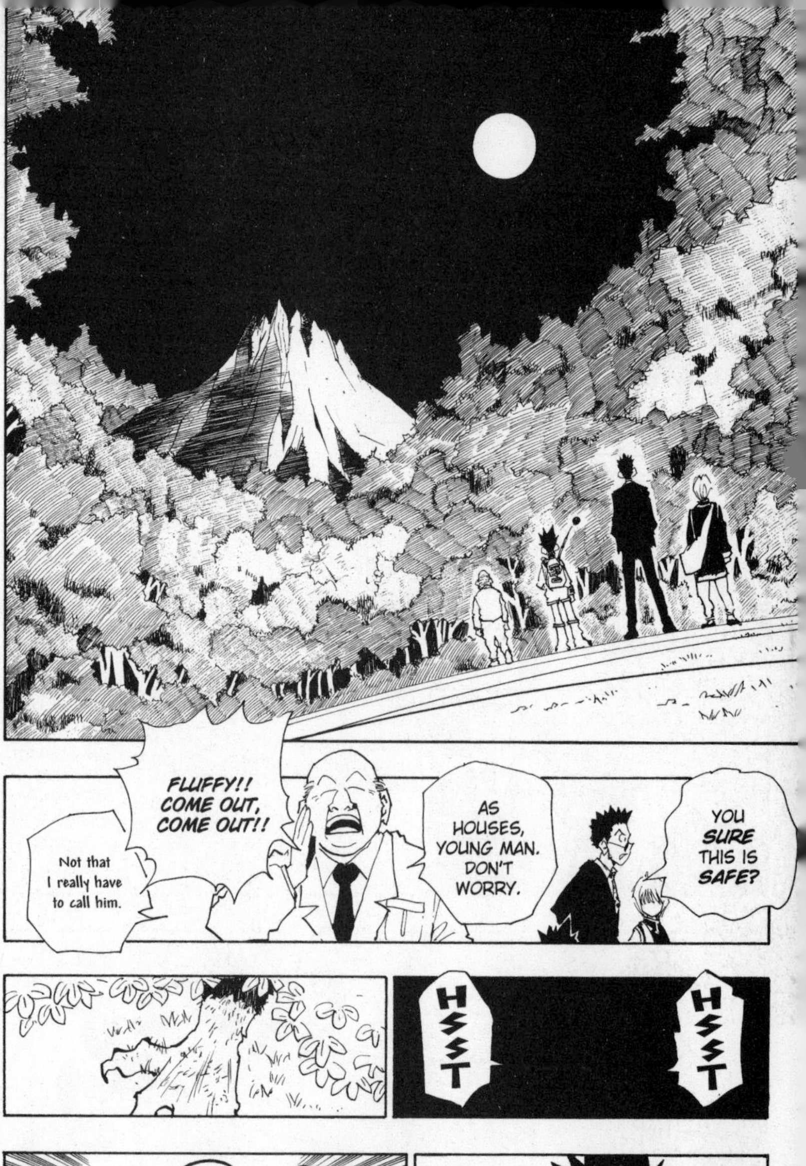
YOU SURE THIS IS SAFE?
AS HOUSES, YOUNG MAN. DON'T WORRY.
FLUFFY!! COME OUT, COME OUT!!
Not that I really have to call him.
HSST
HSST
HAAAH
!!

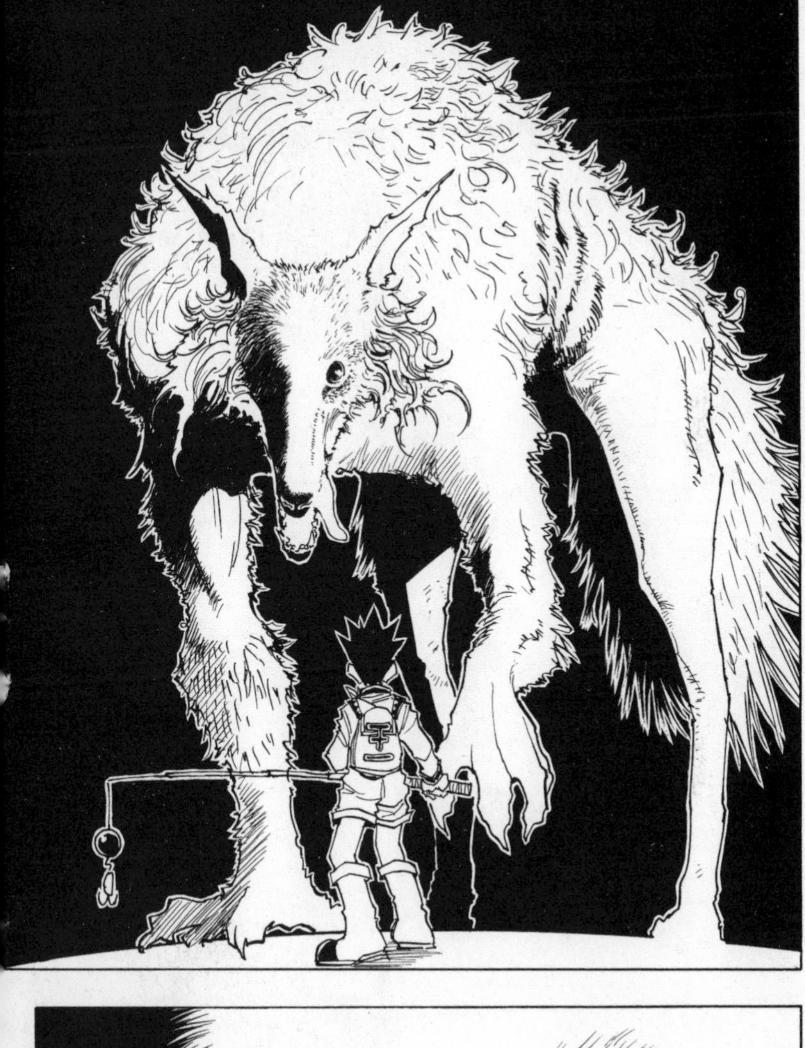
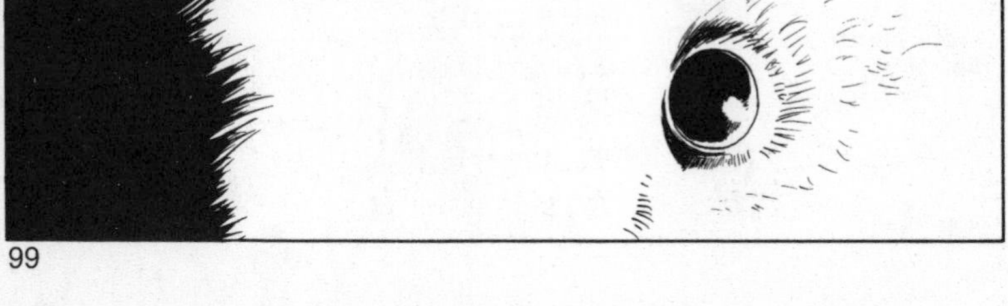

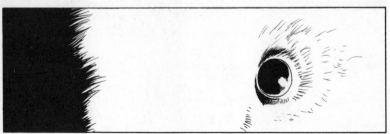

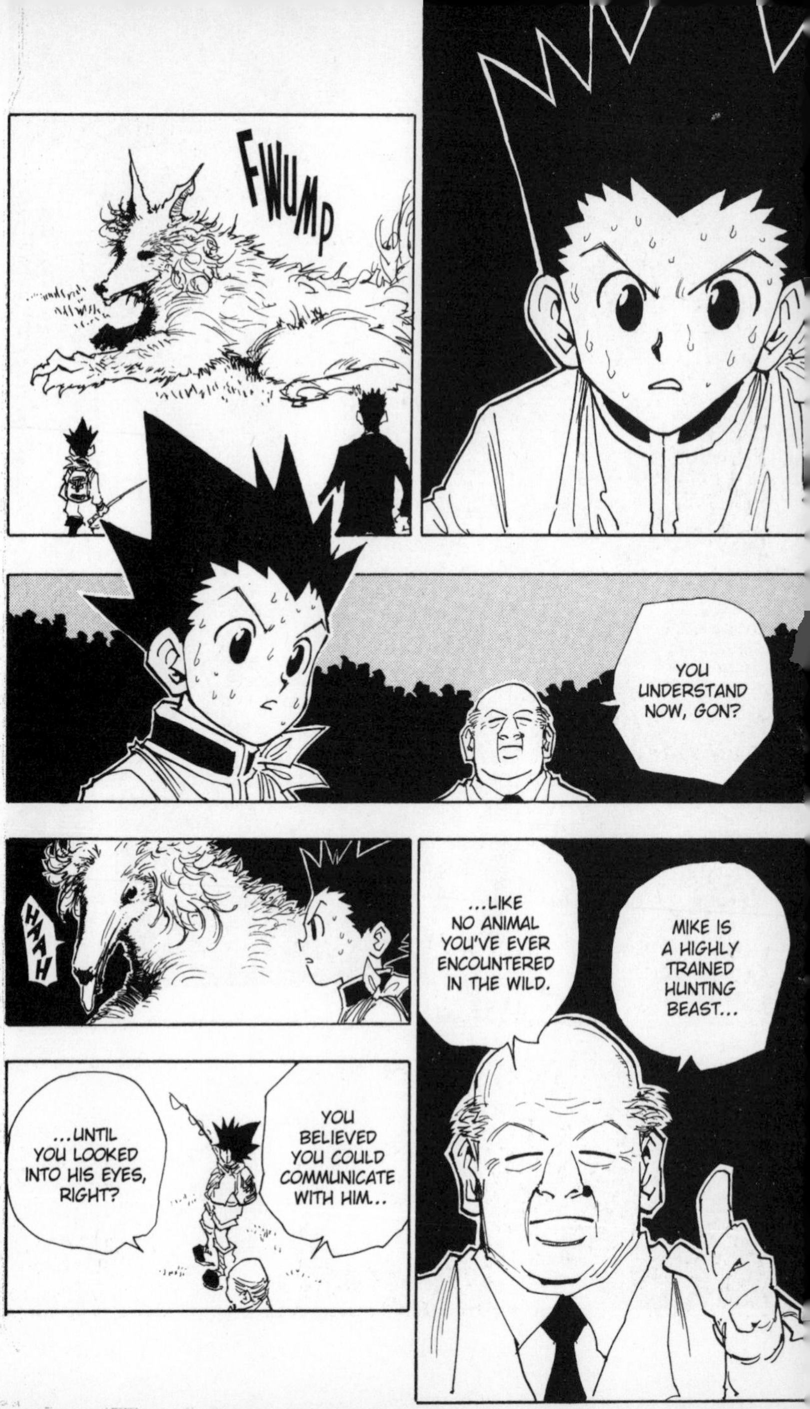
FWUMP
YOU UNDERSTAND NOW, GON?
MIKE IS A HIGHLY TRAINED HUNTING BEAST...
...LIKE NO ANIMAL YOU'VE EVER ENCOUNTERED IN THE WILD.
HAAH
YOU BELIEVED YOU COULD COMMUNICATE WITH HIM...
...UNTIL YOU LOOKED INTO HIS EYES, RIGHT?

READ THIS WAY

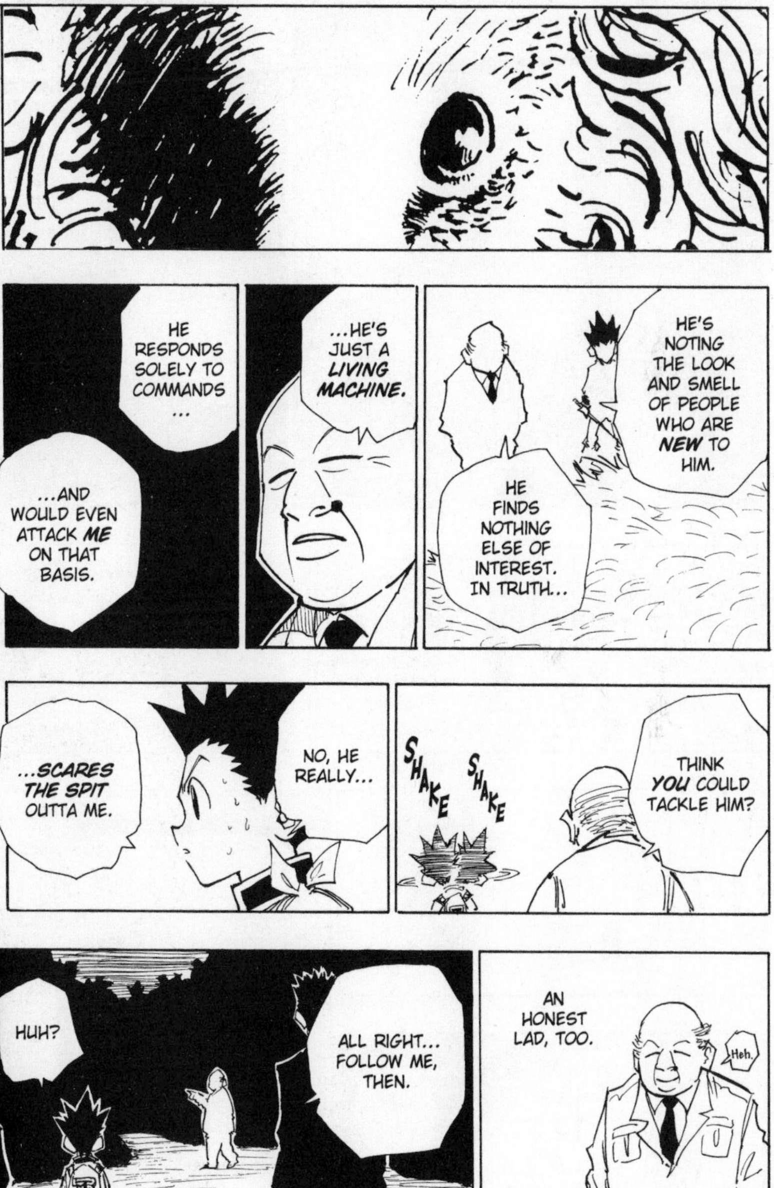
HE'S NOTING THE LOOK AND SMELL OF PEOPLE WHO ARE NEW TO HIM.
HE FINDS NOTHING ELSE OF INTEREST. IN TRUTH...
...HE'S JUST A LIVING MACHINE.
HE RESPONDS SOLELY TO COMMANDS ...
...AND WOULD EVEN ATTACK ME ON THAT BASIS.
THINK YOU COULD TACKLE HIM?
SHAKE
SHAKE
NO, HE REALLY...
...SCARES THE SPIT OUTTA ME.
AN HONEST LAD, TOO.
Heh.
ALL RIGHT... FOLLOW ME, THEN.
HUH?

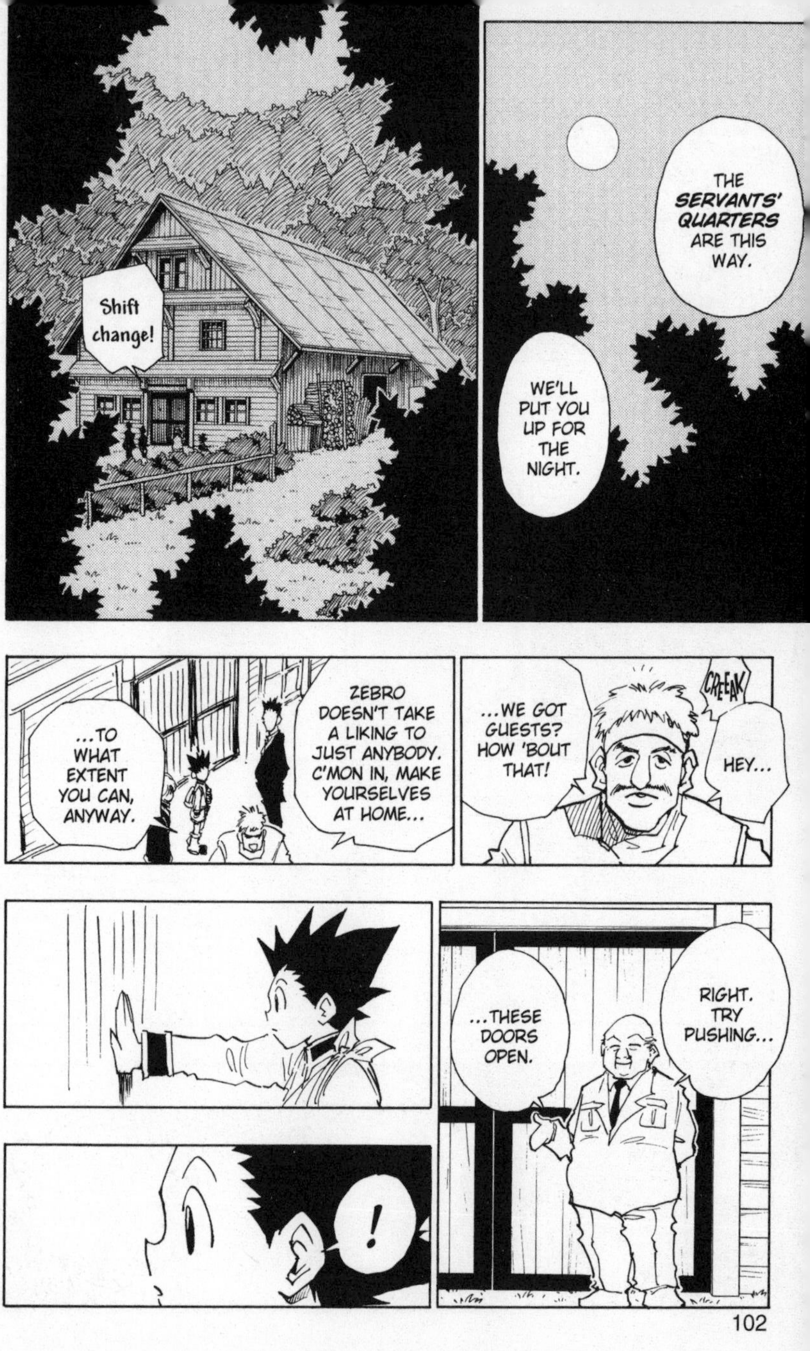
THE SERVANTS' QUARTERS ARE THIS WAY.
WE'LL PUT YOU UP FOR THE NIGHT.
Shift change!
CREEAK
HEY...
...WE GOT GUESTS? HOW 'BOUT THAT!
ZEBRO DOESN'T TAKE A LIKING TO JUST ANYBODY. C'MON IN, MAKE YOURSELVES AT HOME...
...TO WHAT EXTENT YOU CAN, ANYWAY.
RIGHT. TRY PUSHING...
...THESE DOORS OPEN.
!

READ THIS WAY

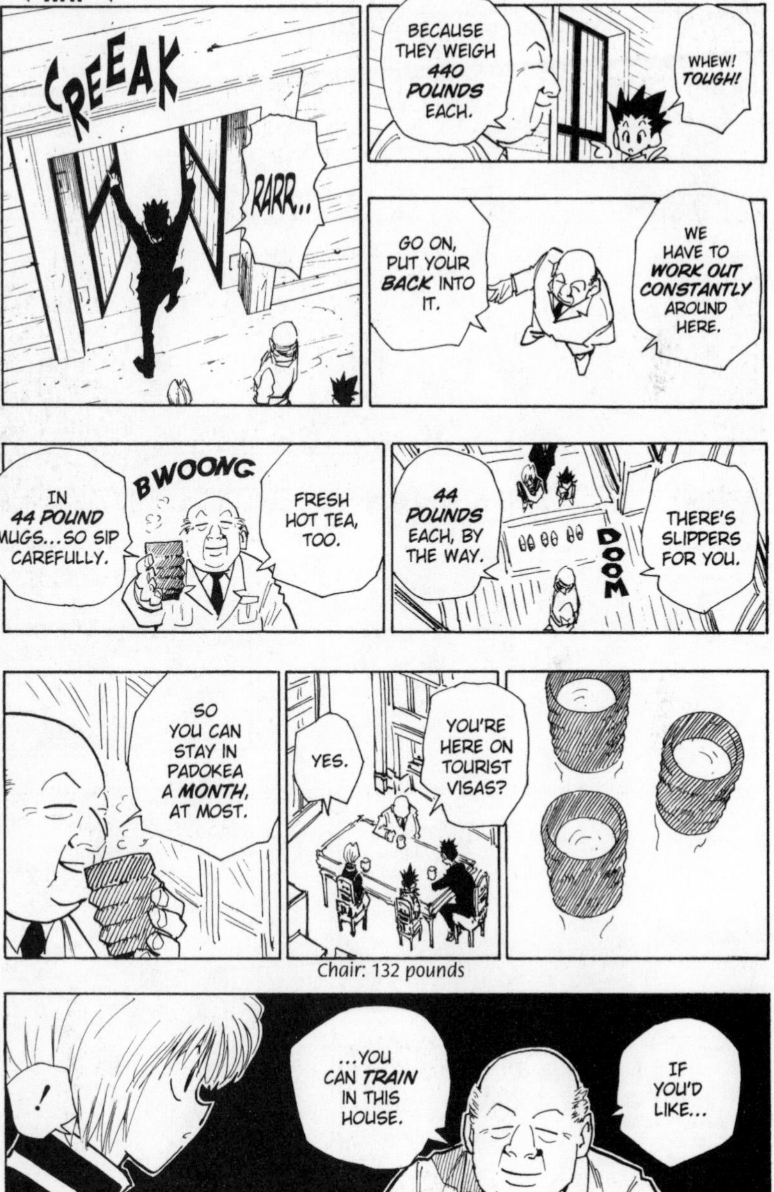
WHEW! TOUGH!
BECAUSE THEY WEIGH 440 POUNDS EACH.
WE HAVE TO WORK OUT CONSTANTLY AROUND HERE.
GO ON, PUT YOUR BACK INTO IT.
CREEAK
RARR..
THERE'S SLIPPERS FOR YOU.
DOOM
44 POUNDS EACH, BY THE WAY.
FRESH HOT TEA, TOO.
BWOONG
IN 44 POUND MUGS...SO SIP CAREFULLY.
YOU'RE HERE ON TOURIST VISAS?
YES.
SO YOU CAN STAY IN PADOKEA A MONTH, AT MOST.
Chair: 132 pounds
IF YOU'D LIKE...
...YOU CAN TRAIN IN THIS HOUSE.
!

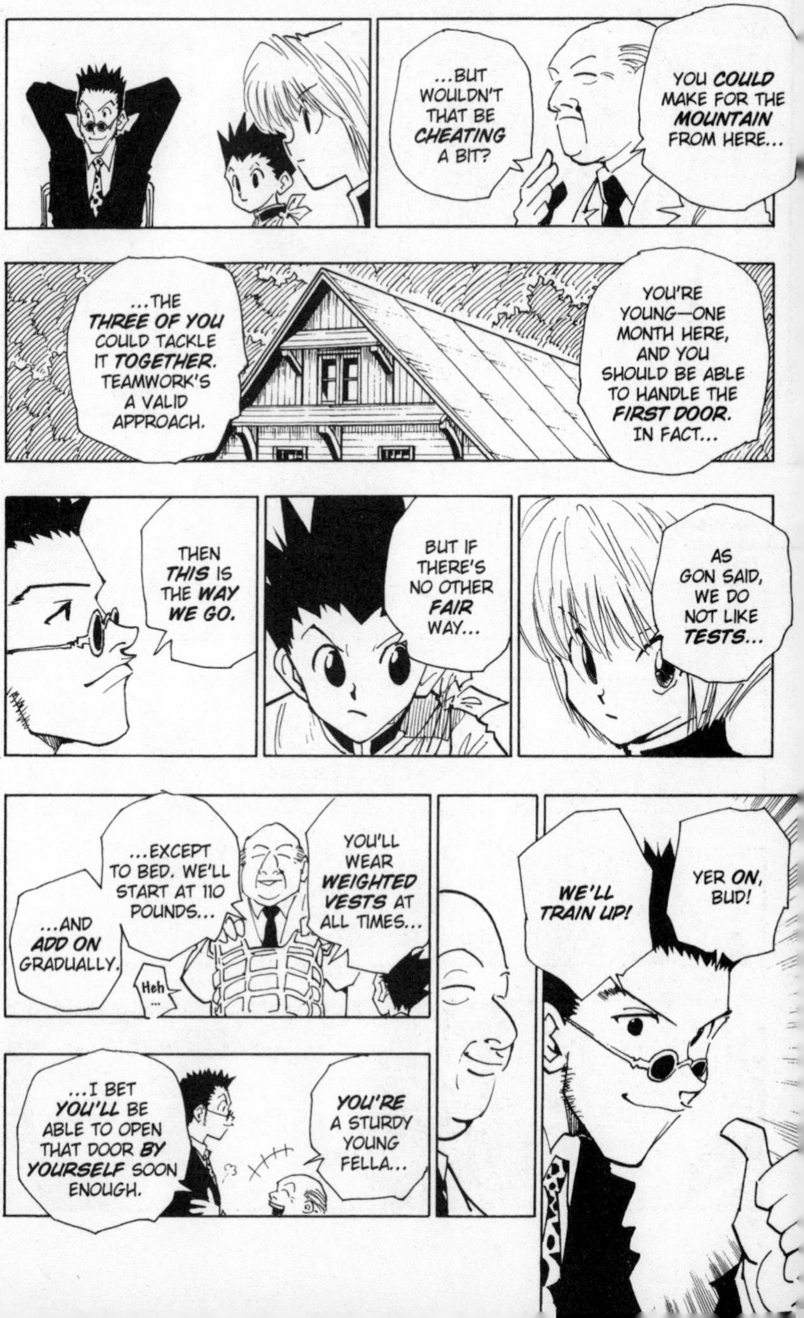
YOU COULD MAKE FOR THE MOUNTAIN FROM HERE...
...BUT WOULDN'T THAT BE CHEATING A BIT?
YOU'RE YOUNG—ONE MONTH HERE, AND YOU SHOULD BE ABLE TO HANDLE THE FIRST DOOR. IN FACT...
...THE THREE OF YOU COULD TACKLE IT TOGETHER. TEAMWORK'S A VALID APPROACH.
AS GON SAID, WE DO NOT LIKE TESTS...
BUT IF THERE'S NO OTHER FAIR WAY...
THEN THIS IS THE WAY WE GO.
YER ON, BUD!
WE'LL TRAIN UP!
YOU'LL WEAR WEIGHTED VESTS AT ALL TIMES...
...EXCEPT TO BED. WE'LL START AT 110 POUNDS...
...AND ADD ON GRADUALLY.
Heh...
YOU'RE A STURDY YOUNG FELLA...
...I BET YOU'LL BE ABLE TO OPEN THAT DOOR BY YOURSELF SOON ENOUGH.

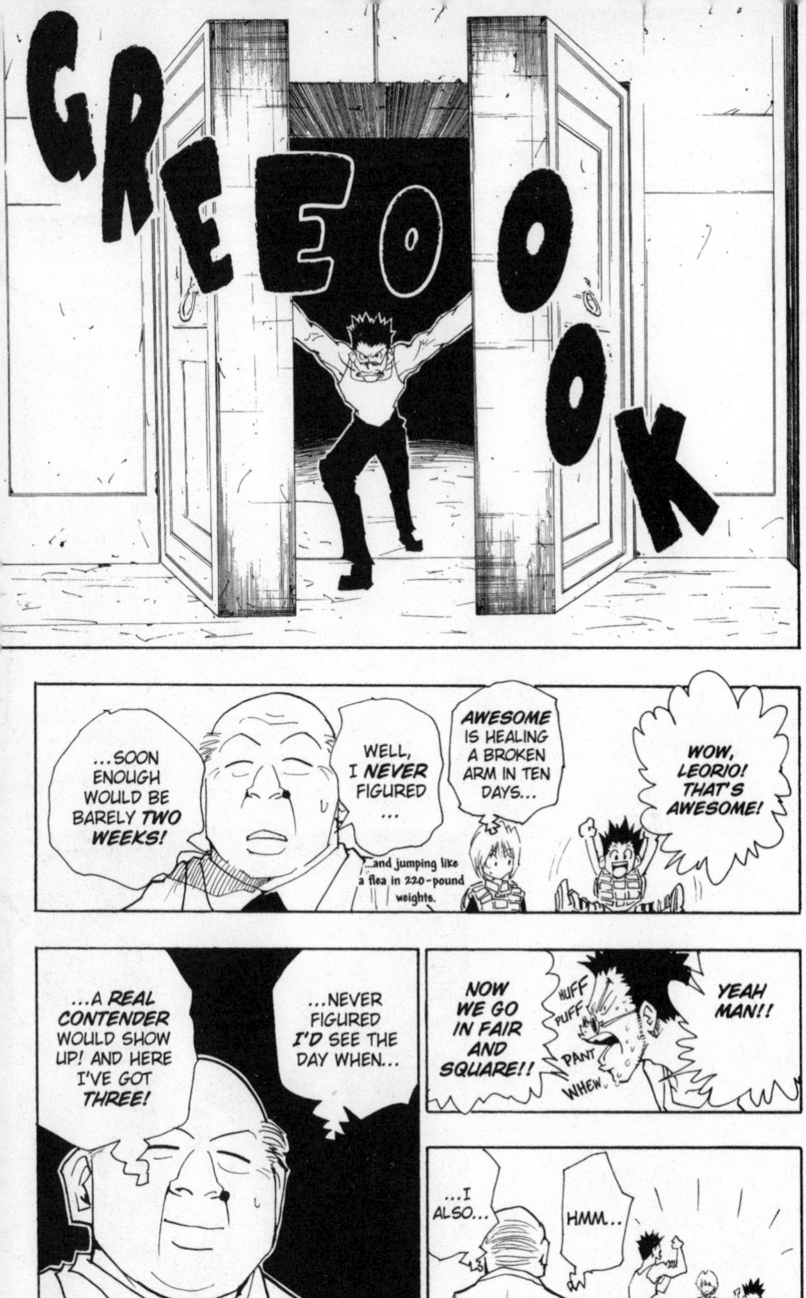
GREEOOOK
WOW, LEORIO! THAT'S AWESOME!
AWESOME IS HEALING A BROKEN ARM IN TEN DAYS...
...and jumping like a flea in 220-pound weights.
WELL, I NEVER FIGURED ...
...SOON ENOUGH WOULD BE BARELY TWO WEEKS!
YEAH MAN!!
HUFF
PUFF
PANT
WHEW
NOW WE GO IN FAIR AND SQUARE!!
HMM...
...I ALSO...
...NEVER FIGURED I'D SEE THE DAY WHEN...
...A REAL CONTENDER WOULD SHOW UP! AND HERE I'VE GOT THREE!

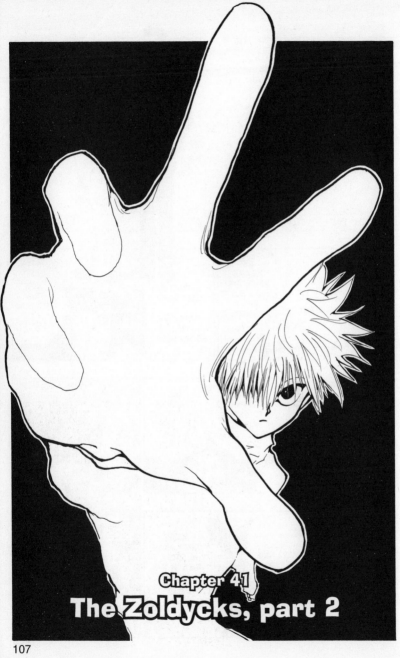

Chapter 41
The Zoldycks, part 2

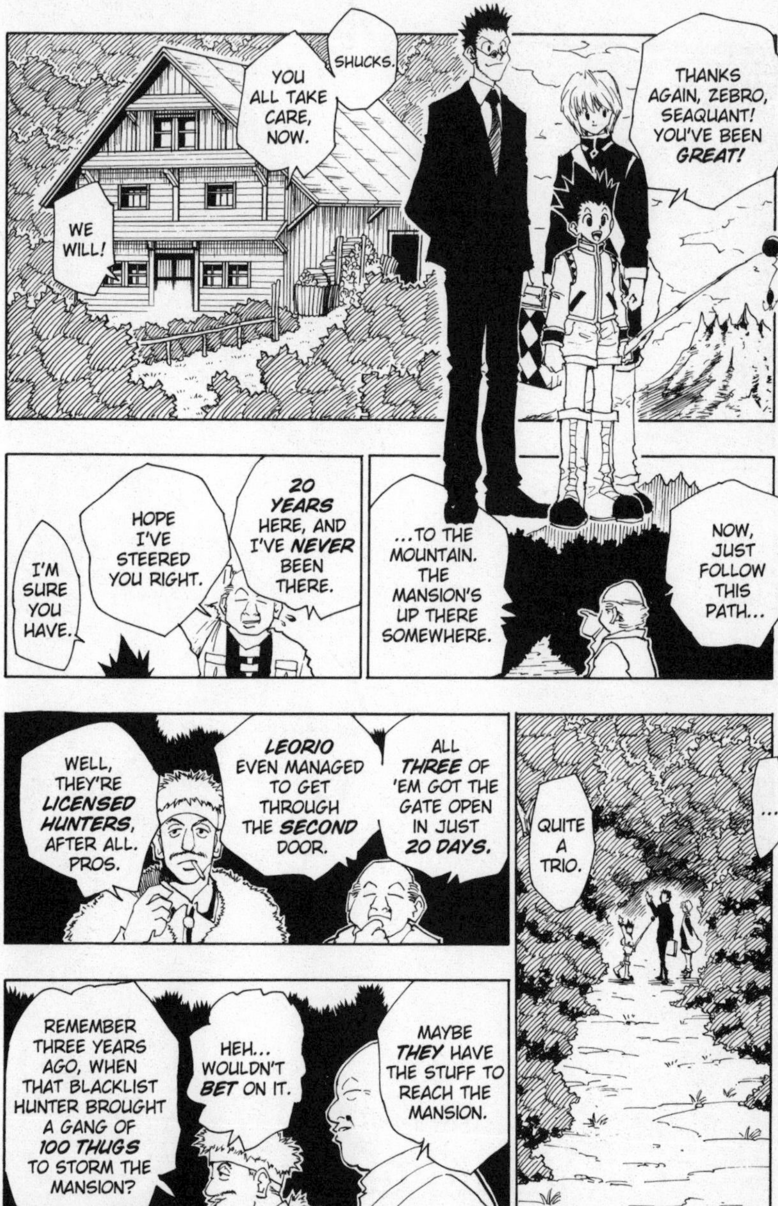
THANKS AGAIN, ZEBRO, SEAQUANT! YOU'VE BEEN **GREAT!**
SHUCKS.
YOU ALL TAKE CARE, NOW.
WE WILL!
NOW, JUST FOLLOW THIS PATH...
...TO THE MOUNTAIN. THE MANSION'S UP THERE SOMEWHERE.
20 YEARS HERE, AND I'VE **NEVER** BEEN THERE.
HOPE I'VE STEERED YOU RIGHT.
I'M SURE YOU HAVE.
...
QUITE A TRIO.
ALL **THREE** OF 'EM GOT THE GATE OPEN IN JUST **20 DAYS.**
LEORIO EVEN MANAGED TO GET THROUGH THE **SECOND** DOOR.
WELL, THEY'RE **LICENSED HUNTERS**, AFTER ALL. PROS.
MAYBE **THEY** HAVE THE STUFF TO REACH THE MANSION.
HEH... WOULDN'T **BET** ON IT.
REMEMBER THREE YEARS AGO, WHEN THAT BLACKLIST HUNTER BROUGHT A GANG OF **100 THUGS** TO STORM THE MANSION?

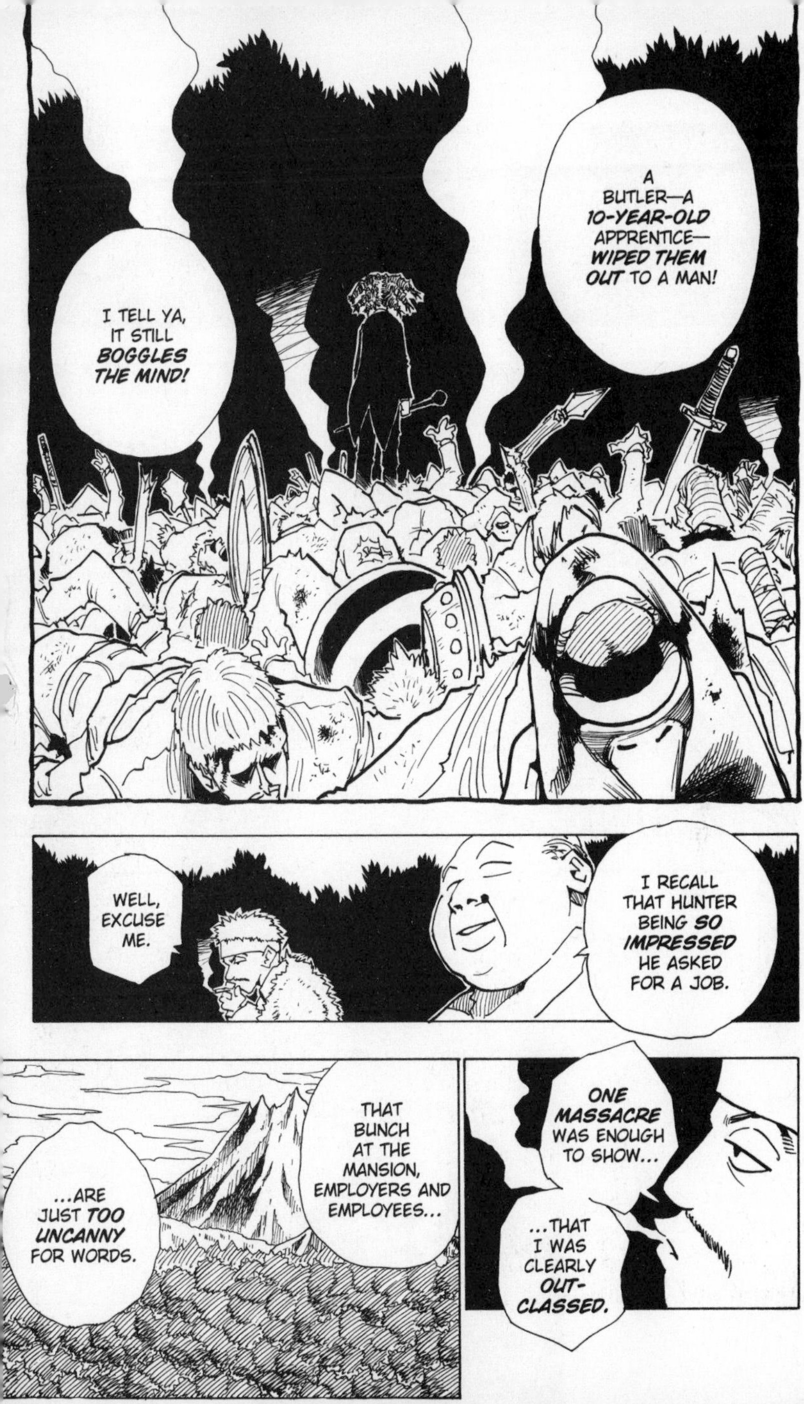
A BUTLER—A *10-YEAR-OLD* APPRENTICE—*WIPED THEM OUT* TO A MAN!
I TELL YA, IT STILL *BOGGLES THE MIND!*
I RECALL THAT HUNTER BEING *SO IMPRESSED* HE ASKED FOR A JOB.
WELL, EXCUSE ME.
ONE MASSACRE WAS ENOUGH TO SHOW...
...THAT I WAS CLEARLY *OUT-CLASSED.*
THAT BUNCH AT THE MANSION, EMPLOYERS AND EMPLOYEES...
...ARE JUST *TOO UNCANNY* FOR WORDS.

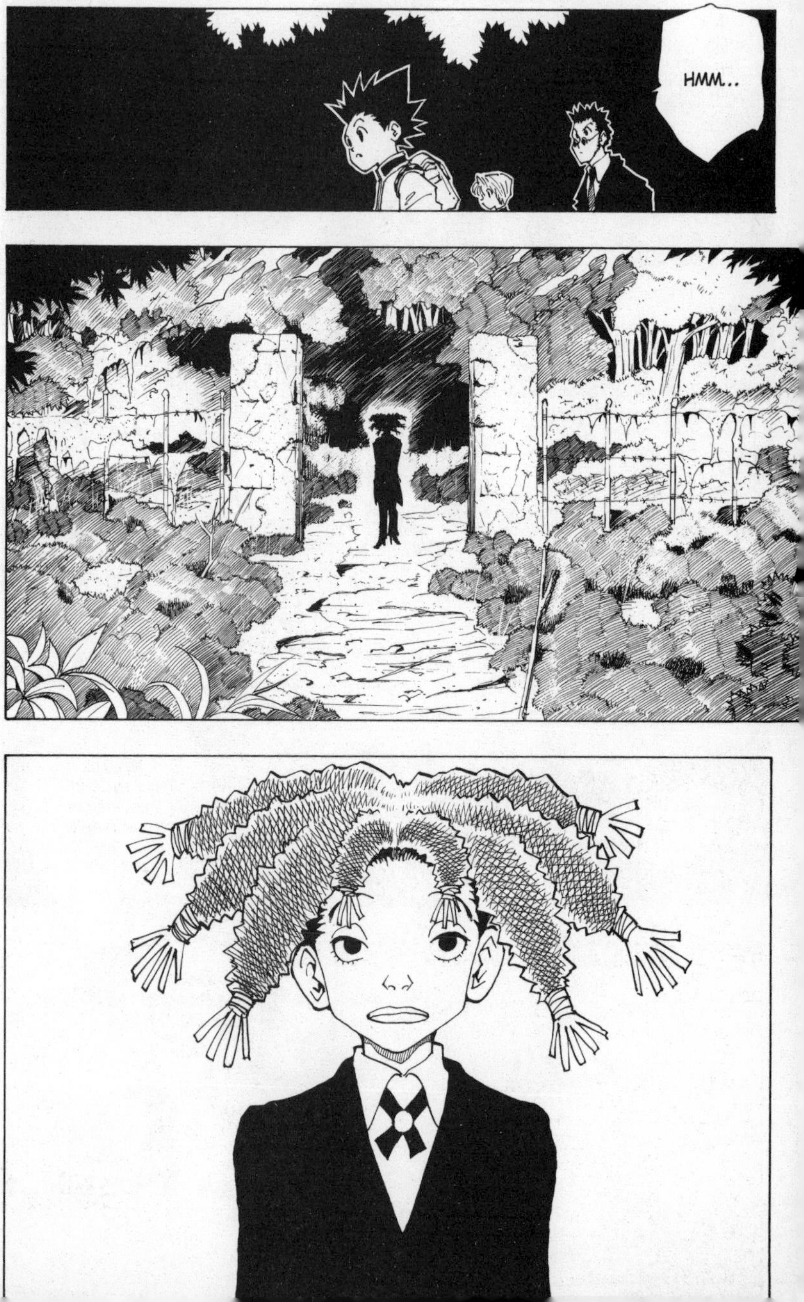
HMM..

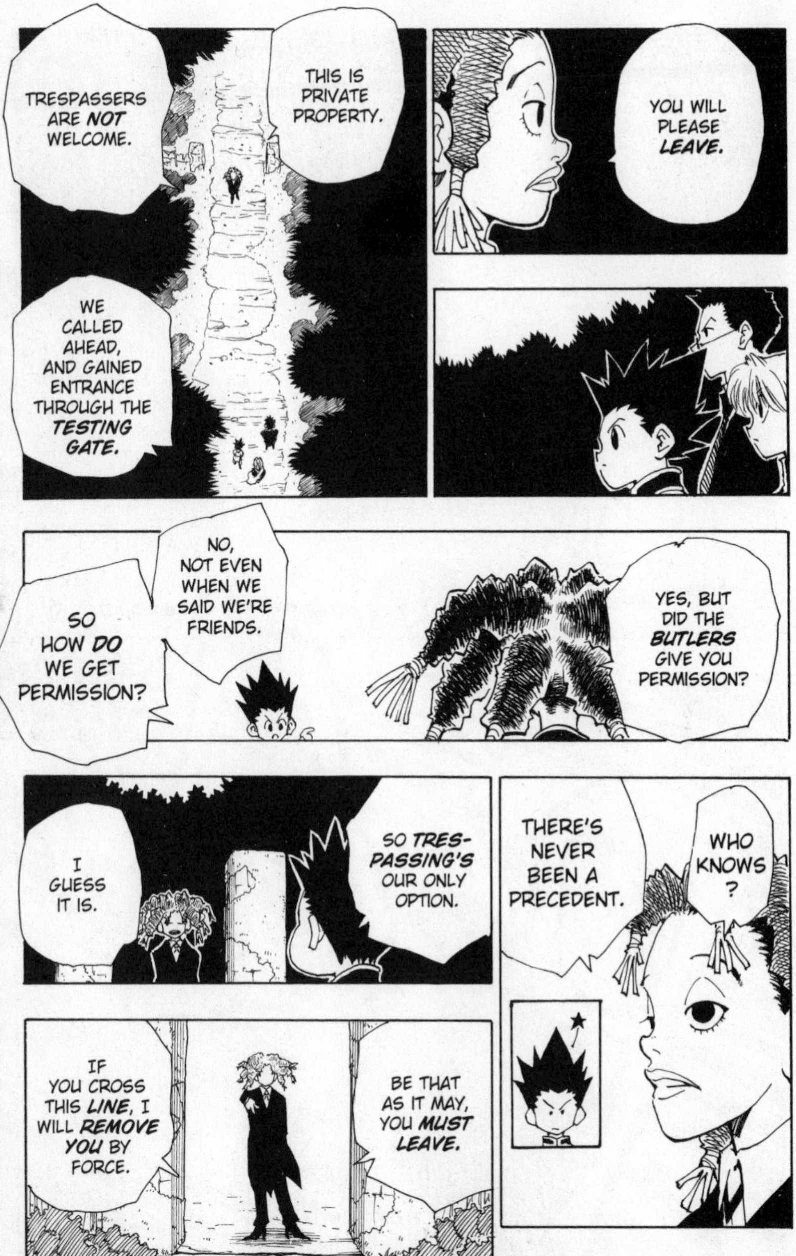
YOU WILL PLEASE LEAVE.
THIS IS PRIVATE PROPERTY.
TRESPASSERS ARE NOT WELCOME.
WE CALLED AHEAD, AND GAINED ENTRANCE THROUGH THE TESTING GATE.
YES, BUT DID THE BUTLERS GIVE YOU PERMISSION?
NO, NOT EVEN WHEN WE SAID WE'RE FRIENDS.
SO HOW DO WE GET PERMISSION?
WHO KNOWS?
THERE'S NEVER BEEN A PRECEDENT.
SO TRES-PASSING'S OUR ONLY OPTION.
I GUESS IT IS.
BE THAT AS IT MAY, YOU MUST LEAVE.
IF YOU CROSS THIS LINE, I WILL REMOVE YOU BY FORCE.

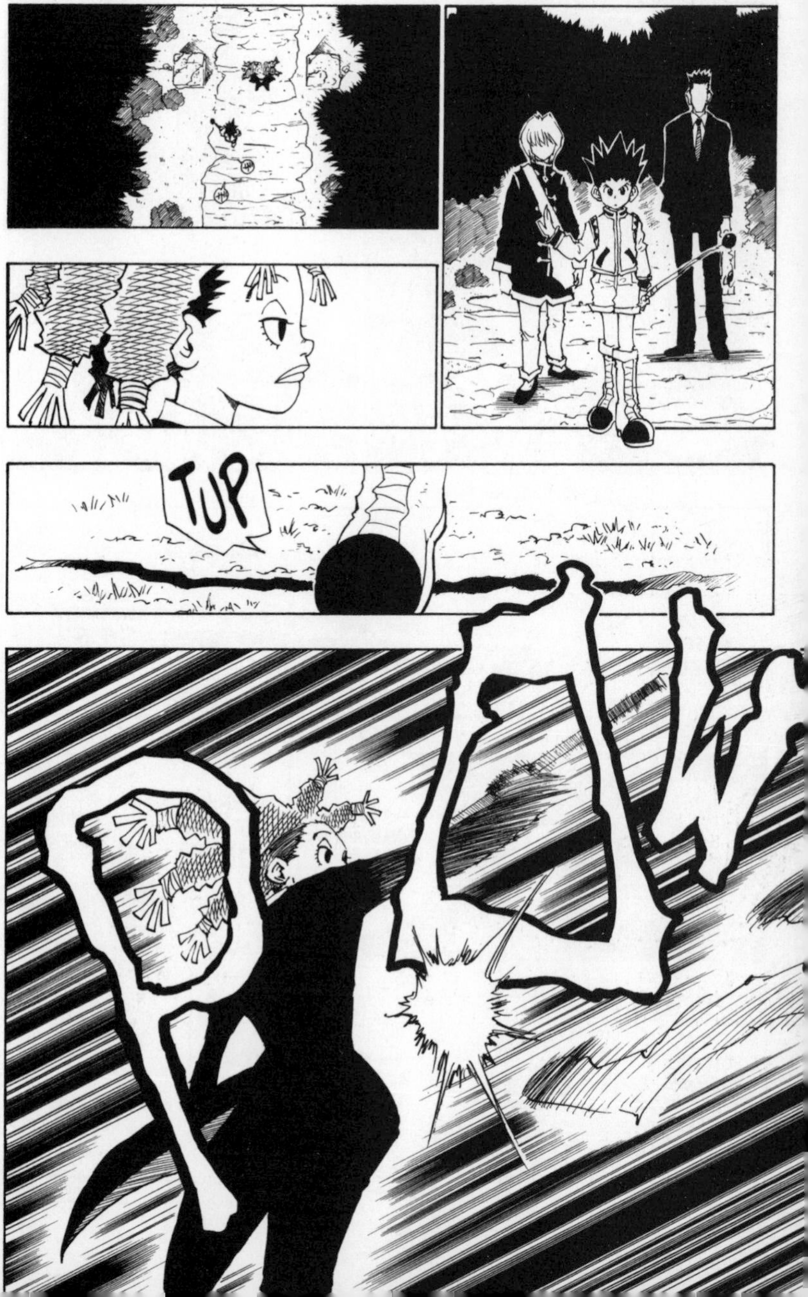
TUP

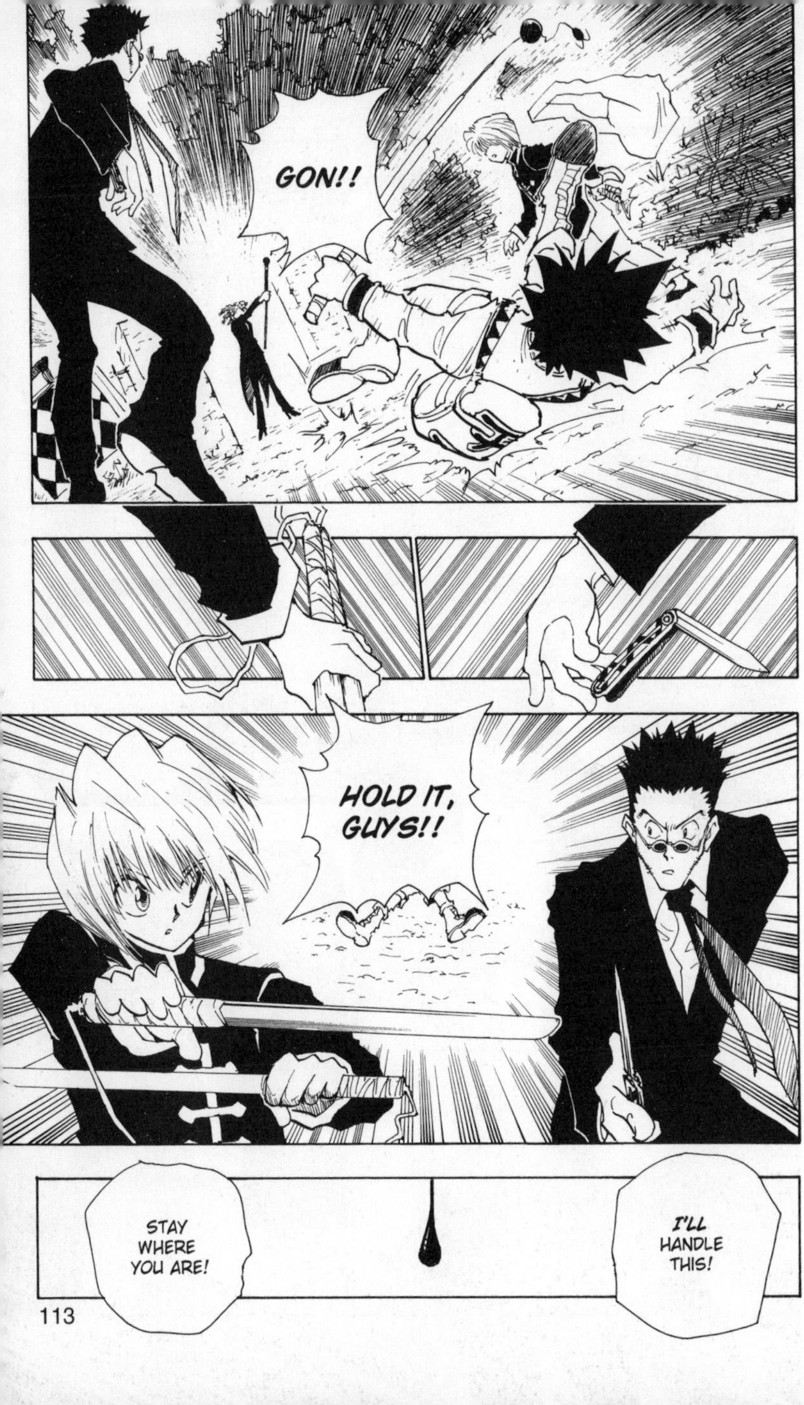
GON!!
HOLD IT, GUYS!!
I'LL HANDLE THIS!
STAY WHERE YOU ARE!

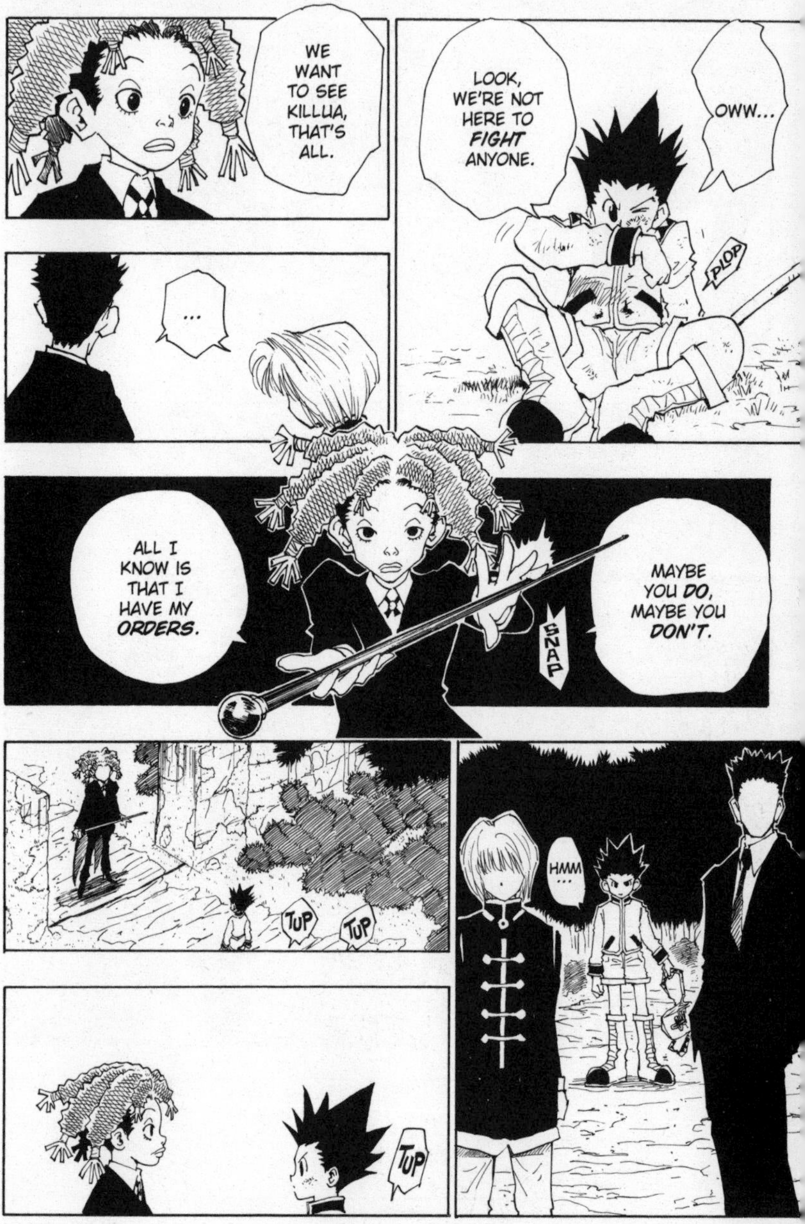
OWW...
LOOK, WE'RE NOT HERE TO FIGHT ANYONE.
PLOP
WE WANT TO SEE KILLUA, THAT'S ALL.
...
MAYBE YOU DO, MAYBE YOU DON'T.
SNAP
ALL I KNOW IS THAT I HAVE MY ORDERS.
HMM...
TUP
TUP
TUP

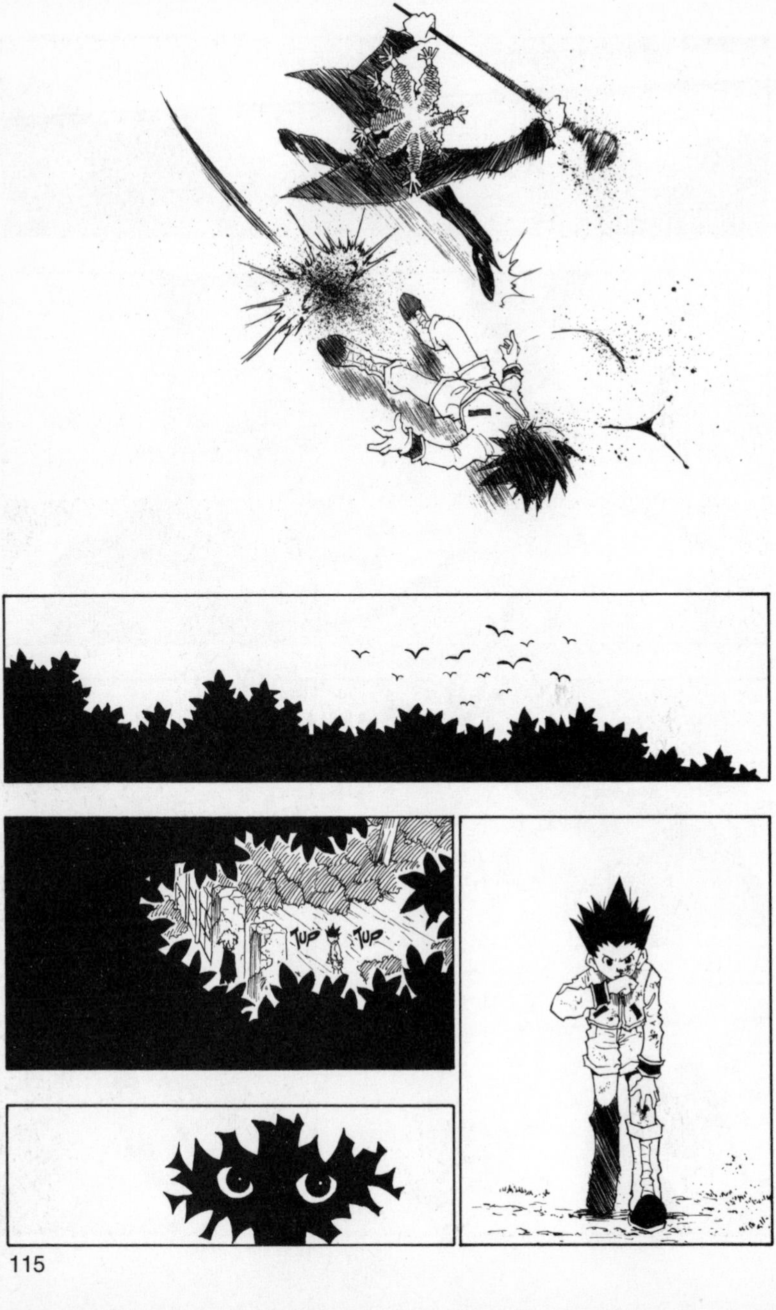
TUP
TUP

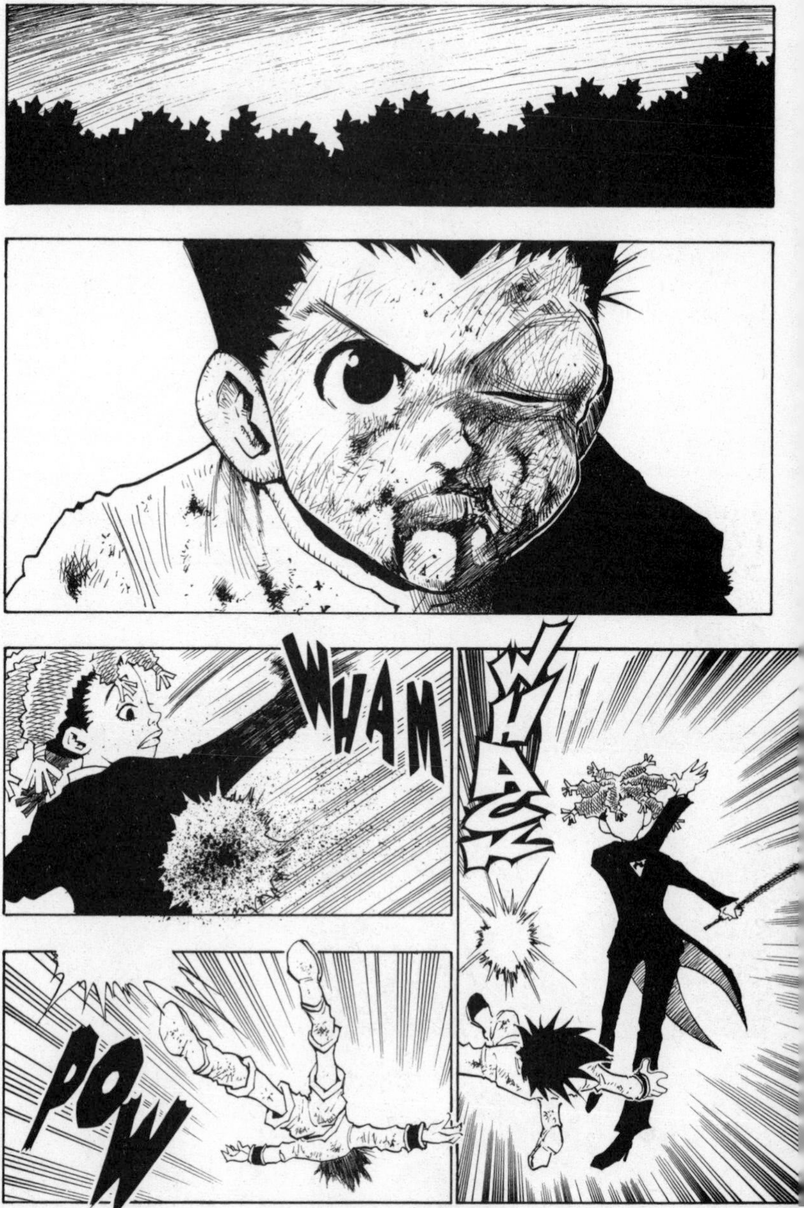
WHACK
WHAM
POW

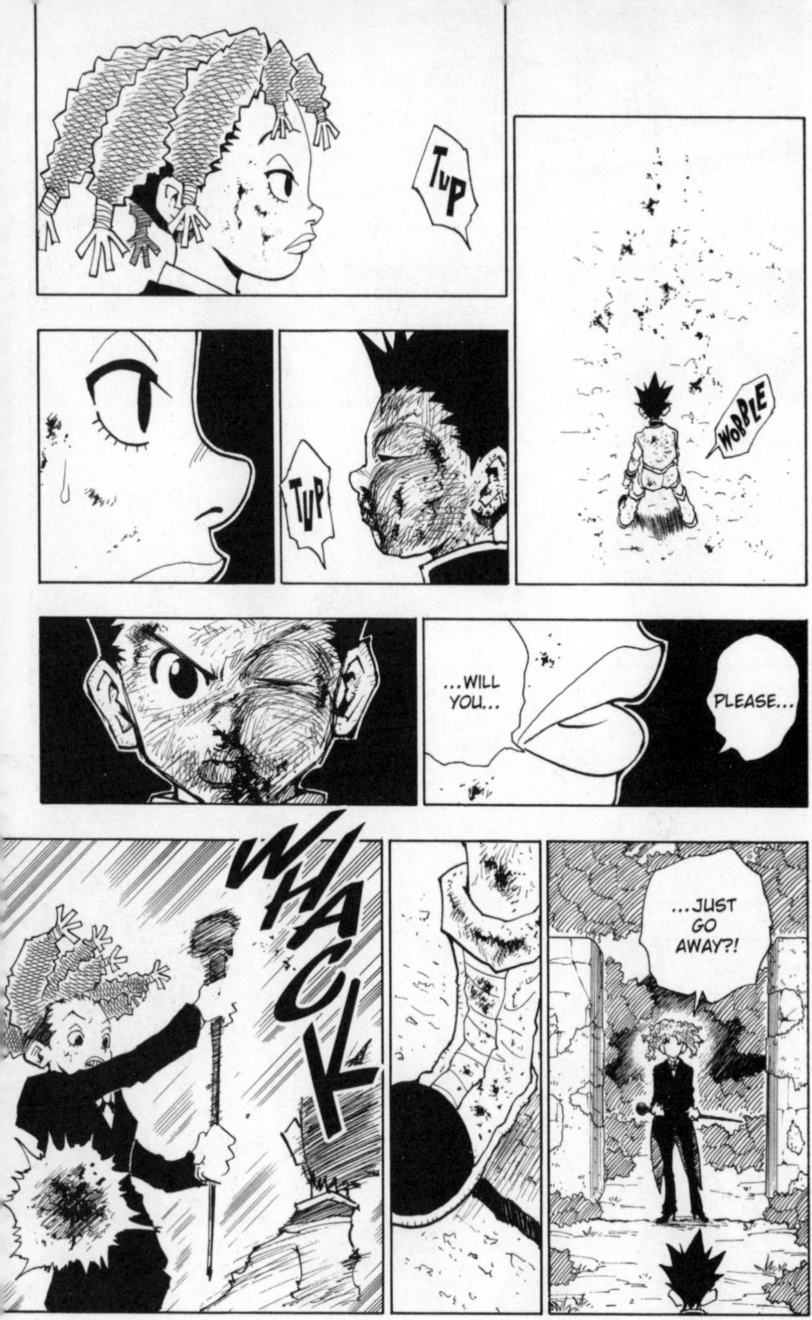
WOBBLE
TUP
TUP
PLEASE...
...WILL YOU...
...JUST GO AWAY?!
WHACK

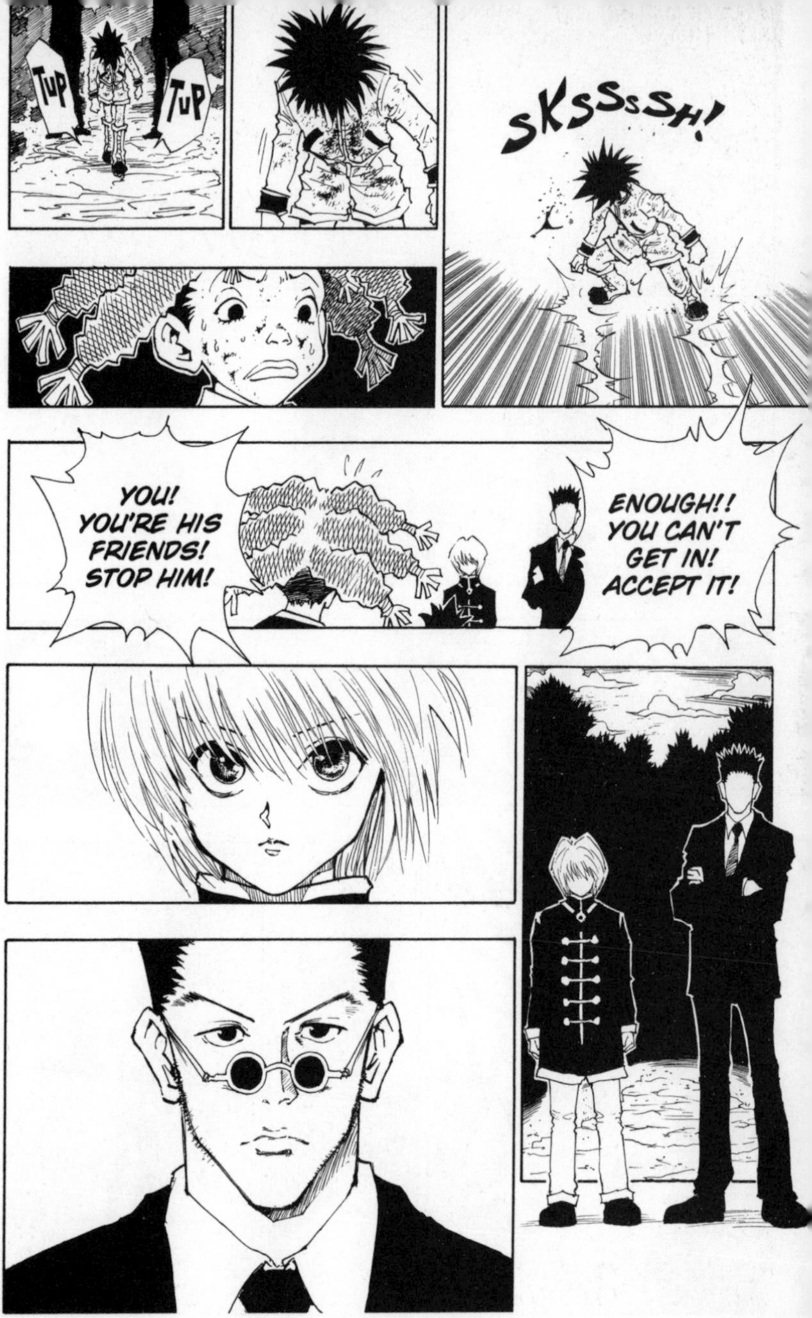
SKSSSSH!
TUP
TUP
ENOUGH!! YOU CAN'T GET IN! ACCEPT IT!
YOU! YOU'RE HIS FRIENDS! STOP HIM!

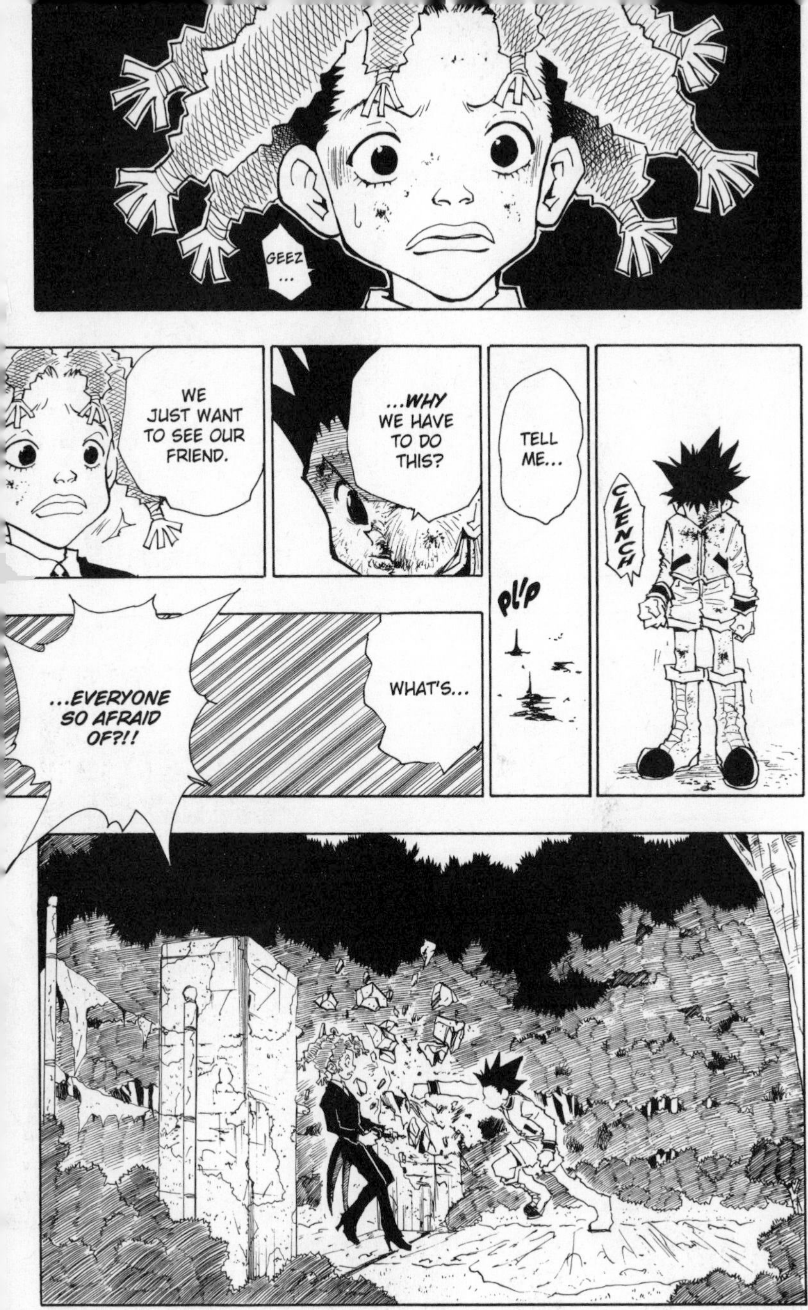
GEEZ ...
CLENCH
TELL ME...
PL'P
...WHY WE HAVE TO DO THIS?
WE JUST WANT TO SEE OUR FRIEND.
WHAT'S...
...EVERYONE SO AFRAID OF?!!

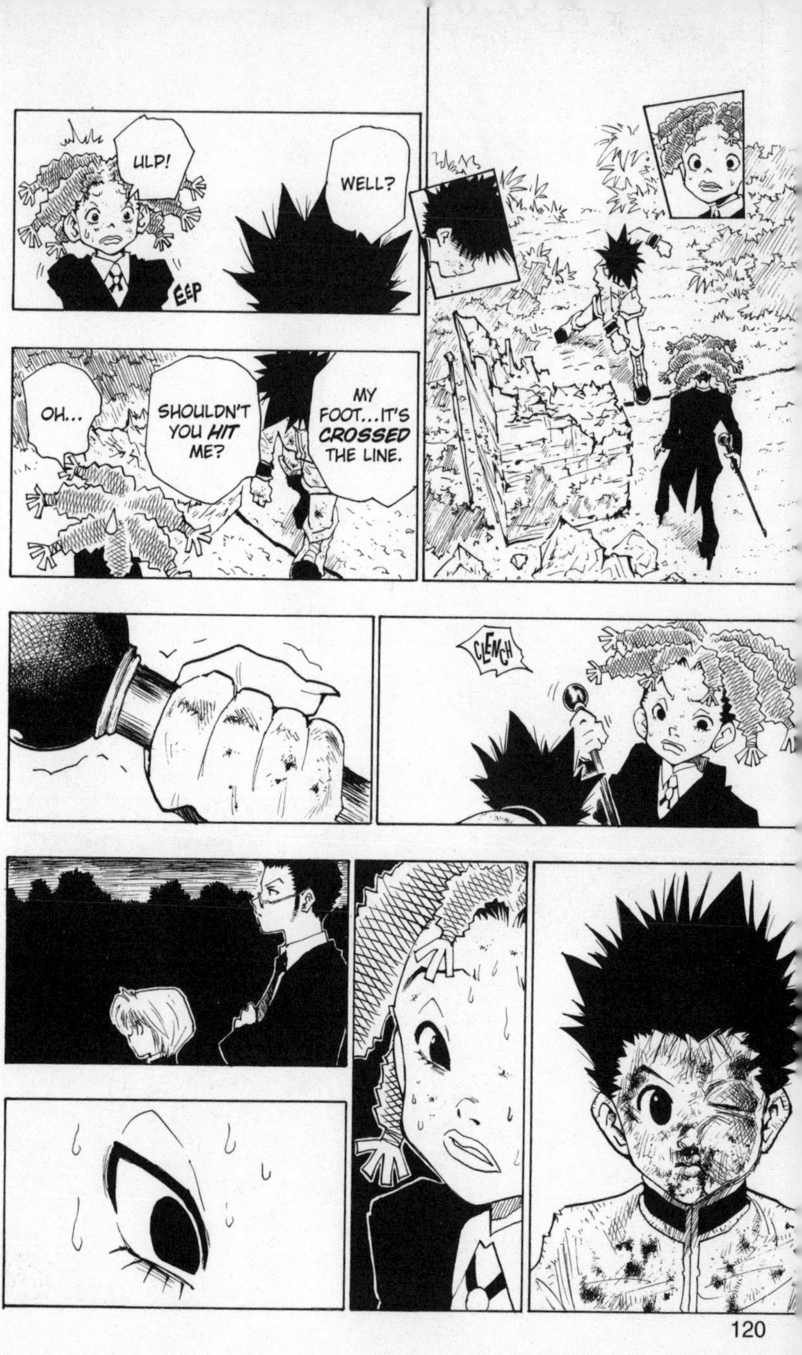
WELL?
ULP!
EEP
MY FOOT...IT'S *CROSSED* THE LINE.
SHOULDN'T YOU *HIT* ME?
OH...
CLENCH

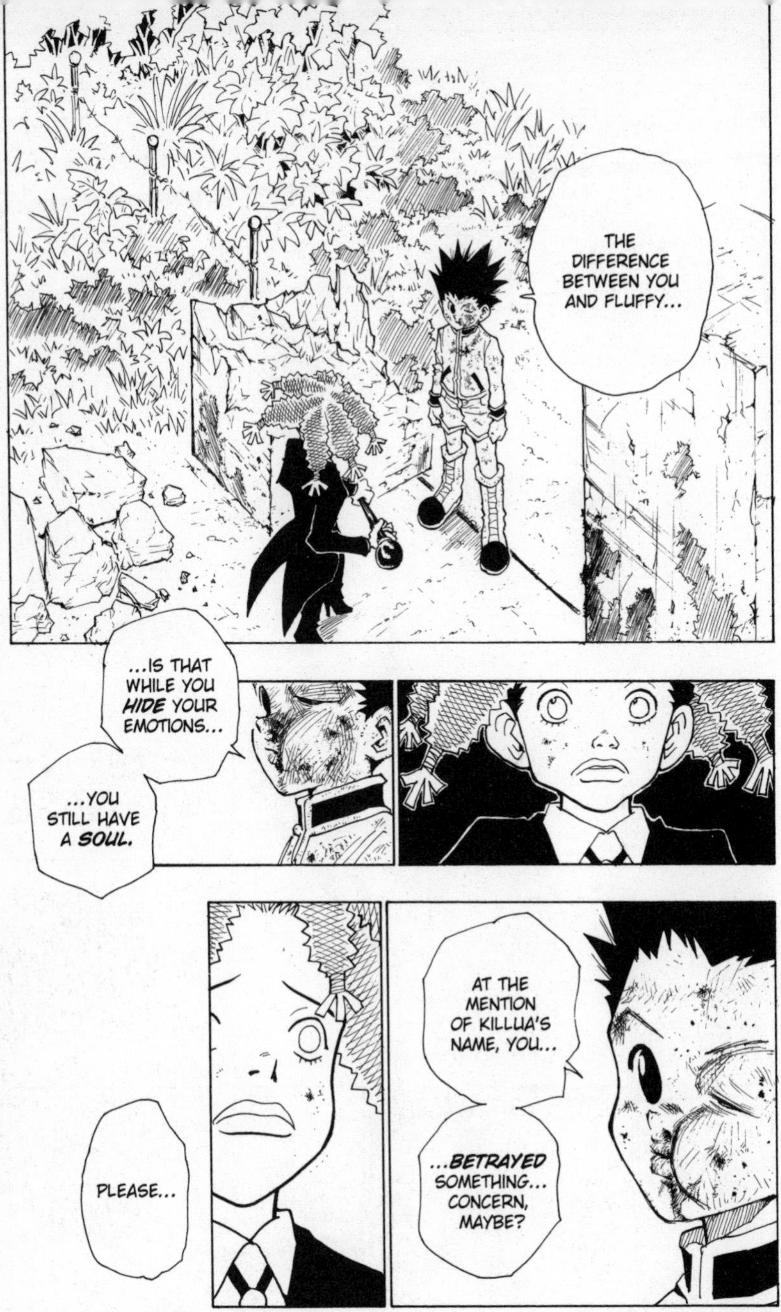
THE DIFFERENCE BETWEEN YOU AND FLUFFY...
...IS THAT WHILE YOU *HIDE* YOUR EMOTIONS...
...YOU STILL HAVE A *SOUL.*
AT THE MENTION OF KILLUA'S NAME, YOU...
...*BETRAYED* SOMETHING... CONCERN, MAYBE?
PLEASE...

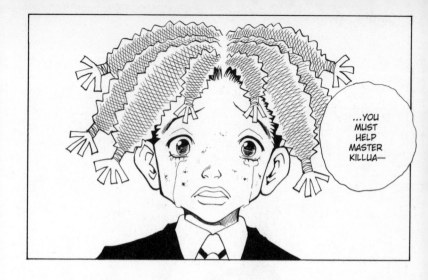

...YOU MUST HELP MASTER KILLUA—

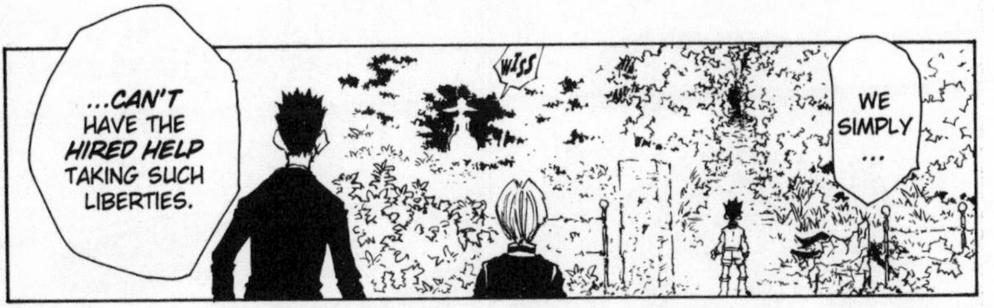
WE SIMPLY ...
WISS
...CAN'T HAVE THE HIRED HELP TAKING SUCH LIBERTIES.

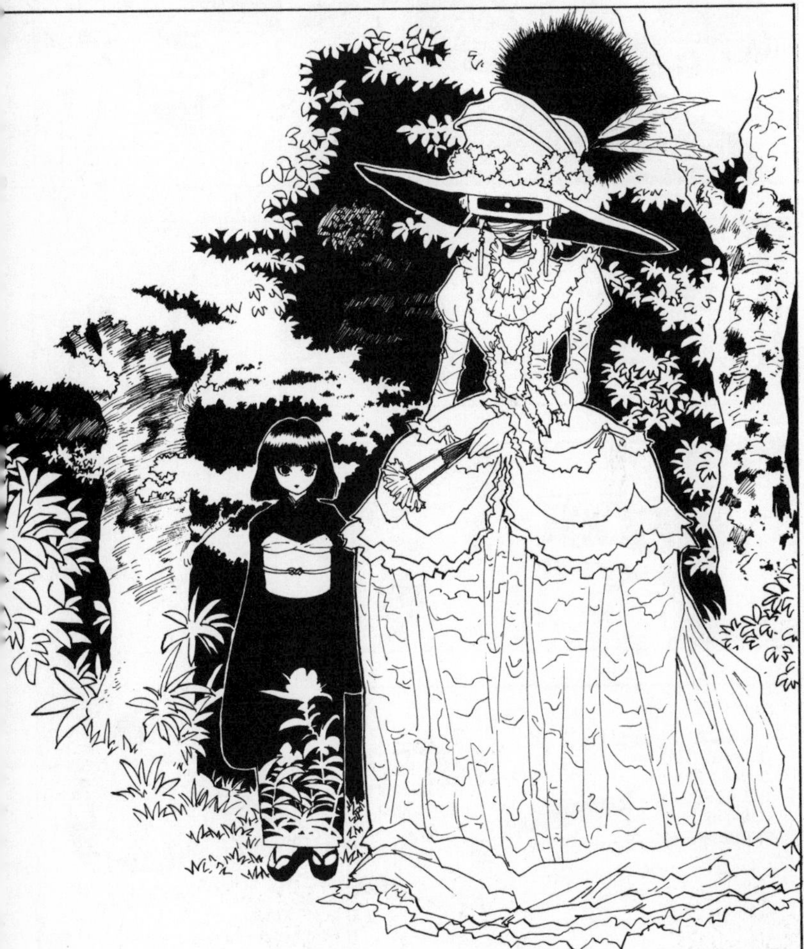

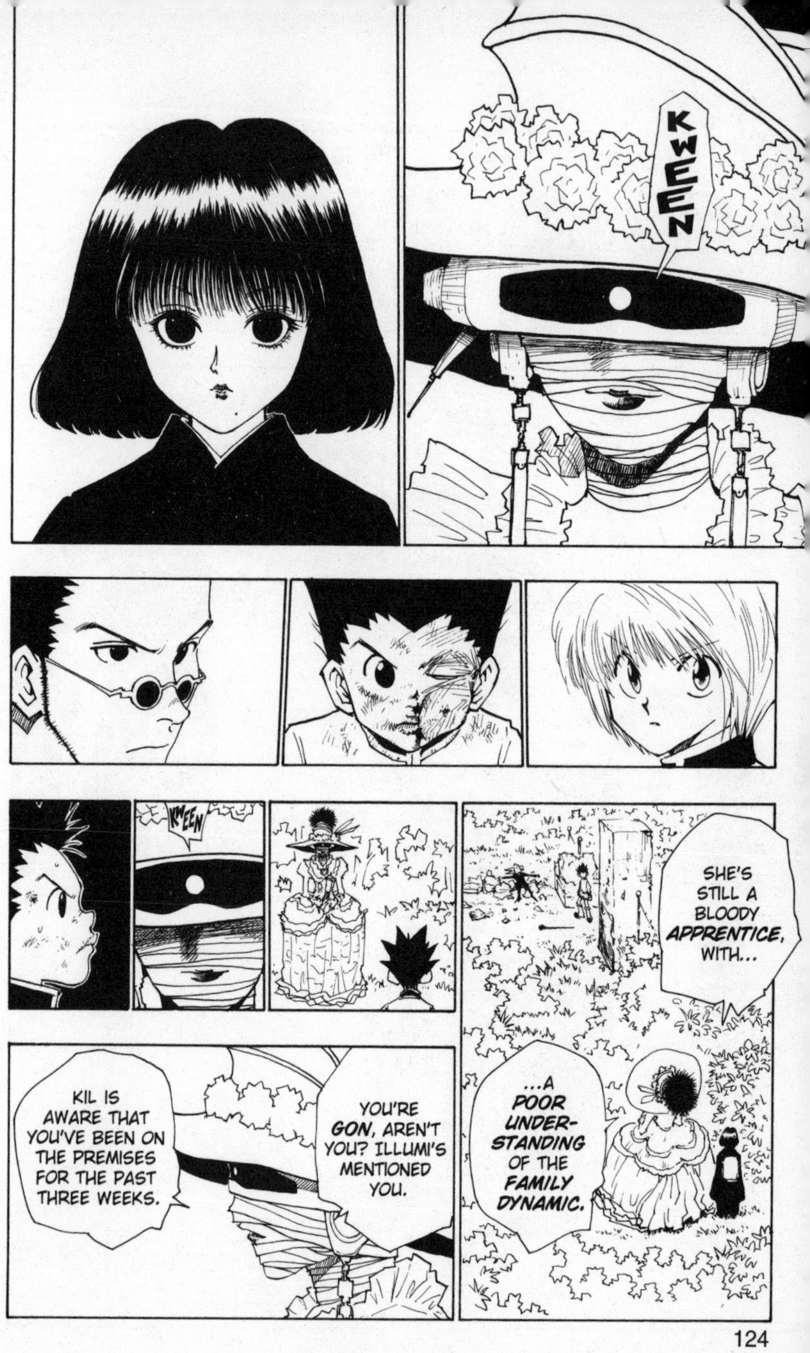
KWEEN
KWEEN
SHE'S STILL A BLOODY APPRENTICE, WITH...
...A POOR UNDER-STANDING OF THE FAMILY DYNAMIC.
YOU'RE GON, AREN'T YOU? ILLUMI'S MENTIONED YOU.
KIL IS AWARE THAT YOU'VE BEEN ON THE PREMISES FOR THE PAST THREE WEEKS.

READ THIS WAY

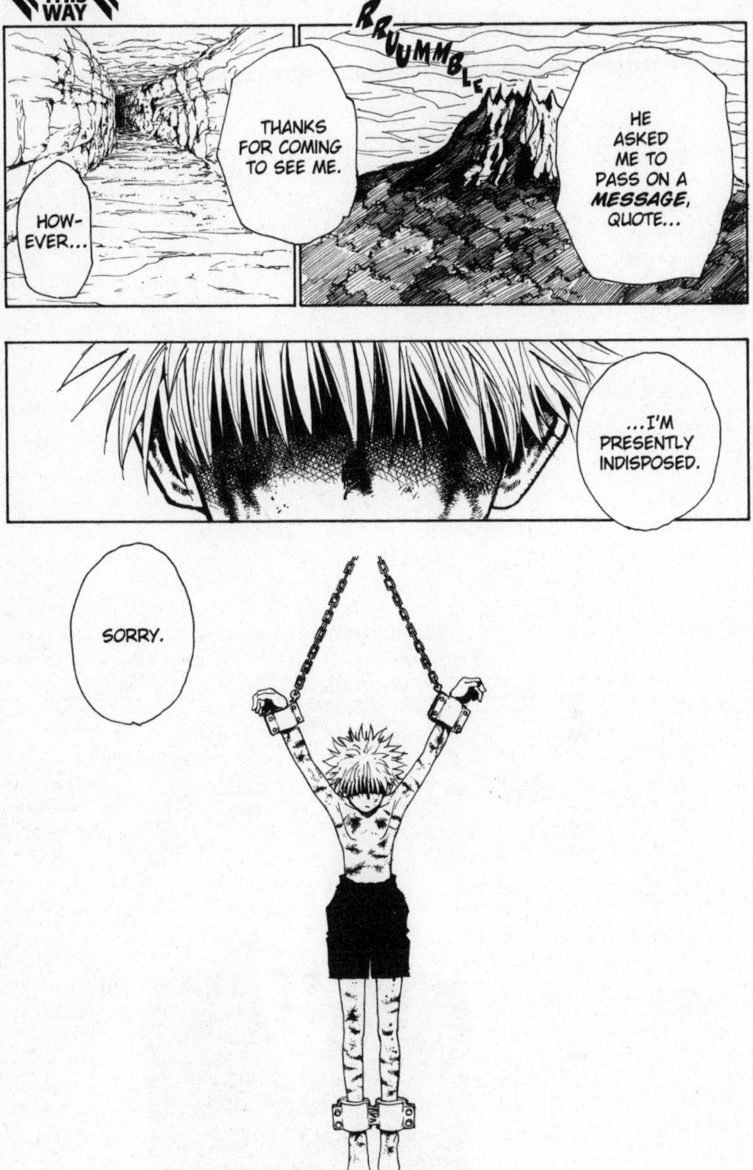
RRUUMMBLE
HE ASKED ME TO PASS ON A *MESSAGE*, QUOTE...
THANKS FOR COMING TO SEE ME.
HOW-EVER...
...I'M PRESENTLY INDISPOSED.
SORRY.

Chapter 42

The Zoldycks, part 3

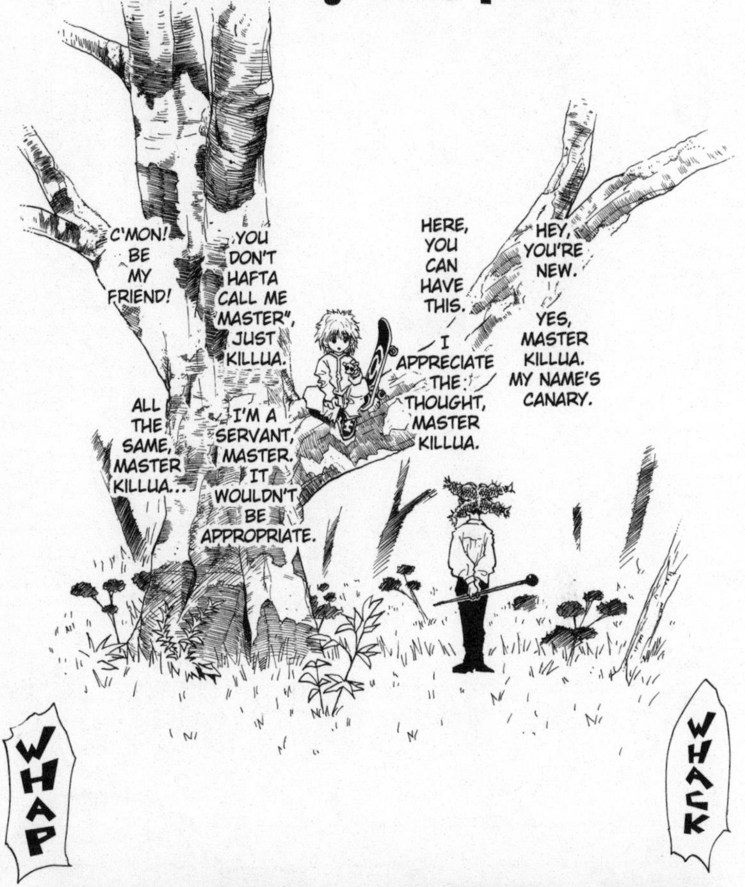
HEY, YOU'RE NEW.
YES, MASTER KILLUA. MY NAME'S CANARY.
HERE, YOU CAN HAVE THIS.
I APPRECIATE THE THOUGHT, MASTER KILLUA.
YOU DON'T HAFTA CALL ME MASTER", JUST KILLUA.
I'M A SERVANT, MASTER. IT WOULDN'T BE APPROPRIATE.
C'MON! BE MY FRIEND!
ALL THE SAME, MASTER KILLUA...
WHACK
WHAP

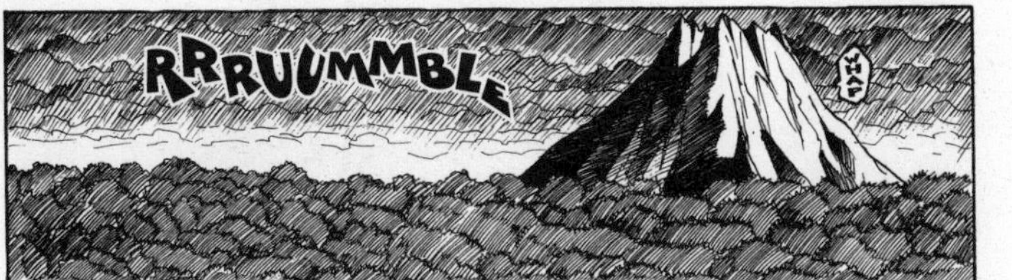
WHAP
RRRUUMMBLE

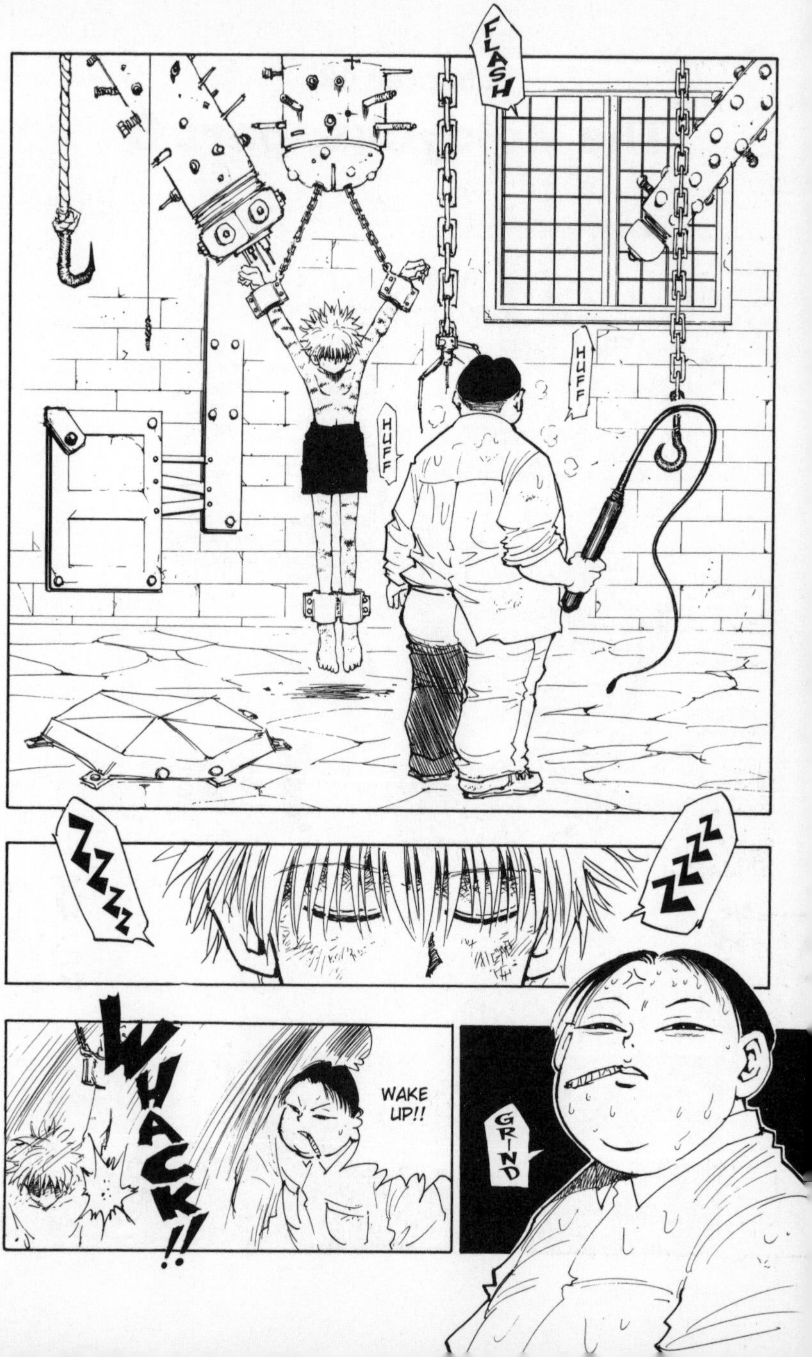

FLASH
HUFF
HUFF
ZZZZ
ZZZZ
GRIND
WAKE UP!!
WHACK!!

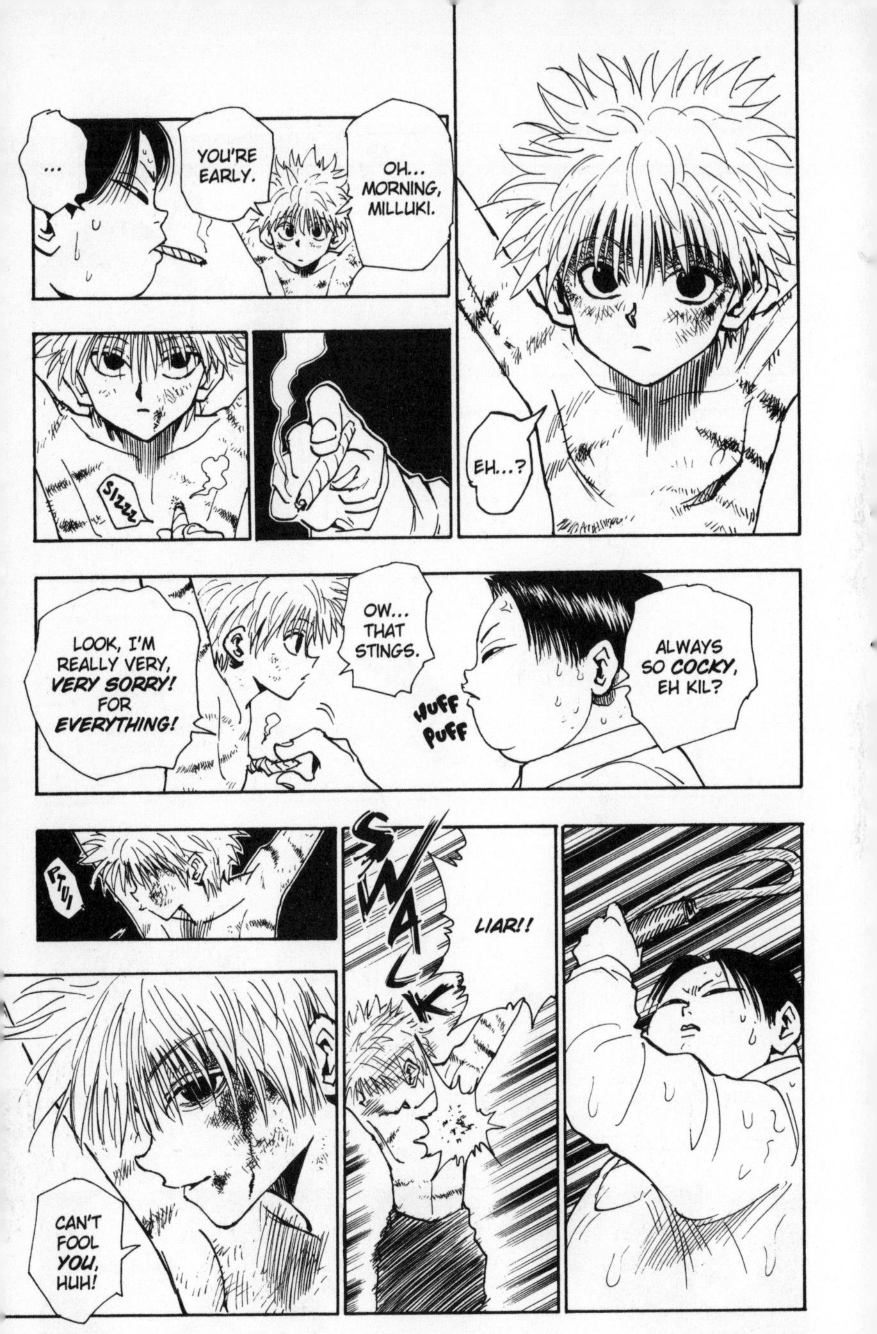
EH...?
OH... MORNING, MILLUKI.
YOU'RE EARLY.
...
SIZZZZ
ALWAYS SO COCKY, EH KIL?
HUFF PUFF
OW... THAT STINGS.
LOOK, I'M REALLY VERY, VERY SORRY! FOR EVERYTHING!
SWAK
LIAR!!
PTUI
CAN'T FOOL YOU, HUH!

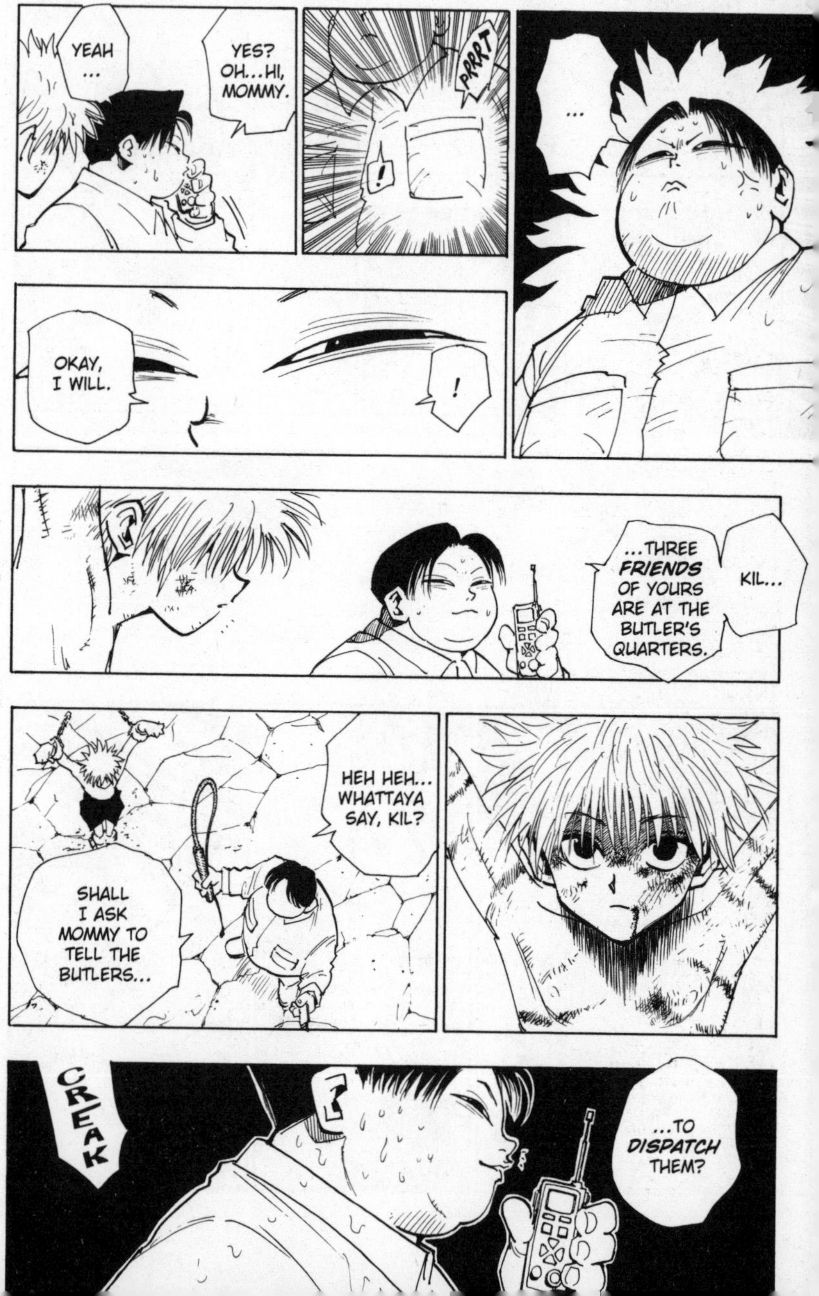
...
PRRRT
!
YES? OH...HI, MOMMY.
YEAH ...
!
OKAY, I WILL.
KIL...
...THREE FRIENDS OF YOURS ARE AT THE BUTLER'S QUARTERS.
HEH HEH... WHATTAYA SAY, KIL?
SHALL I ASK MOMMY TO TELL THE BUTLERS...
...TO DISPATCH THEM?
CREAK

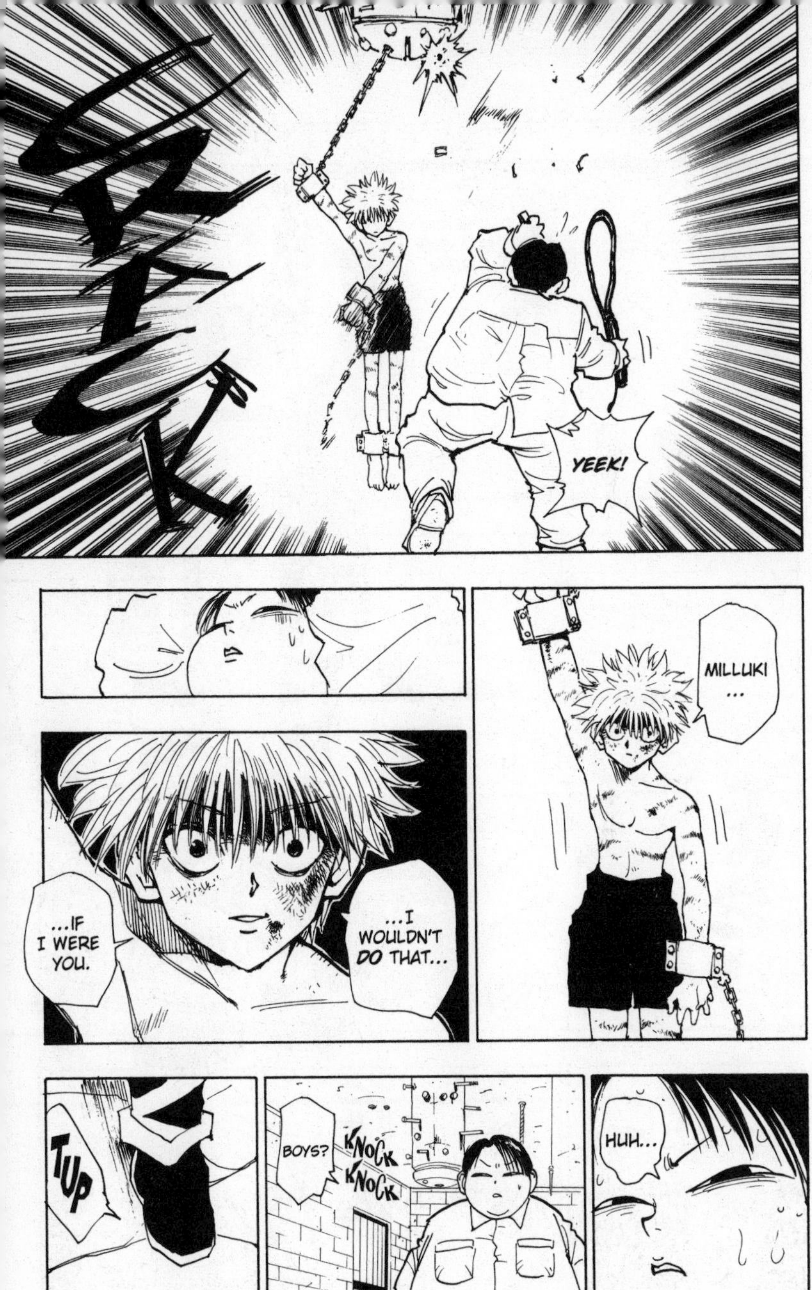
YEEK!
CRACK
MILLUKI ...
...I WOULDN'T DO THAT...
...IF I WERE YOU.
HUH...
KNOCK KNOCK
BOYS?
TUP

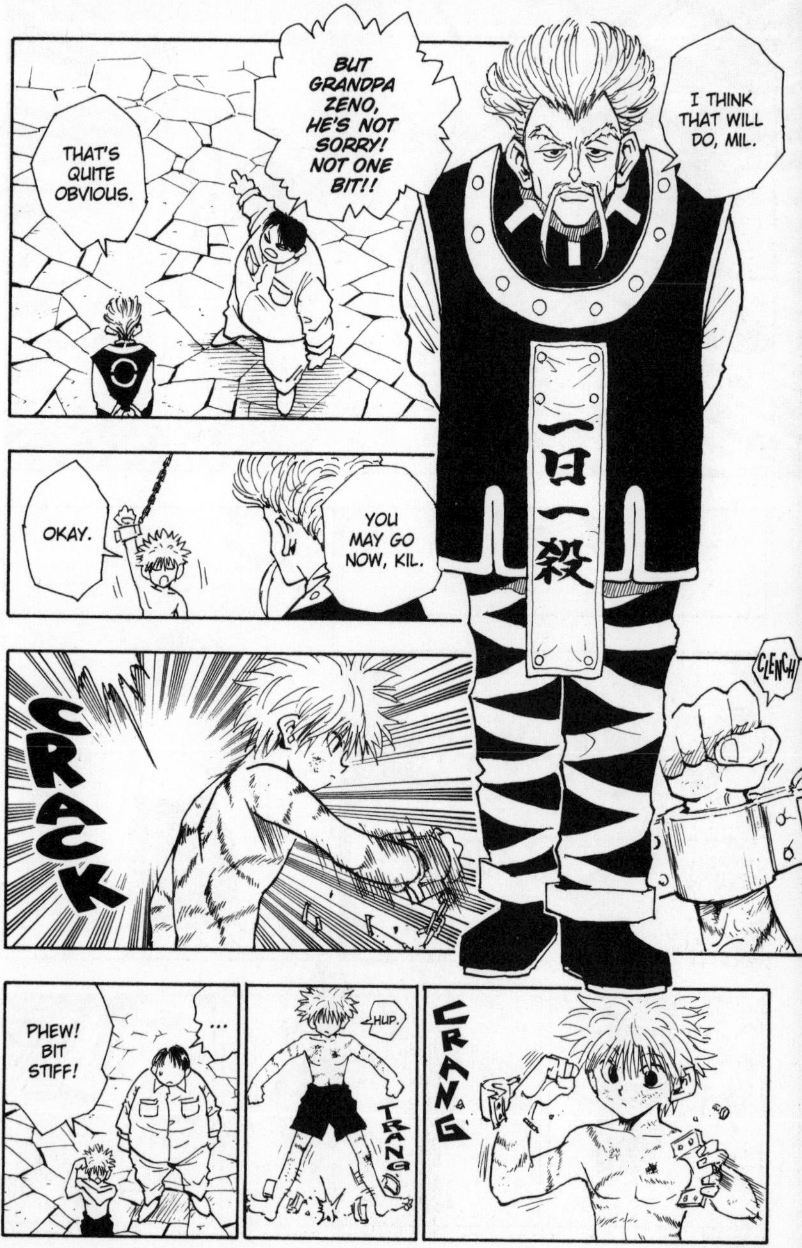
I THINK THAT WILL DO, MIL.
BUT GRANDPA ZENO, HE'S NOT SORRY! NOT ONE BIT!!
THAT'S QUITE OBVIOUS.
YOU MAY GO NOW, KIL.
OKAY.
一日一殺
CLENCH
CRACK
CRANG
HUP.
TRANG
...
PHEW! BIT STIFF!

READ THIS WAY

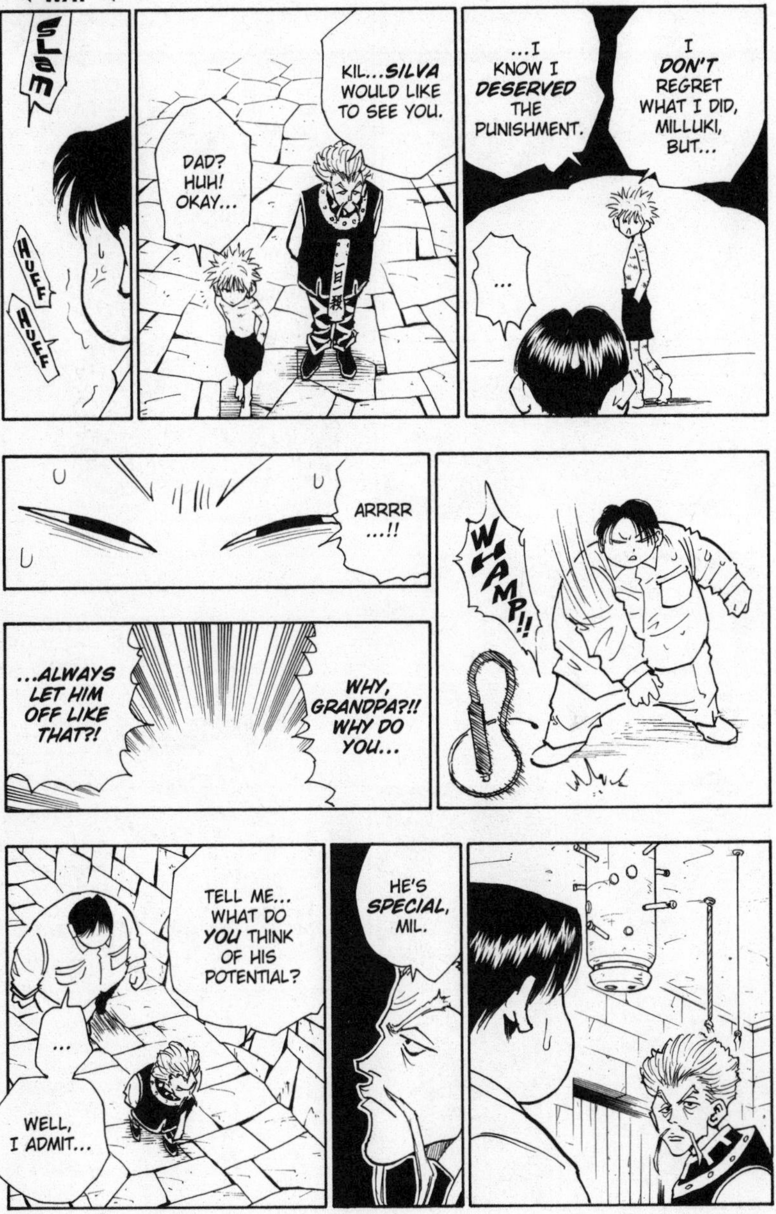
I DON'T REGRET WHAT I DID, MILLUKI, BUT...
...I KNOW I DESERVED THE PUNISHMENT.
...
KIL...SILVA WOULD LIKE TO SEE YOU.
DAD? HUH! OKAY...
SLAM
HUFF
HUFF
WHAMP!!
ARRRR ...!!
WHY, GRANDPA?!! WHY DO YOU...
...ALWAYS LET HIM OFF LIKE THAT?!
HE'S SPECIAL, MIL.
TELL ME... WHAT DO YOU THINK OF HIS POTENTIAL?
...
WELL, I ADMIT...

...HE PROBABLY HAS ONE OF THE MOST AWESOME TALENTS EVER SPAWNED BY THE ZOLDYCKS.
EVEN MOMMY SAYS SO. BUT LET'S FACE IT...
...HE'S ABSOLUTELY NO GOOD AS AN ASSASSIN. HE'S TOO ERRATIC.
HUFF
PUFF
TROMP
TROMP
HE RUNS OFF, HE MAKES FRIENDS... WHAT KIND OF PERSON IS THAT...
...TO HEAD A FAMILY OF WORLD-RENOWNED ASSASSINS?
HUFF HUFF
HMM...
...ALL VALID POINTS.
SURE.
AS FOR ME, I'LL TAKE OUT ANYONE, ANYTIME, FOR THE RIGHT PRICE.
AND MY NEWEST BOMB IS A REAL WINNER!!
TINY ENOUGH TO HARNESS TO A MOSQUITO, IT EXPLODES WHEN SHE SUCKS BLOOD!!
IT'S ONLY GOT THE PUNCH OF A CHERRY BOMB, AND MOSQUITOES ARE NO GOOD FOR PRECISION TARGETING, BUT...
MIL...
...YOU'RE A SHARP KID ...AND AN IDIOT.
WHEEOOOO

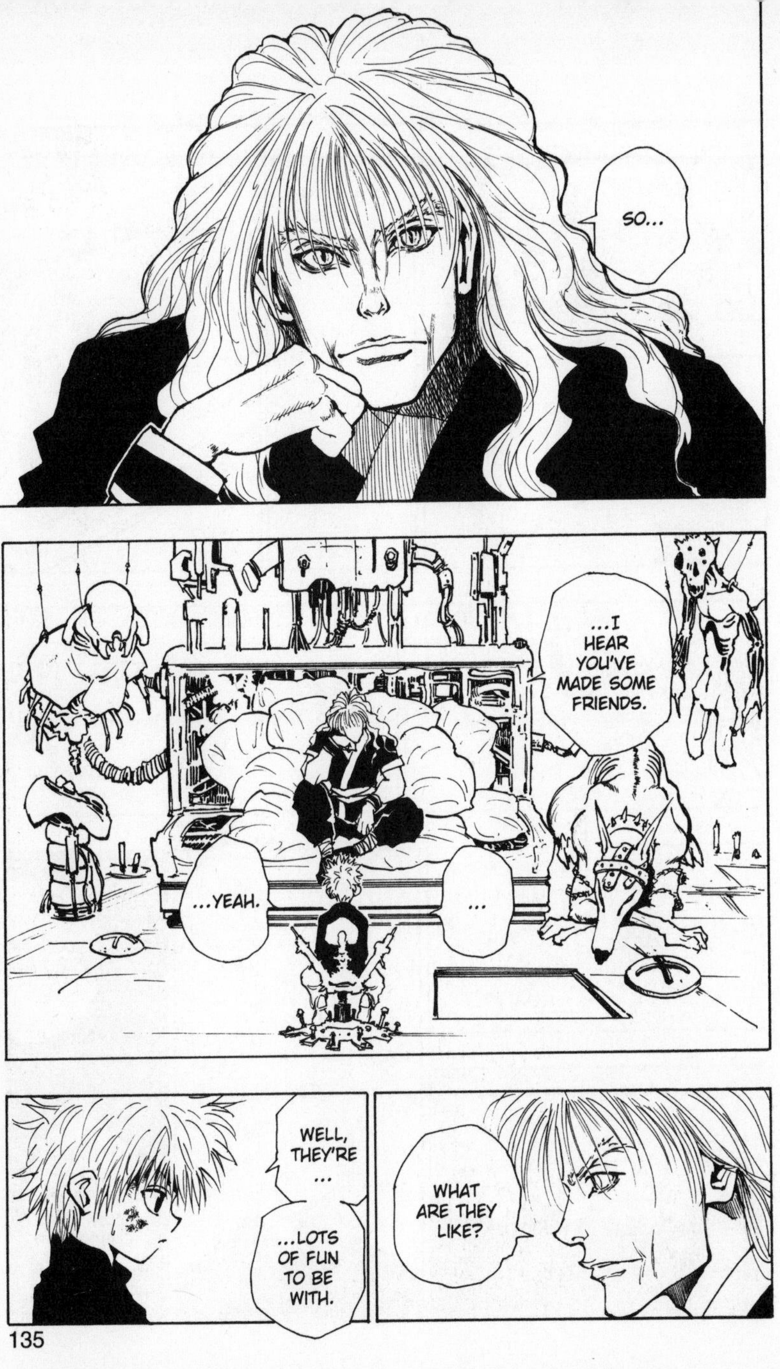
SO...
...I HEAR YOU'VE MADE SOME FRIENDS.
...
...YEAH.
WHAT ARE THEY LIKE?
WELL, THEY'RE ...
...LOTS OF FUN TO BE WITH.

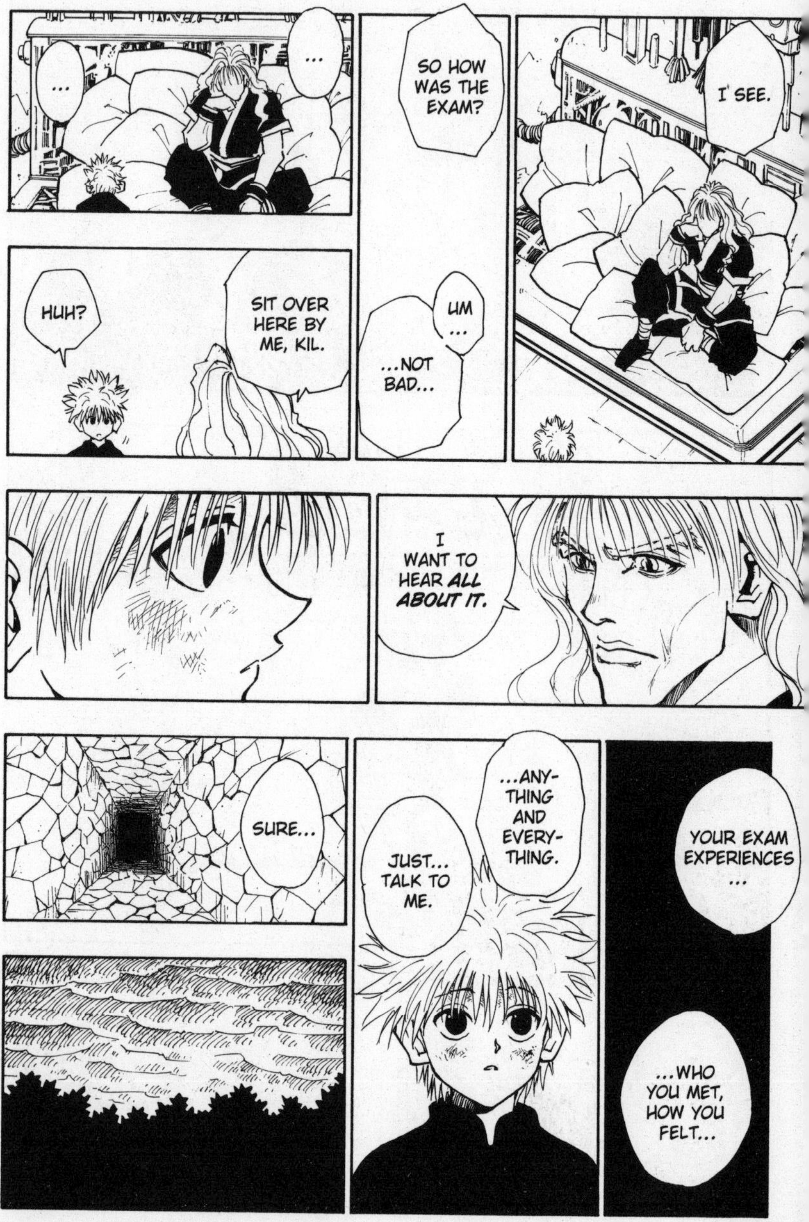
I SEE.
SO HOW WAS THE EXAM?
UM ...
...NOT BAD...
...
...
SIT OVER HERE BY ME, KIL.
HUH?
I WANT TO HEAR ***ALL ABOUT IT.***
YOUR EXAM EXPERIENCES ...
...WHO YOU MET, HOW YOU FELT...
...ANYTHING AND EVERYTHING.
JUST... TALK TO ME.
SURE...

READ THIS WAY

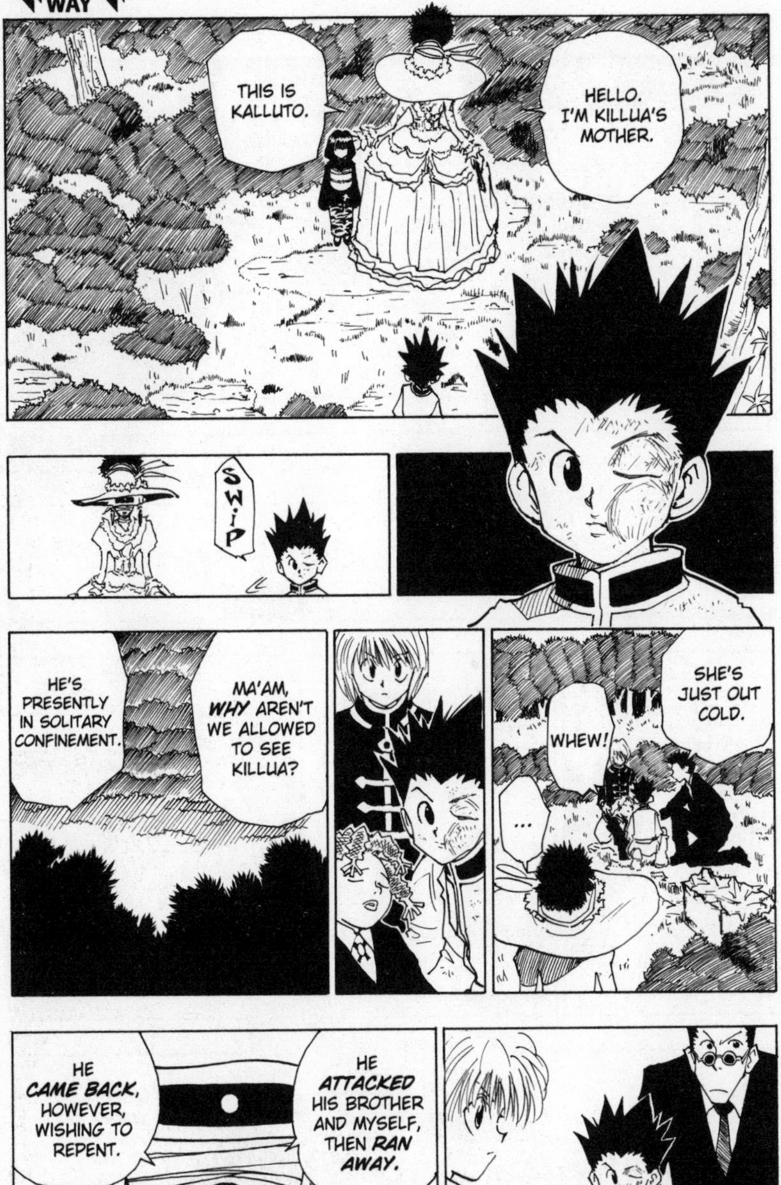
HELLO. I'M KILLUA'S MOTHER.
THIS IS KALLUTO.
SWIP
SHE'S JUST OUT COLD.
WHEW!
...
MA'AM, **WHY** AREN'T WE ALLOWED TO SEE KILLUA?
HE'S PRESENTLY IN SOLITARY CONFINEMENT.
HE **ATTACKED** HIS BROTHER AND MYSELF, THEN **RAN AWAY**.
HE **CAME BACK**, HOWEVER, WISHING TO REPENT.

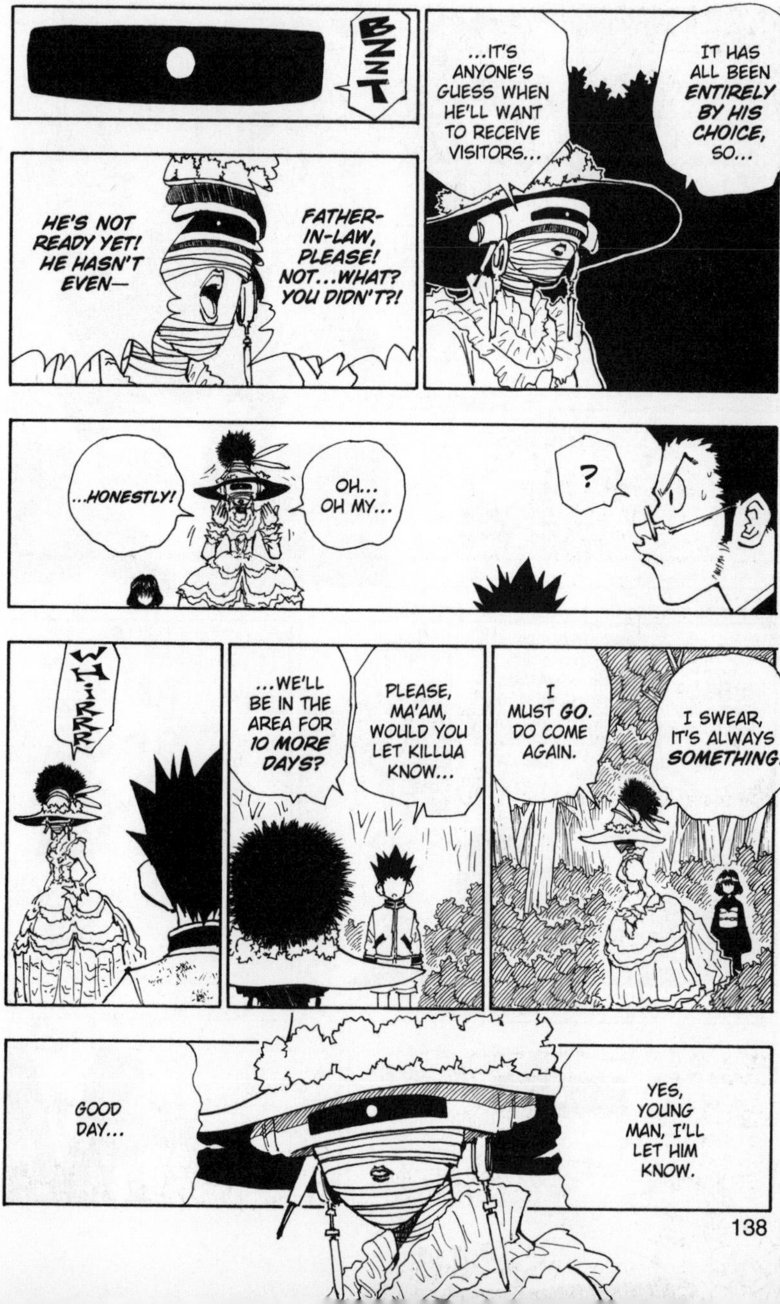
IT HAS ALL BEEN ENTIRELY BY HIS CHOICE, SO...
...IT'S ANYONE'S GUESS WHEN HE'LL WANT TO RECEIVE VISITORS...
BZZT
FATHER-IN-LAW, PLEASE! NOT...WHAT? YOU DIDN'T?!
HE'S NOT READY YET! HE HASN'T EVEN—
?
OH... OH MY...
...HONESTLY!
I SWEAR, IT'S ALWAYS SOMETHING.
I MUST GO. DO COME AGAIN.
PLEASE, MA'AM, WOULD YOU LET KILLUA KNOW...
...WE'LL BE IN THE AREA FOR 10 MORE DAYS?
WHIRRR
YES, YOUNG MAN, I'LL LET HIM KNOW.
GOOD DAY...

READ THIS WAY

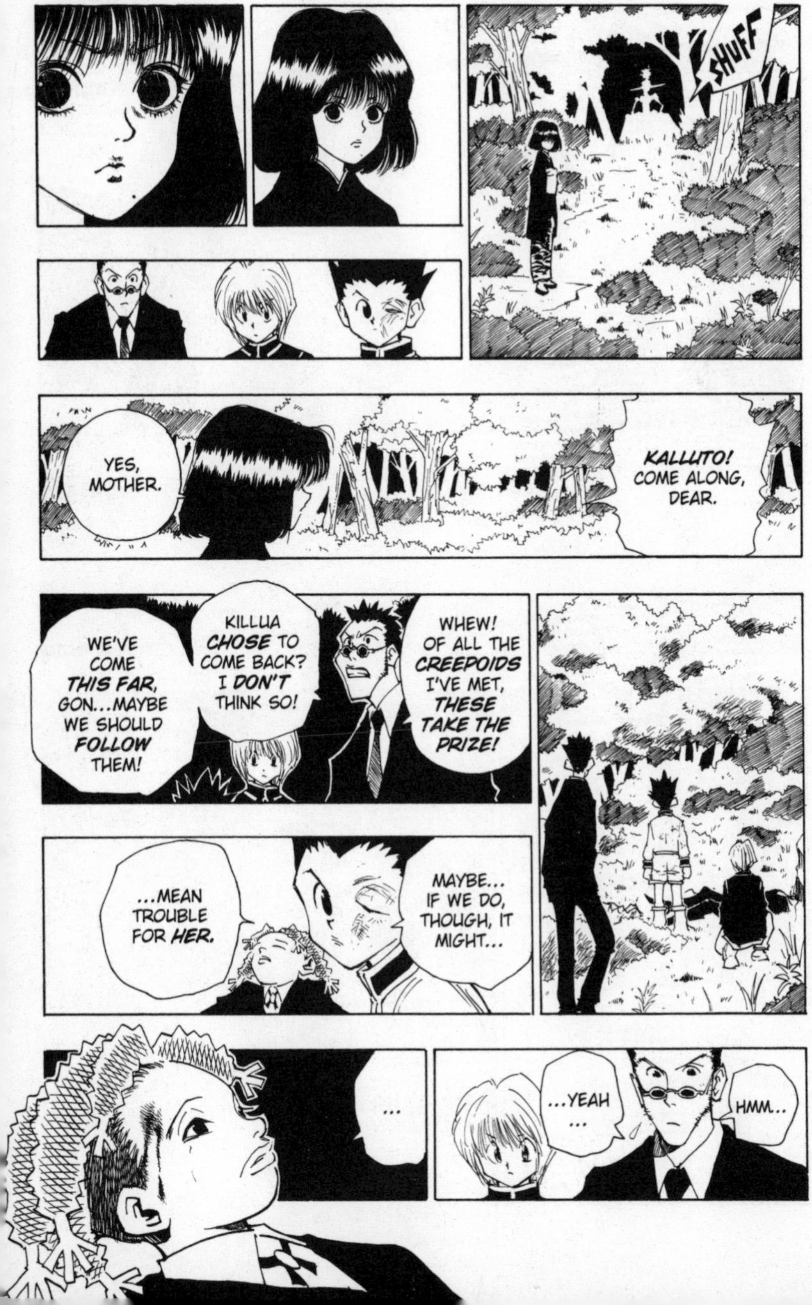
SHUFF
KALLUTO! COME ALONG, DEAR.
YES, MOTHER.
WHEW! OF ALL THE CREEPOIDS I'VE MET, THESE TAKE THE PRIZE!
KILLUA CHOSE TO COME BACK? I DON'T THINK SO!
WE'VE COME THIS FAR, GON...MAYBE WE SHOULD FOLLOW THEM!
MAYBE... IF WE DO, THOUGH, IT MIGHT...
...MEAN TROUBLE FOR HER.
HMM...
...YEAH ...
...

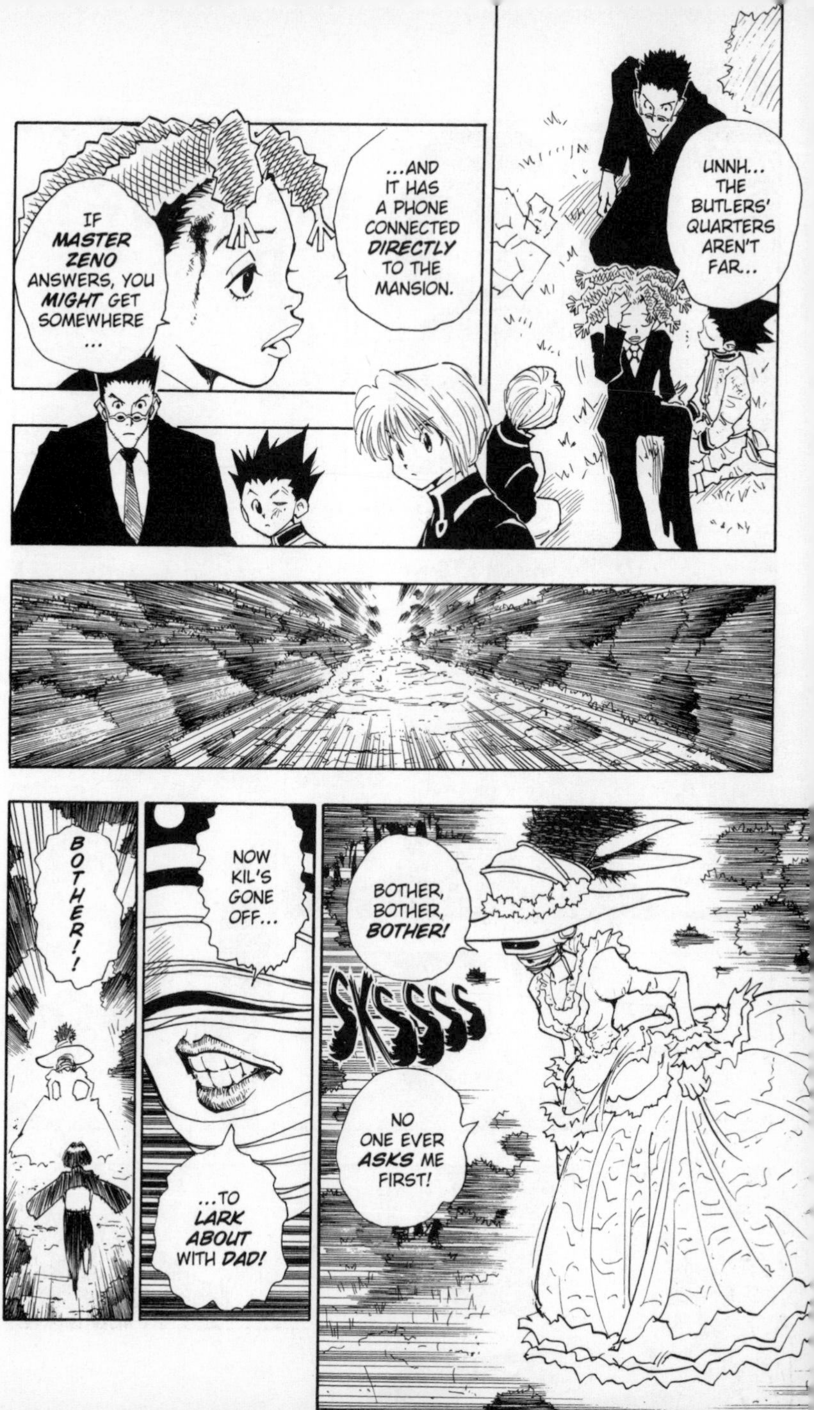
UNNH... THE BUTLERS' QUARTERS AREN'T FAR..
...AND IT HAS A PHONE CONNECTED DIRECTLY TO THE MANSION.
IF MASTER ZENO ANSWERS, YOU MIGHT GET SOMEWHERE...
BOTHER, BOTHER, BOTHER!
SKSSSS
NO ONE EVER ASKS ME FIRST!
NOW KIL'S GONE OFF...
...TO LARK ABOUT WITH DAD!
BOTHER!!

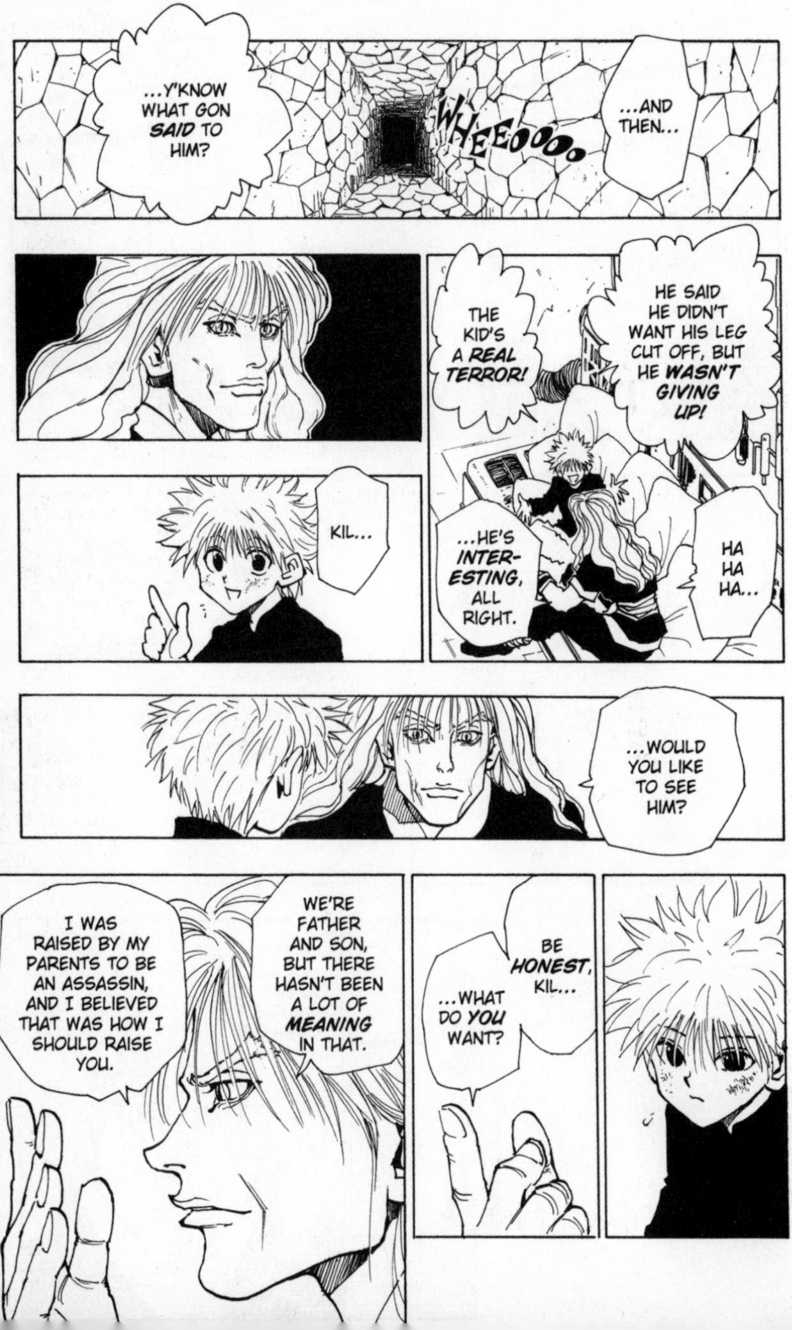
...AND THEN...
WHEEOOOO
...Y'KNOW WHAT GON SAID TO HIM?
HE SAID HE DIDN'T WANT HIS LEG CUT OFF, BUT HE WASN'T GIVING UP!
THE KID'S A REAL TERROR!
HA HA HA...
...HE'S INTERESTING, ALL RIGHT.
KIL...
...WOULD YOU LIKE TO SEE HIM?
BE HONEST, KIL...
...WHAT DO YOU WANT?
WE'RE FATHER AND SON, BUT THERE HASN'T BEEN A LOT OF MEANING IN THAT.
I WAS RAISED BY MY PARENTS TO BE AN ASSASSIN, AND I BELIEVED THAT WAS HOW I SHOULD RAISE YOU.

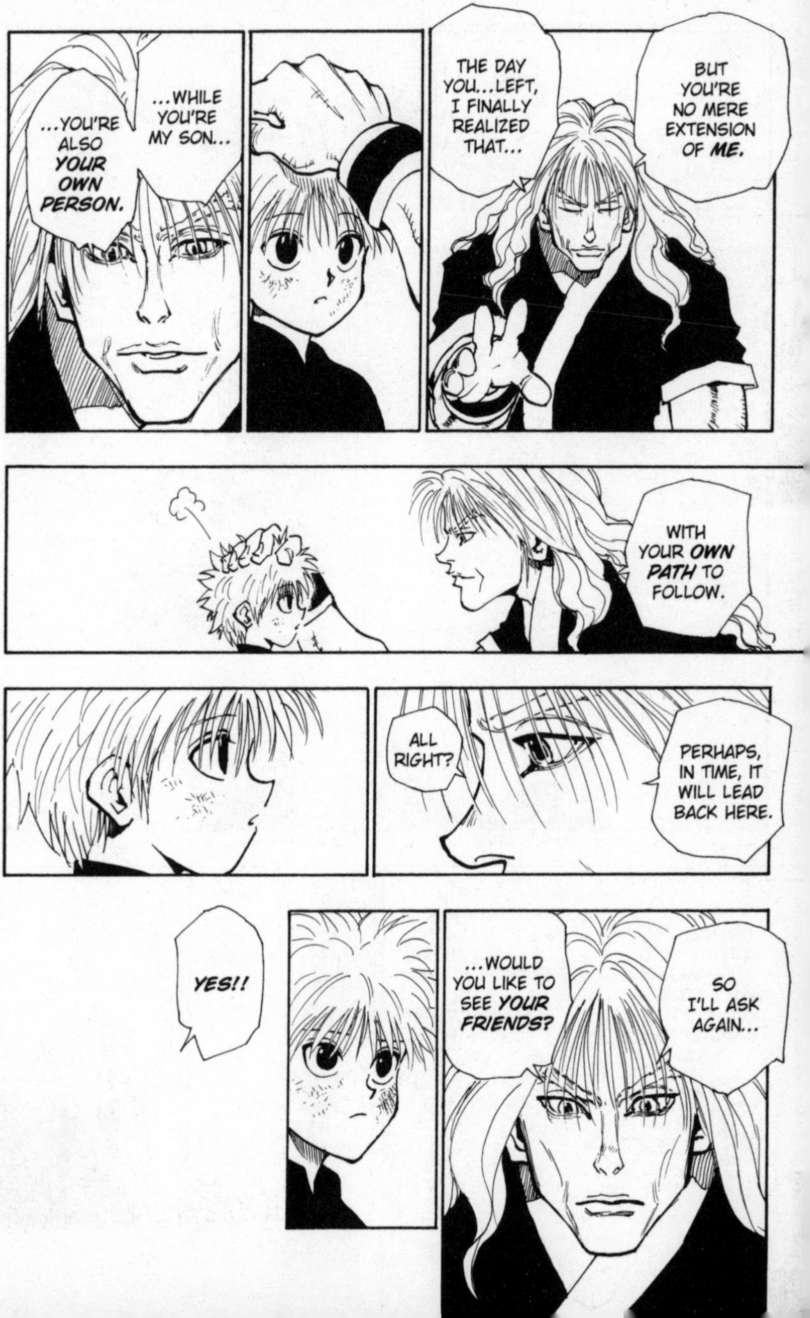
BUT YOU'RE NO MERE EXTENSION OF ME.
THE DAY YOU...LEFT, I FINALLY REALIZED THAT...
...WHILE YOU'RE MY SON...
...YOU'RE ALSO YOUR OWN PERSON.
WITH YOUR OWN PATH TO FOLLOW.
PERHAPS, IN TIME, IT WILL LEAD BACK HERE.
ALL RIGHT?
SO I'LL ASK AGAIN...
...WOULD YOU LIKE TO SEE YOUR FRIENDS?
YES!!

READ THIS WAY

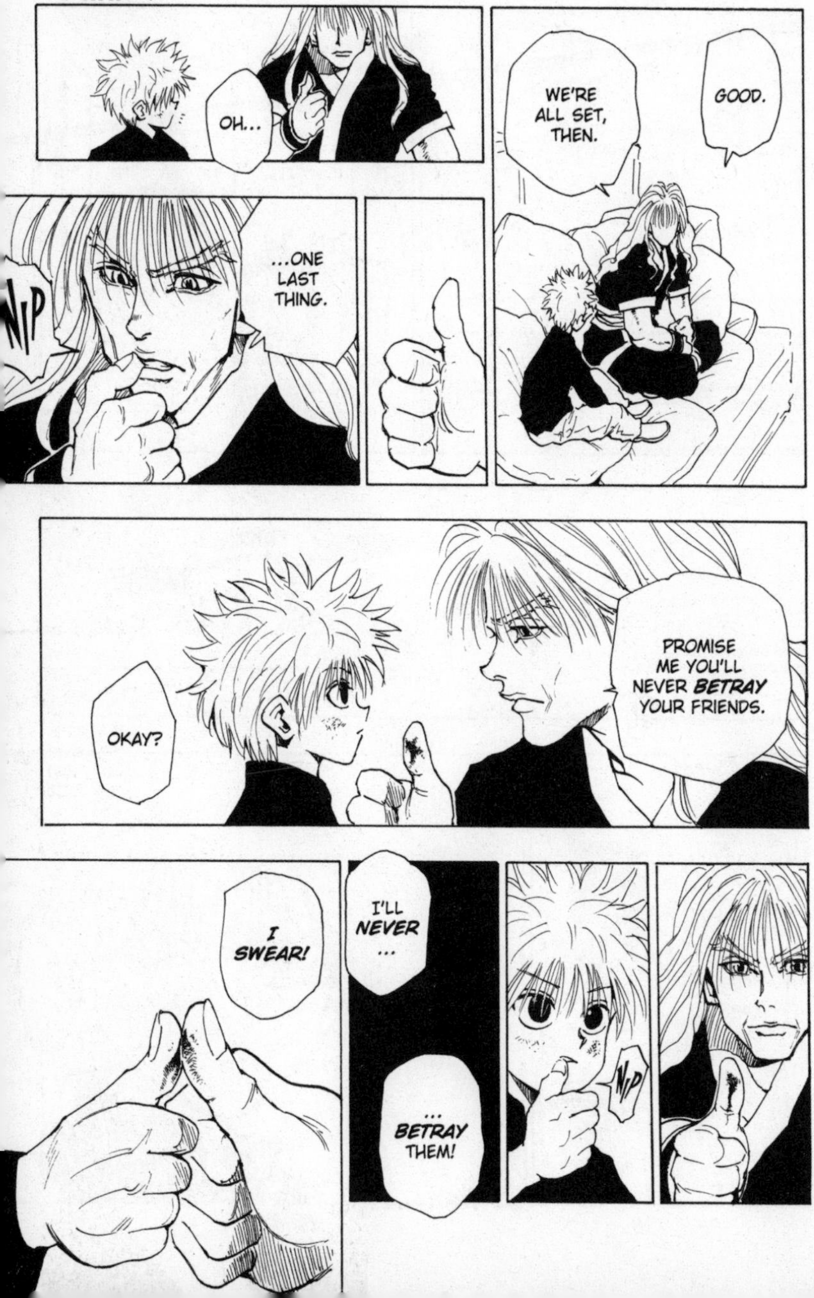
GOOD.
WE'RE ALL SET, THEN.
OH...
...ONE LAST THING.
NIP
PROMISE ME YOU'LL NEVER BETRAY YOUR FRIENDS.
OKAY?
NIP
I'LL NEVER...
...BETRAY THEM!
I SWEAR!

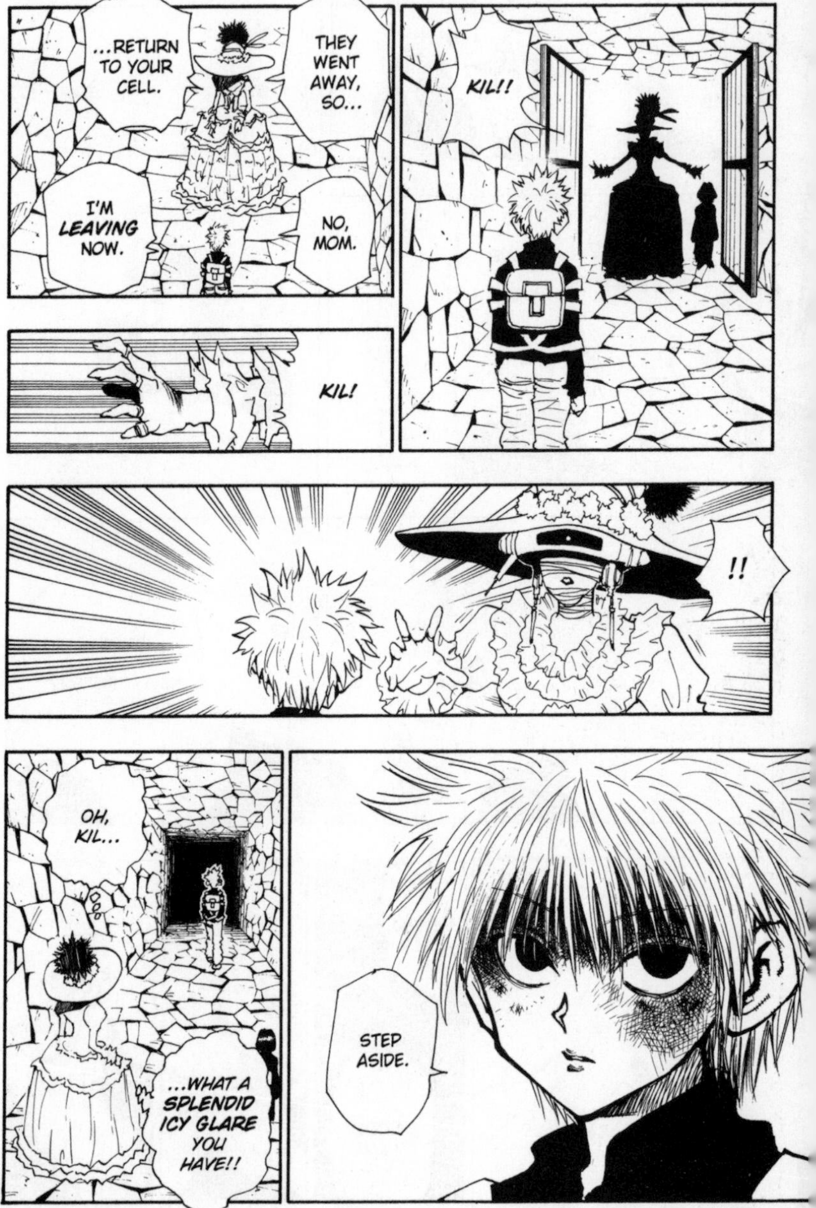
KIL!!
THEY WENT AWAY, SO...
...RETURN TO YOUR CELL.
NO, MOM.
I'M LEAVING NOW.
KIL!
!!
STEP ASIDE.
OH, KIL...
...WHAT A SPLENDID ICY GLARE YOU HAVE!!

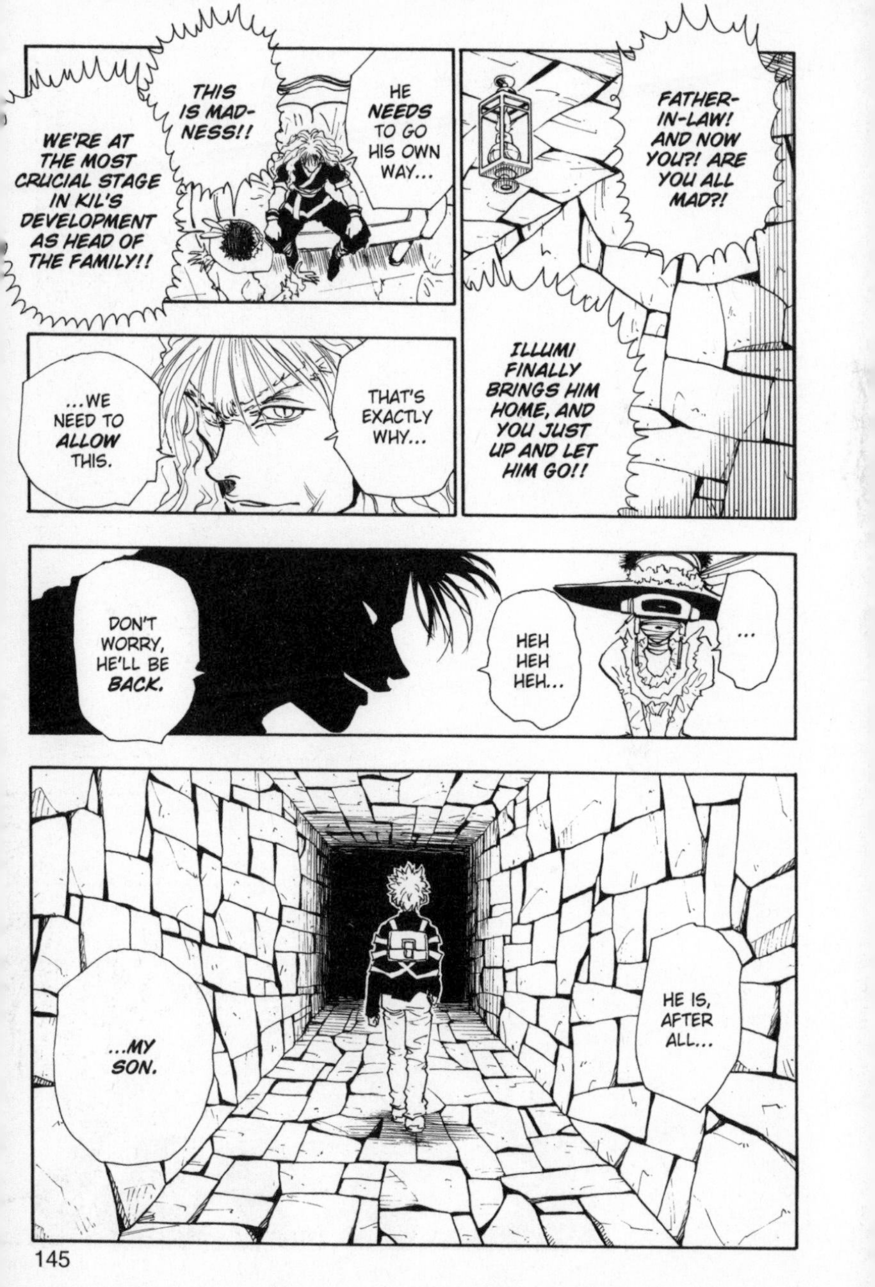
FATHER-IN-LAW! AND NOW YOU?! ARE YOU ALL MAD?!
ILLUMI FINALLY BRINGS HIM HOME, AND YOU JUST UP AND LET HIM GO!!
HE NEEDS TO GO HIS OWN WAY...
THIS IS MADNESS!!
WE'RE AT THE MOST CRUCIAL STAGE IN KIL'S DEVELOPMENT AS HEAD OF THE FAMILY!!
THAT'S EXACTLY WHY...
...WE NEED TO ALLOW THIS.
...
HEH HEH HEH...
DON'T WORRY, HE'LL BE BACK.
HE IS, AFTER ALL...
...MY SON.

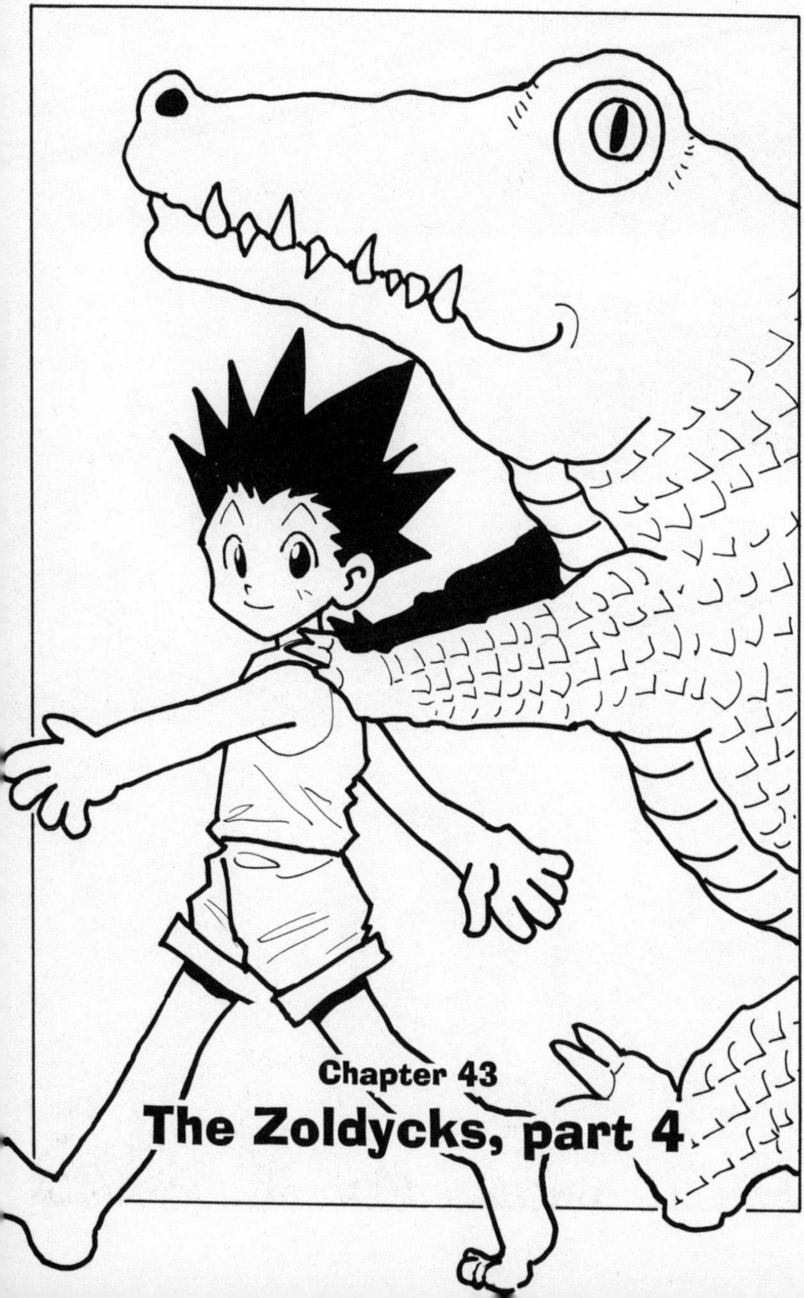

Chapter 43

The Zoldycks, part 4

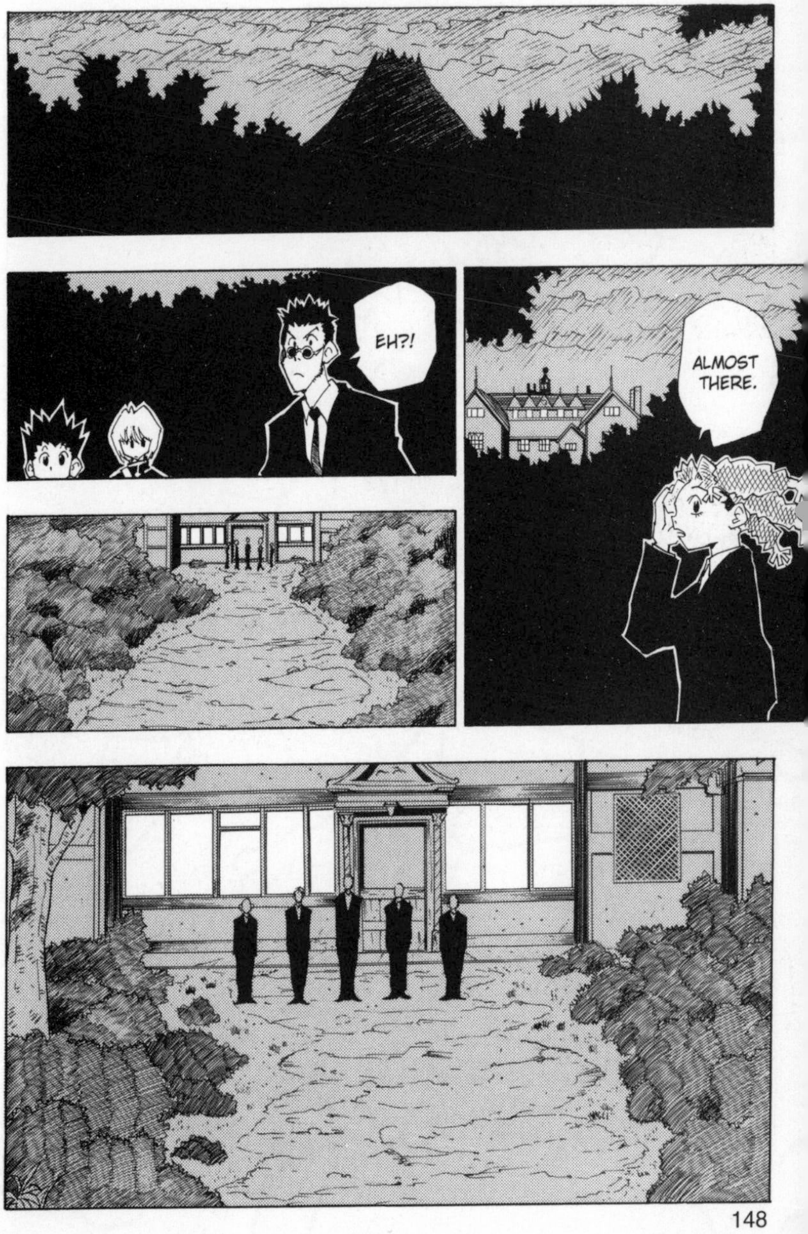
ALMOST THERE.
EH?!

READ THIS WAY

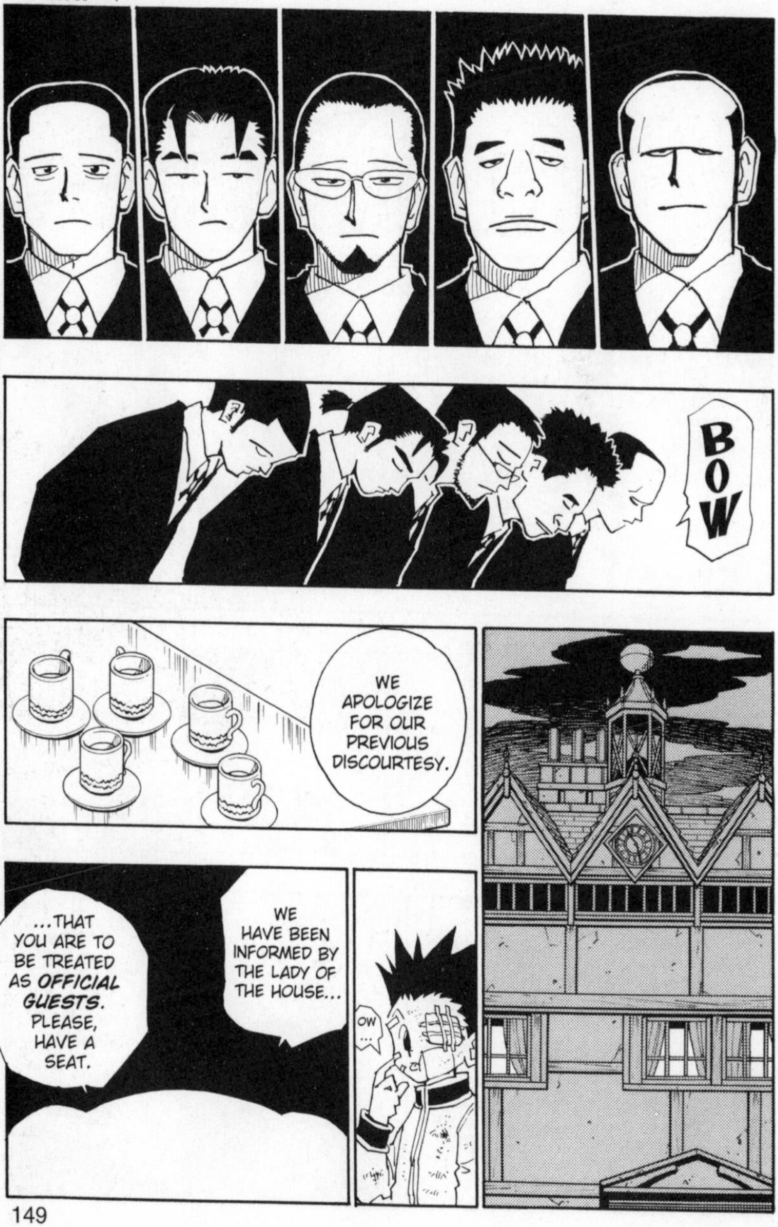

BOW
WE APOLOGIZE FOR OUR PREVIOUS DISCOURTESY.
OW ...
WE HAVE BEEN INFORMED BY THE LADY OF THE HOUSE...
...THAT YOU ARE TO BE TREATED AS ***OFFICIAL GUESTS***. PLEASE, HAVE A SEAT.

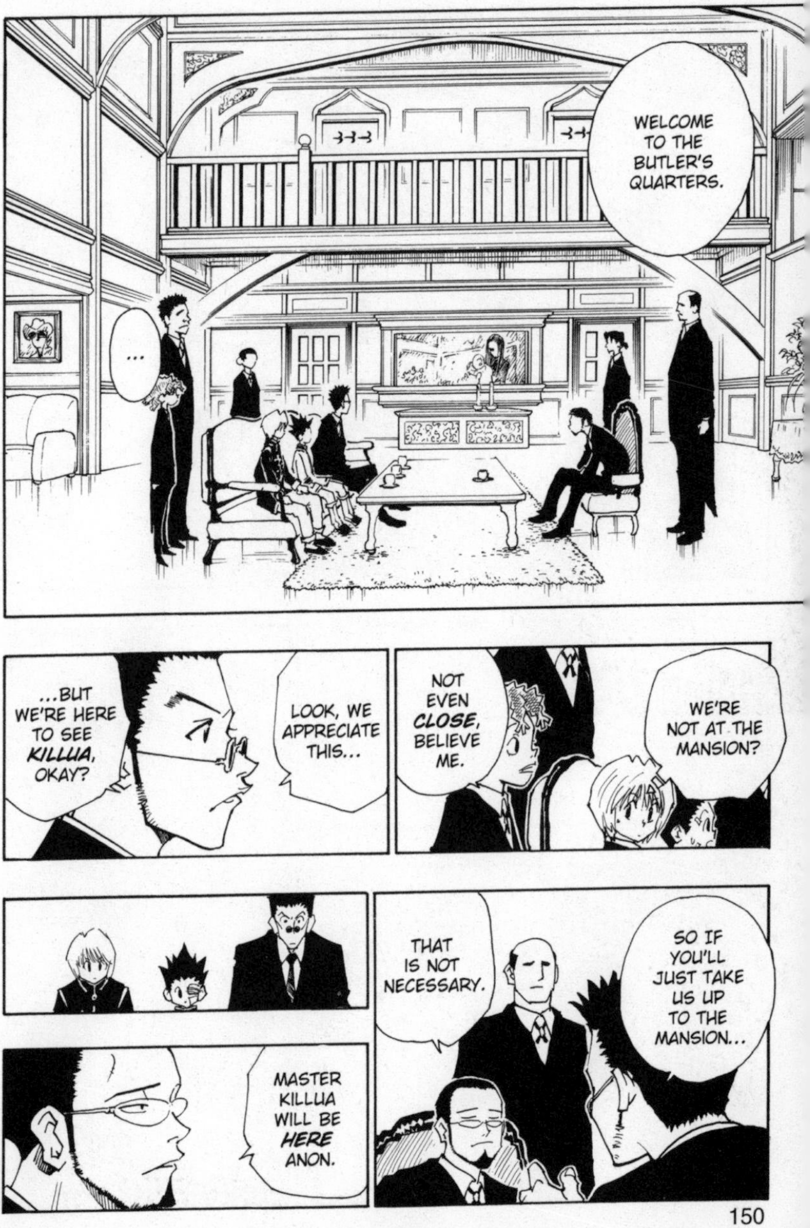
WELCOME TO THE BUTLER'S QUARTERS.
...
WE'RE NOT AT THE MANSION?
NOT EVEN CLOSE, BELIEVE ME.
LOOK, WE APPRECIATE THIS...
...BUT WE'RE HERE TO SEE KILLUA, OKAY?
SO IF YOU'LL JUST TAKE US UP TO THE MANSION...
THAT IS NOT NECESSARY.
MASTER KILLUA WILL BE HERE ANON.

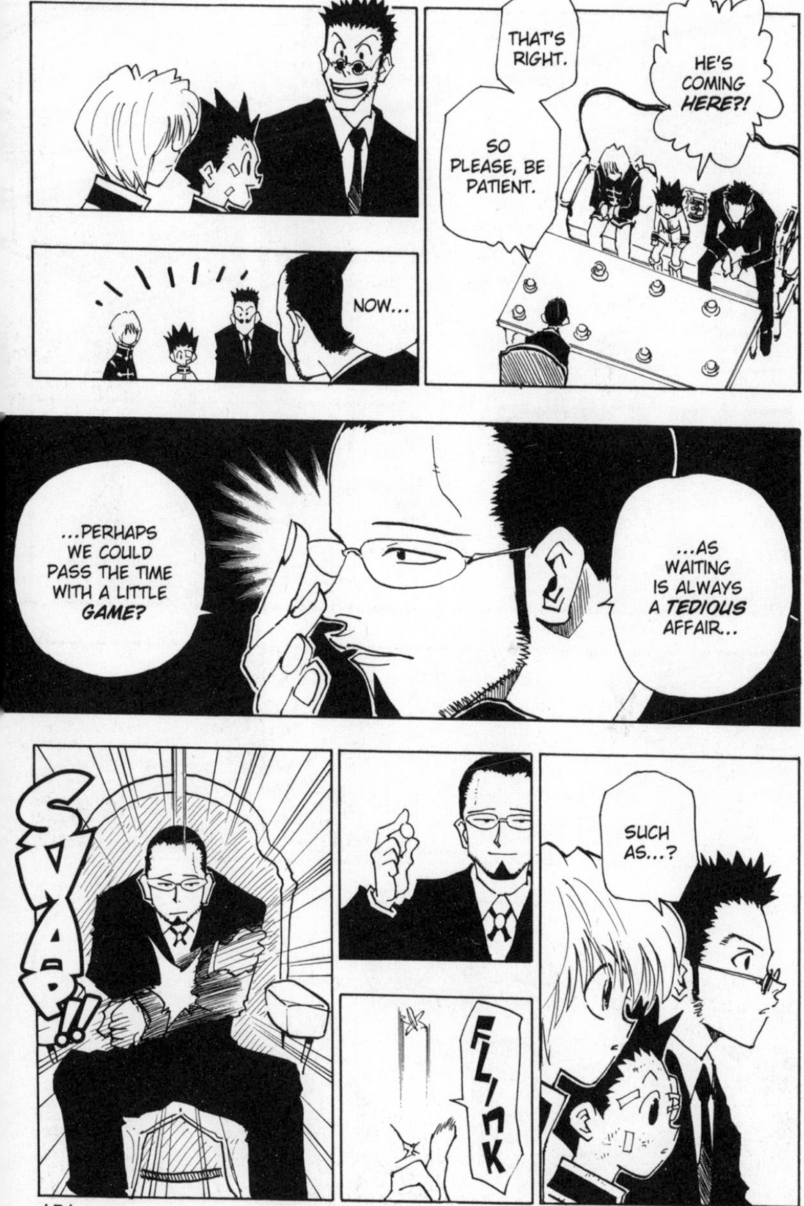
HE'S COMING HERE?!
THAT'S RIGHT.
SO PLEASE, BE PATIENT.
NOW...
...AS WAITING IS ALWAYS A TEDIOUS AFFAIR...
...PERHAPS WE COULD PASS THE TIME WITH A LITTLE GAME?
SUCH AS...?
FLINK
SNAP!!

LEFT HAND!

SO, WHERE'S THE COIN?

I'LL DO IT AGAIN... ONLY **FASTER!**

CORRECT.

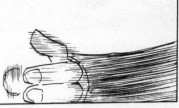
FLINK

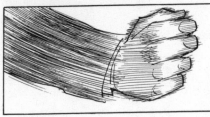

LEFT AGAIN!

AND NOW... WHERE?

SNAP!!

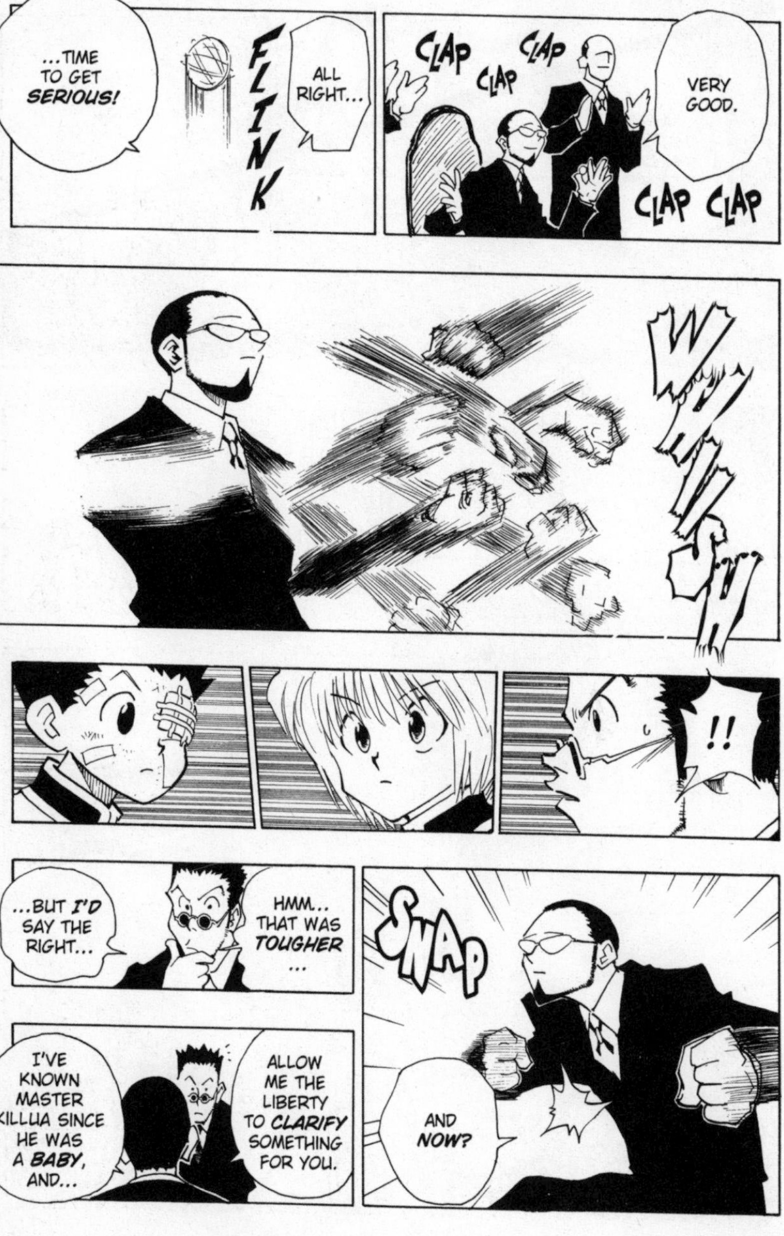
CLAP
CLAP
CLAP
VERY GOOD.
CLAP CLAP
ALL RIGHT...
FLINK
...TIME TO GET SERIOUS!
!!
SNAP
AND NOW?
HMM... THAT WAS TOUGHER ...
...BUT I'D SAY THE RIGHT...
ALLOW ME THE LIBERTY TO CLARIFY SOMETHING FOR YOU.
I'VE KNOWN MASTER KILLUA SINCE HE WAS A BABY, AND...

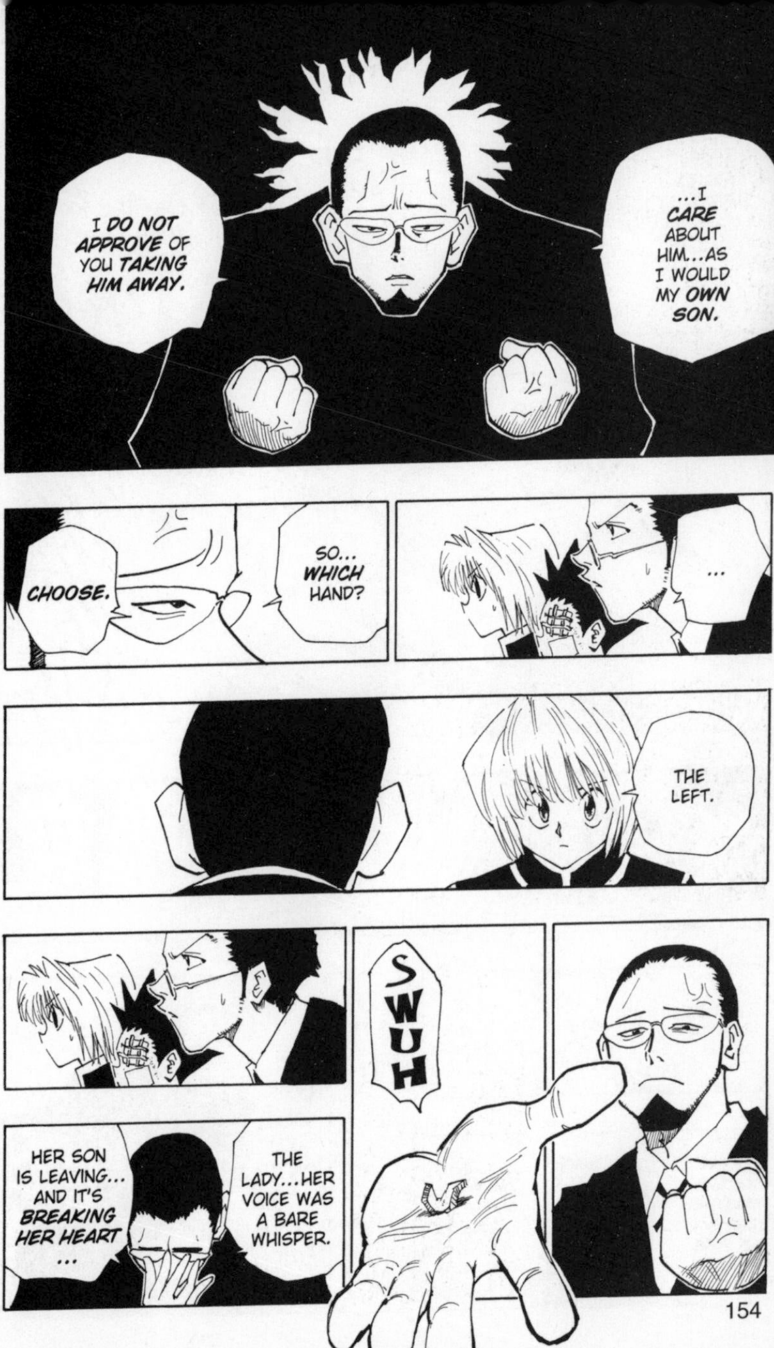

...I CARE ABOUT HIM...AS I WOULD MY OWN SON.
I DO NOT APPROVE OF YOU TAKING HIM AWAY.
...
SO... WHICH HAND?
CHOOSE.
THE LEFT.
SWUH
THE LADY...HER VOICE WAS A BARE WHISPER.
HER SON IS LEAVING... AND IT'S BREAKING HER HEART...

...ALL BECAUSE OF YOU.

...MASTER KILLUA GETS HERE. *MY* RULES. *NO* APPEALS.

I'LL GET THE MEASURE OF YOU MYSELF BEFORE...

SWP

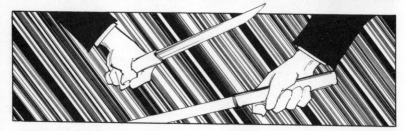

ONE MISTAKE, AND YOU'RE OUT.

IF YOU *ALL* GO OUT BEFORE MASTER KILLUA ARRIVES...

WG

SHING!!

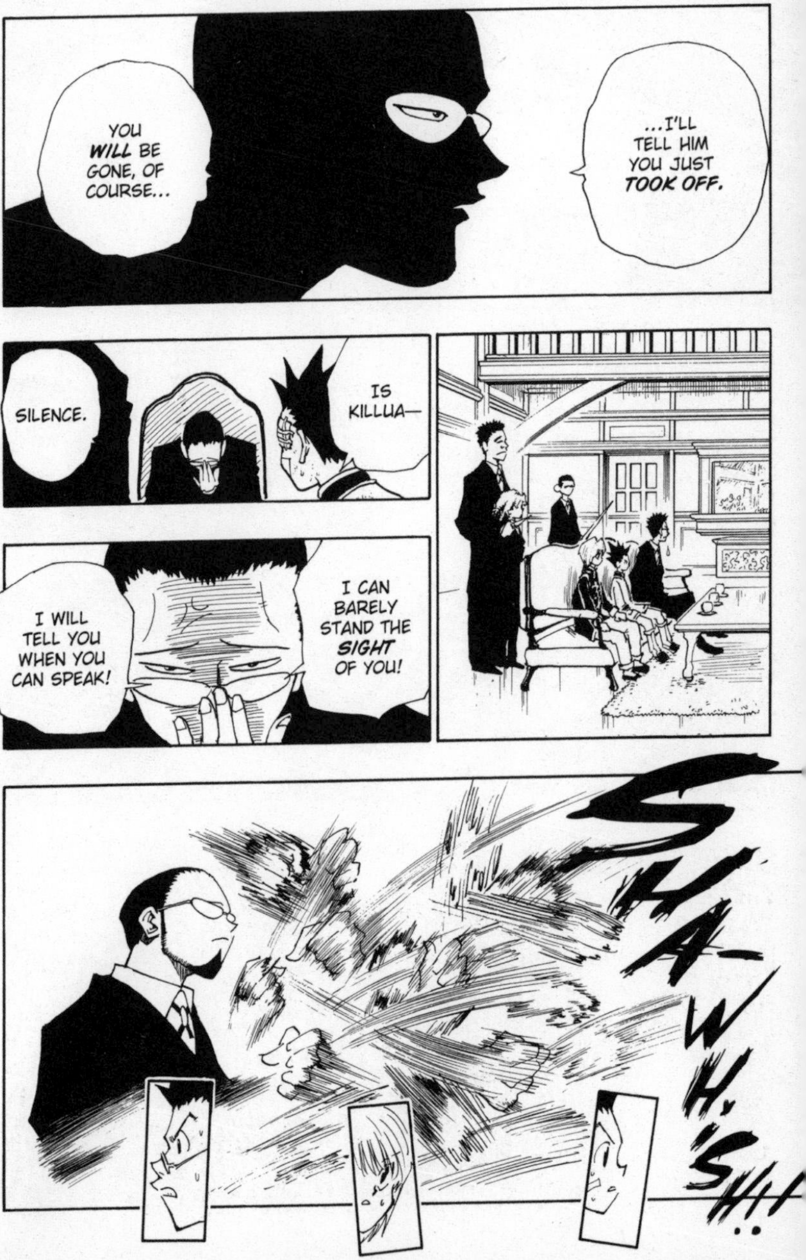
...I'LL TELL HIM YOU JUST TOOK OFF.
YOU WILL BE GONE, OF COURSE...
IS KILLUA—
SILENCE.
I CAN BARELY STAND THE SIGHT OF YOU!
I WILL TELL YOU WHEN YOU CAN SPEAK!
SHA-WHSSH!!

READ THIS WAY

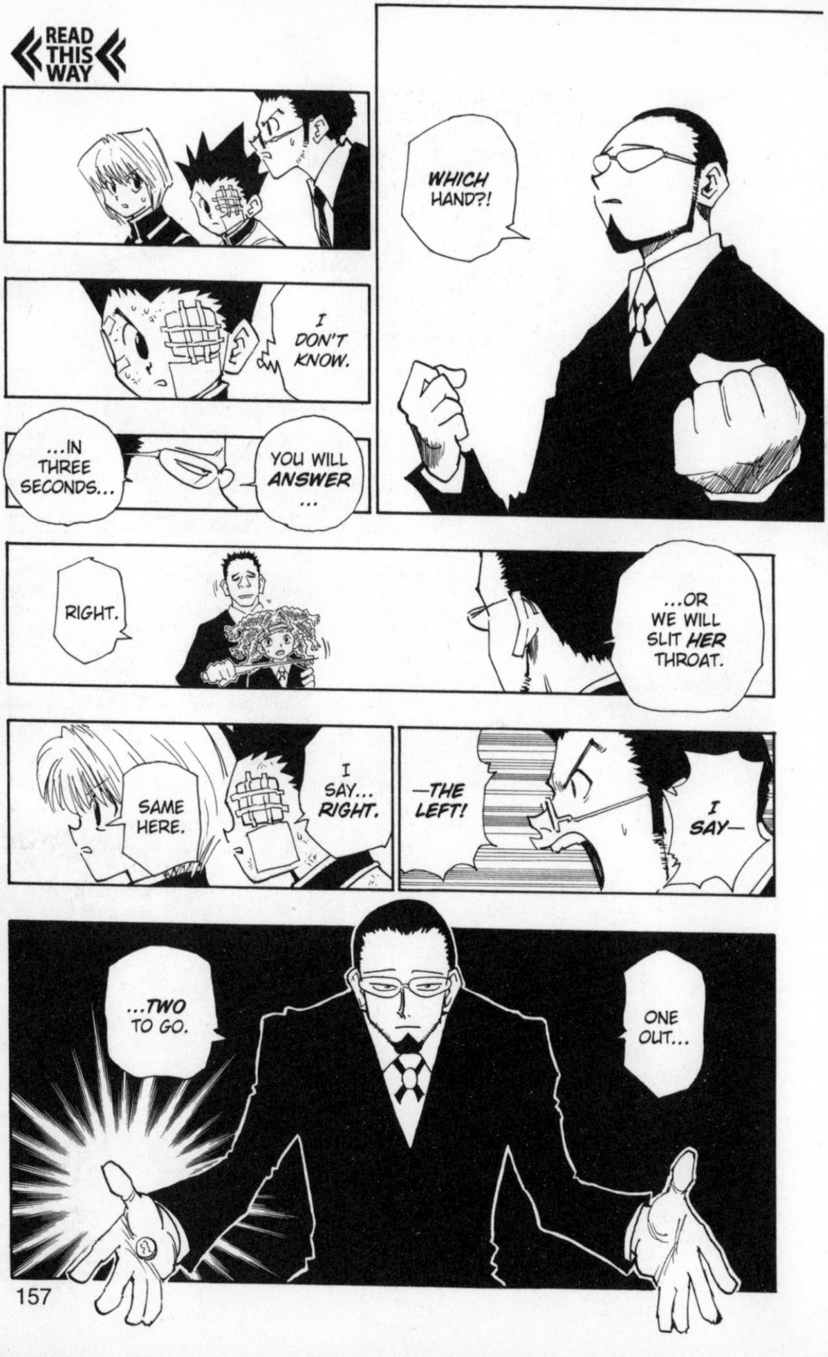
WHICH HAND?!
I DON'T KNOW.
YOU WILL ANSWER ...
...IN THREE SECONDS...
...OR WE WILL SLIT HER THROAT.
RIGHT.
I SAY—
—THE LEFT!
I SAY... RIGHT.
SAME HERE.
ONE OUT...
...TWO TO GO.

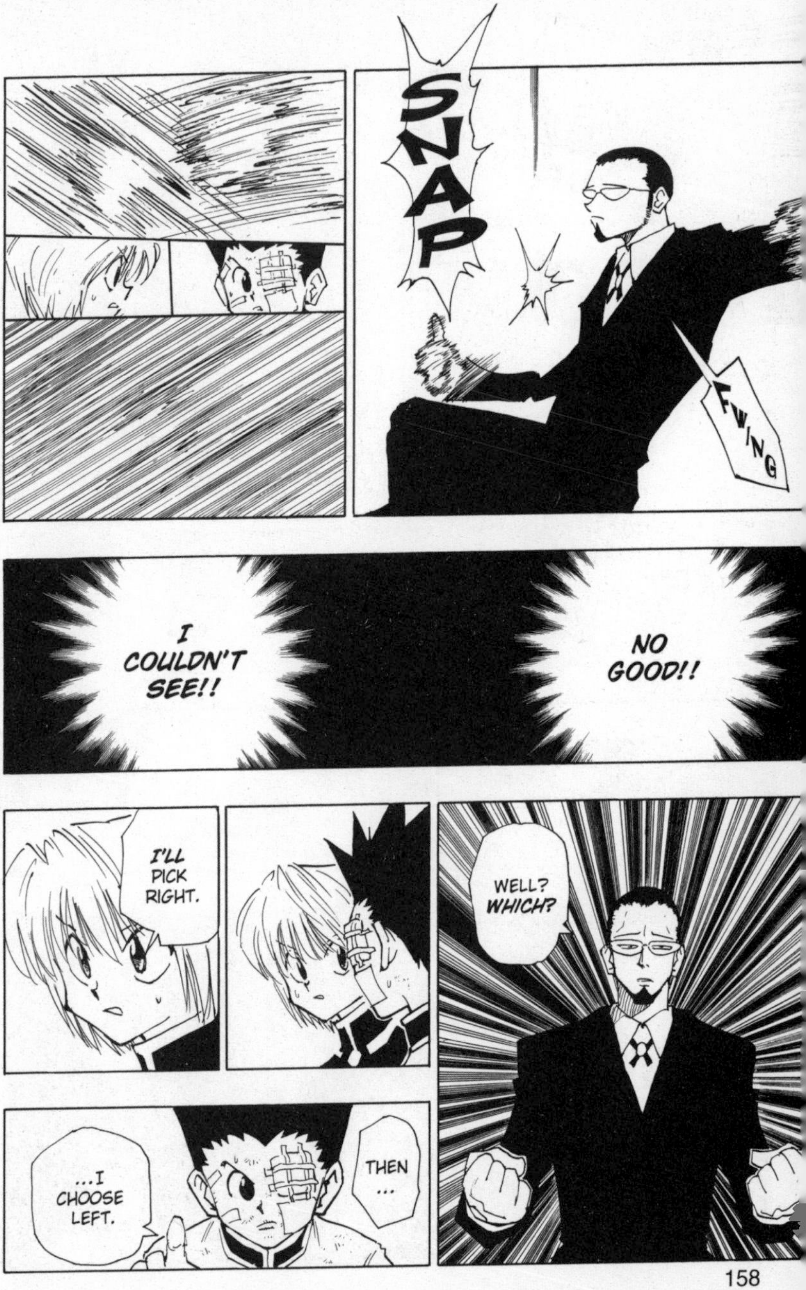
SNAP
FWING
NO GOOD!!
I COULDN'T SEE!!
WELL? WHICH?
I'LL PICK RIGHT.
THEN ...
...I CHOOSE LEFT.

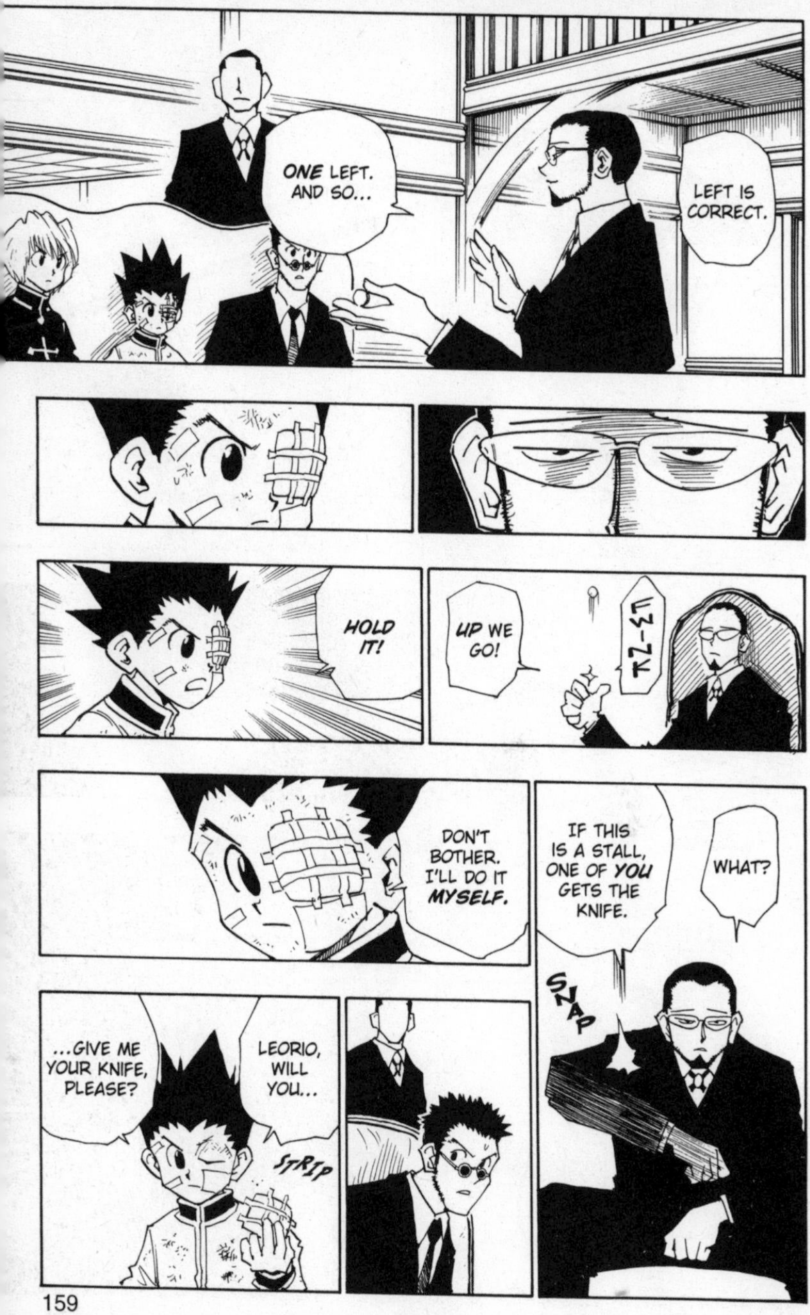
LEFT IS CORRECT.
ONE LEFT. AND SO...
UP WE GO!
HOLD IT!
WHAT?
IF THIS IS A STALL, ONE OF YOU GETS THE KNIFE.
SNAP
DON'T BOTHER. I'LL DO IT MYSELF.
LEORIO, WILL YOU...
...GIVE ME YOUR KNIFE, PLEASE?
STRIP

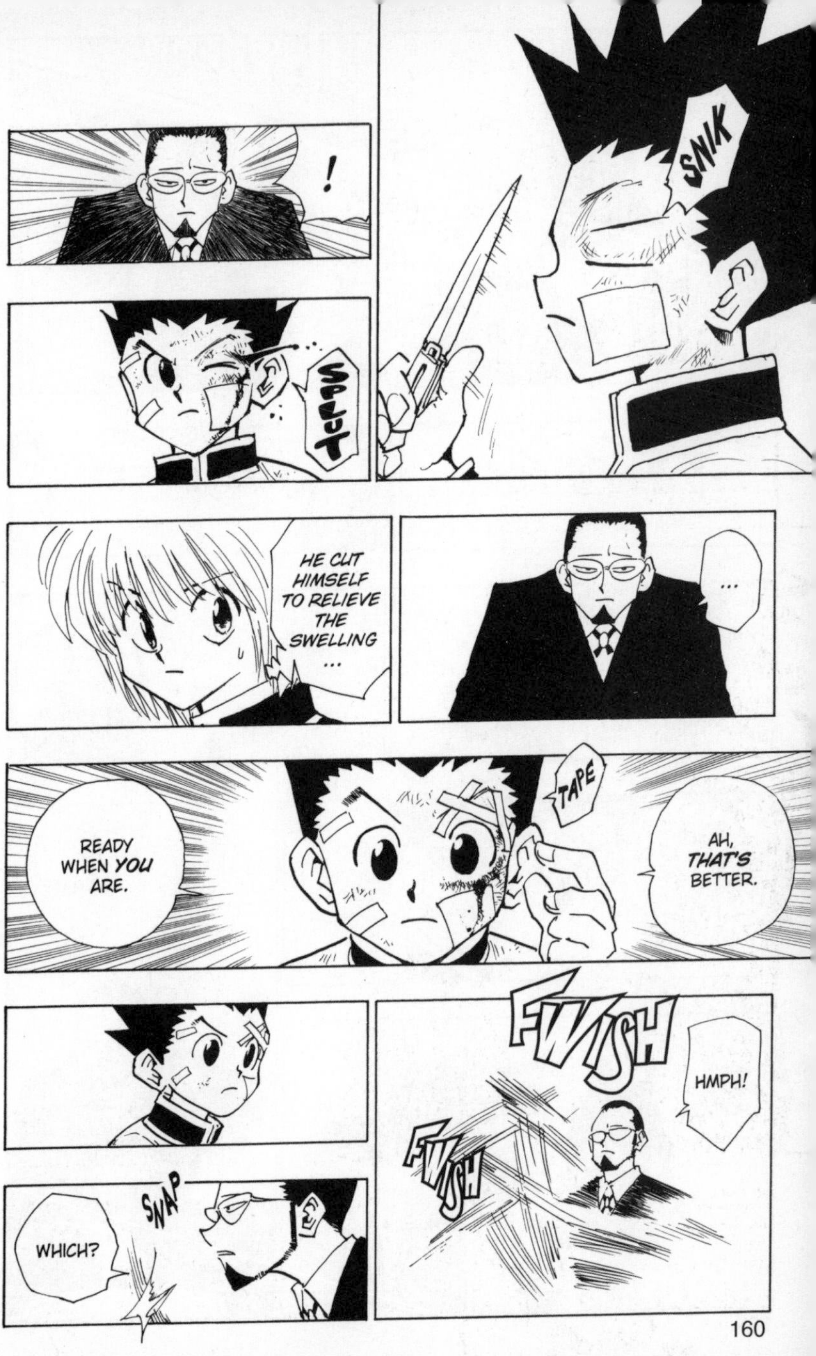
SNIK
!
SPLUT
...
HE CUT HIMSELF TO RELIEVE THE SWELLING ...
TAPE
AH, THAT'S BETTER.
READY WHEN YOU ARE.
FWISH
HMPH!
FWISH
SNAP
WHICH?

READ THIS WAY

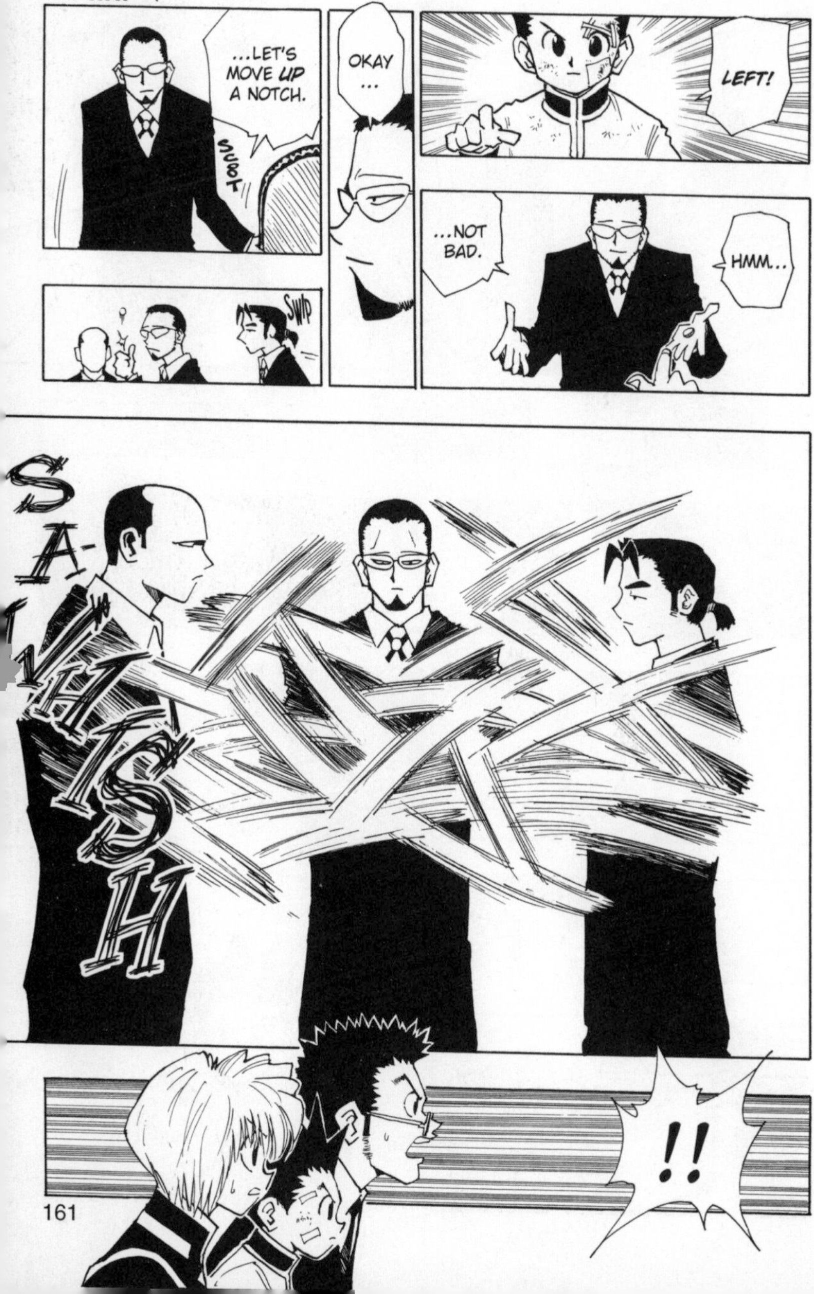
LEFT!
HMM...
...NOT BAD.
OKAY ...
...LET'S MOVE UP A NOTCH.
SCOOT
SWIP
SA-WHISH
!!

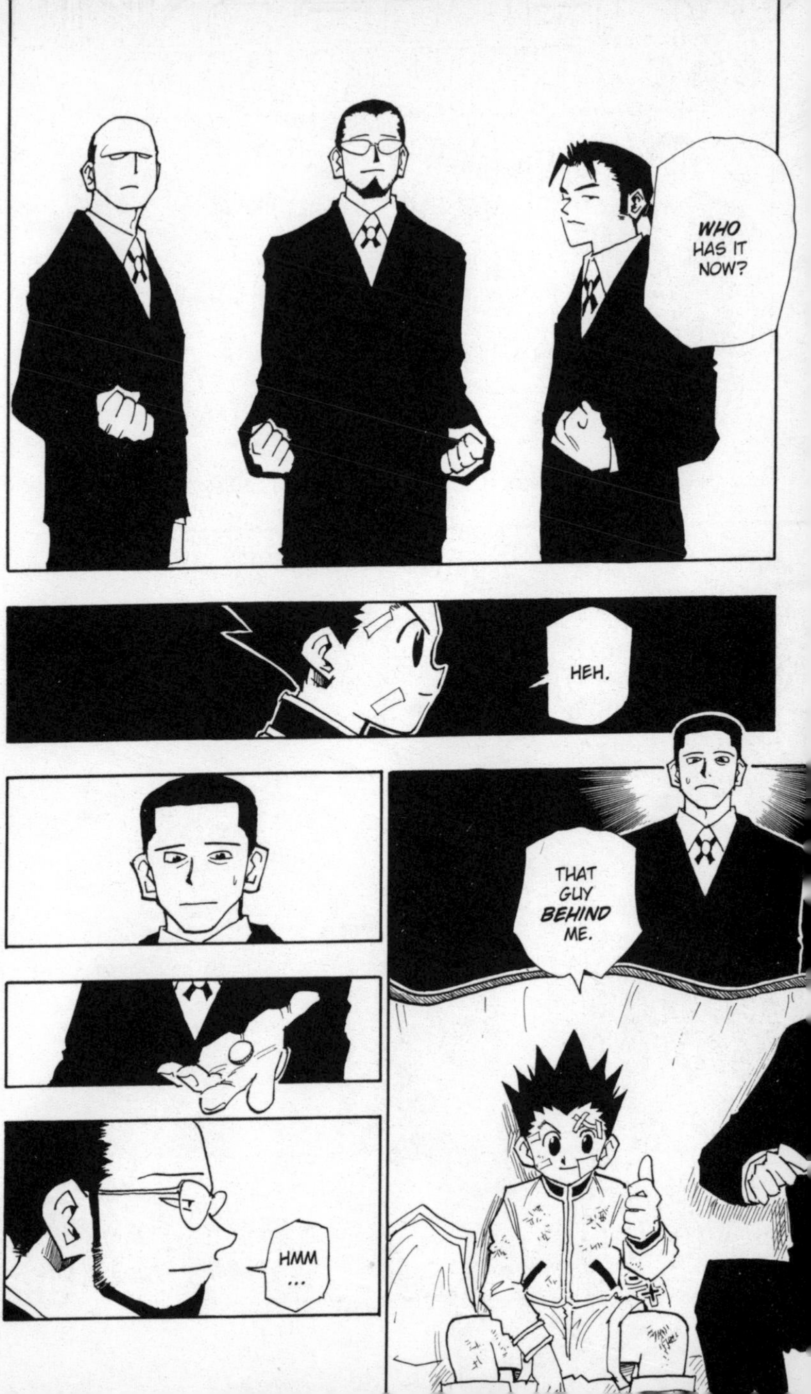
WHO HAS IT NOW?
HEH.
THAT GUY BEHIND ME.
HMM ...

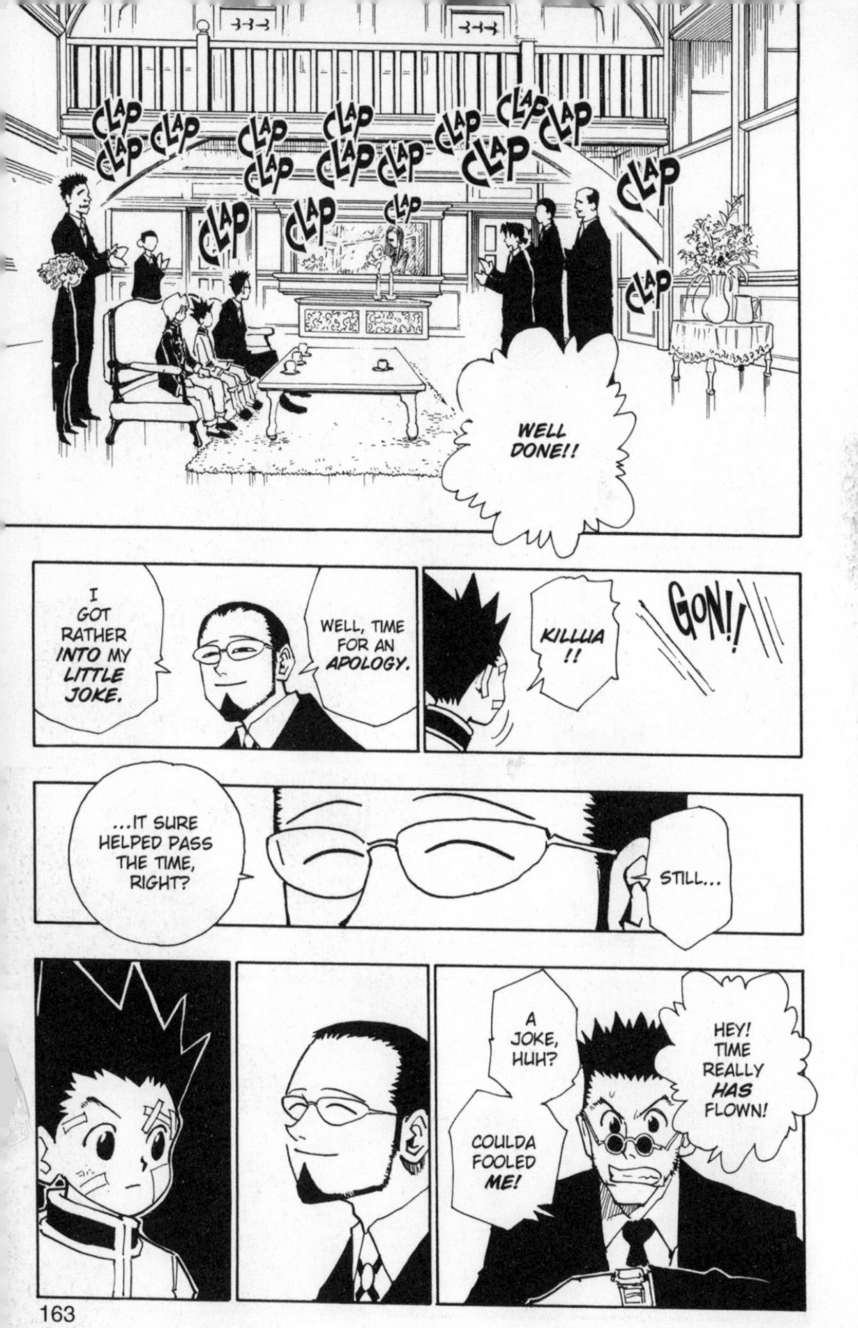
CLAP CLAP CLAP CLAP CLAP CLAP CLAP CLAP CLAP CLAP CLAP CLAP CLAP CLAP CLAP CLAP
WELL DONE!!
GON!!
KILLUA !!
WELL, TIME FOR AN *APOLOGY.*
I GOT RATHER *INTO MY LITTLE JOKE.*
STILL...
...IT SURE HELPED PASS THE TIME, RIGHT?
HEY! TIME REALLY *HAS* FLOWN!
A JOKE, HUH?
COULDA FOOLED *ME!*

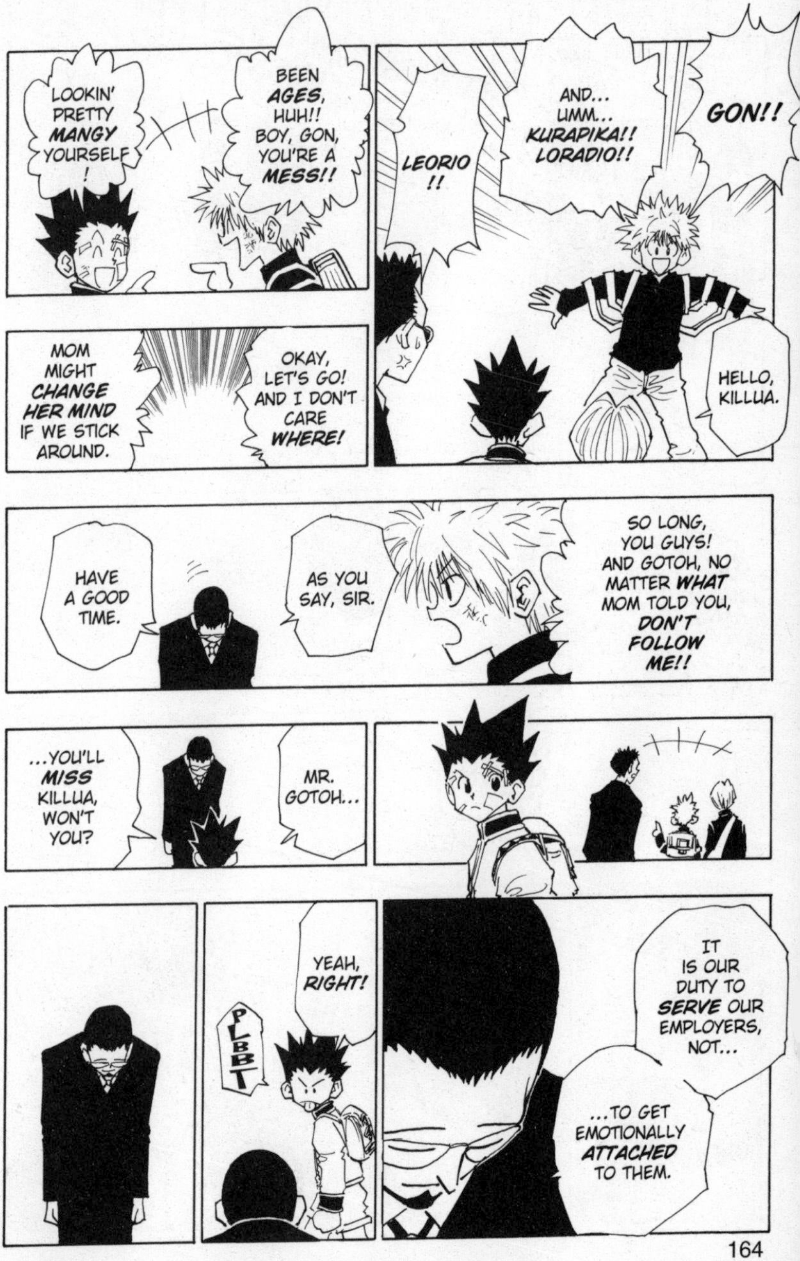
GON!!
AND... UMM... KURAPIKA!! LORADIO!!
LEORIO !!
HELLO, KILLUA.
BEEN AGES, HUH!! BOY, GON, YOU'RE A MESS!!
LOOKIN' PRETTY MANGY YOURSELF !
OKAY, LET'S GO! AND I DON'T CARE WHERE!
MOM MIGHT CHANGE HER MIND IF WE STICK AROUND.
SO LONG, YOU GUYS! AND GOTOH, NO MATTER WHAT MOM TOLD YOU, DON'T FOLLOW ME!!
AS YOU SAY, SIR.
HAVE A GOOD TIME.
MR. GOTOH...
...YOU'LL MISS KILLUA, WON'T YOU?
IT IS OUR DUTY TO SERVE OUR EMPLOYERS, NOT...
...TO GET EMOTIONALLY ATTACHED TO THEM.
YEAH, RIGHT!
PLBBT

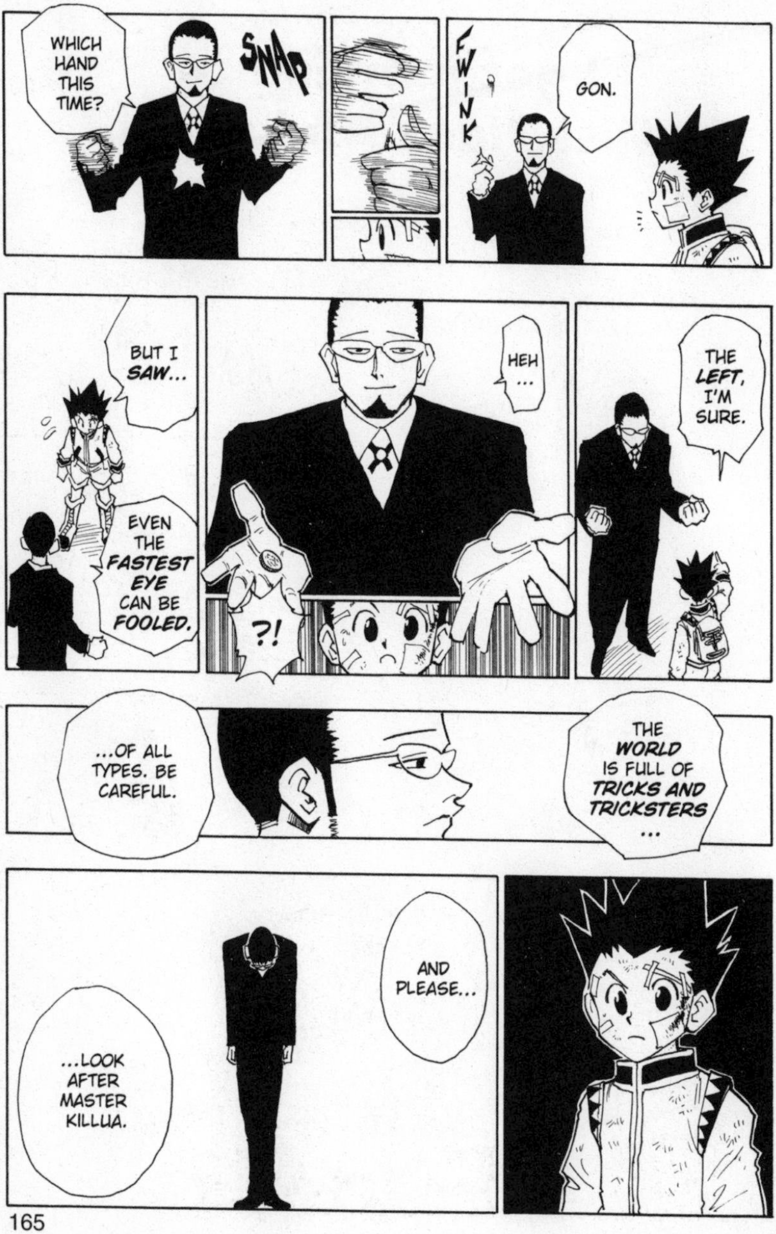
GON.
FWINK
WHICH HAND THIS TIME?
SNAP
THE LEFT, I'M SURE.
HEH ...
?!
BUT I SAW...
EVEN THE FASTEST EYE CAN BE FOOLED.
THE WORLD IS FULL OF TRICKS AND TRICKSTERS ...
...OF ALL TYPES. BE CAREFUL.
AND PLEASE...
...LOOK AFTER MASTER KILLUA.

I got married to Miss Naoko Takeuchi.

① THE PROPOSAL.

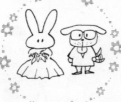

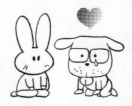

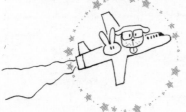

② PREPARING FOR THE WEDDING.

EXHAUSTED...

③ THE WEDDING AND THE RECEPTION.

④ THE HONEYMOON.

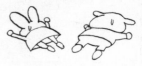

⑤ NOW WE WORK SIDE BY SIDE.

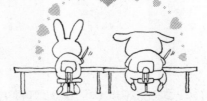

THANKS FOR ALL THE LETTERS WISHING US THE BEST!!

(PLEASE SEND US MORE.)

Chapter 44
The Heavens Arena

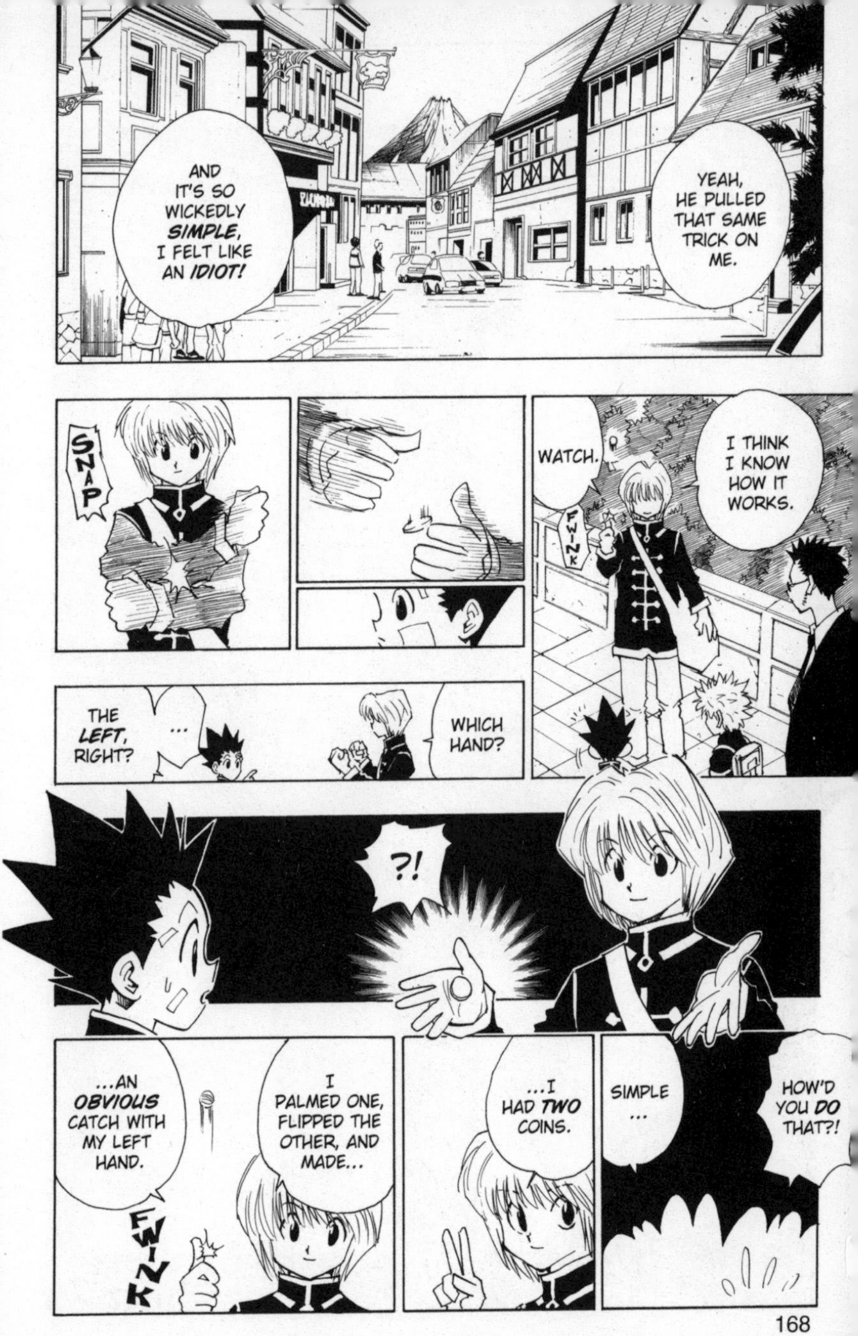
YEAH, HE PULLED THAT SAME TRICK ON ME.
AND IT'S SO WICKEDLY *SIMPLE*, I FELT LIKE AN *IDIOT!*
I THINK I KNOW HOW IT WORKS.
WATCH.
FWINK
SNAP
WHICH HAND?
...
THE *LEFT*, RIGHT?
?!
HOW'D YOU *DO* THAT?!
SIMPLE ...
...I HAD *TWO* COINS.
I PALMED ONE, FLIPPED THE OTHER, AND MADE...
...AN *OBVIOUS* CATCH WITH MY LEFT HAND.
FWINK

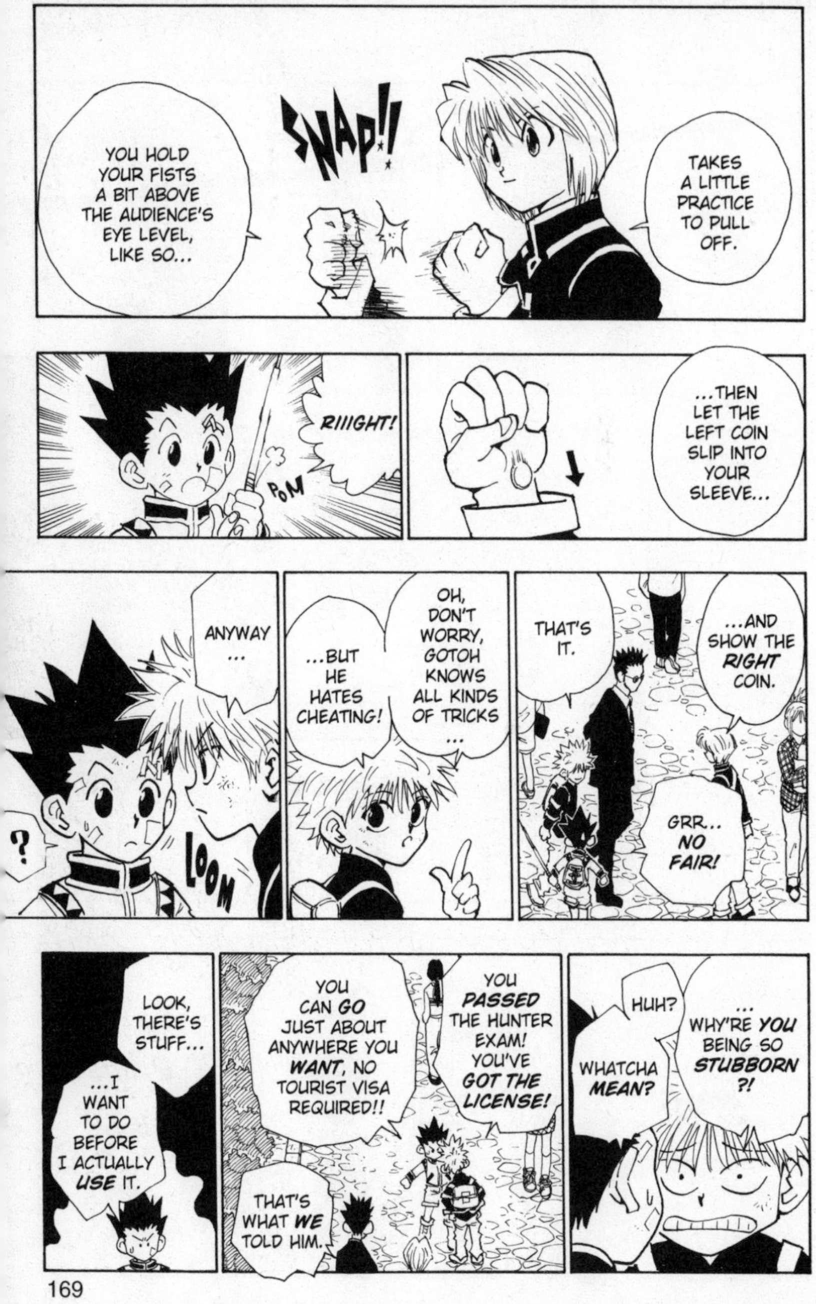
TAKES A LITTLE PRACTICE TO PULL OFF.
SNAP!!
YOU HOLD YOUR FISTS A BIT ABOVE THE AUDIENCE'S EYE LEVEL, LIKE SO...
...THEN LET THE LEFT COIN SLIP INTO YOUR SLEEVE...
RIIIGHT!
POM
...AND SHOW THE RIGHT COIN.
THAT'S IT.
GRR... NO FAIR!
OH, DON'T WORRY, GOTOH KNOWS ALL KINDS OF TRICKS...
...BUT HE HATES CHEATING!
ANYWAY...
LOOM
?
...WHY'RE YOU BEING SO STUBBORN?!
HUH?
WHATCHA MEAN?
YOU PASSED THE HUNTER EXAM! YOU'VE GOT THE LICENSE!
YOU CAN GO JUST ABOUT ANYWHERE YOU WANT, NO TOURIST VISA REQUIRED!!
THAT'S WHAT WE TOLD HIM.
LOOK, THERE'S STUFF...
...I WANT TO DO BEFORE I ACTUALLY USE IT.

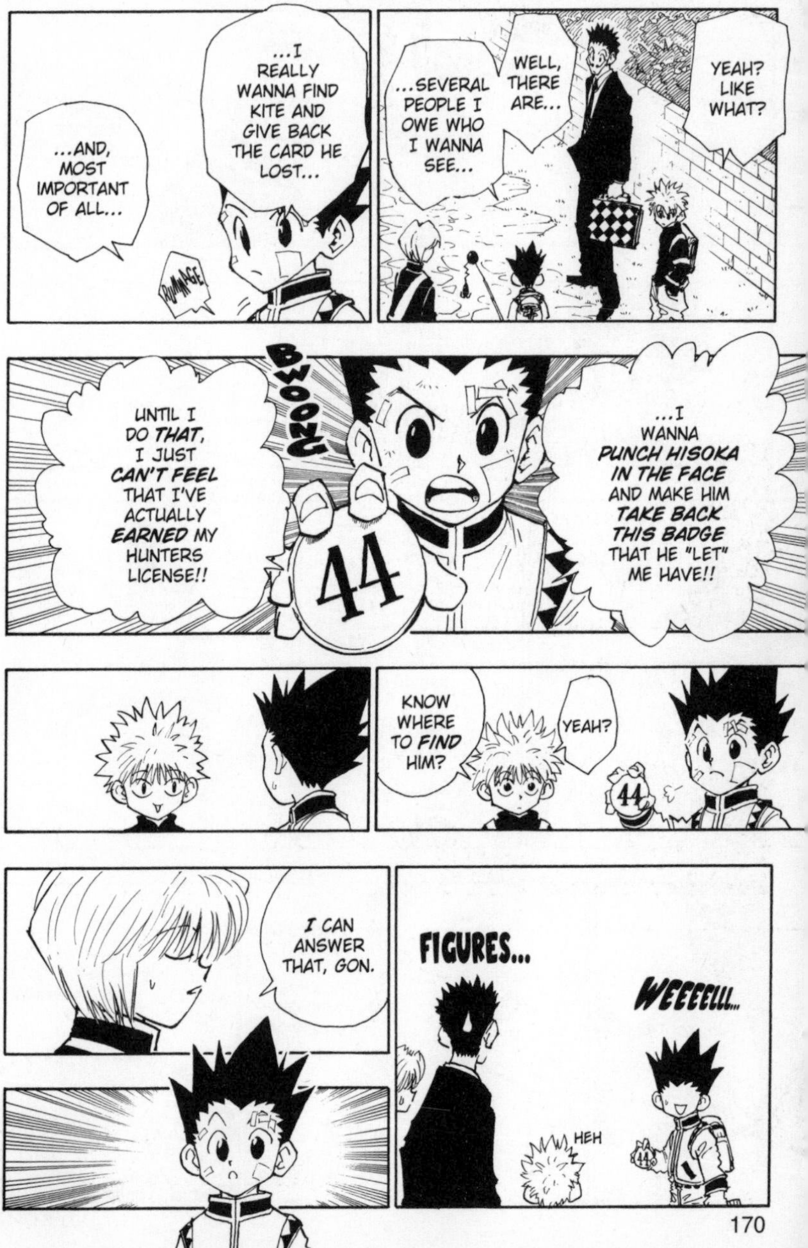
YEAH? LIKE WHAT?
WELL, THERE ARE...
...SEVERAL PEOPLE I OWE WHO I WANNA SEE...
...I REALLY WANNA FIND KITE AND GIVE BACK THE CARD HE LOST...
RUMMAGE
...AND, MOST IMPORTANT OF ALL...
...I WANNA PUNCH HISOKA IN THE FACE AND MAKE HIM TAKE BACK THIS BADGE THAT HE "LET" ME HAVE!!
BWOONG
44
UNTIL I DO THAT, I JUST CAN'T FEEL THAT I'VE ACTUALLY EARNED MY HUNTERS LICENSE!!
YEAH?
KNOW WHERE TO FIND HIM?
WEEEELLL...
FIGURES...
HEH
I CAN ANSWER THAT, GON.

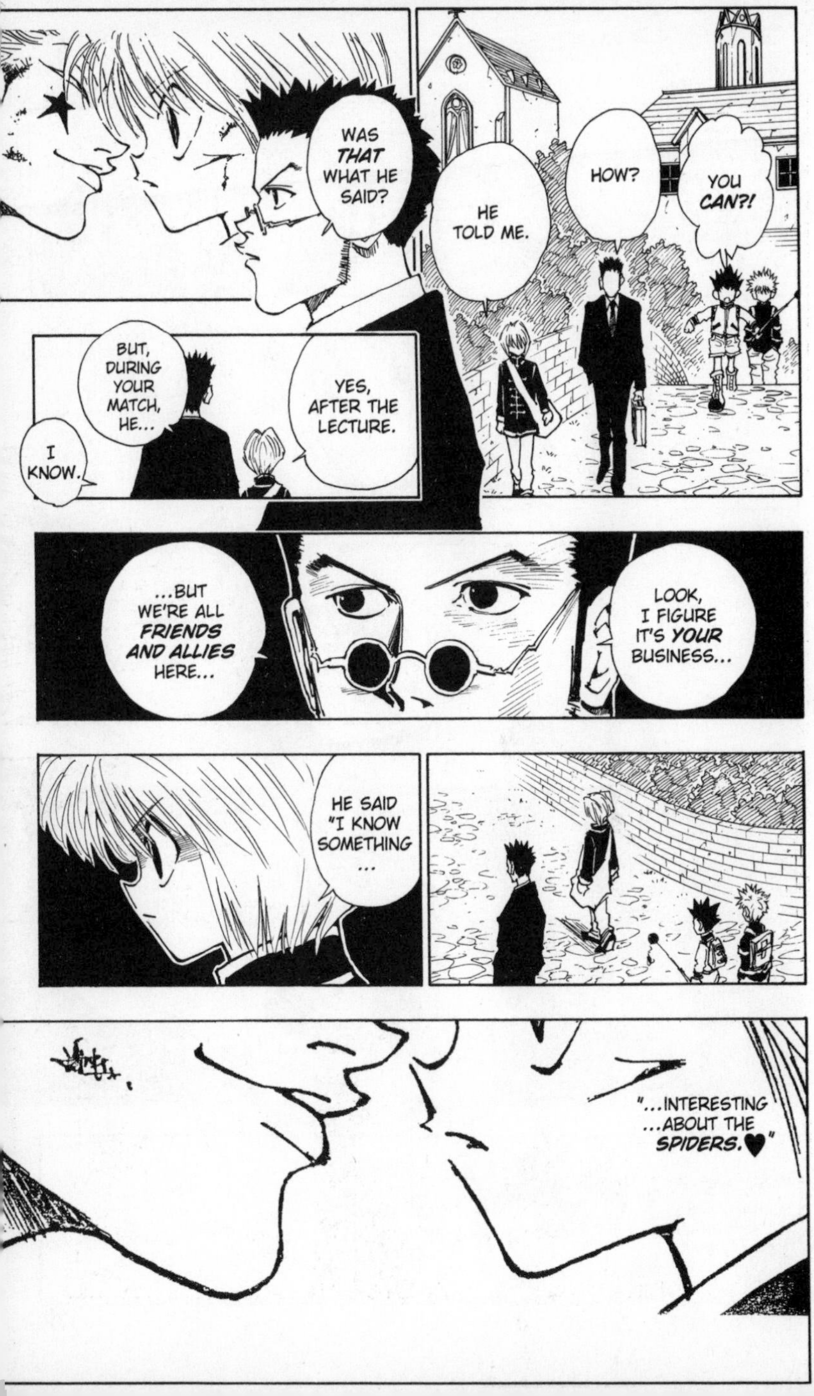
YOU CAN?!
HOW?
HE TOLD ME.
WAS THAT WHAT HE SAID?
YES, AFTER THE LECTURE.
BUT, DURING YOUR MATCH, HE...
I KNOW.
LOOK, I FIGURE IT'S YOUR BUSINESS...
...BUT WE'RE ALL FRIENDS AND ALLIES HERE...
HE SAID "I KNOW SOMETHING ...
"...INTERESTING ...ABOUT THE SPIDERS.♥"

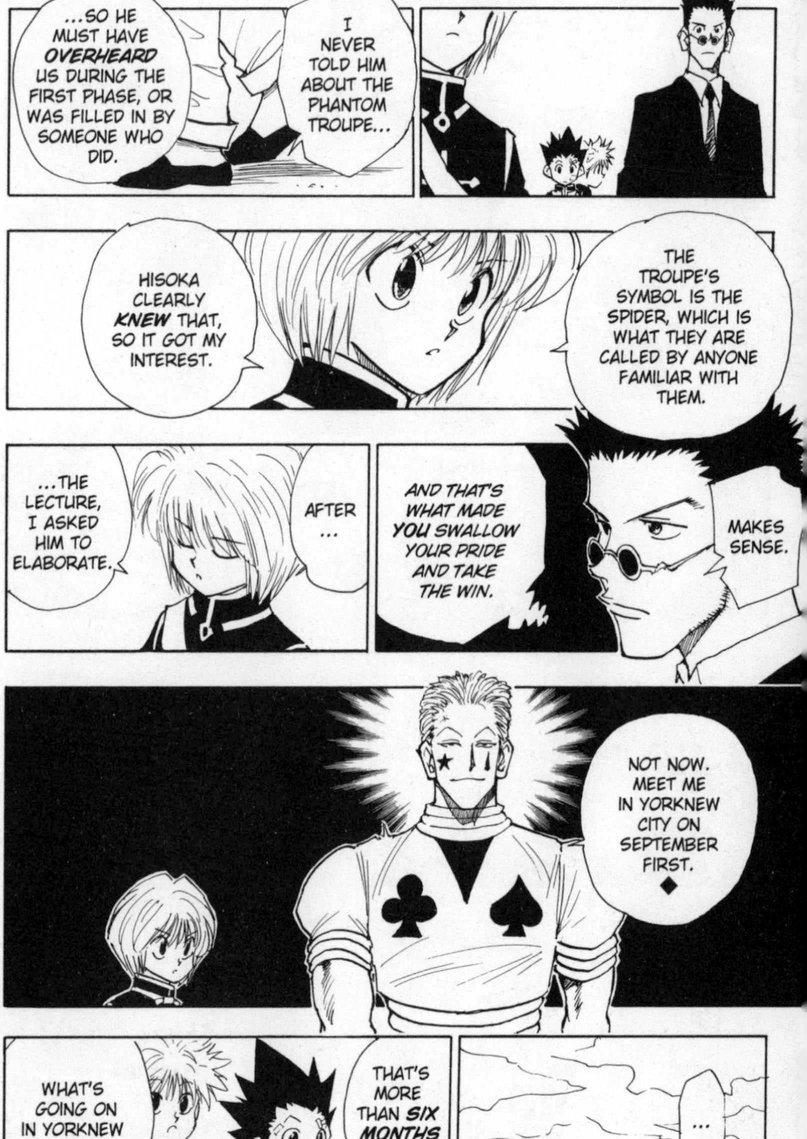
I NEVER TOLD HIM ABOUT THE PHANTOM TROUPE...
...SO HE MUST HAVE OVERHEARD US DURING THE FIRST PHASE, OR WAS FILLED IN BY SOMEONE WHO DID.
THE TROUPE'S SYMBOL IS THE SPIDER, WHICH IS WHAT THEY ARE CALLED BY ANYONE FAMILIAR WITH THEM.
HISOKA CLEARLY KNEW THAT, SO IT GOT MY INTEREST.
MAKES SENSE.
AND THAT'S WHAT MADE YOU SWALLOW YOUR PRIDE AND TAKE THE WIN.
AFTER ...
...THE LECTURE, I ASKED HIM TO ELABORATE.
NOT NOW. MEET ME IN YORKNEW CITY ON SEPTEMBER FIRST. ◆
...
THAT'S MORE THAN SIX MONTHS AWAY.
WHAT'S GOING ON IN YORKNEW CITY THEN?

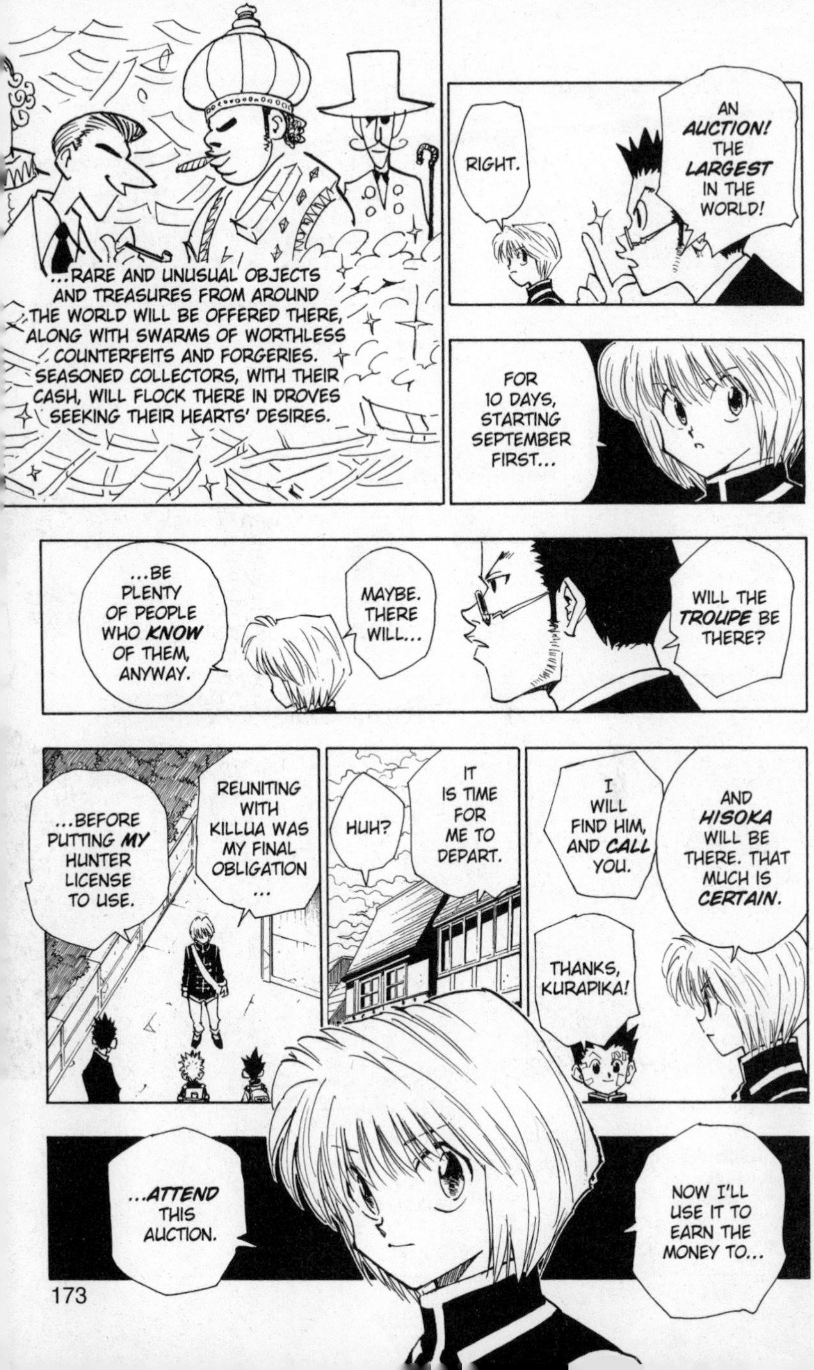
AN *AUCTION!* THE *LARGEST* IN THE WORLD!
RIGHT.
FOR 10 DAYS, STARTING SEPTEMBER FIRST...
...RARE AND UNUSUAL OBJECTS AND TREASURES FROM AROUND THE WORLD WILL BE OFFERED THERE, ALONG WITH SWARMS OF WORTHLESS COUNTERFEITS AND FORGERIES. SEASONED COLLECTORS, WITH THEIR CASH, WILL FLOCK THERE IN DROVES SEEKING THEIR HEARTS' DESIRES.
WILL THE *TROUPE* BE THERE?
MAYBE. THERE WILL...
...BE PLENTY OF PEOPLE WHO *KNOW* OF THEM, ANYWAY.
AND *HISOKA* WILL BE THERE. THAT MUCH IS *CERTAIN*.
I WILL FIND HIM, AND *CALL* YOU.
THANKS, KURAPIKA!
IT IS TIME FOR ME TO DEPART.
HUH?
REUNITING WITH KILLUA WAS MY FINAL OBLIGATION...
...BEFORE PUTTING *MY* HUNTER LICENSE TO USE.
NOW I'LL USE IT TO EARN THE MONEY TO...
...*ATTEND* THIS AUCTION.

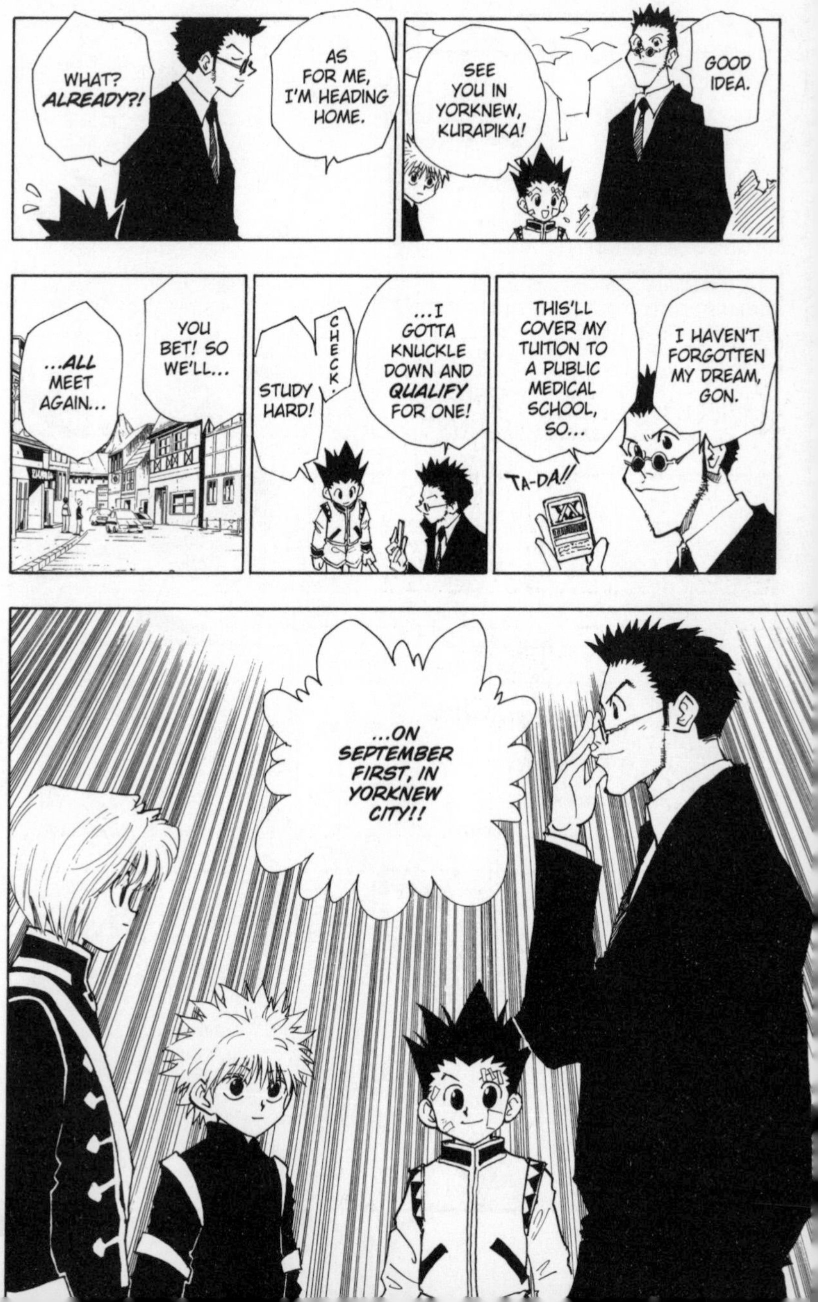
GOOD IDEA.
SEE YOU IN YORKNEW, KURAPIKA!
AS FOR ME, I'M HEADING HOME.
WHAT? ALREADY?!
I HAVEN'T FORGOTTEN MY DREAM, GON.
THIS'LL COVER MY TUITION TO A PUBLIC MEDICAL SCHOOL, SO...
TA-DA!!
...I GOTTA KNUCKLE DOWN AND QUALIFY FOR ONE!
CHECK.
STUDY HARD!
YOU BET! SO WE'LL...
...ALL MEET AGAIN...
...ON SEPTEMBER FIRST, IN YORKNEW CITY!!

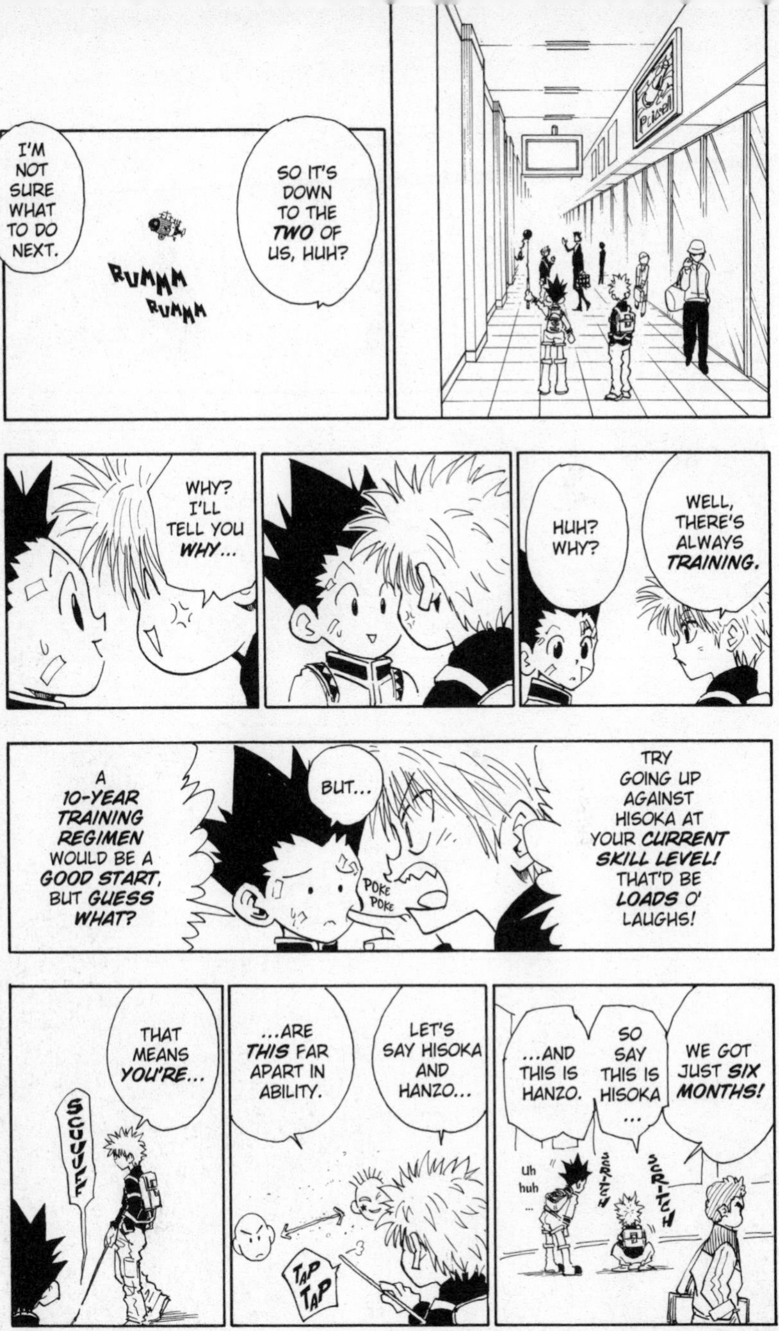
SO IT'S DOWN TO THE TWO OF US, HUH?
I'M NOT SURE WHAT TO DO NEXT.
RUMMM RUMMM
WELL, THERE'S ALWAYS TRAINING.
HUH? WHY?
WHY? I'LL TELL YOU WHY...
TRY GOING UP AGAINST HISOKA AT YOUR CURRENT SKILL LEVEL! THAT'D BE LOADS O' LAUGHS!
BUT...
POKE POKE
A 10-YEAR TRAINING REGIMEN WOULD BE A GOOD START, BUT GUESS WHAT?
WE GOT JUST SIX MONTHS!
SO SAY THIS IS HISOKA ...
...AND THIS IS HANZO.
SCRITCH
SCRITCH
Uh huh ...
LET'S SAY HISOKA AND HANZO...
...ARE THIS FAR APART IN ABILITY.
TAP TAP
THAT MEANS YOU'RE...
SCUUUFF

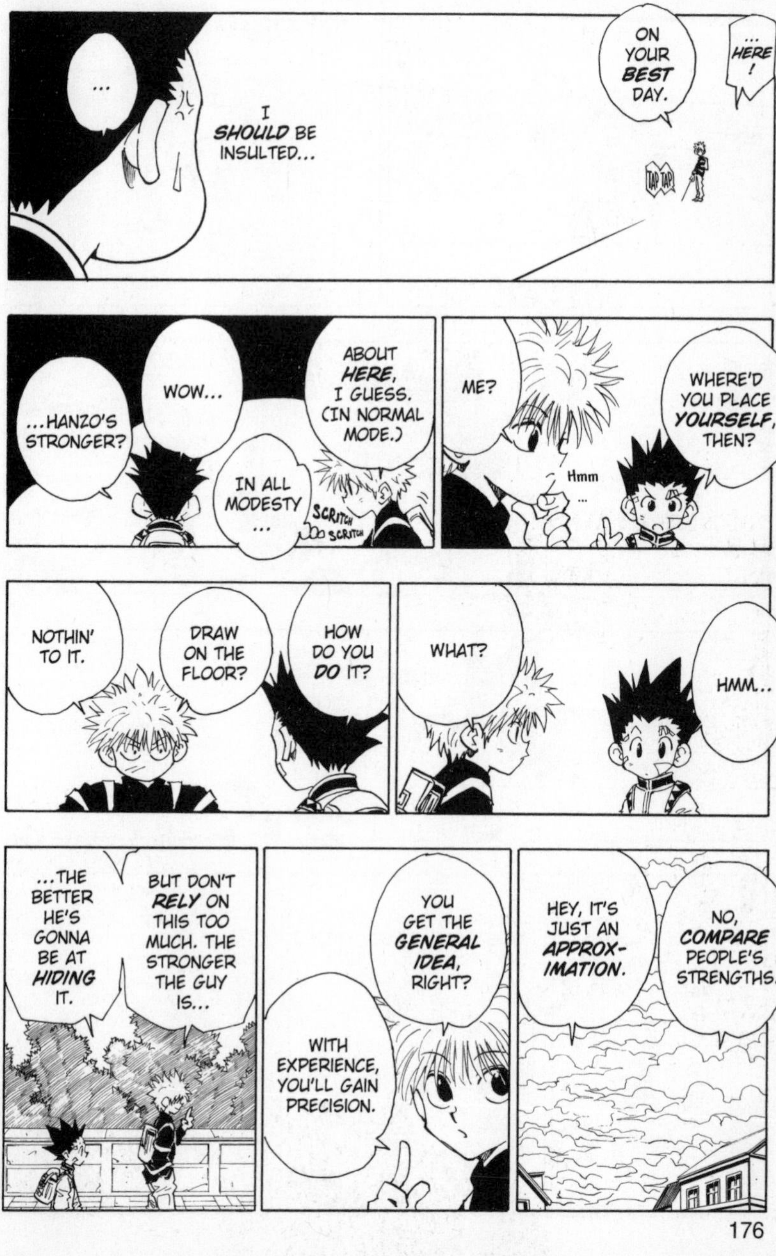
...HERE!
ON YOUR BEST DAY.
TAP TAP
I SHOULD BE INSULTED...
...
WHERE'D YOU PLACE YOURSELF, THEN?
ME?
Hmm ...
ABOUT HERE, I GUESS. (IN NORMAL MODE.)
IN ALL MODESTY ...
SCRITCH SCRITCH
WOW...
...HANZO'S STRONGER?
HMM...
WHAT?
HOW DO YOU DO IT?
DRAW ON THE FLOOR?
NOTHIN' TO IT.
NO, COMPARE PEOPLE'S STRENGTHS.
HEY, IT'S JUST AN APPROXIMATION.
YOU GET THE GENERAL IDEA, RIGHT?
WITH EXPERIENCE, YOU'LL GAIN PRECISION.
BUT DON'T RELY ON THIS TOO MUCH. THE STRONGER THE GUY IS...
...THE BETTER HE'S GONNA BE AT HIDING IT.

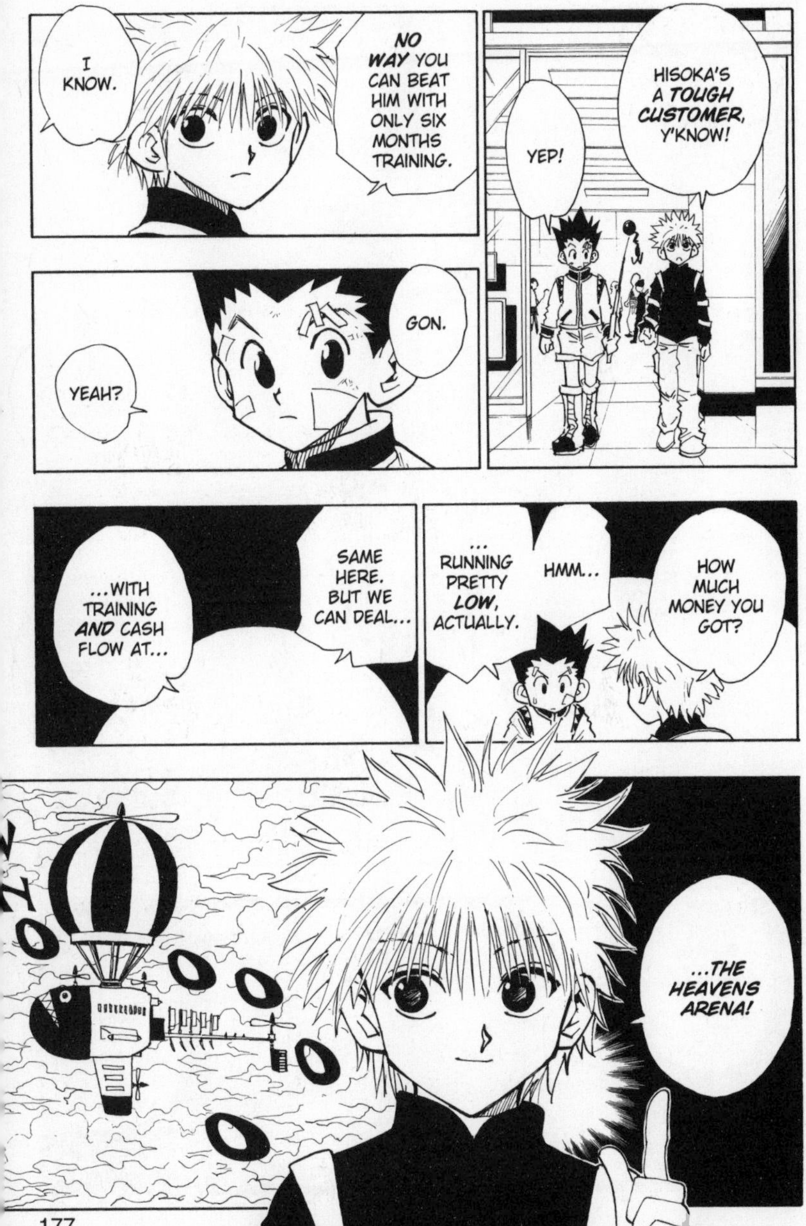
HISOKA'S A TOUGH CUSTOMER, Y'KNOW!
YEP!
NO WAY YOU CAN BEAT HIM WITH ONLY SIX MONTHS TRAINING.
I KNOW.
GON.
YEAH?
HOW MUCH MONEY YOU GOT?
HMM...
... RUNNING PRETTY LOW, ACTUALLY.
SAME HERE. BUT WE CAN DEAL...
...WITH TRAINING AND CASH FLOW AT...
...THE HEAVENS ARENA!

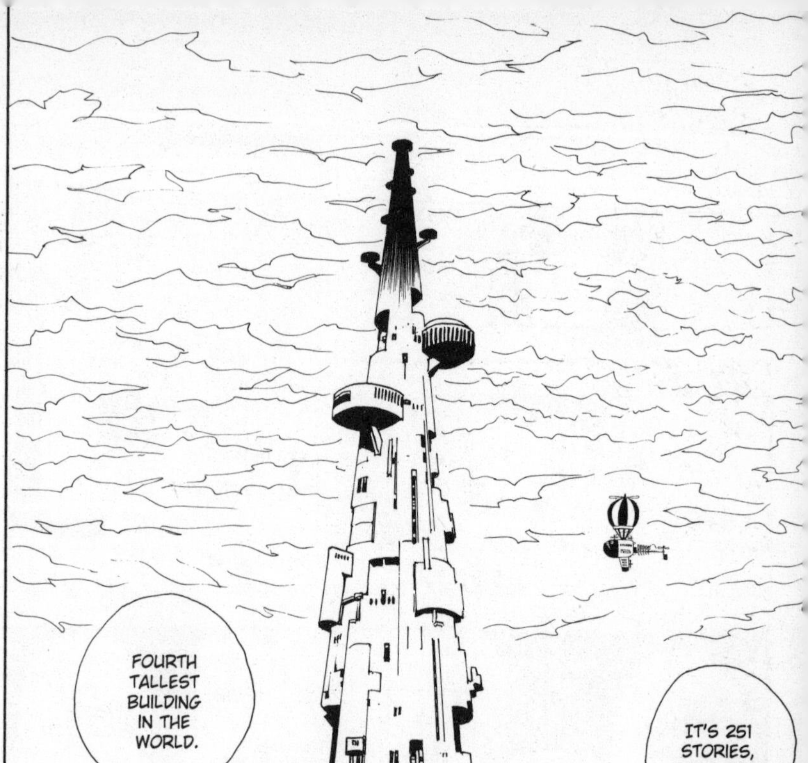
IT'S 251 STORIES, 3250 FEET TALL.
FOURTH TALLEST BUILDING IN THE WORLD.

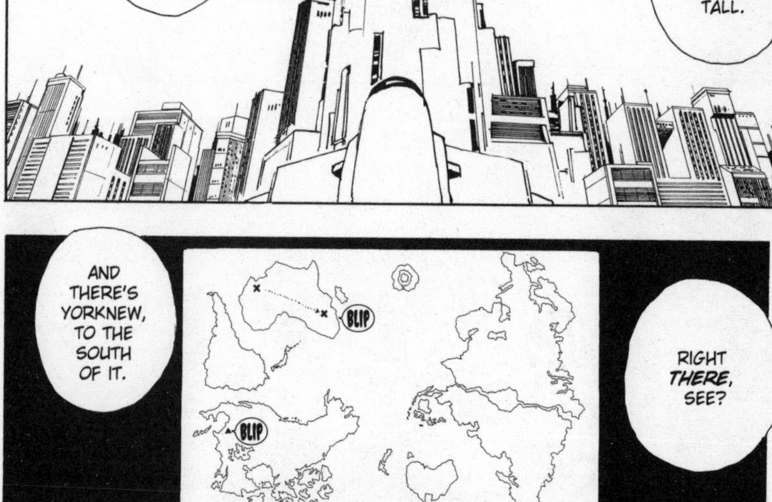
RIGHT *THERE,* SEE?
BLIP
BLIP
AND THERE'S YORKNEW, TO THE SOUTH OF IT.

READ THIS WAY

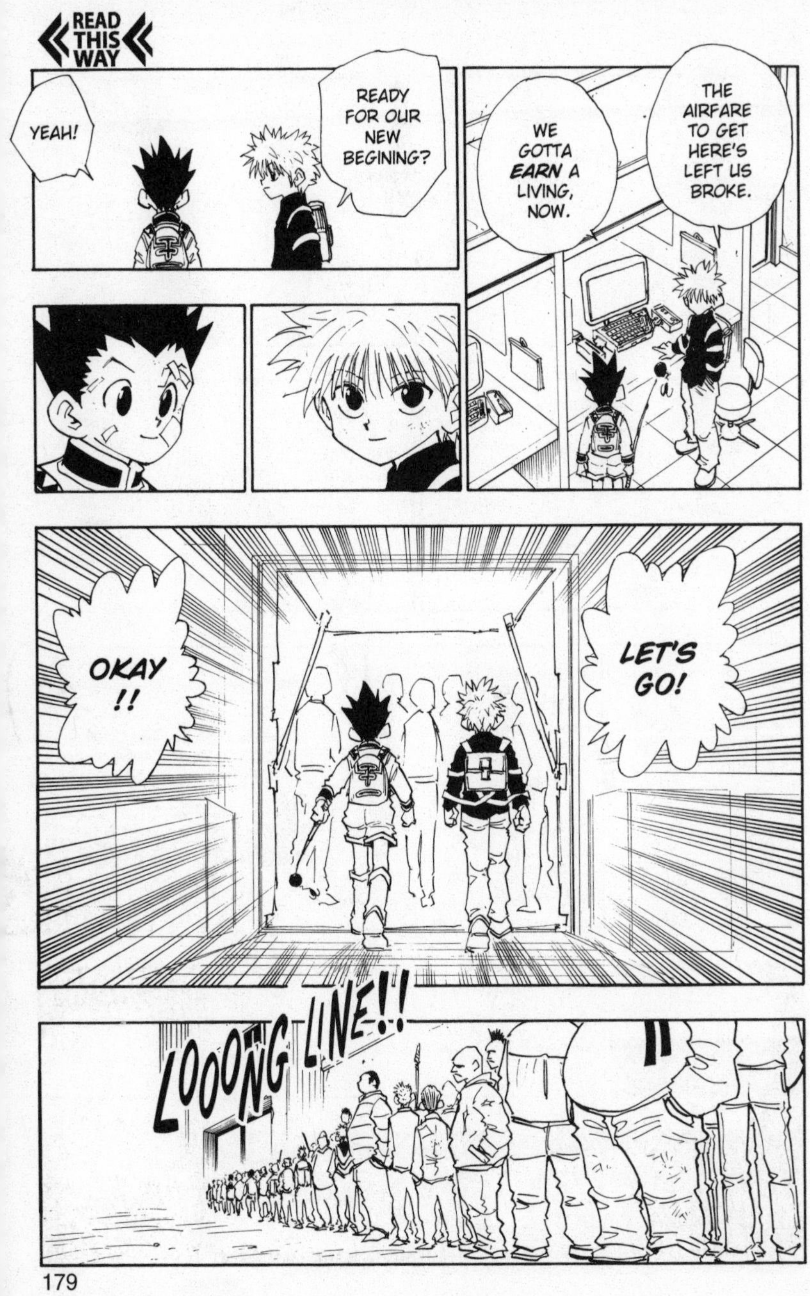
THE AIRFARE TO GET HERE'S LEFT US BROKE.
WE GOTTA EARN A LIVING, NOW.
READY FOR OUR NEW BEGINING?
YEAH!
LET'S GO!
OKAY !!
LOOONG LINE!!

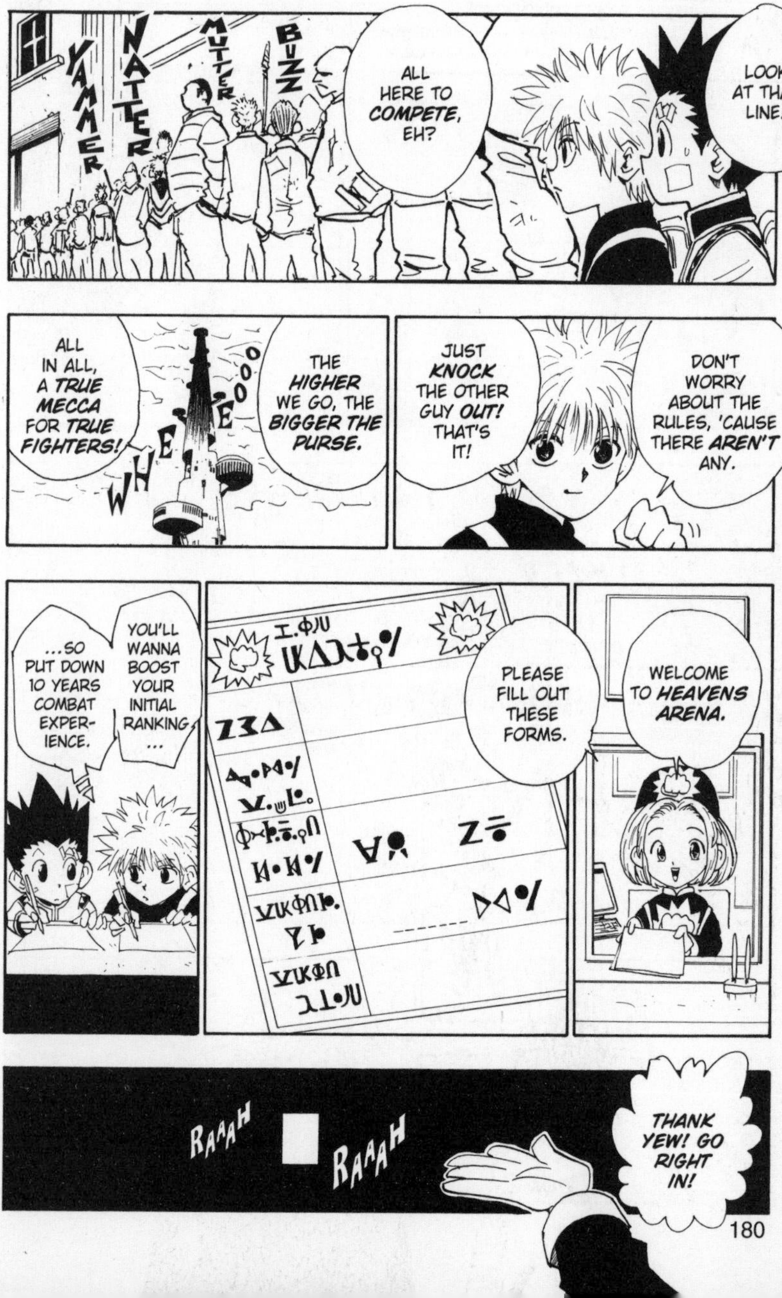
LOOK AT THAT LINE!
ALL HERE TO COMPETE, EH?
BUZZ
MUTTER
NATTER
YAMMER
DON'T WORRY ABOUT THE RULES, 'CAUSE THERE AREN'T ANY.
JUST KNOCK THE OTHER GUY OUT! THAT'S IT!
THE HIGHER WE GO, THE BIGGER THE PURSE.
ALL IN ALL, A TRUE MECCA FOR TRUE FIGHTERS!
WHEEOOO
WELCOME TO HEAVENS ARENA.
PLEASE FILL OUT THESE FORMS.
YOU'LL WANNA BOOST YOUR INITIAL RANKING...
...SO PUT DOWN 10 YEARS COMBAT EXPERIENCE.
THANK YEW! GO RIGHT IN!
RAAAH
RAAAH

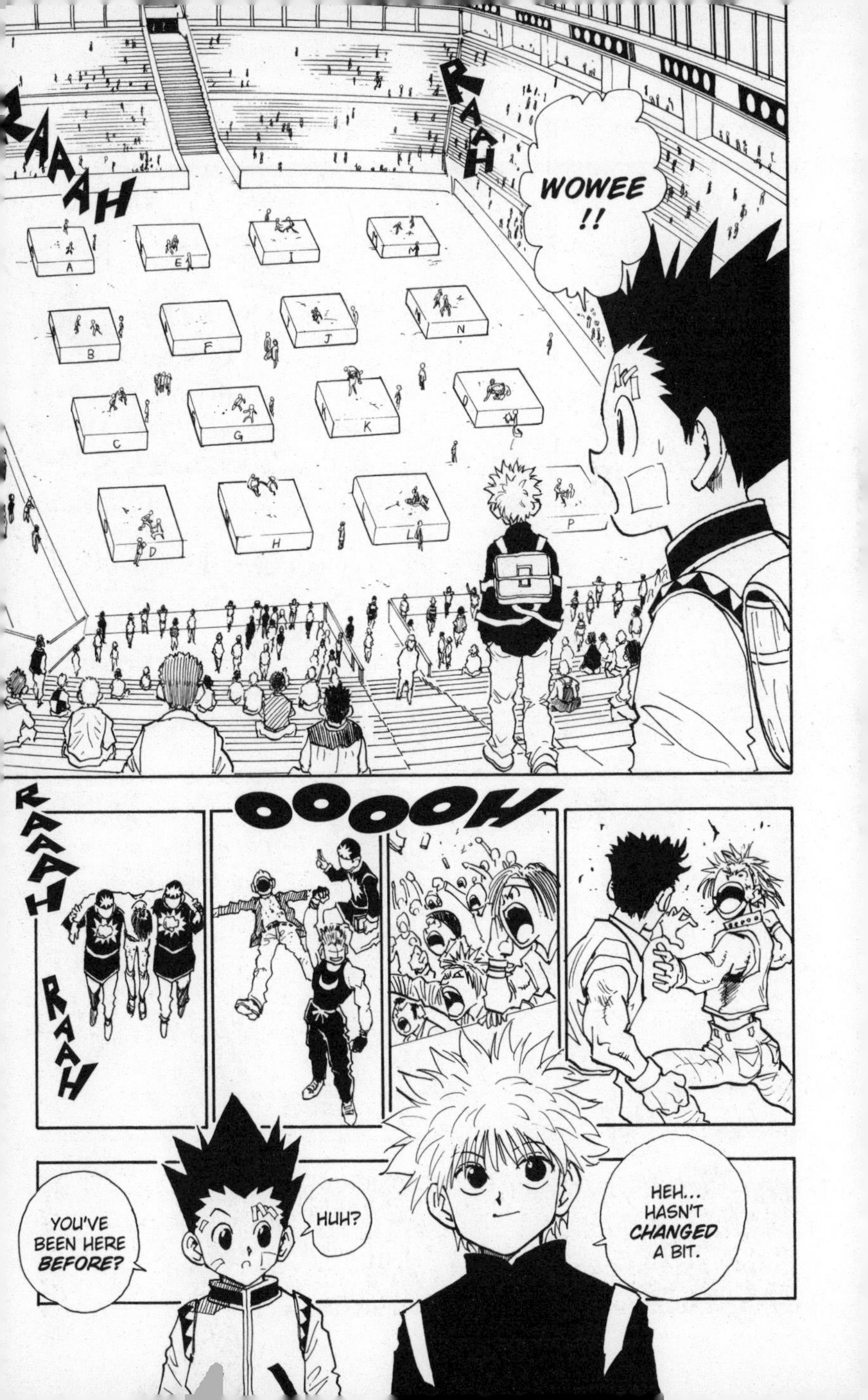
WOWEE !!
RAAH
RAAAAH
OOOOH
RAAAH
RAAH
HEH... HASN'T CHANGED A BIT.
HUH?
YOU'VE BEEN HERE BEFORE?

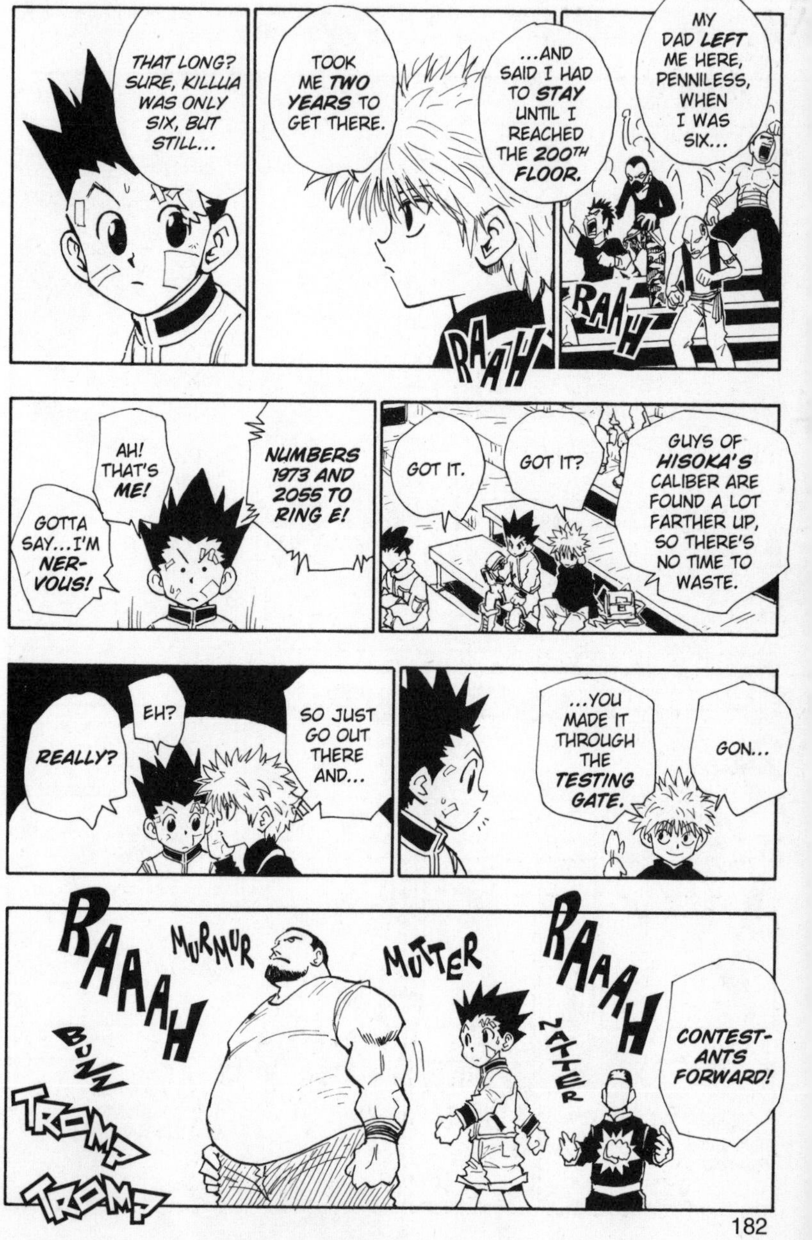
MY DAD LEFT ME HERE, PENNILESS, WHEN I WAS SIX...
...AND SAID I HAD TO STAY UNTIL I REACHED THE 200TH FLOOR.
RAAAH
TOOK ME TWO YEARS TO GET THERE.
RAAH
THAT LONG? SURE, KILLUA WAS ONLY SIX, BUT STILL...
GUYS OF HISOKA'S CALIBER ARE FOUND A LOT FARTHER UP, SO THERE'S NO TIME TO WASTE.
GOT IT?
GOT IT.
NUMBERS 1973 AND 2055 TO RING E!
AH! THAT'S ME!
GOTTA SAY...I'M NER-VOUS!
GON...
...YOU MADE IT THROUGH THE TESTING GATE.
SO JUST GO OUT THERE AND...
EH?
REALLY?
CONTEST-ANTS FORWARD!
RAAAH
NATTER
MUTTER
MURMUR
RAAAAH
BUZZ
TROMP
TROMP

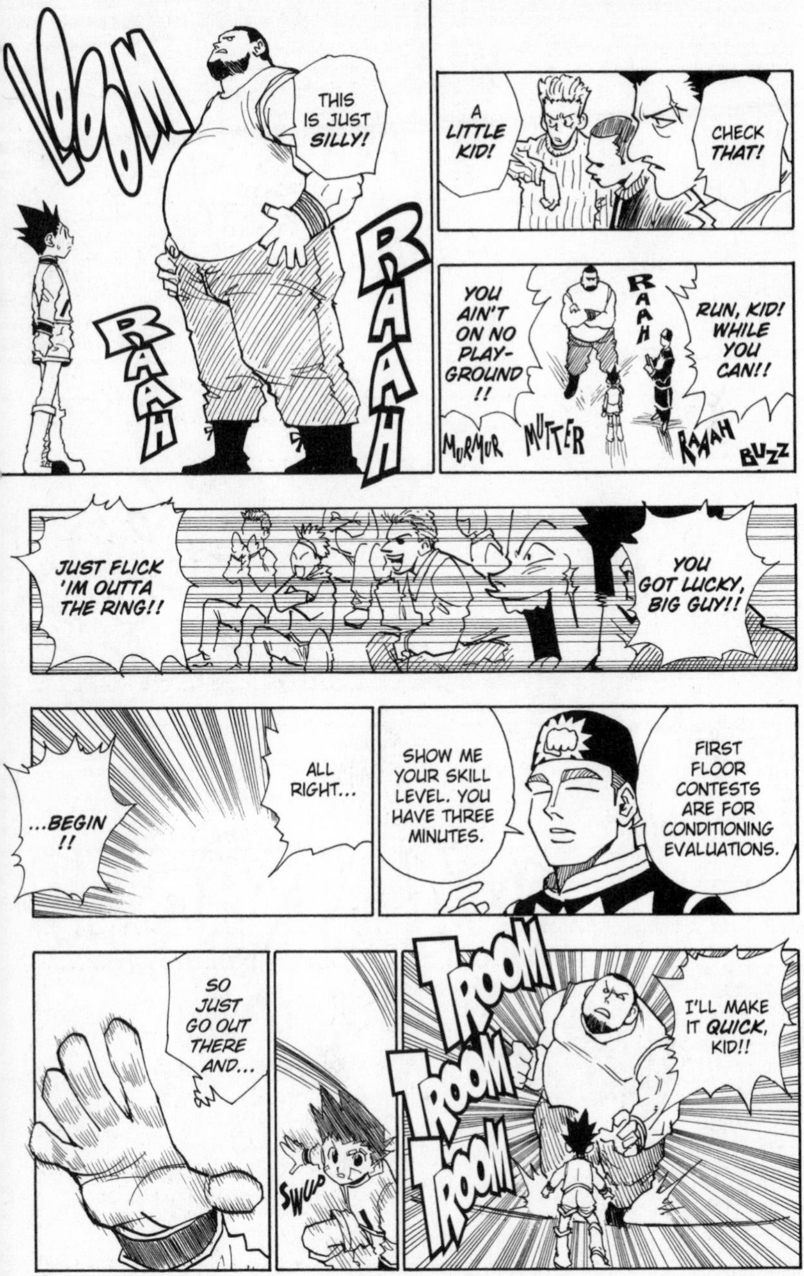
CHECK THAT!
A LITTLE KID!
RUN, KID! WHILE YOU CAN!!
RAAAH
YOU AIN'T ON NO PLAYGROUND!!
BUZZ
RAAAH
MUTTER
MURMUR
RAAAH
THIS IS JUST SILLY!
VOOOM
RAAAH
YOU GOT LUCKY, BIG GUY!!
JUST FLICK 'IM OUTTA THE RING!!
FIRST FLOOR CONTESTS ARE FOR CONDITIONING EVALUATIONS.
SHOW ME YOUR SKILL LEVEL. YOU HAVE THREE MINUTES.
ALL RIGHT...
...BEGIN!!
I'LL MAKE IT QUICK, KID!!
TROOM
TROOM
TROOM
SWUP
SO JUST GO OUT THERE AND...

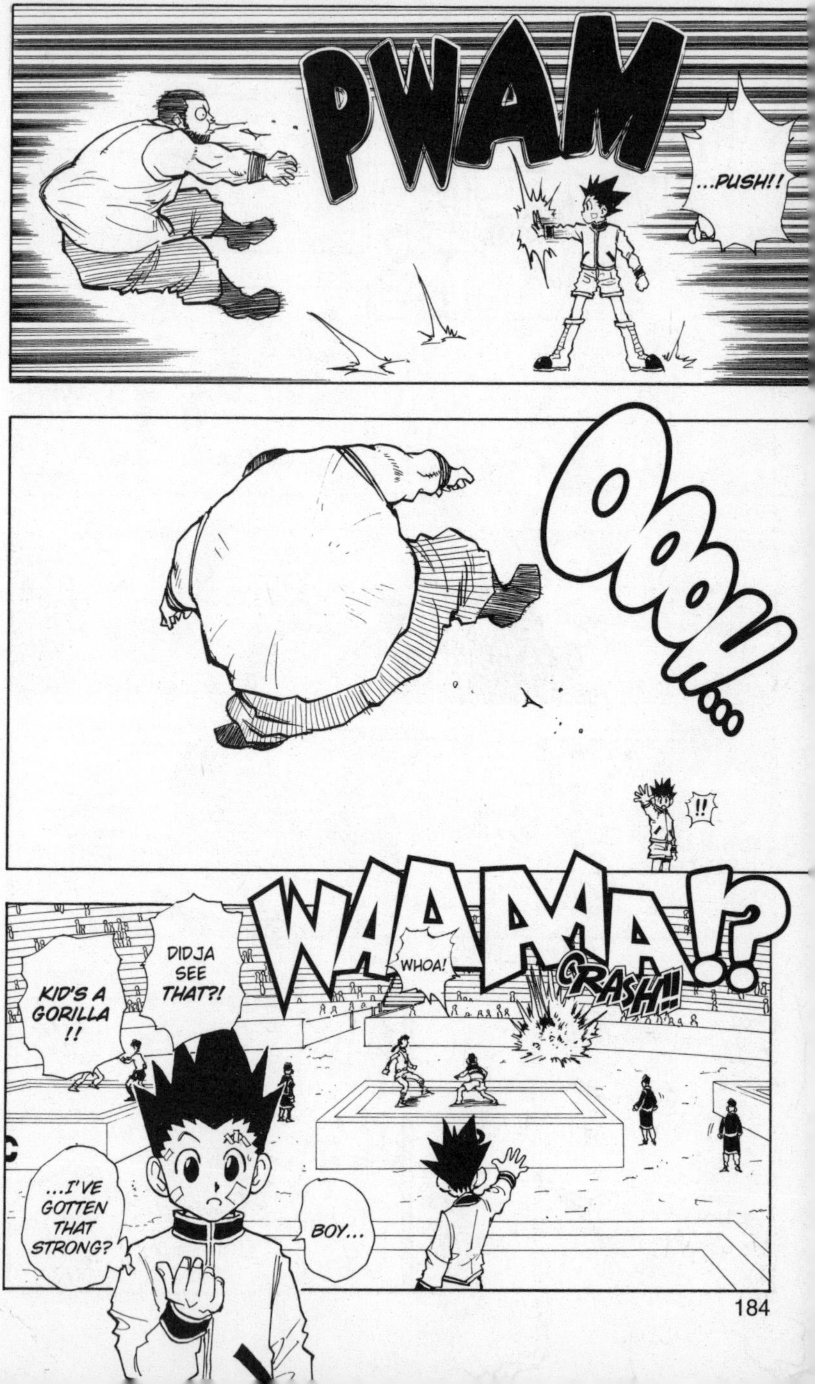
...PUSH!!
PWAM
OOOOH...
!!
WAAAA!?
CRASH!!
WHOA!
DIDJA SEE THAT?!
KID'S A GORILLA !!
BOY...
...I'VE GOTTEN THAT STRONG?

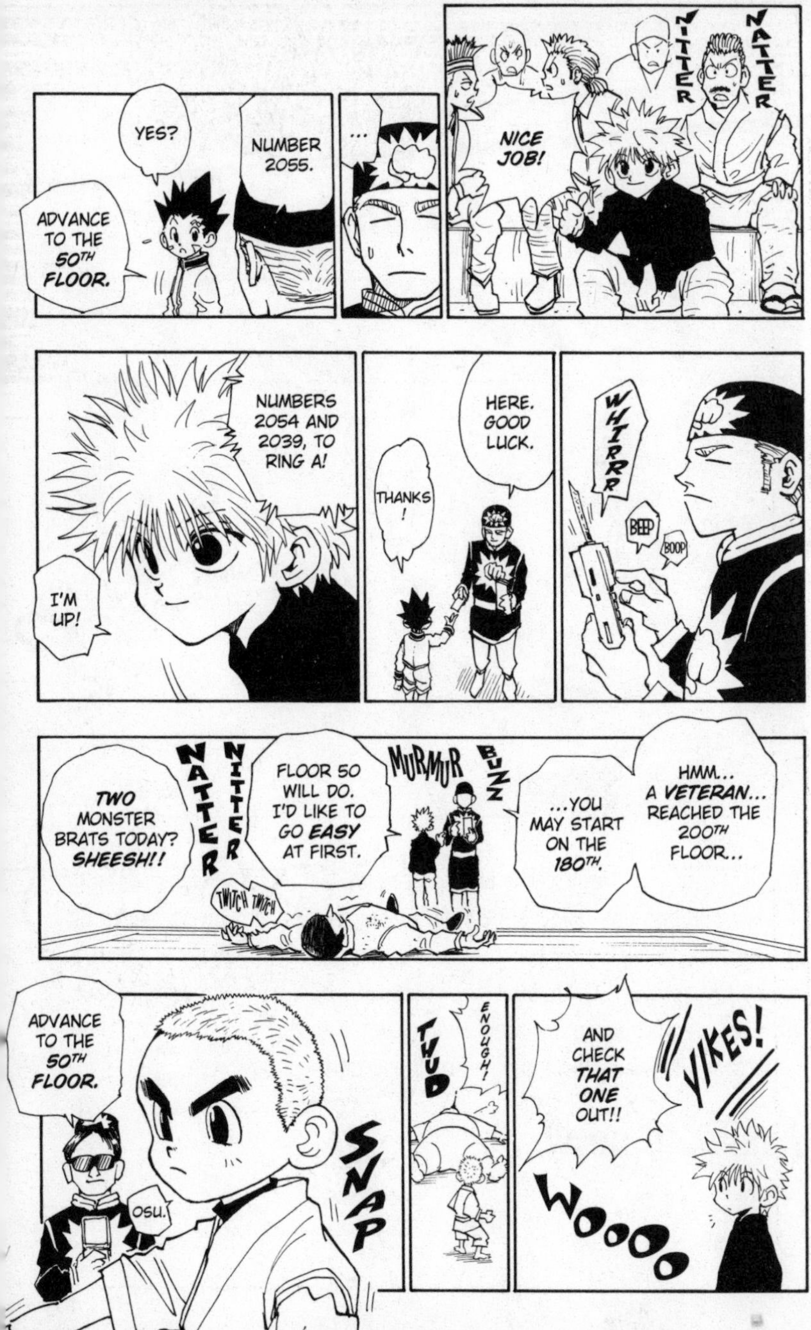
NATTER
NITTER
NICE JOB!
...
NUMBER 2055.
YES?
ADVANCE TO THE 50TH FLOOR.
WHIRRR
BEEP
BOOP
HERE. GOOD LUCK.
THANKS!
NUMBERS 2054 AND 2039, TO RING A!
I'M UP!
HMM... A VETERAN... REACHED THE 200TH FLOOR...
...YOU MAY START ON THE 180TH.
BUZZ
MURMUR
FLOOR 50 WILL DO. I'D LIKE TO GO EASY AT FIRST.
NITTER
NATTER
TWO MONSTER BRATS TODAY? SHEESH!!
TWITCH TWITCH
AND CHECK THAT ONE OUT!!
YIKES!
WOOOO
ENOUGH!
THUD
SNAP
ADVANCE TO THE 50TH FLOOR.
OSU.

Coming Next Volume...

There's a strange force in the Universe called Nen, and a Hunter without it is as good as unemployed! Gon and Killua try to discover its secret at the exclusive training center, the Heavens Arena. There, they are drawn to the mysterious 200th floor, but can't even walk down the hall. Hisoka warns Gon and Killua to stay away from the 200th floor until they understand Nen...but will their impatience be their downfall?

Available now!

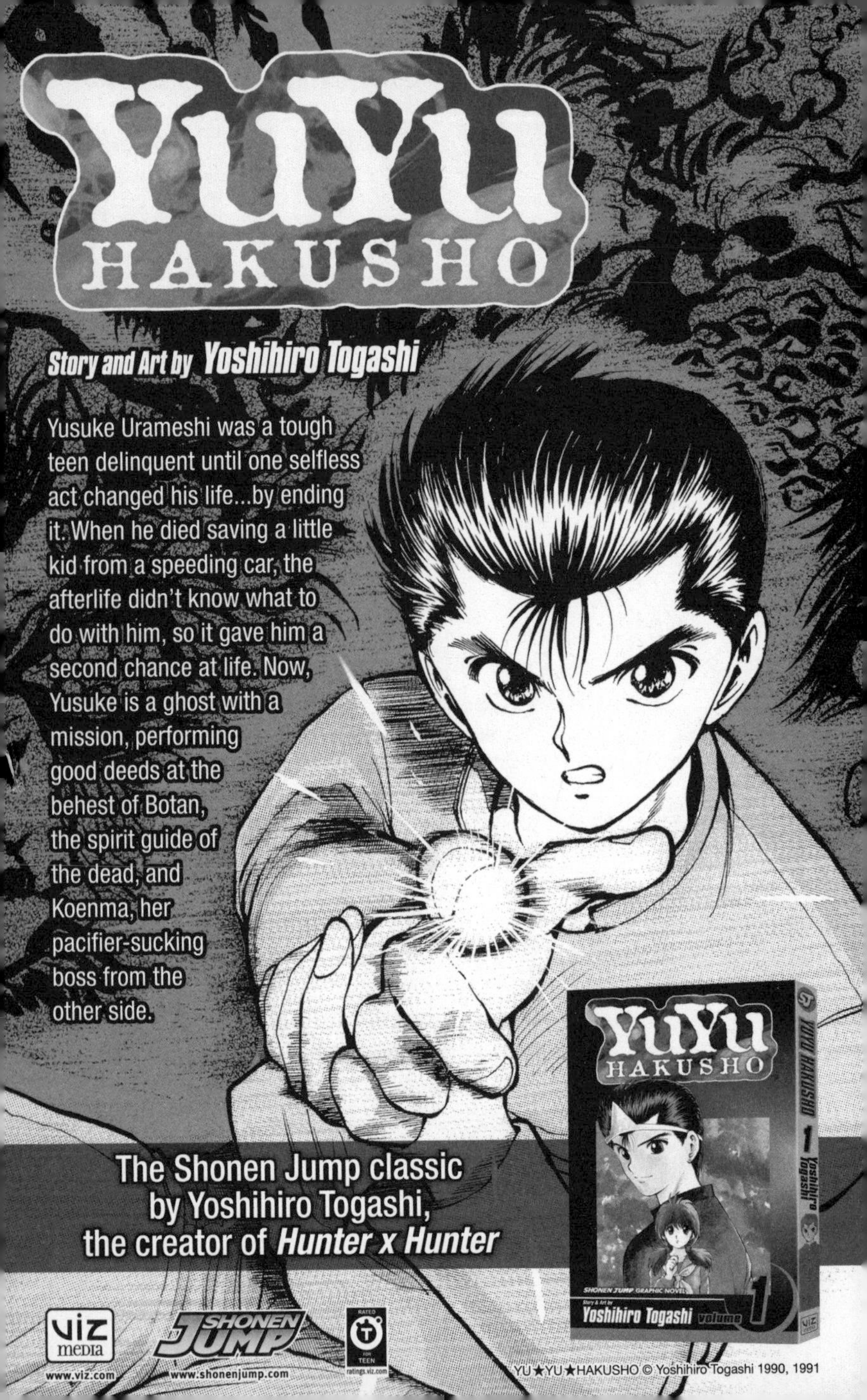
YuYu
HAKUSHO
Story and Art by Yoshihiro Togashi
Yusuke Urameshi was a tough teen delinquent until one selfless act changed his life...by ending it. When he died saving a little kid from a speeding car, the afterlife didn't know what to do with him, so it gave him a second chance at life. Now, Yusuke is a ghost with a mission, performing good deeds at the behest of Botan, the spirit guide of the dead, and Koenma, her pacifier-sucking boss from the other side.
YuYu
HAKUSHO
YUYU HAKUSHO 1 Yoshihiro Togashi
SHONEN JUMP GRAPHIC NOVEL
Story & Art by
Yoshihiro Togashi volume 1
The Shonen Jump classic
by Yoshihiro Togashi,
the creator of *Hunter x Hunter*
viz media
www.viz.com
SHONEN JUMP
www.shonenjump.com
RATED T FOR TEEN
ratings.viz.com
YU★YU★HAKUSHO © Yoshihiro Togashi 1990, 1991

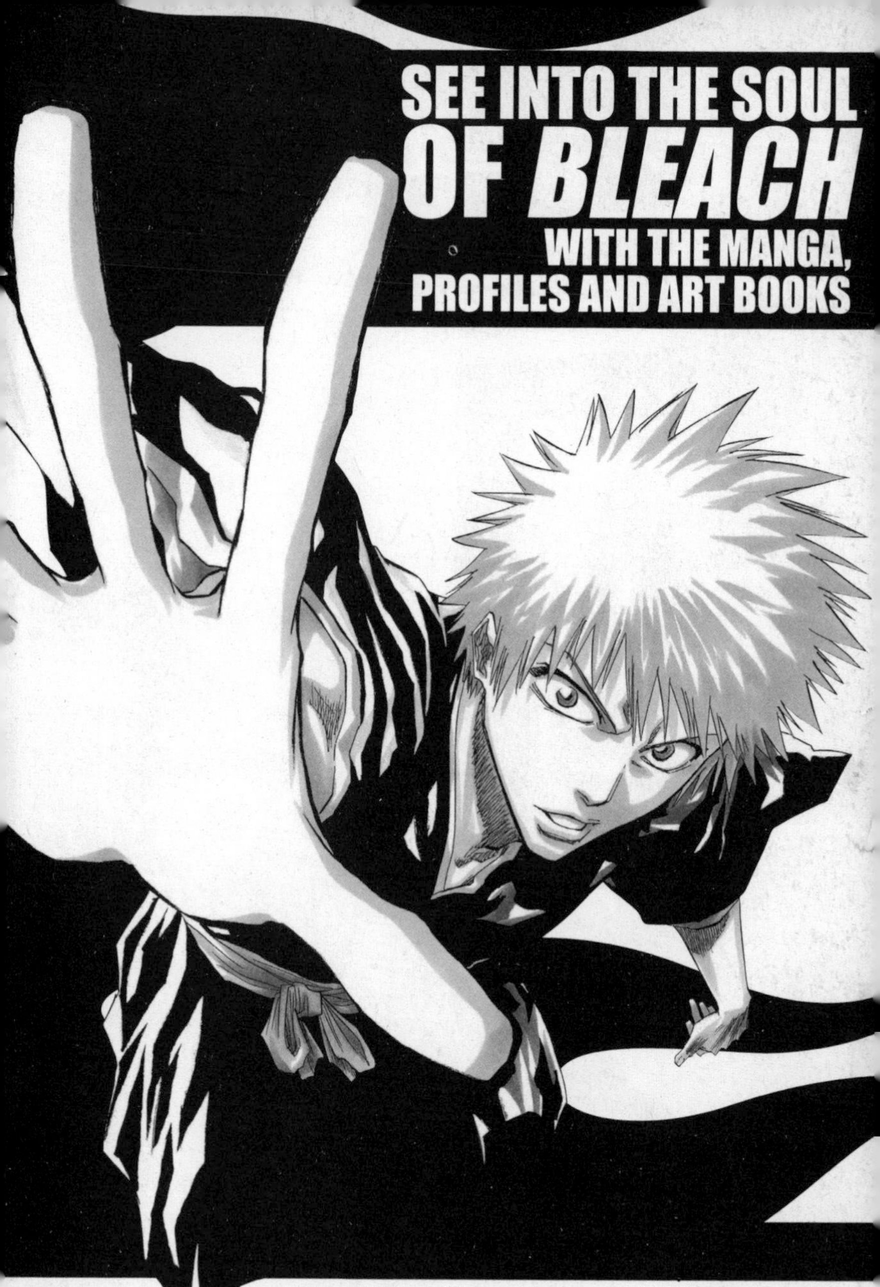
SEE INTO THE SOUL
OF BLEACH
WITH THE MANGA,
PROFILES AND ART BOOKS

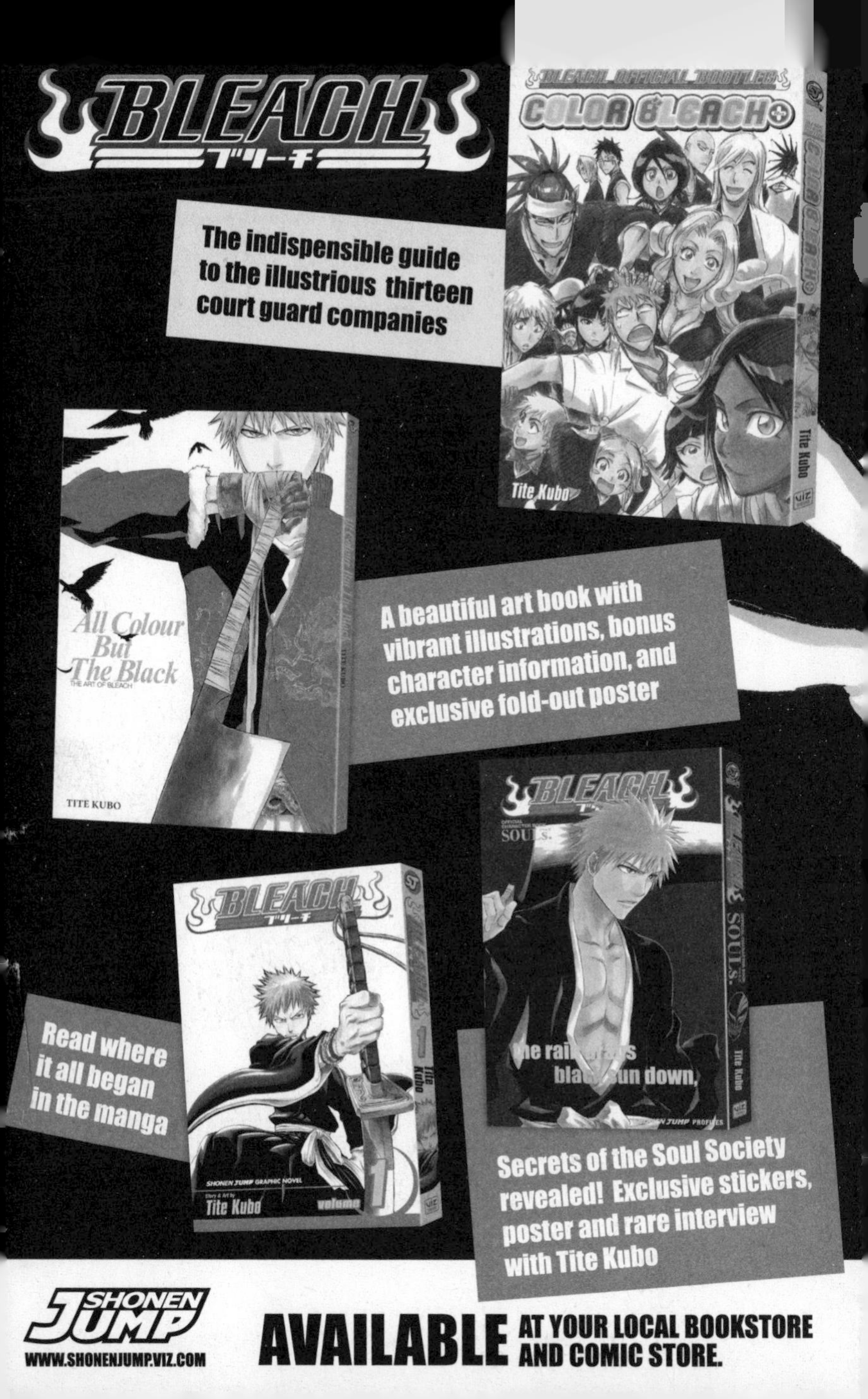
BLEACH
ブリーチ
BLEACH OFFICIAL BOOTLEG
COLOR BLEACH+
Tite Kubo
The indispensible guide to the illustrious thirteen court guard companies
All Colour But The Black
THE ART OF BLEACH
TITE KUBO
A beautiful art book with vibrant illustrations, bonus character information, and exclusive fold-out poster
BLEACH
SOULS.
Tite Kubo
BLEACH
ブリーチ
SHONEN JUMP GRAPHIC NOVEL
Story & Art by
Tite Kubo
volume 1
Read where it all began in the manga
Secrets of the Soul Society revealed! Exclusive stickers, poster and rare interview with Tite Kubo
SHONEN JUMP
WWW.SHONENJUMP.VIZ.COM
AVAILABLE AT YOUR LOCAL BOOKSTORE AND COMIC STORE.

You're Reading in the Wrong Direction!!

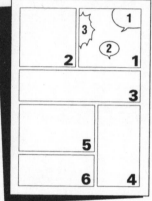

Whoops! Guess what? You're starting at the wrong end of the comic!

…It's true! In keeping with the original Japanese format, **Hunter x Hunter** is meant to be read from right to left, starting in the upper-right corner.

Unlike English, which is read from left to right, Japanese is read from right to left, meaning that action, sound effects and word-balloon order are completely reversed… something which can make readers unfamiliar with Japanese feel pretty backwards themselves. For this reason, manga or Japanese comics published in the U.S. in English have sometimes been published "flopped"—that is, printed in exact reverse order, as though seen from the other side of a mirror.

By flopping pages, U.S. publishers can avoid confusing readers, but the compromise is not without its downside. For one thing, a character in a flopped manga series who once wore in the original Japanese version a T-shirt emblazoned with "M A Y" (as in "the merry month of") now wears one which reads "Y A M"! Additionally, many manga creators in Japan are themselves unhappy with the process, as some feel the mirror-imaging of their art skews their original intentions.

We are proud to bring you Yoshihiro Togashi's **Hunter x Hunter** in the original unflopped format. For now, though, turn to the other side of the book and let the adventure begin…!

—Editor